Treating Drug Problems

Wiley Series on Treating Addiction

Series editors, Robert Holman Coombs and William A. Howatt

TREATING DRUG PROBLEMS
Arthur W. Blume

TREATING ALCOHOL PROBLEMS
Frederick Rotgers

TREATING GAMBLING PROBLEMS
William G. McCown

Treating Drug Problems

Arthur W. Blume

This book is printed on acid-free paper. ♾

Published by John Wiley & Sons, Inc., Hoboken, New Jersey.
Published simultaneously in Canada.

For general information on our other products and services please contact our Customer Care Department within the U.S. at (800) 762-2974, outside the United States at (317) 572-3993 or fax (317) 572-4002.

Wiley also publishes its books in a variety of electronic formats. Some content that appears in print may not be available in electronic books. For more information about Wiley products, visit our website at www.wiley.com

ISBN: 0-471-48483-0

Printed in the United States of America.

10 9 8 7 6 5 4 3 2 1

To Karen, Amanda, and Rachel,
who each in her own way
has taught me valuable lessons
about love, life, compassion, and change.

CONTENTS

Chapter 4: Developing an Effective Treatment Plan

Chapter 5: Recovery Tools, Programs, and Theories

Chapter 7: Posttreatment Recovery Management

SERIES PREFACE

Most books on addiction are written for only 10% of those who deal with addicted people — typically, for experts who specialize in addiction. By contrast, we designed the Wiley Series on Treating Addiction primarily for the other 90% — the many health service providers and family members who, though not addictionologists, regularly deal with those who suffer from various addictive disorders.

All volumes in this series define addiction as "an attachment to, or dependence upon, any substance, thing, person or idea so single-minded and intense that virtually all other realities are ignored or given second place — and consequences, even lethal ones, are disregarded" (Mack, 2002).

Considering that over one's lifetime more than one fourth (27%) of the entire population will suffer from a substance abuse problem (Kessler et al., 1994), many family members and all human services providers will, sooner or later, be confronted with these problems. Unfortunately, few have received any training to prepare them for this challenging task.

For decades, drug problems have negatively affected our families, our economy, and our safety. More than 8 million of America's 75 million children currently have a parent (or parents) addicted to alcohol or other psychoactive drugs. This fuels our nation's foster care and juvenile justice systems, and contributes to an intergenerational problem: Up to 70% of the children of addicts become addicted to drugs themselves (Bernstein, 2002).

Currently, drug trafficking is a $400-billion-per-year industry in our country and represents 8% of the world's trade. According to the White House Office of National Drug Control Policy, Americans currently spend $46–$79 billion annually on just two (of many possible) psychoactive drugs: cocaine and heroin (Kari & Associates, 2004). The Bureau of Justice Statistics (1999) indicates that between 60% and 83% of the nation's correctional population have used drugs at some point in their lives, roughly twice as many as others in the U.S. population.

We proudly introduce you to Arthur W. Blume's exceptionally useful and comprehensive book about Treating Drug Problems. Extremely well informed on this topic, Dr. Blume has superb academic training (doctoral training from the acclaimed addiction program at the Addictive Behaviors Research Center, University of Washington) and more than a decade of hands-on experience as an addiction counselor helping thousands of clients.

His book will serve as an excellent primer and helpful resource for everyone — including experts on this subject — who wants to gain a clearer understanding about the social and psychological dynamics of this problem and what one can do to help addicted clients and associates.

We predict that you will find this book to be an invaluable practical resource.

Robert Holman Coombs, PhD
William A. Howatt, PhD
Series Editors

PREFACE

Working with people who have drug problems is one of the more challenging, interesting, and rewarding domains in the field of mental health care. Treating drug problems is challenging because drug problems can be radically different from one person to another. Drug problems rarely occur in a vacuum, so there are often other biological, psychological, or even social and environmental problems that may co-occur, which makes treating a drug problem even more complicated. In order for a drug problem to be treated effectively, all of these problems have to be addressed satisfactorily in therapy. Treating drug problems also is extraordinarily interesting work because it requires multiple treatment modalities to address these different presenting problems, and because people with drug problems often are interesting and complicated people. Finally, treating drug problems is extremely rewarding, because this is one disorder with which you can see remarkable recovery among the people you treat.

My own career in addictions began by accident as I served as a psychology intern in a public treatment facility many years ago. Toward the end of my internship, the clinic director suggested that I should consider a career in treating alcohol and drug problems, to which I responded, "Why would I want to do that?" Four years and a graduate degree later I was a counselor in a treatment center working with clients and their families to overcome alcohol and drug problems, and loving it. Eleven years and thousands of clients later, I returned to school to complete a doctoral degree because I was interested not only in treating alcohol and drug problems, but also in improving the treatment options for the clients we work with, hoping that by contributing to future research I would aid that process in some small way. Being a therapist first before a researcher has allowed me to view the field with an interesting perspective, and has sensitized me to the points of view of both practitioners and scientists concerning the treatment of drug problems. Because of this history, bridging the chasm between science and practice is of great interest to me. I also believe it is very important to bridge science and practice for our clients' sakes so that addiction science becomes more practical and addiction therapy becomes more scientific.

The field has changed remarkably since I was an intern. Drug problems were essentially treated the same as alcohol problems, inpatient treatment was the first and sometimes only option, and counselors were taught to confront denial early and often. As we have learned more about the biology and pharmacology of drug problems, as well as the psychological, social, and environmental factors that influence the course of a problem (or of the undoing of the problem), prevention and treatment strategies have been changing dramatically. This process has occurred slowly at times, too slowly to be helpful for our clients. Perhaps this is because scientists and treatment professionals often speak different languages and have different tolerances and tempos of change, and at times these differences have caused some suspiciousness and even animosity between addiction researchers and treatment professionals. But the field has changed significantly in spite of these issues, and scientists and treatment professionals generally now recognize that not all drugs or clients are the same, and that effective treatment must recognize individual differences as well as similarities across clients.

These changes, however distressing they may have been to those who work in the field, benefit our clients, who are getting better care than they did when I first started in the field. Advances in psychological and pharmacological treatment options have been impressive and provide a greater number of newer treatment options for those who need them, and even for those who may not want them! Furthermore, the realization that many people with drug problems also have many other problems, including other psychiatric disorders that need to be treated, has prompted many treatment professionals to increase their competence to treat several problems simultaneously in order to insure a more promising outcome for their relapse-prone clients.

The future for treating drug problems is quite promising, with so much research being conducted by so many dedicated people, and with so many dedicated therapists now exploring new and exciting treatment techniques to use with their clients. However, a major challenge in the future concerns whether our society deals with people who have drug problems by treating or imprisoning them. We have reason to believe that treatment will help many people, and at the same time we also have reason to believe that prison may cause some to have worsening problems after release. These contradictory methods for dealing with drug problems in the United States must be resolved in a way that is helpful to the people who have drug problems and to our society as a whole.

The future of treating drug problems is highly promising and will certainly be filled with interesting challenges. In the meantime, there are many options for helping the people you are working with as a counselor or therapist. This book is meant to bridge the gap between science and practice, and to present up-to-date information about drug problems, their sources, and their treatment, in a way that is easily readable by those who need the information most. My hope is that you will find this book interesting and reader friendly, and that it will serve as a stepping stone in your search for better treatment and service options for those about whom you are concerned.

ACKNOWLEDGMENTS

I would like to acknowledge the aid and support of series editors Robert Holman Coombs and William A. Howatt, and thank them for their very helpful suggestions and comments as they reviewed the work in progress. I am very grateful that they invited me to contribute this book to their Treating Addiction series.

CHAPTER 1

Drug Problems: An Overview

TRUTH OR FICTION QUIZ

After reading this chapter, you should be able to answer the following questions:

1. People can recover from drug problems on their own. True or False?
2. Drug problems always get worse over time. True or False?
3. Adolescent drug problems are essentially the same as adult drug problems. True or False?
4. Relapse is a sign that treatment did not work. True or False?
5. Scaring drug users is a highly effective way to motivate change. True or False?
6. Virtual reality may be used in the treatment centers of the future. True or False?
7. Cravings are always biological in nature. True or False?

Answers on p. 47.

Not too many issues in the United States can elicit as many emotions as discussing drug-related problems. It seems that almost everyone in American society has an opinion about drug use, drug policy, and drug treatment. This is likely the result of how drug use in this country has touched so many of us in personal ways. Many people know of someone who has (or has had) a drug problem: a family member, a friend, or a friend of a friend. Drug problems also affect those who have been victimized by drug-related accidents or crime, and many others who care for those harmed by substance abuse. Drug problems can affect all of us by contributing to higher health care and insurance costs, and through higher tax burdens to support services. The abuse of drugs constitutes a major health problem in the United States, with widespread consequences that affect us all in some form or fashion.

Unfortunately, since drug problems have created strong opinions in this country, many opinions are slow to change even when they are inconsistent with the most recent scientific research. As a result, there is a wide array of new research that remains unknown by people who develop drug policies, who treat people with drug problems, and who may know or live with a person who has problems with drugs. Every day we learn more about what we should be doing to help people with drug problems, but unfortunately it takes time for the latest research to trickle down to the people who would benefit from this knowledge.

Partly at fault are scientists, who may find it difficult to talk about the research in ways that are understandable to nonscientists, or who have difficulties communicating the relevance of the research findings for treatment or for policy-making decisions. Partly at fault are policymakers, who often make important decisions for reasons that are more political than scientific. And finally, partly at fault are clinicians, who are suspicious of science or uncomfortable with new techniques, or who may be overly burdened by heavy clinical loads that limit their ability to stay current with the latest in research. Because of these problems in communicating new research findings and translating them into new policies and treatments that will help people with drug problems, progress toward reducing drug problems in the United States has been unnecessarily slowed. It is hoped that this book will be able to bridge this gap by bringing new information about treating drug problems to a wide variety of Americans, particularly those clinicians in the trenches who deserve to know.

Prevalence of Drug Abuse

Epidemiological research suggests that probably 10 to 20% of the population of the United States may have problems related to substance use, with approximately 5% of the population having problems with drugs other than alcohol (Substance Abuse and Mental Health Services Administration [SAMHSA], 2003). The most widely abused substances in the United States are alcohol, tobacco, and marijuana, but the typical pattern is for a person to abuse more than one substance at a time. An example might be that a person may smoke both cigarettes and marijuana, or may use both cocaine and heroin.

Tables 1.1 and 1.2 show the extent to which U.S. citizens report illegal drug use. As can be seen from the Table 1.1, many Americans have used drugs at least once, with marijuana being the most commonly reported substance used either during one's lifetime or during the past year. Perhaps surprisingly, prescribed pain medications are the second most commonly reported drug used by Americans within the last month. The abuse of prescribed drugs is often poorly recognized and does not get the same press as the abuse of street drugs like heroin or cocaine, but it represents a serious health threat to many Americans. Table 1.2 illustrates that men are more likely to use drugs than women, and that there may be some differences across racial and ethnic groups in drug use patterns, which will be discussed in greater detail later in this chapter. Tables 1.1 and 1.2 suggest that drug misuse and experimentation are not uncommon behaviors. Furthermore, a comparison of the lifetime usage numbers to the statistics presented earlier about drug abuse problems indicates that drug misuse does not always mean a drug problem.

Table 1.1: Most Frequently Used Drugs for Nonmedical Purposes (Excluding Alcohol and Tobacco) in the United States in 2001

Drug	Percentage Who Have Used at Least Once in Lifetime	Percentage Who Have Used at Least Once in Past Year	Percentage Who Have Used at Least Once in Past Month
Marijuana/hashish	28.6	7.2	4.0
Pain medications	7.6	2.9	1.2
Cocaine/crack	9.7	1.4	0.5
Tranquilizers	4.8	1.2	0.4
Amphetamines/methamphetamines	5.5	0.8	0.3
Ecstasy	2.8	1.1	0.2
Inhalants	6.2	0.6	0.1
LSD	6.9	0.5	0.1
Sedatives	2.6	0.2	0.1
Heroin	1.0	0.1	0.03

Source: SAMHSA (2001). State Estimates of Substance Abuse. Available at http://www.oas.samhsa.gov/

Note: Percentages are approximate and represent an extrapolation from SAMHSA data and census figures. SAMHSA data do not include drug use among people under the age of 12 years, so these are rough population estimates. Reported drug use does not necessarily mean drug problems.

Table 1.2: Nonmedical Drug Use (Excluding Alcohol and Tobacco) in the United States in 2001, by Gender and Racial/Ethnic Group

Population Group	Percentage Who Have Used at Least Once in Lifetime	Percentage Who Have Used at Least Once in Past Year	Percentage Who Have Used at Least Once in Past Month
Men/boys	35.7	11.4	6.7
Women/girls	30.3	8.6	4.5
African Americans	27.0	8.5	5.2
Asian Americans	15.3	4.4	2.0

(continued)

Population Group	Percentage Who Have Used at Least Once in Lifetime	Percentage Who Have Used at Least Once in Past Year	Percentage Who Have Used at Least Once in Past Month
Hispanics/Latinos	21.2	7.9	4.2
American Indians/Alaska Natives	23.6	9.4	4.3
Native Hawaiians/Pacific Islanders	Unknown	16.0	10.3
White non-Hispanic Americans	31.6	9.1	5.1

Source: SAMHSA (2001). State Estimates of Substance Abuse. Available at http://www.oas.samhsa.gov/

Note: Percentages are approximate and represent an extrapolation from SAMHSA data and census figures. SAMHSA data do not include drug use among people under the age of 12 years, so these are rough population estimates. Reported drug use does not necessarily mean drug problems.

Problems related to substance misuse cost Americans around $140 billion in 1998 (Office of National Drug Control Policy [ONDCP], 2001). Drug problems have been linked to a variety of health problems, including accidental deaths, suicides, homicides, hepatitis and other liver diseases, heart and kidney diseases, cancers, and HIV. Many of these health problems are among the top 10 causes of death in the United States for different age and ethnic groups. For instance, liver diseases associated with substance abuse were the 10th leading cause of death for adults aged 25–34 in the year 2000 (mostly caused by alcohol use, but some caused by drug-related hepatitis), the 6th leading cause of death for adults aged 35–44, the 4th leading cause of death among adults aged 45–54, and the 7th leading cause of death for adults aged 55–64. Infection with HIV, which is highly associated with drug usage, was the 10th leading cause of death in 2000 for

Drug-Use Costs to American Society

- Drug abuse costs American society approximately $140 billion in providing treatment and prevention services, lost earnings or productivity at work, other health care costs, costs associated with crime, and social welfare.
- More than one-half of these costs are directly related to crime.
- Between 1988 and 1995, the White House Office of National Drug Control Policy (ONDCP) estimates that Americans spent $57.3 billion on drugs for nonmedical purposes.

Sources: National Institute on Drug Awareness (NIDA) InfoFacts and ONDCP.

adults aged 15–24, 6th for those aged 25–34, 5th for those aged 35–44, and 8th for those aged 45–54. In addition, the top five killers in the United States *for all age groups* during 2000 (heart disease, cancer, strokes, chronic obstructive pulmonary disease, and unintentional injuries) all have been found to have some direct or indirect association with substance abuse (National Center for Injury Prevention and Control [NCIPC], 2003). Finally, drug problems have been identified as a cause of traumatic brain and spinal cord injuries, cognitive impairment, hypertension, malnutrition, severe burns, and drownings.

What Exactly Is a Drug Problem?

There are many different ways to define having a drug problem, but ultimately it is up to the individual to decide whether she or he has one. Historically, two different angles have been used to define a drug problem. The first looks at how many drugs the person consumes and when, or at what some researchers and therapists call *consumption rates and patterns*. The advantage to considering consumption rates and patterns is that heavy drug use often can lead to health-threatening and other negative consequences for the person using the drugs. However, consumption rates and patterns can be misleading in some instances because of differences in body size, gender differences, and other between-person differences. Because of this, the second angle of defining a drug problem, which has to do with examining the *consequences* of drug use, is also quite useful to consider.

Not surprisingly, consumption and consequences have been found by scientists to be related. However, the relationship is not always as strong as one would think. Some people who use just a very little amount of a drug can have significant difficulties; alternatively, some people can use a substantial amount of drugs with relatively few consequences. Because of these wide variations between individuals, it is a good idea to consider both consumption and consequences when determining whether a person has a drug problem. The next section of this chapter discusses key factors that researchers and clinicians look at when determining whether a diagnosis of a drug problem is appropriate.

> "When solving problems, dig at the roots instead of just hacking at the leaves."
>
> — ANTHONY J. D'ANGELO

The Three C's

Drug problems are often typified by what has been called the *three C's* (*c*ompulsive use, loss of *c*ontrol, and *c*ontinued use despite adverse consequences). Although some people who have drug problems experience all of the C's, there are many who do not. However, a person with a drug problem will likely have experienced at least one of them, so assessing for them is quite useful when evaluating for a drug problem. The three C's are described in detail in the following sections.

The Three C's and What May Contribute to Them

1. **Compulsive** use, and it may be related to . . .
   - Reinforcement
   - Cravings
   - Habit
2. Loss of **control**, and it may be related to . . .
   - Drug-induced myopia
   - Cravings
   - Beliefs that the person will lose control
3. **Consequences**
   - Types of consequences can vary from person to person.
   - Consequences can vary in importance from person to person.
   - Consumption *and* personal beliefs can contribute to consequences.

Compulsive Use

First, drug problems often are linked to what is called *compulsive drug use*. Compulsive use of drugs generally means that a person uses drugs automatically and habitually without thinking about the consequences of the behavior. Three important aspects related to compulsive drug use include *reinforcement* for substance use, *cravings* for the substance, and *habit*. To begin with, compulsive use of drugs is reinforced because the early stages of drug use reward the person either by stimulating the pleasure centers of the brain (e.g., the nucleus accumbens) or by taking away withdrawal or psychiatric symptoms, pain, or negative emotional states. Reinforcement is quite potent, making it likely that the person will use the drug again.

However, as the person increasingly uses the substances, tolerance develops. The euphoria of drug use may diminish or become more unpredictable, with highs or symptom relief occurring less frequently over time. The person may find that the pleasurable rewards come only intermittently. Many behavioral researchers, beginning with B. F. Skinner, have studied the powerful effects of intermittent or variable reinforcement in maintaining a particular behavior. *Variable reinforcement,* which means that the reinforcement happens randomly and becomes unpredictable to the person engaging in the behavior, contributes to keeping a person hooked on a behavior (reinforcement is discussed in greater detail later in this chapter).

Second, compulsive users of drugs often report they experience *cravings* for the substances that they prefer. Cravings have been described to me as gripping urges to use substances that will sometimes seem to come "out of the blue." Cravings seem to have both physical and psychological components. Physical cravings seem to occur as a direct result of withdrawal symptoms. When the drug is not being administered after a period of continuous use, the body experiences neurochemical imbalance; aversive symptoms, ranging from shakes to seizures, can occur. Cravings may be the result of the person's interpreting bodily signals that trigger the desire to ingest the substance in order to avoid physical withdrawal symptoms.

In addition, chronic or heavy drug abuse can sometimes alter a person's physiology, so that a chronic neurochemical imbalance may result. Such an imbalance can contribute to chronic symptoms of anxiety or depression. It is unclear whether these imbalances can be completely reversed over time with abstinence, but we do know that these symptoms and the underlying neurochemical changes that contribute to them may continue for months or even years after the drug was last used. Former clients of mine have told me about experiencing what they thought were physical cravings — some after months of abstinence — that in reality were being cued by their symptoms of anxiety or depression. The good news is that newer pharmacological agents can be very helpful in moderating physical withdrawal symptoms, and in reducing or alleviating depression and anxiety that can trigger a craving for drugs.

The other kind of craving a person may experience is psychological. Psychological cravings are triggered by the context of the drug experience rather than by the drugs themselves, and the user often misinterprets these cravings as a desire for drugs when what they actually want is a drug-related experience. A very common psychological craving occurs when a person misses experiences associated with using situations, such as socialization or recreational activities. The person will initially believe that the craving is physical but when you investigate further using behavioral analysis (explained in greater detail in Chapter 4), the craving is not physical at all, but related to missing an experience associated with using substances. The use of drugs has been paired so closely to an experience of socialization that the craving may be misattributed to needing the drug when in reality the person is craving an experience given up to avoid drug-using situations. Even though psychological cravings are not physiologically triggered, they can be extremely powerful experiences and often place a person at high risk for *relapse* (discussed later in this chapter and in Chapter 7). Treatment for psychological cravings focuses on exposure to emotional triggers, and changing behavioral responses and beliefs related to expectancies about substance use (see discussions about therapies in Chapter 5).

Psychological cravings also can be linked to a user's *expectancies,* or beliefs about what substance use will do for him or her. Positive expectancies about substance use can be related to what is termed *euphoric recall* of substance use experiences, which simply means that a person remembers the good times of using while perhaps forgetting or minimizing the memory of bad times. Positive expectancies often glamorize the drug use experiences by selectively remembering the pleasant using experiences while ignoring the not-so-good experiences. Expectancies will be discussed in greater detail later in this chapter.

Third, compulsive drug use also is related to *habit.* Habitual behavior is deeply ingrained in our memory processes and often leads to automatic responses without a moment of pause for the person to consider the actions before they occur. Habitual memory is part of *implicit memory,* which is the type of memory related to automatic behaviors such as driving a car or riding a bike. Can you imagine unlearning how to drive a car? But in a sense, that is exactly what a person who has abused drugs must do in order to break a compulsive behavior that may have lasted for many years. Behavioral scientists often will say that "the best prediction of behavior in the future is what has been done in the past," and with good reason, since habits, bad or good, are very difficult to change.

Habitual behavior tends to operate on autopilot, too. An example of how the automatic processes of habitual memory operate would be an instance in which you are cleaning house on autopilot, and then you stop for a moment and have no memory of having dusted the table even though it looks clean. Habitual behavior often means acting without thinking, so that you often have no awareness of what you are doing at a particular moment (or why). The same is true for compulsive drug use, when a person may use a drug without even being aware of what he or she is doing. Habit can place the person in a high-risk situation before he or she even knows it.

Loss of Control

Loss of control also is typical among people who abuse drugs, and some drug users will describe their habits as being out of control. Loss of control has been described as an inability to predict when or how many drugs will be consumed. Some drug users describe loss of control as *powerlessness,* meaning that the desire for substances controls their behavior.

Researchers have not clearly determined what may cause loss of control. However, we do know from alcohol research that intoxication can lead to what has been called *drug myopia:* impaired perceptual abilities caused by intoxication, causing a person to become more nearsighted, so to speak, to what is happening around him or her in the environment. Furthermore, drug-induced myopia limits a person's awareness at the exact moment when he or she is at greatest risk for being out of control, thus increasing the person's risk for experiencing a variety of problems. Drugs often impair higher brain functions associated with judgment, decision making, planning, and awareness. The impairment of these important brain functions makes it more likely that the person will be unable to regulate drug use, and he or she may overindulge in drugs without even realizing it. Loss of control is likely related to the diminished awareness of how many drugs have been used while the person was intoxicated. Myopia during intoxication also can adversely affect interpersonal relationships, since the person may misinterpret social interactions. Many fights occur while a person has impaired judgment while under the influence of drugs. Intoxicated drug users are vulnerable to risky behavior not only because of impaired physiological capabilities but also because of impaired thought and perceptual processes.

CLIENT HANDOUT

Do You Have a Drug Problem?

1. Have you found it difficult to predict when you will use too many drugs?
2. Do you find yourself trying to control or cut down on your drug use from time to time?
3. Do you have cravings in which you want to use a certain drug or use drugs in general?
4. Have drugs caused you some problems or hardships recently, such as being short on money or contributing to family and relationship stress?
5. Have you used drugs even when you thought it was a bad idea or after they had caused you some major problems or hardships?
6. Do you have regrets, guilt, shame, or other negative feelings about your recent drug use?
7. Have you used drugs in situations that were very risky for you?

If you answered yes to more than one of these questions, and you are currently using drugs, then you may want to consider getting a professional evaluation, just to be on the safe side.

Another possible contributor to loss of control may be the experience of cravings, discussed previously. Many of my clients have reported that their cravings contribute to deviation from their treatment goals or to a lapse or relapse. However, when conducting an analysis of a person's behavior, therapists often discover that the craving may have been only the first step toward a feeling of loss of control, rather than the direct cause of it. This will be discussed in greater detail in Chapter 7 concerning relapse research; however, to describe it briefly here, cravings may have been a first step, but the research on relapse suggests that negative emotions rather than the physical cravings themselves may be the ultimate trigger for loss of control (Marlatt, 1985; also see section on emotional factors later in this chapter).

Loss of control also has been linked in some research to expectations. In a famous study, alcohol-dependent subjects were studied to see whether they lost control because of tasting alcohol or because of *believing* they were tasting alcohol. At the time of the study, it was believed that loss of control in alcohol-dependent people was triggered by actually ingesting alcohol. In this study, however, people who were alcohol dependent and drinking alcohol (but thought they were drinking tonic water) did not lose control, whereas people who were alcohol dependent and were *not* drinking alcohol (but were told that they were) did report loss of control (Marlatt, Demming, & Reid, 1973).

What is being described is a *placebo effect,* and placebos have been used effectively for years to treat people medically even though placebos have no active medical properties. Some people, including some drug users, are highly suggestible, so that their beliefs about what is being used may be more powerful than the actual chemical properties of the substance. We do not know how powerful the placebo effect is under all conditions, but beliefs about substance use probably do play a part in loss of control.

Other research has found that people who expect to lose control while using drugs often do so, which provides additional support for the power of beliefs to affect behavior. Cognitive researchers often refer to this as a *self-fulfilling prophecy*. However, in some cases, what appears to be a self-fulfilling prophecy actually represents an accurate perception by the person of his or her capabilities. In fact, personal confidence in one's ability to negotiate a difficult situation without losing control is a potent predictor of drug use. Researchers found that people who have low confidence in their ability to control their using-behavior in certain situations often show greater loss of control in those situations. In many cases, when beliefs predict outcomes, it often is difficult to sort out whether the person's beliefs make something happen or the person is making a realistic appraisal of how well he or she will cope with the challenging circumstances. Regardless of cause, the research does suggest that beliefs may play an integral role in the experience that drug users describe as losing control (see the discussion of cognitive risk factors later in this chapter).

The experience of losing control often described by people with drug problems must be taken seriously. Assessing those situations in which people report a loss of control may provide clues to whether overuse is related to perceptual impairment, to cravings, or to a person's belief system. Interventions to prevent loss of control will described more fully in Chapter 5.

Continued Use in Spite of Consequences

Drug problems often have associated negative consequences. However, the consequences cannot be assumed to be important to the person experiencing them. Even though the consequences appear to us to be harmful, there are many times when the drug user may not have that awareness, or may not even interpret the consequences in the same way that you or I might. Some of the gulf between what others see as a problem and what a drug user may see as a problem is likely due to myopia. The drug user simply may not have awareness because of impairment. However, the drug user also may not consider the consequences to be important or related to his or her drug use. When this occurs, the drug user may not be motivated to change, or may even be unaware that behavior change is desirable. Furthermore, awareness of negative drug use consequences often is confounded by simultaneous awareness of pleasurable consequences, and the research suggests that the pleasurable consequences are more likely to be remembered than the negative ones (remember euphoric recall?). The net effect would be that a person may selectively filter out negative experiences in favor of recalling the positive experiences of using drugs.

Because consequences are different things for different people, researchers have been busy studying how to use consequences to encourage motivation to change drug use. For example, some research suggests that motivation may be enhanced if the person believes consequences are directly attributable to substance abuse and that the consequences are in personally important domains (Blume & Marlatt, 2000). However, there does not seem to be any silver-bullet type of consequence that will motivate change in all people. In addition, a person with a drug problem must believe that the adverse consequences outweigh the pleasurable effects in order to be motivated to change (see Chapter 3 for greater detail on motivating change).

To complicate matters, consequences seem to be perceived differently by young adults than they are among older adults. Because consequences are perceived differently, their ability to motivate change is different among young drug users than it is for older ones. For example, some research suggests that tactics that use fear to motivate change among young adults are not very effective, simply because young adults do not believe those types of consequences can happen to them. In addition, young drug users often do not experience immediate health consequences and sometimes are spared other types of nasty consequences by the safety nets of families and other social institutions.

So, even though negative consequences often are associated with drug problems, they often are not experienced the same way from person to person. Discussing consequences can help encourage behavior change if the therapist knows which ones to highlight. This kind of clinical judgment usually comes from the therapist's seeing a drug problem through the eyes of the client with whom he or she is working (see Chapter 3 for ideas on how to do this).

Myths Versus Facts Concerning Drug Problems

In addition to common elements that may identify a drug problem, such as the three C's, there are also common misperceptions related to drug problems. Many of these misperceptions have taken on lives of their own, such that people thoroughly believe these myths about drug problems are true even though science has plenty of evidence that they are not. Some of these misperceptions result from the chasm that exists between science and the treatment of drug problems, and still others are perpetuated because the media or other public sources speak with authority on that about which they know little. This section is meant to set the record straight, because these myths only hurt the people we are attempting to help. A very interesting article was written more than 10 years ago, entitled "Taboo Topics in Addiction Treatment: An Empirical Review of Clinical Folklore" (Chiauzzi & Liljegren, 1993). In this article, the authors attempt to set the record straight on several critical issues related to substance abuse. I highly recommend reading this article if you have an opportunity and are interested in learning more about myths that have been perpetuated in the treatment of drug and alcohol problems. In the remainder of this section, I will discuss 10 common myths about drug problems. Some of these myths are mentioned in the "Taboo Topics" article.

Myth Number 1: People must get treatment in order to get better. In several research studies, investigators have tracked people with substance-related problems over time to see what happens. The results from these studies suggest that some people who get treatment get better; some people do not get treatment and get worse; and, less obviously perhaps, some people who get treatment do not get better. But what is most interesting is that a sizeable minority of people with drug problems receive no treatment but get better anyway, and many stop using drugs all together. Even though the prevailing wisdom among some in the field is that you have to get treatment in order to get better, the science does not support that assertion. This is good news because there are not enough treatment resources to serve everyone, and it means some people have the resources to solve their own drug problems. Spontaneous or natural recovery is described in greater detail later in the chapter.

Myth Number 2: People with drug problems must identify themselves (some feel publicly) as addicts in order to get better. It may be helpful for some people with drug problems to label themselves as addicts, but it is clearly not helpful for everyone. In fact, for a sizeable number of people with drug problems labeling seems to be harmful and may harm their chances for recovery. The general rule of thumb in psychotherapy about labeling is that it must be useful to the person. To be useful to a client, the label must be consistent with the client's worldview and must provide for a direct solution to overcome the problem being labeled. For some clients, being labeled as addicts or as powerless over drugs is contrary to their worldviews and does not provide a solution within their way of thinking for overcoming their drug problems. My solution is to let the client decide whether he or she wants to label himself or herself, and whether that label will be helpful as the client finds solutions to a drug problem. For some people, labeling will not be helpful.

Myth Number 3: You cannot trust a person with a drug problem to tell you the truth about drug use. Actually, telling the truth about drug use is probably related more to the level of trust the user has toward others rather than to the drug problem itself. If the drug user trusts you, then he or she may be forthcoming about drug use. However, discussing drug use openly is complicated by the fact that many substances are against the law to use. Because of this, the drug user (from his or her perspective) has to be very careful what to say to another person. Yes, a drug user may lie about the drug use if he or she does not trust you. But the research suggests that if the drug user trusts you, then what is said is likely to be much more accurate than what you can find out from a loved one or a friend. After all, a loved one or a friend does not have the constant contact necessary to know exactly what drugs the client has used.

Myth Number 4: There is a certain type of personality that leads people to addictions. An addictive personality is something that scientists have sought for many years with very little success. The belief has been that if such a personality is identified, then this knowledge might be useful for finding a cure. However, even though some people clearly have compulsive tendencies, researchers have found a wide variety of personality types who have problems with drugs. What contributes to the belief that a specific personality type may be at risk for a drug problem is the high co-occurrence of particular disorders (e.g., Antisocial Personality Disorder) or the high incidence of particular behavior patterns (e.g., impulsiveness) with drug problems. On the other hand, researchers have found that opposing personality types, such as introverts and extroverts, can have drug problems and may even use drugs under similar circumstances (e.g., social situations), but for different reasons. Perhaps more useful than seeking an addictive personality would be identifying the function of drug use for the person (which will be discussed in greater detail later in this chapter and in Chapter 4).

Myth Number 5: Exposing a drug user to a drug-using cue is risky during treatment or in early recovery. Although it may seem intuitively to be true that a person may be tempted when confronted with a drug-using cue, such as a bong or a razor blade, and that exposure to these cues should be avoided, it is absolutely the wrong way to think about the problem. How likely is it that clients will be able to avoid all cues related to their drug use for the rest of their lives (or even in early recovery)? And, if you do not prepare the client for exposure to a particular cue during therapy, then how can you expect him or her to cope with exposure to the cue later, when a therapist is not around? Cue exposure (Chapter 5) has been found by research to be incredibly helpful to clients trying to overcome drug problems. The truth is that we should try to expose our clients to these drug-using cues while they are in therapy (in a safe environment) so that they have the necessary skills and confidence to cope with those cues later when they are not in a safe environment.

Myth Number 6: Therapists are the most important conveyers of behavior change in treatment. Actually, this is true only in a negative sense, such as when therapists generate resistance in their clients. Research has shown that therapist behavior can increase and decrease client resistance. If therapists are directly confrontational in therapy, then client resistance rises, and when therapists reduce confrontation resistance falls (even in the same session!). However, clients ultimately make decisions regarding behavior change, and therapists can only encourage (or discourage) that process. Therapists can grease the wheels for improvement, but the client ultimately moves toward change, sometimes in spite of a therapist. This should be a relief to a therapist or counselor because the responsibility for change is on the client.

Myth Number 7: All people with drug problems are in denial, and that denial should be challenged. Related to our discussion under Myth Number 6, we know that challenging a client in an adversarial way actually decreases the likelihood of successful treatment, and often leaves a client feeling hostile toward seeking treatment in the future. Therefore, confronting denial is generally not a good idea. Furthermore, what has traditionally been labeled as denial may not be denial at all. If a person is not aware of the consequences of drug use, there are other possibilities besides denial, such as cognitive impairment or myopia — or perhaps the person simply has not experienced major consequences associated with drug use. Furthermore, I have worked with many people with drug problems who were very aware of the consequences and of the desirability for change, but felt discouraged. Discouragement often can be misinterpreted as denial when in fact it is a problem with confidence and not motivation. Confronting discouragement will not instill hope. And finally, I have worked with some clients who were perceived as being in denial by other therapists, but who later admitted they simply hadn't trusted those therapists enough to open up. Many times the mistrust was driven by therapist confrontation, personality mismatch, or the circumstances of treatment (court-ordered). However, what may be perceived as denial by a therapist or counselor is often nondisclosure related to distrust.

As you can see, the appearance of denial may be a sign of other impediments. I personally do not find the word *denial* helpful because I have seen the label used in therapeutic settings to denigrate a particular client. Denial has become a nasty and overused word in treatment, and I have witnessed its being used in anger by some therapists and counselors as a weapon against their clients. I would suggest avoiding the term all together in treatment since there is no research to support that it needs to be identified or confronted in order for a person to get better.

Myth Number 8: Illegal drugs are generally more addictive than non-illegal drugs. Research has not found this to be true categorically. Part of the difficulties with legislating drugs is that political and economic forces often pressure policymaking decisions. For instance, we know that alcohol is arguably more dangerous than some of the drugs that are illegal, such as marijuana. Certainly tobacco is an incredibly destructive drug to millions of Americans, too. In some cases, the legality or illegality of drugs makes little sense when considering the relative addictive properties of the chemical and the relative costs to society related to the misuse of the substance.

The federal government developed a schedule of controlled substances in order to determine the level of control necessary to protect the well-being of the populace. This schedule was designed to take into account the relative potential for harm of a given substance, as well as its relative potential for medical benefit. In theory, as the numbers increase on the schedule (see Table 1.3), these substances are meant to represent decreasing amounts of risk to a user and increasing possibilities for medical benefits (a Schedule-1 substance having the highest risk for addiction and no medical value, a Schedule-5 substance having the lowest risk for addiction and greater medical value). In reality, the schedules do not necessarily reflect what the research has found concerning potential risks for addiction and potential medical benefits. The schedules do not always make scientific sense because politics have a played a part in their development.

Table 1.3: Schedule of Controlled Substances

Schedule Number	Description of Level of Threat/ Value From Substances	Examples of Substances in This Schedule
1	High abuse potential with no medical value in U.S.	Heroin, LSD, marijuana
2	High abuse potential with possible medical value in U.S.	Cocaine, amphetamines, strong opioid medications
3	Medium abuse potential with possible medical value in U.S.	Acetaminophen (Tylenol) with codeine, some barbiturates
4	Medium to low abuse potential with possible medical value in U.S.	Tranquilizers, phenobarbital, propoxyphene hydrochloride (Darvon)
5	Modest abuse potential with possible medical value in U.S.	Mild opioid analgesics, some cough syrups, etc.

Source: U.S. Drug Enforcement Agency (2001). Information available at http://www.usdoj.gov/dea/.

Myth Number 9: All drug problems are the same and should be treated the same; and *Myth Number 10: Drug problems are progressive and chronic.* I have saved these two myths until last because the next few sections will discuss the science related to these in great detail. To answer briefly, drug problems are not the same across all people, and therapy should not be developed with a one-size-fits-all philosophy.

Patterns to Drug Problems

Transient Versus Chronic Problems

Drug problems are not necessarily consistent across all people who use drugs. There are some people I have worked with as a therapist who reported to me that they were hooked pretty much from the start, but in all honesty, the majority of my clients had different stories. The more common story is that some people begin by using drugs recreationally, then somewhere along the way get into trouble with that use. Furthermore, there are some people whom therapists never see who can and do use drugs recreationally without problems. So using drugs does not automatically mean that addiction is around the corner, nor does having a drug problem necessarily mean it will always get worse.

With those people who develop drug problems, they do not necessarily experience consistent problems over time. Some clients do have continuous problems, a situation often called *chronic* drug dependence by therapists. However, some clients move in and out of problems, so that sometimes they seem addicted and other times they do not. Therapists often refer to this as an *episodic* or *transient* pattern. Continuous or chronic drug problems often are described as *dependence* by treatment professionals, whereas the more transient or episodic problems are often referred to as *abuse,* although even this distinction is not always clear-cut (see next section). The Institute of Medicine (IOM; 1990) did an investigation of alcohol abuse as an example, and found that drinking problems changed drastically over time, and that most people had transient problems whereas only a very small percentage of people who drank alcohol had severe problems.

Figure 1.1 provides some perspective (using the IOM model) in terms of how many people who use drugs have severe drug problems. As you can see in this figure, many people do not use drugs at all, followed by a sizeable minority who are recreational users, some who may have mild or occasional problems or none at all, and then a very small minority who have drug problems and who may require help. Drug use does not necessarily translate into drug problems, nor does drug use mean a person needs treatment.

Dependence Versus Abuse

The *Diagnostic and Statistical Manual of Mental Disorders, Fourth Edition, Text Revision* (*DSM-IV-TR;* American Psychiatric Association, 2000) specifies that the symptoms of substance-related disorders may include tolerance; withdrawal; loss of control; unsuccessful efforts to cut down or quit; a great deal of time committed to finding, using, or recovering from using substances; impairment in specific areas of one's life; and continued use in spite of negative consequences. To meet criteria for *dependence,* the individual must have three or more of these

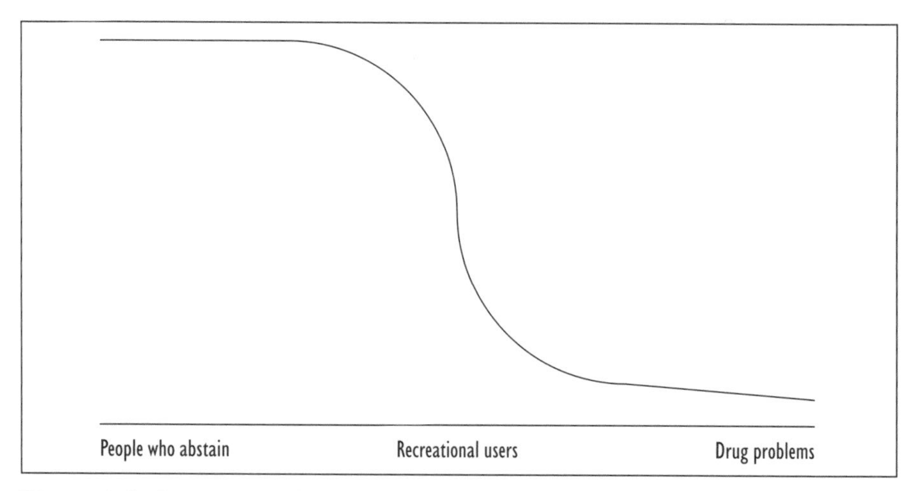

Figure 1.1: Continuum of drug problems.

Note: The slope of this graph is merely to show the relative number of people who abstain, use drugs, or have drug problems, in order to provide some perspective.

symptoms. To meet the criteria for *abuse,* the individual must experience negative consequences of drug use to such a degree that it impairs at least one area of life function (e.g., work, family, social life).

A person can meet criteria for abuse or dependence for one drug and not others, although there is concern about what has been referred to as *cross-addiction.* Cross-addiction means that a person who is dependent upon one substance may be dependent upon another, very similar one. An example might be a person who is diagnosed as dependent upon tranquilizers and who, you may fear, is also addicted to a similar substance such as alcohol. However, the research is not entirely clear on whether cross-addiction occurs, and I have known clients who had very specific problems with one substance who did not generalize into problems with other, similar substances. A person also may meet criteria for abuse or dependence for multiple substances; generally, this is referred to more simply as *substance abuse* or *substance dependence.*

Theoretically, drug "abuse" does not need to involve any evidence of physical dependence, according to the *DSM-IV-TR,* although we know that even social users can experience tolerance and withdrawal. More typically, *abuse* means that a person is experiencing negative consequences related to drug use in a specific life domain, such as impairment in a relationship or problems at school or work. Drug dependence, on the other hand, often involves physical tolerance and/or withdrawal (but does not have to, according to the *DSM-IV-TR* definition), and/or impairment in multiple areas of one's life. The odd thing about the *DSM-IV-TR* definition is that a person can be diagnosed with drug dependence even if he or she is not experiencing symptoms of physical addiction. In addition, since the diagnosis can be made by meeting three criteria out of a possible seven, two people can be diagnosed as dependent on the same substance and have entirely different presentations.

The *DSM-IV-TR* presumes that these diagnoses are linear in that there can be *progression* from abuse to dependence, but not vice versa. One criterion for a diagnosis of substance abuse is that a person has *never* been diagnosed with dependence on that substance. This definition suggests that a person who is abusing drugs can get worse (i.e., become dependent), but once dependent remains diagnosed as drug dependent (although the dependency can be "in remission"). This is much different than the way other psychiatric problems are generally conceptualized. For instance, people who experience Major Depression are not thought of as depressed even when they are not exhibiting depressive symptoms. Major Depression is described as an *episode* rather than a condition, but drug problems often are considered to be a *condition.* As you'll see later in this chapter, research on the natural course of drug abuse and dependence has found that people generally oscillate between experiencing multiple problems to sometimes experiencing fewer or no problems at all, *even while still using drugs.* This body of research, referred to as *naturalistic studies* on the course of substance problems, calls into question the assumption that drug dependence is a life sentence for all people.

As you can tell, there are some problems and inconsistencies with how we currently diagnose drug problems. One size does not fit all when describing or treating drug problems. Although determining a diagnosis may be important for determining the type of treatment and for obtaining third-party reimbursement, the more important issue for treating a drug problem is determining whether the person has risk factors that would predict more problems in the future, and then to intervene upon those risk factors. Later in this chapter we will examine the predictors of worsening problems and who may be at risk.

Psychological Versus Physical Dependence

Another way to conceptualize drug problems is to examine psychological versus physical dependence on a substance. *Psychological dependence* is defined by beliefs: A person thinks he or she needs the substance in order to cope. *Physical dependence,* on the other hand, is defined by actual physical changes related to drug use that may result in withdrawal symptoms and tolerance. However, to confuse matters, recreational users also may experience tolerance and withdrawal, so it is important to be careful when using these distinctions to define whether a person has a drug problem.

Conceptualizing dependence as both psychological and physical acknowledges that drug problems can have psychological, environmental/social, and biological roots (more follows on these roots in this chapter). Some researchers have suggested that some drugs, such as cocaine, may not be physically addictive but can be psychologically addictive since they may be highly reinforcing and very pleasurable. Personally, I find the distinctions between psychological and physiological dependence irrelevant, since both processes seem interrelated. However, conceptualizing drug dependence in this way does suggest the importance of both psychological and medical models to treat people who have drug problems, which will discussed more fully in Chapter 5.

Spontaneous Remission and Maturing Out

Some people who have drug problems are able to help themselves out of those problems without treatment. Researchers have studied people with substance-related problems over decades of their lives to determine what is the natural course of problems among different people. The results of these naturalistic studies have been quite interesting and challenge the view that all drug problems are chronic and progressive. Many untreated people with substance-related problems in these studies were found to have a more cyclical course in their addictions, rather than a linear and progressive course. Some people were able to successfully abstain without treatment even after a period of what would have been described as severe dependence. The research has found that many people with drug problems move through cycles of severe abuse followed by periods of control, sometimes followed by relapse, so that the trajectory may be cyclical rather than strictly linear. If anything, the natural course of addictions research

CASE STUDY

Edison the Experimenter

Edison is a newly married, 23-year-old civil engineer with a brand new career. He has a great future in front of him — but it didn't always seem that way. When Edison was in high school, he was busted once for smoking marijuana at school and was suspended for a few days. His principal put him on an "at-risk students" list. In college, Edison made mediocre grades his first two years, majoring in partying and minoring in missed classes. However, in his junior year, he found his passion in an engineering class, and began to spend more time on his studies and less time smoking marijuana. As a senior, he met Kate, whom he loved dearly. After a while, the partying just did not seem as important. When he graduated, he left his partying days behind him, as many youthful drug users do!

suggests that there are individual differences among people with drug problems and that not everyone follows a traditional trajectory with regard to progression of symptoms.

In addition, the trajectory of drug problems also can differ according to a person's age. Young adults diagnosed with drug-related problems in adolescence or early adulthood have shown the ability to mature out of those problems. *Maturing out* is a phrase coined to describe why so many adolescents often naturally outgrow drug problems. Many of these adolescents could easily be diagnosed by *DSM-IV* criteria as having drug abuse or dependence during adolescence or young adulthood or while in college, but ultimately go on to lead productive and healthy lives without abusing substances. The research shows that maturing out typically occurs among young adults after they have graduated, gone to work, or entered into long-term love relationships. The common denominator for maturing out, we think, is that increased responsibilities usually lead to decreased drug-related problems. Many young adults show the capacity to move beyond youthful drug experimentation and abuse when challenged with increased life responsibilities.

Clinical Versus Nonclinical Populations: Why Some Do Not Mature Out

There are, however, subgroups of young adults who may not mature out of drug problems as easily as others. Those who seem to have problems maturing out usually have other problems that preceded the onset of drug use. For instance, researchers have found that young adults who have a history of Conduct Disorder or who have other psychiatric disorders (such as schizophrenia, Bipolar Disorder, depression, Anxiety Disorder, or a major personality disorder) mature out of drug problems at much lower rates than those who do not have these additional problems.

POINTS OF CONTROVERSY

Moderate Use After a Problem?

One of the hottest debates in substance abuse research for decades has been whether people with drug and alcohol problems can ultimately return to moderate use. At least in the alcohol research literature, the evidence is clear that some people who meet criteria for alcohol dependence early in life eventually no longer meet that diagnosis in spite of still drinking. Research also has found that many adolescents with alcohol and drug problems are able to mature out of those problems over time as life responsibilities increase. Although not as much research has been concerned with the use of substances other than alcohol, I certainly have met people who had problems with "harder" drugs earlier in life who were using nothing stronger than marijuana recreationally later in life. If nothing else, this controversy has taught researchers and clinicians alike that not all drug problems are the same, and therefore that not all drug problems should be treated in the same way.

Progression

Some people who do not mature out of their drug problems may eventually use drugs continuously with progressively worsening problems. In the 1940s, Jellinek developed a model for this continuous and progressive disease trajectory based on personal observations and self-reports from severely alcohol-dependent clients. The trajectory showed a steady and steep slide from prodromal or early stages of addiction to chronic late-stage addiction, which ended with either the death, imprisonment, or recovery of the person. We do not know what progression may look like for other substances besides alcohol, which was the only substance Jellinek studied. However, for years many treatment professionals have believed that this trajectory with its prescribed progression of symptoms and consequences was the typical course for all addictions.

Clearly, some people have increased difficulties over time with their drug use and may experience greater losses or worsening consequences, but this is not true for everyone with drug problems. Sometimes when working in treatment settings, it feels like it is true, but in treatment settings we see a very limited sample of all drug users, a sample whose members often do have worsening problems. There are many people who never darken the doors of treatment who are different than the clients generally seen by treatment professionals.

Interestingly, Jellinek later modified his model by proposing that there were five different types of trajectories for alcoholics, three of which he did not consider to be chronic, progressive, or even related to disease (Jellinek, 1960). In effect, Jellinek was ahead of his time by suggesting more than 40 years ago that the trajectory for substance-related problems is not the same for all users of substances.

Drug Problems: A Biopsychosocial Model

Drug problems likely have multiple causes. To begin with, drug problems seem to be rooted in biological processes. No surprise here, since the biological processes related to addiction have gotten a great deal of press. Psychoactive drugs influence neurochemistry in such a way as to stimulate the pleasure center of the brain. In this way, drug problems are biologically based. Many researchers are also searching for possible genetic links that may place a person at risk for developing a drug problem.

However, drug problems also have psychological and social factors that seem to contribute to the development and perpetuation of the problem. Researchers refer to this as a *biopsychosocial* model (see Figure 1.2) since biology, psychology, and social/environmental factors are all important for understanding and treating a drug problem. Notice that the arrows on this model go two ways, indicating that not only do these factors influence a drug problem, but the drug problem can influence these factors. Psychological factors may include personal variables such as the way a person behaves, thinks, and feels. Social factors often are related to personal interactions but also can be related to environmental factors. The social and psychological factors are very important to understand in the development and perpetuation of drug problems because these are the areas that we will most likely be able to intervene upon and possibly change. We have not determined how to change biology yet, although some progress has been made in *pharmacotherapy* (which will be discussed in Chapter 5).

Within the broad categories of biological, psychological, and environmental processes, researchers have identified certain factors that seem to increase the risk of experiencing drug-related problems. There are several different categories of risk factors that tend to cluster together. However, many of these risk factors

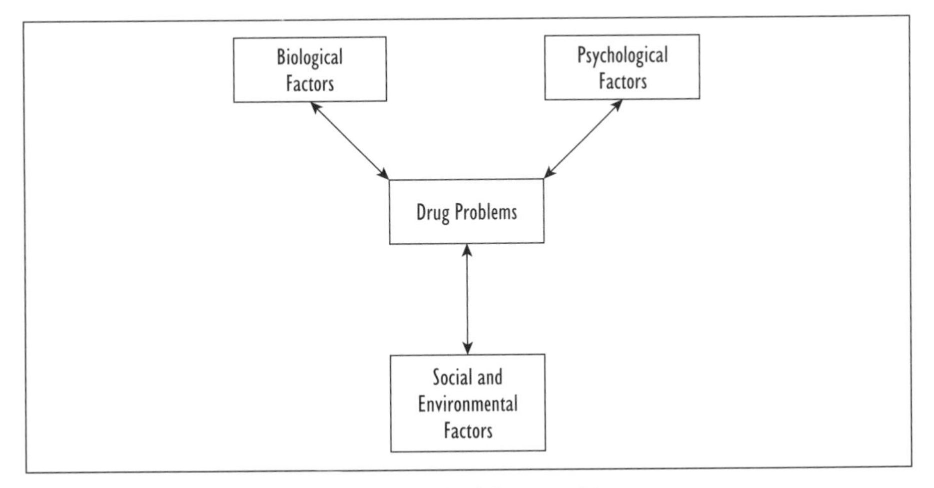

Figure 1.2: The biopsychosocial model of drug problems.

influence each other, so it is difficult to talk about one without remembering the others. For the purpose of simplicity, I will classify the risk factors in biological, environmental, behavioral, cognitive, and emotional categories, although it should be understood that these risk factors may interact with one another.

Biological Risk Factors

Therapists and researchers have found that a family history of addictions may be a particularly potent risk factor for drug problems, and the risk seems even higher if a member of the nuclear family has abused substances. Health care professionals have noted that intergenerational substance abuse commonly occurs within families. However, it is not clear how much of the propensity to experience drug problems within families is genetic rather than behavioral. Twin studies have suggested that drug abuse may have a genetic component, but more than a decade of work has not clearly identified the specific genes responsible. Furthermore, even if a gene pattern emerged for, say, opioid (e.g., heroin) dependence, there is no guarantee that a similar pattern would be identified for dependence on another type of drug (say, cocaine). To further complicate matters, intergenerational transmission of substance abuse also can be explained by behavioral factors, such as modeling by parents' or siblings' using drugs in order to escape, avoid, or cope with stress or problems. Intergenerational transmission of substance abuse within families is likely a combination of genes, which may cause a person to be vulnerable or sensitive to drug use, and of maladaptive modeling by family members who use substances to cope.

Although genetic research is not conclusive to date, there is compelling evidence that the greatest biological risk factor for having a drug problem is to have a *co-occurring psychiatric disorder*. As mentioned previously, epidemiological research has determined that the co-occurrence of drug problems with psychiatric disorders is quite high, with estimates that 1/3 to 2/3 of all drug-dependent people have at least one co-occurring psychiatric disorder. There is evidence to suggest that certain mood and anxiety disorders may be transmitted across generations in families, so it is possible that what is thought to be an intergenerational transmission of a drug problem may actually be related to intergenerational transmission of psychiatric conditions that may cause a person to be at risk for a drug problem. Many clients with co-occurring disorders believe that their drug problems may have started as an attempt to *self-medicate* their psychiatric symptoms (self-medication will be discussed in greater detail subsequently). For many clients with co-occurring disorders, though, it is difficult to parse out what came first, the psychiatric symptoms or the drug problem.

Environmental Risk Factors

Environmental risk factors also influence the development and course of drug problems. For instance, poverty has been linked to higher rates of drug problems, and impoverished neighborhoods usually have higher rates of drug abuse. In addition, stress has been identified as a risk factor for the development and perpetuation of drug-related problems. Many of my clients have told me that their drug use started as a way to reduce stress or to relax. Many different types of psychological stressors may contribute to drug abuse, including those related to family, money, and job stress; unemployment; daily hassles; or major life changes or crises. There has been speculation on the part of some researchers that crowded living conditions, often associated with increased psychological stress, also may be associated with drug abuse, although this would be difficult to determine absolutely since crowding and poverty usually go hand in hand.

The same can be said for education, which is generally considered to be a protective factor from problems, meaning that increased educational training usually means a person is at less risk for drug-related problems. However, education, too, is highly associated with income, so it is unclear what is really protective from drug problems — financial security or higher education. On the other hand, college students tend to have increased rates of drug usage while they are in school (as mentioned previously) before the use tends to subside after graduation, so education is not always protective from drug use but perhaps reduces the likelihood lof long-term destructive abuse.

Other environmental stressors linked to drug problems include physical or emotional abuse, traumatic events, and oppression. A significant body of research has studied the relationship of abuse and trauma with drug problems (see the discussion on shame later in this chapter). Many people who go on to develop drug problems in life have a history of being physically, emotionally, or sexually abused, although ascertaining exactly how many people have been victimized is difficult because of the sensitivity of the topic. Epidemiological estimates that I have seen suggest that 10% to maybe more than 50% of all people with drug problems may have been abused in some way, depending upon the definition of abuse and the population being studied. The association of abuse with drug problems is significant and certainly warrants attention. However, asking a person about abuse has to be done very skillfully and with caution (see Chapter 5 for greater discussion).

One area of research related to abuse or neglect has to do with how well a person fits within his or her social environment. One researcher, Marsha Linehan (1993), has talked about how a poor fit with the social environment (viz., not fitting into the family, school life, or other important social networks) may cause psychiatric problems if the poorness of fit causes the person to feel like an outsider or to feel constantly invalidated or put down. Many of my clients have told me that they have not felt part of their families or that they did not fit well into society in general, or have described themselves as black sheep. Abuse and neglect lead to an invalidating environment, but so can mismatches of personalities within families or mismatches of behavioral patterns with social norms. Furthermore, there is evidence that the way emotion is expressed in families can be associated with a poorness of fit that can influence the course of drug problems.

Many of my clients have talked about this as contributing to the feeling that they did not belong or were not accepted in their families (see the discussion later in this chapter about familial factors).

Many clients from ethnic-minority groups also feel a poorness of fit with the majority culture. Majority culture often has vastly different expectations for behavior and relationships and vastly different values than those held within many ethnic-minority cultures. Some researchers have suggested that being competent in a culture may be an important skill to have for good psychological health. Some of this research suggests that the ability to function competently in all the cultures in which a person dwells, such as the home culture and the culture of the larger society, may be associated with less risk of drug problems, presumably because a person has the requisite skills to successfully negotiate his or her different worlds.

Furthermore, many of the ethnic-minority clients I have worked with report experiencing varying degrees of prejudice and cultural isolation as well as reporting some degree of culture shock and problems adjusting to the majority culture. Some clients report using drugs to seek relief or escape from the environmental stressors related to prejudice and cultural shock. Others have candidly told me that their drug use was an act of defiance toward what they consider to be an oppressive majority society.

In addition, societal expectations about substance use seem to be related to the susceptibility of societal members to experience drug-related problems. Many respected researchers believe that exposure to responsible substance use in society early in life may promote more moderate substance use in those societies where such behavior is sanctioned. One striking example is the Netherlands, which legalized marijuana use in coffee shops two decades ago but currently has lower marijuana abuse rates than the United States. We have no idea whether this kind of societal exposure would work with more potent substances than marijuana, although the same results have been found for alcohol in France, which has a much lower cirrhosis rate than the United States even though French citizens usually drink for longer portions of their life spans.

> "[I]t would be madness to settle on medical treatment for the body of a person by taking an opinion poll of the neighbors. . . ."
>
> —PLATO

In particular, the United States has an interesting history of tension between trying to solve drug problems through the legal system versus through treatment services. In some ways, these approaches are diametrically opposed to each other, since one approach focuses on punishment whereas the other focuses on care. More recently, these two approaches to dealing with drug problems have been merged creatively in so-called *drug courts,* which have mandated treatment to inmates as an alternative to prison time. Research clearly supports that treatment is more effective than imprisonment in resolving drug problems. In addition, prisons in the United States are bursting at the seams, with more than one million people incarcerated on drug-related charges. Other societies, including Australia and some nations in Europe, have been relying more heavily on prevention and treatment instead of the court system, and have either reduced legal penalties or decriminalized drug use entirely while increasing the resources dedicated to helping those with problems or at risk for developing problems. It is unclear at this time whether the overburdened prison systems may cause U.S. public policy on incarcerating drug users to be reconsidered in the future, but the data are quite clear that treatment, as opposed to imprisonment, saves taxpayers money in the long run.

In addition to biological and environmental factors that influence the onset and course of drug-related problems, there also are many individual risk factors. These variables can include those related to a person's actions or behavior, those related to the way a person thinks, or those related to the experience of emotions. The next few sections will discuss in detail these personal variables that can be related to drug problems in some people.

Behavioral Risk Factors

As mentioned, researchers have been searching for many years for a personality pattern or a psychological profile for people who have drug problems, without success, in spite of the belief by many that such a personality type exists. However, behavioral principles may explain the addictive behavior patterns that we may see even if people with drug problems exhibit varying personality types. For instance, *positive reinforcement,* which is akin to receiving a reward or something pleasurable after a specific behavior occurs, will encourage the person to repeat that behavior. Positive reinforcement can happen after a person has used a psychoactive drug if he or she begins to feel relaxed, numbed, excited, or high — in other words, if the experience is pleasurable.

However, reinforcement does not necessarily happen all the time or even regularly. For example, even though many of us work every day, we do not necessarily get paid at the end of that day for what we did. And in some instances reinforcement is unpredictable, like when you receive an unexpected phone call that is rewarding to you from a close friend. When reinforcement doesn't occur in a predictable way, it is referred to as being on a *variable* or *intermittent* (random or unpredictable) schedule (or pattern). Behavioral researchers have found that a variable reinforcement schedule produces behavior patterns that are much more difficult to change than behavior patterns reinforced regularly.

The variable reinforcement pattern is complicated by certain beliefs that people have about what drugs can do for them. Many clients I have worked with engage in a type of thinking about drug use that is very similar to what is called the *gambler's fallacy:* the belief that the odds favor getting lucky the next time after a losing streak, even though the reality is that the odds of winning remain the same regardless of what happened before today. Many of my clients tell me (wishfully) that the next high will be a good one, even if the last 10 have not been good, believing (errantly) that the odds favor it. The reality, of course, is that the occasional rewards keep people hopeful that the next time will be the jackpot high that they are seeking (maybe even as good as the ones they experienced prior to the development of tolerance).

Drug use also can be negatively reinforcing for a person. Negative reinforcement makes it likely that the person will repeat the behavior, just as positive reinforcement does, but in a slightly different way. In *negative reinforcement,* the reward occurs when the behavior is followed by removal or reduction of something aversive to the person, or of a negative consequence, therefore making it likely that the behavior will be repeated. Sometimes negative reinforcement may involve the lifting of a punishment. Drug courts use negative reinforcement by suspending or reducing a prison sentence if the person complies by completing treatment successfully. In another case, negative reinforcement may involve the reduction of nasty physical withdrawal symptoms. In this instance, using drugs

THINGS TO REMEMBER

Reinforcement Can Help Drug Use Become a Habit

Reinforcement is something that happens after a behavior that makes it likely that the behavior will be repeated, and it can be both positive and negative. Reinforcement is different than punishment. Reinforcement encourages repeating a behavior, whereas *punishment* discourages repeating a behavior.

Some find it difficult to understand differences between positive and negative reinforcement, and often confuse negative reinforcement and punishment:

- *Positive reinforcement* = pleasurable consequences related to substance use
- *Negative reinforcement* = reduced emotions, withdrawal, or psychiatric symptoms

Positive and negative reinforcement play a part in establishing the addictive process.

Reinforcement often happens more than once, and sometimes with a pattern:

- *Continuous* reinforcement means that drug use is reinforced after every use, but this pattern is less likely after tolerance develops.
- *Variable* or *intermittent* reinforcement happens after tolerance develops, and occurs in a random and unpredictable fashion that keeps the person returning to the drug for the next good high.
- People with drug problems often experience variable reinforcement — both positive and negative — when they use, because the drug makes them feel better, but only occasionally and unpredictably.

may be reinforced if the use helps the person avoid getting the shakes or chills. Just like positive reinforcement, negative reinforcement can be on a variable or intermittent schedule, meaning that sometimes using a drug averts withdrawal symptoms, but not always. Drug problems may develop as a consequence of having drug use "shaped" by the pattern of seeking pleasure and avoiding discomfort. In the beginning of the vicious cycle, the compulsion to seek and use drugs may begin in order to seek highs and avoid lows, but eventually, as the behavior becomes habit and the reinforcement becomes less predictable, the pattern may take on a life of its own.

Clients often talk about using drugs to *self-medicate* pain or emotional discomfort, or symptoms related to other psychiatric disorders. Self-medication also can be thought of in terms of negative reinforcement. The person may believe that drug use reduces aversive psychiatric or physical symptoms, such as depression, anxiety, or chronic pain — and occasionally it may. However, the research suggests that drug use probably will worsen the symptoms over the long term rather than improve them. But since the drug use has been negatively reinforced at times by symptom reduction, the client may continue to use the substances under the belief that the drugs will medicate the symptoms *this* time.

Finally, drug problems often are a function of poor coping skills. Sometimes people will turn to drugs to cope with stress or avoid problems. Drugs may become a kind of solution for people when they do not have other means for coping or solving problems. There is a body of research that suggests that many people with drug problems have difficulties with skills such as assertiveness or problem-solving abilities. Because they are not able to assert themselves effectively with other people, they often find themselves having difficulties in social relationships or being socially awkward. Others may feel trapped because they are unable to solve problems methodically. There are solutions for these difficulties, namely teaching these skills, which will be discussed in Chapter 5.

Cognitive Risk Factors

A person's belief system also can influence drug use patterns. Many clients have certain beliefs about what the drug will or will not do for them. These beliefs about the effects of a drug are called *expectancies.* Expectancies can include positive or negative beliefs about the effects of using the substance. Expectancies are very powerful beliefs and difficult to change. In fact, research has found that positive expectancies about drug use can remain ingrained even after a person has not used the drugs for some time! Positive expectancies make it hard for people to want to change since they believe that using the drugs will do good things for them, such as reducing anxiety or depression or improving their social lives. Related to expectancies is what some psychological scientists have called the *self-fulfilling prophecy,* which concerns how a person's beliefs about outcomes can lead that person to act a certain way in the future (in effect, confirming what the person believed to be true all along). In this research, as mentioned earlier, if people believe something will happen a certain way, they may actually act in ways that make the predicted outcomes happen without being aware of doing so. The consequences of using drugs can often be a function of what a client believes about the outcome.

Another important cognitive risk factor concerns whether people believe they have the ability to control their behavior in certain situations. Researchers have found that *self-efficacy* (Bandura, 1997), or the perception of control and mastery in a particular situation, can influence whether a person has problems with drugs. If people have low self-efficacy (i.e., low competence and little confidence) in particular situations for coping without using drugs, then they may lose control of their drug use in those situations. It is unclear whether low self-efficacy may be a realistic appraisal of one's ability or whether these beliefs are like a self-fulfilling prophecy. Regardless of the reason, self-efficacy seems highly influential of drug use patterns. As previously suggested, hopelessness and discouragement may lead a person to give up trying to overcome a drug problem.

THINGS TO REMEMBER

Thoughts Can Influence the Course of Drug Use

Cognitions are beliefs that contribute to drug use behavior. The following are important beliefs that have been associated with drug use:

- Expectancies about the drug use
- Self-efficacy about drug use behavior
- Awareness of consequences of drug use
- Level of motivation to change drug use
- Neurocognitive problems associated with drug use

Common emotions associated with addictive processes include the following:

- Anger
- Sadness and grief
- Shame and guilt
- Regret and rumination
- Boredom
- Happiness

Many chemically dependent clients have difficulties identifying and regulating their emotions, much to their detriment.

Cognitive Problems Related to Substance Abuse

Additionally, chronic drug use has been linked to neuropsychological problems that in turn make it harder to stop the cycle of abuse. Psychoactive drugs by definition affect the brain, and long-term or acute exposure to psychoactive substances can be toxic. Furthermore, we know that drug abuse can increase the risks of stroke, brain injury related to accidents, malnutrition, or liver damage, all of which can adversely affect brain function as well.

Memory difficulties among people with drug problems are common, including noticeable short-term memory deficits. These memory problems seem to be more noticeable when a person is under stress, or when confronted with a new and complicated problem to solve or a learning task, which of course would complicate the ability to change behavior. The research suggests that long-term memory may be less affected than short-term memory, which is both good and not-so-good news. The not-so-good news is that long-term memory is suspected to be the source for memories associated with positive expectancies for drugs, which may explain why expectancies remain entrenched.

Chronic or acute drug use also has caused problems with other, higher brain functions related to the ability to solve problems, control impulses, think abstractly, and be attentive, and to plan, initiate, and stop behavior. These would be important skills to alert a person to the fact that his or her drug use may be causing problems, to allow the person to consider alternatives, and ultimately to enable the person to change behavior successfully. There is some reason to suspect that impairment of higher brain functions and memory may be partially responsible for perceptual problems related to drug use. Lacking awareness about having a drug problem or about the desirability of reducing or stopping drug use may be related to not tracking very well cognitively. As mentioned earlier, what is called *denial* by treatment professionals may really be cognitive impairment.

Researchers used to believe that cognitive problems developed only after chronic abuse of substances, but more recent evidence suggests that these problems can develop rapidly. Certain people might be more vulnerable than others to the effects of substances on their brains. Some adolescent drug users have shown evidence of cognitive problems, and recent research has found that the adolescent brain may be highly vulnerable to toxic effects of chemicals. Some substances, such as methamphetamine and cocaine, can cause mini-strokes that drug users may not even be aware of, and these mini-strokes can cause subtle but potentially important changes in memory and higher brain functions.

What has been difficult to determine is whether the neuropsychological problems are consequences of the abuse, or whether some of these cognitive problems may have preceded drug use. For example, many people who have drug problems also exhibit signs of hyperactivity or attention problems, but it is unclear whether these problems preceded the drug use or whether the drug use caused the problems. In addition, some people seem to have problems with impulse control or exhibit antisocial behavior even before using the substances, and these difficulties may be related to premorbid neuropsychological problems, such as an undiagnosed head injury. We do not know for sure, but it seems likely that for some people neuropsychological problems may have made them vulnerable to developing drug problems.

Additionally, impulse-control and attention problems, hyperactivity, and even antisocial behavior could be caused by a prenatal exposure to psychoactive drugs that escaped detection. Research has linked these conditions with known prenatal toxicity, and the consequences of low levels of prenatal exposure to psychoactive substances can sometimes be missed. In these instances, the symptoms are more likely to be observed as behavioral and attributed to other causes (such as Attention-Deficit Disorder). Recent research also suggests that children of mothers who may have used substances during pregnancy also may be at risk for drug problems later in life (Baer, Sampson, Barr, Connor, & Streissguth, 2003).

There is some good news, in that brain function begins to improve in most cases when drug abuse is stopped, and the improvement may continue for many months. Improvement often begins after the *detoxification* period, when mental confusion and some acute cognitive problems often improve rather dramatically. Other cognitive problems, some of which can be subtler and more difficult to detect, may persist for several months or years, as mentioned; but eventually many are reversible.

Emotional Risk Factors

Emotions also can play a role in the development of a drug problem. To begin with, many people who have drug problems have difficulties labeling what they feel. When queried about their feelings, many clients cannot tell you what they are feeling at that moment, often confusing one emotion with another (e.g., anger for shame or embarrassment) or a thought with an emotion (e.g., when asked, "How do you feel about that?" the individual may reply, "It was unfair" instead of "I was angry and hurt"). Understanding why many drug users have problems identifying their emotions is not difficult. Many people are using drugs in order to alter their moods and emotions, so obviously this alteration can blunt emotions over time. Many of my clients have made no bones about using drugs to avoid or escape certain emotions. So it is no great surprise that people with drug problems would have difficulty knowing what they are feeling, since the function of their drug use may have been to avoid feeling for many years.

People with drug problems often have difficulties expressing their emotions as well as identifying them. This difficulty has been attributed by some researchers to having *emotional dysregulation,* which simply means lack of skill at controlling or expressing emotions. Like cognitive problems, the problem of emotional dysregulation may be a consequence of substance use over time. However, the emotional vulnerability of the person may predate the substance use. If the person was emotionally vulnerable, substance use to avoid emotions may have seemed like a very attractive option. Many clients have shared with me that they feel emotionally vulnerable, or describe their experience of emotions as more intense than it must be for other people. Certainly some people seem to be highly sensitive to emotions expressed by others, often wearing their hearts (or emotions) on their sleeves, so to speak. Research seems to support the notion that some people are more sensitive to emotions than others, just as other evidence exists that some people with seasonal depression are more sensitive to amounts of sunlight than the average person. In addition, some of the emotional vulnerability being described may be attributed to *temperament.* Developmental researchers have suggested that a person's disposition toward expressing emotion and interacting with others may be set at an early age. A person's temperament also may influence how that person reacts to the emotions and behavior of other members of his or her family (see more on temperament under familial considerations in this chapter).

Furthermore, many substance users were reared in families that expressed emotions inappropriately. Parents and others in the home may not have been very skilled at expressing emotions themselves, and modeled inappropriate expressions of emotions for the children. This would certainly have been true in families in which substances were being abused, or where trauma, abuse, and neglect occurred. For instance, if emotional volatility was normative in the family, then a person reared in that family might consider emotional volatility as normative in the real world. On the other hand, if emotional expression was punished, then a person reared in that family might be averse to expressing emotions as an adult. In my experience, clients reared in families where emotions were taboo or underexpressed often have problems confusing emotions with thoughts.

Other clients may be very good at expressing one particular emotion, so well in fact that they will often express it to the exclusion of other emotions. An example is the client who has no problem identifying that he or she is angry, and is angry often, but rarely expresses emotions other than anger. It is almost as if the anger drowns all the other emotions out. Some of my clients have drowned out certain emotions to avoid other, more aversive feelings, such as embarrassment or sadness.

The expression of emotions in inappropriate ways can cause a vicious cycle for a person. For example, expressing emotions inappropriately can cause problems with interpersonal relationships. If a person is perceived as emotionally awkward or volatile, others may go out of their way to limit contact with that person. The result may be increased social isolation, which in turn may reinforce the belief by many clients with drug problems that they are social misfits (recall the earlier discussion about environmental risk factors). In addition, the disinhibiting effects of drugs may exacerbate emotional dysregulation, potentially making the dysregulation that much worse.

THINGS TO REMEMBER

Emotions Can Trigger Drug Use

- Difficulties experiencing and expressing emotions can sometimes be at the heart of a drug problem.
- Some people may be emotionally vulnerable and may use drugs to control the experience of emotions, but using often causes consequences that can lead to increased emotional vulnerability.
- Some people with drug problems have difficulties with *emotional dysregulation*, which means they may under- or overreact to the experience of emotions.

In general, strong emotions can be potentially risky for people with drug problems, especially for people who are using drugs to cope with emotions. For instance, the expression of anger is very commonly associated with aggression, and frequently drug problems and aggression go hand in hand. Part of the reason for this association is likely the high co-occurrence of Conduct Disorder and Antisocial Personality Disorder with drug problems. Anger is a very commonly experienced emotion for people with these disorders. A person who is aggressive while using drugs also complicates his or her situation since aggressive acts often cause more problems.

Even for those clients without conduct problems, anger often is an integral part of the drug problem. Frequently the person is angry because of neglect or abuse, or the person may have been frustrated because of not being able to cope adequately with life problems. Some of my clients have described anger as a shield that helps them deflect painful events and protects them from people perceived to be hurtful. The shield of anger also may be used when a person feels like he or she is losing control, which happens frequently when a drug problem is involved.

But anger is not the only emotion that plays a part in drug problems. Grief and sadness also are commonly experienced by people with drug problems, but they are often hidden behind the shield of anger. Grief and sadness may predate the substance abuse, and the person may use drugs to avoid thinking about the events that prompt the sadness or grief. Grief and sadness may be related to past events involving abuse, neglect, or loss, or sometimes it is a by-product of depression. But grief and sadness also may develop because of the consequences of drug problems. People who have drug problems are at great risk to incur a number of aversive consequences, such as major and stressful life changes and losses, unemployment, relationship and family problems, financial and property losses, exposure to violence, loss of contact with (and possibly the death of) family or friends, illness, poverty, homelessness, loss of self-respect, and potentially even the loss of important values or spiritual meaning and purpose. It is rare to find a person with a drug problem who has not experienced a major loss or does not have some major regret. Although the loss itself is not always attributable to drug use, the person may be using drugs to avoid remembering the loss.

Interestingly, the research suggests that for many people the day-to-day hassles of living are more difficult to cope with than the larger-than-life changes we each occasionally experience. People often are able to meet the major life challenges, but get battered over time by trying to live with the little daily hassles. *Daily hassles* are perceived as never-ending annoyances that can cause a great deal of frustration and stress to build up slowly over time. Sometimes daily hassles influence drug use more than crises. I have had some clients who are able to rise to the challenges of major life events, but then falter when trying to negotiate day-to-day living activities.

Another potentially toxic emotion linked to drug problems is the experience of *shame.* Shame as a consequence of being abused has been cited by many people with drug problems, especially women, to be related to subsequent drug use. Even if a person was not abused prior to using drugs, he or she is at high risk for being abused while using drugs, because people often are vulnerable to being victimized when impaired. Previous research has found that many adults are under the influence of psychoactive substances when they are victimized, and of course the research also finds a strong link between substance impairment and perpetration of violence. Shame does not necessarily have to be the result of abuse or victimization, though. Shame can accumulate as the direct result of the perception of personal failings or falling short of personal goals related to drug problems.

Another emotion linked with drug problems is *guilt,* which, unlike shame, is related to violating personal principles, rules, or interpersonal trust. However, the assumption that all people with drug problems feel guilty about their behavior is in error. For example, people with drug problems who also have Antisocial Personality Disorder will not likely feel guilt or remorse, which can complicate motivating behavior change in those people. Since antisocial personality frequently co-occurs with drug problems, treatment professionals cannot assume that all clients will feel guilt as a result of drug use. One caveat is worth noting here: Antisocial Personality Disorder by definition includes scrapes with the law and problems with authority. Although the co-occurrence of this (and of many other disorders) is associated with drug problems, there has been speculation that people who use drugs may be overly diagnosed with this disorder simply because drug use is a crime. One must be careful to account for the illegality of drug use when determining whether a person is truly antisocial or whether the person is simply a drug user who got caught doing illegal drugs.

Many drug users without antisocial features will feel some degree of guilt as a result of their drug use and associated behaviors. Frequently, clients will have behaved while under the influence of drugs in ways that may have violated their principles, or may have taken advantage of others. Clients may have hurt other people, conned other people, violated their own belief systems, or violated the trust of others. Behaviorally speaking, the best way to combat guilt is to use correction or overcorrection, which will be discussed in Chapter 5. Research on the determinants of relapse have found that shame and guilt can derail efforts to stop or reduce drug use, and that many times people will use drugs again in attempts to avoid feeling ashamed or guilty (Marlatt, 1985). This sets a drug user up for a vicious cycle of experiencing noxious shame and guilt, followed by substance use to ameliorate these feelings, which then places the person in situations where he or she is vulnerable to doing something else that will increase shame or guilt.

In addition, both *rumination* (unhelpful thoughts that spin around like a treadmill in a hamster cage and stop forward progress in life) and *regret* are associated with drug problems for a couple of important reasons. To begin with, rumination and regret often are the result of poor choices related to poor judgment. Obviously, being impaired by drug abuse can cause poor judgment and a wide range of consequences that can contribute to ruminative thoughts and regret. Drug problems cause interpersonal problems, lost opportunities, or even violations of trust with people who are important to the drug user. Rumination and regret also may be related to missed opportunities or to not reaching personal goals or expectations. Since drug use often impairs a person's ability to think and reason clearly, negative consequences that can contribute to rumination and regret are often the result. However, experiencing rumination and regret is not necessarily the end of the story, because my own research suggests that uncomfortable experiences such as these may prompt a person to consider changing his or her substance use (Blume & Schmaling, 1998; Blume, Schmaling, & Marlatt, 2001).

CASE STUDY

Joy for Joyce

Joyce, a 36-year-old woman who was trying to overcome a problem with Xanax (alprazolam), had found that things were going quite well in her life. She had a much better relationship with her children since she stopped using the Xanax, work was much easier than before, and she was dating a person who seemed much nicer than the others she had dated before she quit the drugs. It was not always easy, though. When she first stopped, she felt so anxious that she thought her insides were going to shake out, and she found herself alternating between being really irritable and being really tearful. After a while, her moods leveled out and she began to experience great satisfaction in her life. That joy scared her and she thought about using again because she was not sure how to cope with this experience of joy. In some ways she felt guilty about feeling so good after feeling numb for so long. Today, she is grateful to have that joy, and all the other emotions — including the not-so-good ones, because they remind her that she is alive instead of numb.

Rumination and regret also may be frequently experienced simply because depression and anxiety often co-occur with drug problems. Rumination and regret are common symptoms of depressive and anxiety disorders. When a person ruminates, the obsessive thinking tends to keep the person depressed because the problems seem unsolvable. Problem solving is paralyzed by the hopelessness, worry, and regret that engulf a person. It is difficult to determine whether the depression or anxiety preceded or are a consequence of the drug problems, so it is important to treat the drug problems and depressive symptoms/anxiety simultaneously when they co-occur. This will be discussed in detail in Chapter 5.

For some people, *boredom* has been associated with excessive drug use. There is a growing body of research looking at how unstructured time is related to substance abuse, especially among young adults. Unemployment also can be a risk factor for increased substance use. Many of my clients have told me that they frequently used drugs to overcome boredom and fill the time. Similarly, risk- or sensation-seeking behavior is associated with drug problems, and boredom in combination with risk seeking and impulsiveness can be particularly dangerous for some drug users. Some psychiatric disorders that commonly co-occur with drug problems are defined by these particular behaviors — for example, constant feelings of boredom or emptiness are common with Borderline Personality Disorder, and risk- or thrill-seeking is also common among people with Conduct Disorder or Antisocial Personality Disorder. So for some people with drug problems, structuring time and finding ways to have exhilarating experiences without drugs will be important for behavior change to occur.

Finally, and surprisingly to some, *happiness and joy* can cause problems for some people with drug problems. The reason? The experience of happiness and joy may be so overwhelming to a person who otherwise has difficulties with emotional dysregulation or who has not experienced much happiness or joy in his or her life that it may cause the person to feel off balance or uncomfortable with the experience. Regardless of whether the emotions are positive or negative, some people do not know how to handle emotional experiences appropriately. Some of my clients have told me that happiness and joy were paired with drug use to celebrate an occasion, which of course often led to a loss of the happiness and joy after the celebration. Others described their first experiences of joy in many, many years as foreign and awkward, and some had the opinion that they were not entitled to experience joy (probably as a result of shame and guilt). Many times they would sabotage the experiences of happiness and joy by using drugs to avoid the strangeness of these emotional experiences.

Some clinicians and researchers have noted that drug problems seem inextricably linked to problems with emotions. Certainly, many studies have found evidence for links between emotions, especially extreme emotional experiences, and drug abuse, and such links are frequently described in the personal stories told by drug users. However, the relationship between emotions and drug use is complicated and likely influenced by all the other risk factors discussed previously in this chapter.

In summary, there are many internal and external factors associated with the development and perpetuation of drug problems. Genetic factors or a family history of substance use are beyond our control to change at this time, but these factors may help us identify people at risk and target them with prevention strategies. However, environmental, behavioral, cognitive, and emotional risk factors are changeable. Until more is known about biological and genetic precursors to drug problems and how to treat those risk factors, intervening upon the environment, behavior, cognitions, and emotions provides the greatest hope for helping a person who is experiencing or may be at risk for experiencing a problem with drugs.

Epidemiology of Certain At-Risk Populations

There are differences in drug use and drug problems across different subgroups of the population. For example, drug use patterns may differ slightly across ethnic-minority groups (see Table 1.4), so it is important to be aware of which drugs are more commonly used by the community you serve. Specific ethnic-minority groups have higher prevalence rates for drug problems than the national norm. Epidemiological research has found that American Indians and Alaska Natives have the highest psychoactive-substance dependence rates of any ethnic group (13.9%; SAMHSA, 2003), but they also have much higher abstinence rates than the national norms. On the other hand, Asian Americans have the lowest rates (3.6%) of abuse of any ethnic group. There also are gender differences within ethnic groups that are not readily apparent. As an example, substance dependence rates are much greater for Hispanic/Latino men than women.

In addition, people with psychiatric disorders commonly have co-occurring drug problems, perhaps as an attempt to self-medicate the symptoms of these disorders. Therapists should be aware that several types of psychiatric disorders commonly occur with drug problems (see Chapters 2, 4, and 5 as well). Among the most frequently co-occurring disorders with drug abuse are mood disorders, such as depression and Bipolar Disorder; anxiety disorders, including Panic Disorder, Posttraumatic Stress Disorder, and Social Phobia; schizophrenia; Antisocial Personality Disorder; and Borderline Personality Disorder. In addition, people who have chronic physical pain have an elevated risk of abusing opioid pain medications, especially if their physicians have been undermedicating the pain (which tempts the person to seek more medication). In many cases, though, people with chronic pain had problems with substance use before the injury (sometimes the injury was a result of that abuse), and many others have co-occurring psychiatric disorders as well that complicate things.

Although these different populations are known to have higher than average prevalence rates for drug problems, they do not seem to be seeking treatment or

Table 1.4: Substances Most Commonly Used for Nonmedical Purposes (Excluding Alcohol and Tobacco) During Previous Month Among Members of Racial/Ethnic Groups in the United States (Ages 12 and Older) 2001

Racial/Ethnic Group	Most Commonly Used Drug Type	2nd Most Commonly Used Drug Type	3rd Most Commonly Used Drug Type
African Americans	Marijuana (5.6%)	Prescription drugs (1.6%)	Cocaine (0.8%)
Asian Americans	Marijuana (1.7%)	Prescription drugs (0.8%)	Hallucinogens (0.6%)
Hispanics/Latinos	Marijuana (4.2%)	Prescription drugs (1.9%)	Cocaine (1.0%)
American Indians/ Alaska Natives	Marijuana (8.0%)	Prescription drugs (2.3%)	Hallucinogens (0.2%)
Native Hawaiians/ Pacific Islanders	Marijuana (7.1%)	Prescription drugs (1.1%)	Inhalants (0.2%)
White non-Hispanic Americans	Marijuana (5.6%)	Prescription drugs (2.3%)	Cocaine (0.7%)

Source: SAMHSA (2001). State Estimates of Substance Abuse. Available at http://www.oas.samhsa.gov/

therapy in large numbers. In the United States, state and national statistics concerning how many have sought and successfully completed treatment are disturbing, suggesting that many of these high-risk groups may be grossly underserved (also see Chapters 4 and 5). It is unclear exactly what is preventing successful treatment seeking and completion by these high-risk populations, but the National Institutes for Health (NIH) is encouraging research to investigate these disparities in mental health services. To give you a sense of who is being served, Table 1.5 shows the recent figures, by age and racial-ethnic group, for how many of those who need treatment are actually receiving it.

Influences of Age and Gender

Young people tend to be at greater risk to use and abuse drugs than older adults, but many tend to mature out of this behavior, as mentioned earlier. Many drug users will give up drug use when they begin to assume vocational and family responsibilities. A minority of recreational drug users seems to go on to develop problems later in life. The length of time passing between the first use of a substance, and whether (or when) the user becomes dependent upon that substance, seem to be a function of the person's physiology, the potency of the

Table 1.5: People Needing Drug Treatment in 2000 Who Actually Received It

Population Group	Percentage of Those Needing Treatment Who Received It
By age	
Ages 12–17 years	11.4
Ages 18–25 years	8.6
Ages 26+ years	26.3
By gender	
Men	15.0
Women	19.0
By race or ethnicity	
African Americans	18.7
Asian Americans	< 5.0
Hispanics/Latinos	9.0
American Indians/Alaska Natives	8.7
Native Hawaiians/Pacific Islanders	30.0
White non-Hispanic Americans	17.8
Total for all U.S. in 2000	**16.6**

Source: SAMHSA (2000). Treatment Episode Data Set. Available at http://www.dasis.samhsa.gov/dasis2/index.htm

Note: For some racial-ethnic groups with small populations (such as American Indians and Native Hawaiians), the percentages may not be as accurate as those for larger groups because of sampling techniques.

substance, and the amount being consumed. Generally speaking, the aging process causes drug-related health problems to increase substantially, so that adult users often have health concerns after chronic abuse of a drug that young users may not experience after abusing drugs for the same amount of time. One major exception would be the rate of infectious diseases passed between drug users sharing needles, a rate unaffected by the age of the user.

Adolescence is a time of *novelty seeking* related to curiosity and learning skills for survival that maybe part of a natural maturation process. Adolescent brains are not fully mature, especially the frontal lobes, which have to do with problem solving, decision making, and judgment. We are not totally certain whether novelty seeking may be an important behavioral component associated with brain maturation, or if it may be a behavioral by-product of not having fully developed brain functions that may lead to poor choices. Regardless of the explanation, it is common for adolescents to seek novelty — which may explain why young people are interested in experimentation in general and with drugs in particular. The downside to novelty seeking is that it can lead to risk-taking behavior, and sometimes adolescents miscalculate the risks and consequences of certain activities. Underestimation of risk can cause problems for young adults, even if they are using drugs only periodically. Binge substance use is typical for many young adults, and there is some evidence that binge patterns may be more destructive than regular, maintenance-type patterns. The differences in the cognitive processes of young adults may explain why many traditional strategies for preventing and treating drug problems that work with older adults often will not work for youth.

Gender differences with regard to risk for drug problems exist as well. Men tend to be at greater risk for drug problems than women, although with the passage of time, greater numbers of women are experiencing drug problems. Women have tended to abuse prescription drugs at proportionally greater rates than men, whereas men are more likely than women to use injectable drugs. As gender equality increases in American society, it will be interesting to see whether gender differences in drug use patterns diminish — a trend we have seen with other health risks, such as heart disease.

For women of childbearing age, a very small percentage report using drugs during pregnancy. However, just like with alcohol, using drugs during pregnancy carries the risk of significant birth defects as well as significant withdrawal symptoms for infants who are born in intoxicated states. Many psychoactive drugs pass freely from mother to child through the wall of the uterus. In addition, some substances (e.g., cocaine) will pass from mother to child in milk through breastfeeding. There also is evidence that drug use can deform male sperm cells, but it is unclear whether these defects may then contribute to birth defects. Perhaps thankfully, in many cases drug use will reduce fertility in both women and men.

Familial Considerations

As mentioned, drug problems often seem to run in families. Although genetics and biology may be partially to blame, it also is likely that families are modeling the behavior. When the children see their parents using substances to cope or to relax, they discover through *observational learning* (having it modeled for them) that substances may be functional in this way. In addition, we have already discussed the relationship of abuse with drug problems, and certainly abusive families are breeding grounds for all varieties of mental health problems.

Other factors within families can be associated with drug problems. For one, a child's *temperament* may indirectly have some effect. If a child's temperament clashes with parental temperament or family temperament, it may cause a misfit for the child in the family structure. The child may feel alienated in the family and may seek peer support. If the child's temperament clashes with other social institutions, such as school, then the child's alienation may contribute to seeking other, like-minded peers, some of whom may be using drugs. This may be a first step toward a cycle of drug use and alienation.

Parental monitoring also has been associated with behavior problems. If children feel they are neglected or ignored, then they are more likely to engage in risk-taking behavior because the monitoring of their behavior is absent. Related to this, a lack of structure or consistency in rules and discipline can contribute to behavior that may lead a child to a drug problem. In effect, families that alienate family members are at risk for having a family member with a drug problem.

Furthermore, these principles seem to apply to success in overcoming a drug problem once it has begun. Family alienation is a sticky issue for clients seeking help with a drug problem. Sometimes loss of family contact reduces the amount of social support a recovering drug user may have after getting help, which can make progress more of a struggle. Other times the family may still be communicating with the client, but not in helpful ways. I have witnessed times when family members would unload on clients who were undergoing or had just completed treatment, and certainly their anger may be legitimate. However, the research concerning recovery from mental health disorders suggests that nonsupportive emotional expressions like these can adversely affect recovery. This makes sense when we consider that emotional dysregulation is often a contributing factor to a drug problem in the first place.

Treatment Success/Failure

The sidebar on page 41 provides some data on who is seeking treatment for drug problems. Treatment for drug abuse can vary greatly. The traditional treatment model consists of individualized and group treatment, and modalities can range from intensive inpatient to outpatient. Other people seek individualized psychotherapy for their drug problems, and some opt for pharmacological services such as maintenance on methadone (a drug often prescribed and distributed in neighborhood clinics as an alternative to heroin). As mentioned, these differences will be described in greater detail in Chapter 5, but I wanted to mention them here to highlight the difficulties in assessing how effective treatment can be. One problem with understanding success and failure in treatment is that there are multiple ways a person can get help for a drug problem, and these different treatment modalities have different standards by which they measure success. Defining treatment success is a matter of much dispute, and some definitions of success may be controversial across treatment models. For example, some treatment models view success only in terms of abstinence, whereas others view success as reduction of harmful drug use. These different models will be described more in Chapter 5.

Who Is Seeking Treatment?

- In fiscal year 1995, 1.9 million people were admitted to publicly funded treatment facilities.
- 46% of those admissions were drug (but not alcohol) related.
- 56% of those admitted were White Americans, followed by African Americans (26%), Hispanics/Latinos (7.7%), American Indians/Alaska Natives (2.2%), and Asian Americans and Pacific Islanders (0.6% combined).
- The most commonly abused drug reported by those admitted was cocaine (38.4%), followed by heroin (25.5%) and marijuana (19.1%).

Source: NIDA InfoFacts.

Federal data collected from across the nation suggest that between 42 and 52% of those who enter drug treatment complete the recommended length of the program. The people who would be less likely to complete would be those in the high-risk categories discussed earlier in this chapter. *Relapse-prone* clients or those who do not fit well within a certain treatment modality also are at risk for early departure from treatment. Other data suggest that the outcomes after treatment are mixed. The research suggests that many people may get better after treatment, but that only a minority of clients remain abstinent for a year or more after discharge (Miller, Walters, & Bennett, 2001). Because of these findings, treatment professionals might want to broaden their definitions of success, because clearly some people with drug problems get better even while still using drugs after treatment. Progress, rather than perfection, may be a worthy goal.

What may be more interesting is the compelling evidence that *client-therapist match* may be the most important predictor of successful outcome for clients after drug treatment. The evidence suggests that the way a therapist treats a client will not only affect treatment outcome, but also may influence whether the client seeks help in the future if needed. Therapists who aggressively confront clients often generate resistance, and if clients feel they have been disrespected, then they are significantly less likely to seek help again in the future. These findings speak to the power of the therapeutic relationship to make or break treatment.

Therefore, *goodness of fit* between therapist and client is crucial. There are three important factors that may be related to goodness of fit. First, the therapist should consider the client's goals for therapy in developing the treatment plan (see Chapter 4). Sometimes therapists allow their own agendas to dictate the treatment plan, which may lead the client to feel invalidated (not taken seriously). Second, the therapist should be respectful toward the client, which means being an advocate instead of an antagonist. Clients do not generally consider the old model of confronting early and often to be respectful, and that old model has been associated with poor treatment outcomes. Finally, individualized treatment plans should be truly individualized, which suggests that one style of therapy will not necessarily work well for all clients. I realize that it is difficult in treatment facilities with large client-to-therapist ratios to individualize therapy, but it is important to find creative ways to do so in order to ensure positive outcomes.

Therapists may wish to use these suggestions to guide their conduct with their clients in order to promote a healthy therapeutic alliance. Consumers (drug users seeking treatment) and their families also may wish to use these three goodness-of-fit treatment factors as guidelines when shopping for an appropriate therapist. Consumers will want to consider whether the model of treatment fits well with their own needs and worldviews as well (see Chapter 5 for more details on treatment models).

Recovery/Relapse Rates

As mentioned, only a small minority of clients sustains abstinence for a year after treatment. This means that most people will have a slip or a relapse, but this should not be discouraging to those who know or work with a person who has been in treatment. Relapse should be considered a normal part of the change process, and an opportunity rather than a disaster. *Relapse* is defined as a return to old using patterns, which differentiates it from a *lapse* — a brief slip into using that may or may not lead to a relapse. It is unclear how many relapse episodes are normal for people with drug problems to experience before they succeed at abstaining, but smoking research has found that the average is more than 10 serious quit attempts before a person can successfully stop smoking tobacco. Because of these findings, relapse is considered progress toward change, rather than a failure in the change process (see the discussion of relapse prevention in Chapter 7 for greater details). Therefore, therapists and people with drug problems should not be discouraged by relapse rates, because relapse simply points out where a correction in the recovery plan needs to take place in order for the client to succeed in the future. Relapse is an opportunity to learn rather than a failure in treatment.

The Unrecognized Treatment: Prevention Programs

One of the most underrecognized forms of treatment is *prevention.* With regard to drug treatment, an ounce of prevention is worth a pound of the cure. The best treatment for drug problems is to prevent them from occurring in the first place. Many prevention programs currently in place target adolescents and young adults.

Recent campaigns for prevention include programs like Drug Abuse Resistance Education (D.A.R.E.), a school-based program designed to support a decision to "say no" to drug use. Some advertising campaigns target people who may already be using drugs, and these campaigns try to link drug use to contributions to a variety of social ills, such as accidents, theft, and even the supporting of terrorism. These recent advertising campaigns have not been evaluated by researchers to determine whether they are effective, but in general, similar advertising campaigns in the past have not been found to be effective. Many of these campaigns have used *fear* as a principle motivator for behavior change. However, for many people, especially young adults and adolescents, fear campaigns do not work to change behavior. The problem with using fear campaigns is twofold. First, young adults and adolescents are not at a point in their lives developmentally such that they believe the fear message will happen to them. Since the fear message generally is associated with death, and adolescents and even young adults have little concern about death and dying because of their developmental stage, these campaigns fall flat. Second, older adults often dismiss fear campaigns as something that may happen to the other person but likely will not happen to them.

Project D.A.R.E. and other abstinence-based programs do not have good track records for success. The problem for "just say no" programs is that they do not teach a person how to respond to high-risk situations in effective ways to avoid saying yes, and they do not teach young adults what to do in case they have already said yes — and finally, these programs often have presenters (such as police officers) who can be easily discredited by teens and young adults as biased and not the kinds of spokespeople who will adequately present all the facts. Because of these problems, programs like these have not shown good research outcomes: Participants of these programs did not have any more reduced levels of substance use over time than people who did not participate in the programs, and in some studies, participants actually did worse over time with substance use than nonparticipants.

Other, more successful prevention programs have been documented to save an amazing amount of money when compared to the money spent on treatment, and because prevention programs also save many lost months and years of productivity for young adults who end up abusing drugs, developing effective new prevention programs is an extremely important strategy for treating drugs. Unfortunately, significantly more money is spent on treatment each year in our society than is spent on prevention.

Clearly, prevention is an extremely important strategy for treating drug problems at the earliest stage. An effective prevention program must level with adolescents and young adults about drug use, should not use fear as the principle motivator for behavior change, and should assume that many curious young adults will experiment with drugs. In addition, skills must be taught that will allow the young adults who do use drugs experimentally to control that use, and that will reduce the danger of drug-using activities in order to reduce harm to young and naïve drug users. Prevention programs are the first and best line of defense against drug problems developing in the first place. However, our society has not invested in or developed effective prevention programs in the same way that we have invested in and developed treatment programs. It is unfortunate, because it is almost as if we have built our house of treatment services without a strong and necessary foundation of prevention. Our house of treatment is the weaker for it, too.

What the Future Holds: What Is Next for Treatment?

Many of the changes in treatment protocols over the last decade have been driven primarily by two factors: economics and new research. As mentioned, when I started in the addictions field, 28-day inpatient treatment was the norm. Third-party reimbursement (by insurance companies and governmental agencies) has pushed the industry to shorter (if any) inpatient stays, with the bulk of the treatment being conducted in an outpatient modality to control costs. This change is not necessarily a bad thing, since the research suggests that outpatient therapy is as effective as inpatient services for most clients. In addition, highly successful brief interventions and therapies have been developed and widely tested that can be conducted in a few sessions, sometimes even just one (see discussions about motivational enhancement therapy and interviewing in Chapters 3 and 5).

I believe these particular trends will continue into the future as medical and mental health resources become more stretched in American society. Furthermore, the integration of multiple modalities of treatment is likely to become more commonplace, so that clients may receive all sorts of services as part of treatment. Treatment for clients with co-occurring disorders is likely to be more common, and pharmacotherapy will be a routine part of treatment along with psychological therapy. It is more likely that cravings will be managed with new *prophylactic* medicines during treatment. Therapists and counselors will need to become skilled in using empirically supported therapies specifically targeted at disorders that commonly accompany drug problems, such as cognitive behavioral therapies for depressive and anxiety disorders (see Chapter 5 for more information). In addition, neuropsychological evaluations may become more necessary, since research has determined that significant cognitive problems frequently occur among people who abuse drugs.

The demographics of the country are changing, and it is predicted that some time around the year 2050 White Americans will be outnumbered by all the other racial-ethnic groups. This suggests that treatment in the not-so-distant future will have many new cultural issues to consider. Language barriers will be increasingly important to overcome, and many clients will have radically different worldviews than the majority who are treated now. It is likely these differences in worldviews will affect how treatment is designed. For instance, folk healers from particular cultures are invited to be part of treatment in some areas of the country today, and this will probably become a necessity for most areas of the country in 50 years. Another consideration is whether traditional support groups will work for people with worldviews that differ greatly from those of the majority culture, because there is some evidence now that they do not (e.g., Arroyo, Miller, & Tonigan, 2003).

Additionally, technological advances will offer new and exciting ways to treat clients. Already, Web-based services are being used for primary and secondary prevention of substance abuse, principally among young adults. It may be that some treatment services will eventually be offered at common Web sites over the Internet. Virtual reality also offers the potential for clients, at the flip of a switch, to have *imaginal exposure* (simulated real-life situations, sought in order to practice skills) to high-risk relapse situations. Already virtual reality is being used for the treatment of other psychological disorders, mainly anxiety, and it is only a matter of time before some enterprising treatment center uses virtual reality to train their clients in drug refusal skills. This technology offers the opportunity to take relapse prevention to a new and rather realistic level.

Finally, prevention must play a larger role in treating drug problems before they occur. The best money we can spend is to nip a drug problem in the bud. Unfortunately, drug prevention programs have not fared well in the past, and new programs must be developed that not only reach those people at risk, but do not alienate them at the same time. The prevention message must focus on public health rather than moral concerns, and should be a message that will not be dismissed by those who need to hear it most.

All of these changes may cause some nervousness in the field, since therapists and counselors will have to know how to treat more than simply drug problems alone. However, in the end, I believe greater competence in all of these areas will help the clients we treat immensely, and ultimately may reduce the risk of relapse after discharge from therapy. A great deal of this book will be dedicated to providing detailed information that may help therapists develop new competencies in preparation for the exciting future in the treatment of drug problems, and for consumers to make informed choices on how to treat their drug problems.

Summing Up

Defining a drug problem is complex, and its definition is complicated by a great number of cultural myths that have no scientific support. Many beliefs in our culture about what constitutes a drug problem simply do not agree with the research. The use of drugs is not necessarily a gateway to a drug problem, and even when a drug problem develops, it may change over time without any intervention at all. The biopsychosocial model suggests that drug problems, when they occur, are influenced by an interaction of biological, psychological, and social factors that vary greatly from person to person and across different cultures.

The greatest hope for intervening upon a drug problem is treating the factors we know how to change at the present, which are mainly psychological and environmental. Because drug problems may look different from one person to the next, therapists and counselors must individualize treatment services to serve the unique problems of individuals, even if the treatment is delivered in groups. Prevention methods would be our first and best weapon, but they currently are underfunded and lag years behind the development of treatment services. In the future, treatment will be influenced by rapidly changing demographics and by technological advances. Treatment and therapy do work, and will only get better in the future with these changes.

Key Terms

Biopsychosocial. A model wherein a drug problem is believed to develop because of an interaction among biology, psychology, and the social environment.

Co-occurring disorders. The occurrence of other disorders along with the drug problem; also called *dual diagnosis* or *comorbid disorders*.

Craving. A strong desire to use drugs, which can be physically or psychologically cued.

Denial. A way to describe a person's apparent unawareness of a drug problem.

Detoxification. The period when a person is withdrawing from a substance.

Drug myopia. Drug-induced distortion of a person's perceptions of reality such that the person is blinded to what is happening around him or her.

Maturing out. A natural phenomenon whereby many youthful drug users naturally evolve out of a drug problem as they mature.

Natural recovery. The phenomenon whereby many people with drug problems are able to overcome those problems by themselves.

Novelty seeking. A natural youthful tendency to seek out new and interesting experiences.

Parental monitoring. The amount of time that parents actively spend with their children.

Pharmacotherapy. Therapy that uses medicines to treat problems.

Prophylactic. Preventive measures to stop a problem before it starts.

Relapse. A return to old substance use patterns after a period of cessation.

Self-medicating. The attempts of some drug users to reduce symptoms of another problem by using drugs.

Temperament. Similar to personality, it is the way a person may get along with others.

Recommended Reading

One recommended resource is *How Drugs Influence Behavior: A Neurobehavioral Approach,* by Jaime Diaz (New York: Prentice-Hall, 1996). This book is written in such a way that even nonresearchers can understand the effects of certain types of drugs upon the body.

Another I recommend is *Addiction and Change,* by Carlo C. DiClemente (New York: Guilford Press, 2003). This book provides a detailed review of the research that concerns how to change a substance-related problem.

TRUTH OR FICTION

QUIZ ANSWERS

1. True; 2. False; 3. False; 4. False; 5. False; 6. True; 7. False

CHAPTER 2

Recognizing a Drug Problem

TRUTH OR FICTION QUIZ

After reading this chapter, you should be able to answer the following questions:

1. Determining that a person has a drug problem is generally easy to do. True or False?
2. Tough-love approaches are always the best strategies to use if your loved one has a drug problem. True or False?
3. Depression and anxiety commonly occur with drug problems. True or False?
4. Many people with drug problems are also anxious in social situations. True or False?
5. Therapy and treatment can improve lives dramatically. True or False?
6. Ambivalence about drug use is normal. True or False?
7. A referral will generally hurt a client. True or False?

Answers on p. 88.

One of the most difficult things to determine is whether a person has a drug problem. For therapists, the determination often is made by use of second- or thirdhand information, by use of a relatively short assessment of behavior, or by use of a very limited amount of contact with the client (hours of clinical time, rather than days; for other professionals, contact with the client may be even briefer). In addition, since the visit may not necessarily be made with a drug problem in mind, even less information about drug usage and consequences may be forthcoming from the client. For family members and friends, it is difficult to sort out the truth about whether a loved one or a friend may have a drug problem, since such issues can be quite emotionally charged and strong personal feelings can be involved. Proceeding thoughtfully and carefully when one suspects a drug problem can help avoid losing the trust one has with a client, loved one, friend, or coworker.

There are some signs and symptoms that serve as warning flags for a possible drug problem, but these signs and symptoms do not provide 100% certainty that the problem is related to drugs. Sometimes these problems are signs and symptoms of a wide variety of problems besides drug abuse. Therefore, it is prudent to look for several corroborating signs that a drug problem may be present. The presence of only one sign alerts you to the possibility of a drug problem, and to keep your eyes open for other signs of trouble. Please remember that one sign cannot be taken as proof positive that a drug problem exists.

Here is an example of why you have to be careful when trying to identify a problem by one sign alone. Treatment professionals often have used the occurrence of a drinking-and-driving offense as an indication that someone likely has an alcohol problem. The rationale behind this is the opinion that most social drinkers would not drive while under the influence of alcohol, or that the odds of their getting caught are much lower than those of someone (like a person with an alcohol problem) who would drive while impaired more frequently. However, a recent study found that social drinkers are just as likely to get arrested and charged with a drinking-and-driving offense as someone who has a drinking problem, which challenges the conventional wisdom. In light of this new evidence, should therapists now ignore drinking-and-driving offenses as irrelevant to the identification of a drinking problem? Absolutely not! The research has made it clear that using this criterion for identifying possible problem-drinking behavior may produce *false positives* along with true positives, so it should be a flag for concern but not a banner to herald an absolute problem. However, savvy professionals know that such an offense offers a great opportunity to assess for other warning flags related to drinking problems. The same logic is used for detecting a drug problem (other than one with alcohol). One sign or symptom does not a problem make, but keeping your eyes open for other signs or symptoms is warranted.

The next few sections of this chapter will discuss in some detail what therapists and other professionals, as well as friends or loved ones whom they may be counseling, should look for when a drug problem is suspected in a client, loved one, close friend, coworker, or employee. Keep in mind that there are exceptions to every rule. For example, some people are able to use drugs without obvious problems. Other people use drugs experimentally once or a very few times and have significant problems by happenstance, but are able to change their behavior rapidly because of these problems (and usually do not use drugs again). Keep in mind that these signs and symptoms may be from another mental health problem, or even from a co-occurring mental health problem (which will be discussed in greater depth later in this chapter). The signs and symptoms presented are meant as a guide but not necessarily a guarantee. When in doubt, remember that a thorough professional evaluation is warranted before you jump to conclusions. The next section offers a discussion

> "Problems are only opportunities in work clothes."
>
> — HENRY J. KAISER

of what a loved one, friend, or employer should look for when he or she notices a problem and believes it may be drug related. Following this discussion will be a section on what you as a therapist, counselor, or other professional should look for in terms of abnormal behavior that may be drug related in order to determine whether a more comprehensive evaluation should be completed.

Symptoms of a Drug Problem: What Family, Friends, and Coworkers May Observe

As mentioned earlier in this book, a drug problem usually involves biological, psychological, and social or environmental factors. With this model in mind, you can conceptualize signs and symptoms of a drug problem within these three domains. Drug problems can cause changes in health or appearance; in personality, mood, and emotions; in routine, responsibility, and reliability; and in relationships, work behavior, and other social and recreational activities. Often the people in close proximity to a person suspected of having a drug problem detect these changes more quickly than a stranger (or even a therapist) can, but not always. Sometimes people with drug problems are very good at covering them up. Many times people with drug problems can have difficulties in one area of their lives while appearing quite normal in other areas. So even though, for example, a problem may be detectable to a love partner, there is no guarantee that coworkers or close friends will see the same problem, or even suspect that problems exist.

Significant and negative physical changes can herald a drug problem, and one noticeable symptom can be the development of a significant health problem or a noticeable change in health status. There are many health conditions (as mentioned in Chapter 1) linked to drug problems, and some of these are potentially life threatening. Another sign of a drug problem is reduced cognitive function. If a person is experiencing memory problems or lapses in memory, it could be a sign of a problem with drugs (although it could be symptomatic of other things as well). Other cognitive problems besides change in memory abilities may be more difficult to pin down. Since drug use can affect many other brain functions, there may be noticeable changes in higher thinking processes or even in behavior. Sometimes a person becomes clumsy and perhaps seems accident prone. Other times a person may appear mostly normal but show signs of making very poor decisions, perhaps acting impulsively and often taking risks without realizing he or she is doing so. Unfortunately, although these cognitive changes may be obvious to the observer, the person in question may not be aware of them at all.

However, some observable physical changes are subtler than those previously mentioned and are not obviously debilitating to the person in question. For instance, sometimes problems with irritability and morning sluggishness that may linger late into the day can be a sign of withdrawal symptoms. Drug use also can cause rashes, acne, sores, and other skin problems that did not exist before.

Sometimes friends, coworkers, or loved ones may notice changes in speech patterns or in a person's behavioral pace, such that a person may seem more accelerated or retarded in activities or exhibit unusual sleeping patterns. People with drug problems sometimes let their appearances go, not caring so much about how they look in public. Changes in appearance may include anything from grooming to clothing. Sometimes significant weight changes, usually a weight loss, may be noticeable, as well as changes in fitness level. In addition, some people who have drug problems experience photosensitivity, so they will be bothered by light and may compensate by wearing sunglasses indoors or opting for low lighting in their environment.

However, physical changes are not the only potential signs of a drug problem. Noticeable changes may be observed in personality, mood, or emotions. Family members have told me in the past they knew something was wrong because loved ones seemed like strangers or had changed into completely different people. Family members reported a variety of negative changes they observed in the ways their loved ones interacted with other people. Mood changes included being more hostile, frustrated, anxious, depressed, or even paranoid. Behaviorally, the person may appear more restless, sneaky, reclusive, or secretive because of these moods. Emotionally, a person with a drug problem may seem short-tempered or moody, with *emotional lability* (extreme and often unexpected mood change) sometimes present. Frequently, emotions are expressed in unexpected or inappropriate ways for a particular situation (i.e., not consistent with the way others might respond, or perhaps not even consistent with how the person may have responded in the past before drug use). In other cases, emotional responses may be quite exaggerated for the situation (e.g., getting really angry about a little thing) or noticeably underexpressed (such that the person does not seem to care about something that she or he used to care about). In many instances the response will seem either too intense or too laid back for the given situation.

A third area of change that loved ones, friends, or coworkers may observe would be a fundamental change in the person's day-to-day behavior, or in personal interests or goals over the long term. To begin with, a change in a person's routine may be one possible warning sign of a drug problem. The person may neglect daily responsibilities or appear to be less reliable than before. The routine generally changes slowly as a drug problem develops, so it may be difficult to detect changes immediately. Eventually a person with a drug problem may neglect various activities that used to be important to her or him, or may reduce activities with family or friends — for example, no longer wanting to walk the dog (which used to be a fun and important task for the person), forgetting to cut the grass or pay the bills, not playing with the children, or perhaps forgetting where the car is parked and walking home. Behavioral changes may show up as tardiness or even missing appointments, and these changes may worsen over time. The person in question may forget to do certain work-related tasks or assignments, and may fail to show for certain meetings or events, and then try to cover with vague or unreasonable excuses. Sometimes the person in question may get defensive if those excuses are questioned or challenged. In more severe circumstances, people with drug problems may blame others, including those closest to them, rather than admit to what is really going on. If such a pattern persists, the behavioral changes may result in fundamental changes in the person's basic values and overall lifestyle. These fundamental changes in lifestyle often will be at odds with what may have been important values in the past. One obvious clue is that the behavior of a person with a drug problem becomes less predictable over time.

Relationships are another area of interpersonal behavior where loved ones could notice warnings signs of a drug problem. For example, family members may notice a significant change in level of intimacy with a partner. As mentioned, the partner may seem like a stranger, and this stranger syndrome can adversely affect conversations, joint decision-making activities, and level of interest in couple or family activities. Partners also may exhibit disinterest in sexual intimacy, or perhaps even an inability to achieve an erection or have an orgasm. Sometimes problems with intimacy are perceived as neglect and disinterest; in other instances partners may argue more. In still other instances, abusive behavior may result. Most domestic violence can be linked to substance abuse in some form. A person with a drug problem may abuse loved ones with words, physical violence, or emotional cruelty, or in extreme cases may abuse someone sexually. This aggressive behavior affects both partners and children, and abuse in the household may not always be obvious to a casual observer. Drug-using children also can exhibit aggressive tendencies, which usually come across as being argumentative or defiant. However, in some cases children can be abusive toward a parent or sibling. Children with drug problems also will opt out of family activities, and will exhibit many of the overt changes in behavior already discussed. Usually the changes are most notable in academic performance and in the home life.

Other family and relationship problems may emerge as a result of a drug problem. Financial problems or even financial mismanagement may be a sign that something is wrong. If bills are not being paid, money is slipping away inexplicably, or bill collectors are calling, then it may be a sign of a drug problem. Also, certain personal items such as jewelry, appliances, or other items may turn up missing without explanation (having been either lost or hocked). Financial problems can be exacerbated if there are other co-occurring conditions, such as a mental disorder typified by impulsive behavior, or a compulsive gambling problem.

Sometimes a person with a drug problem will distance him- or herself from the family by seeking seclusion in a private area of the house (like a basement or a shed) in order to use drugs. In some cases people with drug problems may make this location off-limits to other family members, or may insist on time alone at specific times of the day. Loved ones may discover drug paraphernalia by accident in those areas of seclusion or in other places frequented by the person.

When confronted with such evidence, it may be that the person will deny it or react angrily against "accusations." The discovery of such items does not necessarily mean the person has a drug problem, but one might be more suspicious if there was clear intent to hide such behavior.

Friends also may note behavior changes warning of a potential drug problem. Many times close friendships are adversely affected by the drug problem. The close friend may seem to drift away with little explanation, or may associate him- or herself with unknown strangers or even people who seem out of character for the person. In other cases arguments may ensue, potentially over something quite trivial. Drug-using friends may be irritable and difficult to be around. Many people I've worked with in therapy have reported the loss of at least one significant friendship because of drug use, and often express regret about that loss after the fact. In some cases, friends can detect a drug problem before family members do, simply because family members may be too close to the situation to actually be aware of what is happening in an objective fashion. Friends also may be more attuned to the other behavioral changes mentioned earlier in the chapter.

Employers and coworkers also may notice certain behavioral changes that cause concern. A drug problem contributes to worker unreliability, which is often easy for coworkers to spot. For instance, a reduction in productivity may be noticed, with expected work not being completed on time or the quality of work becoming sloppy. The worker may begin to show a pattern of tardiness or increased absenteeism. This change in reliability also may include taking long or excessive breaks or long lunch hours. Coworkers may see unusual behavior from the person with a drug problem, and may perceive the person as high-strung, irritable, or argumentative. There also may be indications of irresponsibility with company property, such as damaged or lost work-related items and equipment, or perhaps even a misplaced or damaged company vehicle.

Children and adolescents may show similar signs of a problem at school, with truancy often being the principle sign. Dropping grades and failure of classes are cause for concern. Aggressiveness also can be a sign of a drug problem among some children and adolescents. This aggressiveness may result in bullying behavior among peers, which is a widely underreported problem in schools today. Students with drug problems may sleep in class. On the other hand, sleeping in class could also be a sign of a *parental* drug problem rather than one in the child or youth in question, so caution needs to be exercised in interpreting this behavior. Parental drug use can cause significant disruption of sleep patterns for children due to stress, domestic violence, and the placement of increased family and sometimes work responsibilities on the child. So it cannot be assumed that students who sleep in class are using drugs, and the problem may be as innocent as late-night phone calls or television viewing (but you can safely assume that something is not right).

Other changes in activities that might suggest a drug problem include a reduction in social or recreational activities. Often a person with a drug problem will withdraw from social activities with which she or he used to be actively engaged. Many times this change will be observed as a loss of interest in recreation or the neglect of a hobby that used to be very important for the person. In certain cases a person may withdraw from social situations unexpectedly. In other circumstances a person may seem like he or she is socializing through "partying a lot," which of course may be quite literally true. Changes in interests like these seem quite pronounced, and may be viewed as a radical shift in personal tastes and interests regarding social activities and hobbies, when in fact the issue may be that the time and activities are focused on drug use. However, like all of the signs mentioned in this section, a change in interests or activities may be related to many different things, so you cannot simply assume these changes are related to a drug problem without further evaluation.

Signs of a Drug Problem: What Professionals May Observe

First, it is worth noting that assessment is the most important thing a therapist can do while working with someone who may have a drug problem. A thorough, well-conducted assessment of a person's behavior is the foundation for the type and quality of therapy he or she will receive. If the assessment is weak or poorly conducted, then therapy will be weak as well. With this being said, a professional should always assess the different life areas previously discussed for significant changes in behavior and for dysfunctional patterns (including health and appearance; cognitive function; personality, mood, and emotional experiences; family, friendships, and other social relationships; and finances, school, work, hobbies and interests, and recreational activities). The professional may have access to collaborative information from loved ones, friends, or coworkers, which can help in the assessment process. However, some research has found that professionals may get a more accurate picture of a drug problem from the drug user rather than from a family member simply because a great deal of the drug-using behavior is hidden from the family. Assessment tools and methods will be discussed in much greater detail in Chapter 4.

Besides assessing for the various signs already discussed, the professional may observe certain behaviors during in-session contact with the person that may suggest whether a problem is drug related. For example, a person's reluctance to discuss drug use with you may suggest the possibility of a drug problem. Usually reluctance is related to distrust of mental health services or of the significant amount of power that you may hold over the person you are interviewing. If you understand the issues around power imbalance in therapeutic relationships and the importance of establishing an alliance to build trust for the sake of the therapeutic relationship, then you can avoid this potential roadblock to gleaning information from the client and working toward progress in therapy. However, if you move forward in the interview without recognizing or acknowledging these concerns, then it is likely that the meeting will be frustrating for both you and the other person. Many people with drug problems are very reluctant to talk about drug use to a stranger (understandably so, if you consider the potential legal consequences).

The reluctance to discuss a drug problem also is related to the fear by many drug users that they will get "the lecture" from you. Many of my drug-using clients have told me about their reluctance to discuss drug problems openly because of fears about being judged harshly for their behavior. Several confided that they had been lectured to by counselors, therapists, and other professionals in the past and did not care to repeat those experiences ("humiliating," "judgmental," and "parental" are terms I have heard used to describe past lectures from health care professionals to my clients). So in response to the lecture, clients may choose to argue with you or "check out" of the interaction. Since some people with drug problems have come to expect the lecture, they may carry out a preemptive strike of their own, baiting the professional in session in order to speed up the argument. In this way the client is testing the professional to see how trustworthy he or she is, and if the lecture ensues (as the client fully expects), then the interview is, for all practical purposes, over. As a professional, you should be aware that you will be tested for trustworthiness by the person in the room with you, and if you fall into the lecture-the-client trap, then you might as well be lecturing to the wall.

Sometimes clients blame others or circumstances for the problems they are having rather than blame the drugs. Be aware, however, that this is a common stereotype, since many people believe that blame is typical of someone not yet ready to change drug use behavior. However, it is not always the case that people will blame if they have a drug problem, and sometimes blaming behavior is more related to personality than it is to drug abuse. You cannot simply assume that a person with a suspected drug problem will use excessive amounts of blame, just like you cannot assume it is a drug problem if the person blames a great deal. Even though I have seen blaming behavior in some clients with drug problems, it is not fair to say that blame is a defining characteristic of a drug problem.

Other things that professionals can look for in session include inappropriate mood or emotional reactions as well as physical symptoms — pupil dilations or constrictions; needle tracks or other skin changes, including a yellowish tint (hepatitis); restlessness, sweating, and other sympathetic nervous system–type (fight or flight) responses; signs of intoxication, including slurred or incoherent speech and difficulty with attention, concentration, and other mental processes; significant bruising or nosebleeds; and emaciation, which may reflect malnutrition and weight loss. Drug testing may provide some data about the person you are seeing, but what do the data really mean? *Toxicology* screens can provide evidence of drug use, but this is not necessarily evidence of drug problems. Furthermore, these screens are not necessarily infallible. There are sometimes false positives, and in other instance some people with drug problems are quite skilled at getting around such testing in a number of ways.

An additional tip-off to a possible problem is to ask yourself what it is that brings this person in to see you today. Did the person have an accident of some kind? Research has found that many household, worksite, and auto accidents are related to substance abuse. Did the person attempt suicide? The research suggests that substance abuse is a problem for many people who attempt suicide. In a very real sense, professionals have to piece together the evidence as if they were psychological detectives, and in many cases the evidence may be indirect, vague, or circumstantial, which makes it difficult to accurately determine the truth about the person being interviewed. Ultimately, progress on determining the true source of a problem will require that the client or patient trust you enough to share his or her perception of what the problem may be. How to build this trust, even in a short amount of time, will be discussed in Chapter 3.

THINGS TO REMEMBER

Symptoms That Collaterals May See That Could Suggest a Drug Problem

- Changes in health or physical appearance
- Changes in cognitive abilities such as memory, decision making, or judgment
- Changes in personality, mood, or emotions, especially emotional extremes
- Changes in behavior, routine, values, or interpersonal relationships
- Loss of interest in hobbies, social events, or recreation that used to be important to the person

Additional signs that professionals may observe:

- Information provided by others about the client
- Reticence about discussing drug use
- Blaming others or circumstances rather than the drug use for problems
- Inappropriate moods or emotions in session
- Physical signs related to drug use
- The circumstances behind the visit
- Work or school problems
- Involvement in accidents or acts of violence, either as a victim or as a perpetrator

Remember that these symptoms and signs could also point to other problems besides drugs, so make sure to get a comprehensive assessment!

When Collaterals Come for Help First

There are many instances when a family member *(collateral)* will seek help for a problem before the person with the drug problem does. Often, however, the family member will not be forthcoming about the drug problem, or it will not be otherwise obvious that drug abuse is indirectly involved. Excellent examples of these types of situations include the family members' seeking help as victims of domestic violence or parental neglect, or are injured in accidents.

As a professional, you should be educated on your legal responsibilities for reporting incidents of domestic violence to civil authorities. These responsibilities can vary widely from state to state, but typically involve an assessment of the risk of further harm to the person who has been hurt. Again, I want to emphasize that professionals must be familiar with the processes in their states for protecting the health and well-being of people from perpetration, and those legal expectations and your ethical obligations as a professional will guide your responses (see also the discussion on responding to crises in Chapter 3). There also are many resources on how to handle victimization through therapy, support systems, temporary housing, and other important services to ensure the well-being of victimized clients.

In addition to perpetrated violence, it is critical to remember that victims of household, worksite, or auto accidents may not have a drug problem, but the occurrence of the accident may point toward a drug problem in someone else who is involved. Within family situations, a partner may have caused an accident that contributed to injury of a family member. Sometimes a tragic situation like this will allow a brief window of opportunity to identify and intervene upon a drug problem. It is commonly understood that when a family member is a victim of abuse, there is the strong possibility of a drug-related problem in the perpetrator. Under these circumstances, many professionals would know to assess for a drug problem somewhere in the family system. However, many professionals forget to consider drug problems as a possibility in the family system when accidents occur.

For example, many professionals may not be aware that child neglect is often the result of drug abuse by one or both parents. Many children who are injured or killed due to accidents (e.g., those caused by fires, poisoning, or falls) or even those admitted to emergency health care because of neglect or as a result of nonadherence to medical requirements (as with a fatal asthma attack) can be linked to a family in which one or more parents have a drug problem. Parental neglect can be caused by many things, including momentary distraction, of course, and everyone who has been a parent knows there are times when your attention may be momentarily drawn away from your children. However, the research suggests that many children who play with matches, fall down stairs, swallow household chemicals (or heroin, for that matter), get locked in closed cars during an August heat wave, or experience some other trauma or critical life-threatening events often are neglected because drug use has interfered with parental monitoring.

In schools, professionals may witness children acting out in class, underachieving, daydreaming, or having other behavioral or scholarship problems. Remember that attention or concentration problems and restlessness can be caused by things other than Attention-Deficit/Hyperactivity Disorder (ADHD). If a child attends school and appears unkempt, disheveled, and poorly clothed for the circumstances (e.g., underdressed for winter), this too may represent parental neglect related to drug use. In addition, infants who are born under the influence of substances provide strong evidence for a maternal drug problem.

As you can see, there are many different symptoms and signs that may point to a drug problem. However, the difficulty is that these same symptoms and signs may point of other kinds of problems as well, and may produce a false positive with regard to a drug problem. It is critical not to confront a person about such a problem prematurely, but rather to provide an environment where he or she feels comfortable in disclosing without the fear of being judged harshly.

What family members, friends, coworkers, and professionals must do is piece together the evidence to see if a pattern emerges among the symptoms and signs that would suggest a strong likelihood of such a problem. With all this being said, though, it is up to the person with the problem to admit to having that problem, and then to do something about it. Collaterals can open the door to awareness of the drug problem and maybe for the desirability of change, but ultimately the drug user must walk through that door for something different to happen.

Recognizing the Existence of More Than One Problem

It may not be the end of the story even when a drug problem has been identified. As you may remember from Chapter 1, a great many people who have drug problems also have other mental or physical health problems. Some of these problems may be a result of drug use, but for some people the health problems may have preceded the drug problems. Regardless of which came first, it is necessary to identify problems that may accompany the drug problems if the client is going to receive the proper care needed for successful treatment.

There are specific symptoms that family members, friends, coworkers and professionals can look for to help determine whether there are other problems besides drug use. Identifying other mental or physical health concerns can help a person advocate for specialized services for a client or his or her loved one, friend, or coworker in order to provide for the best care possible. However, identification of these signs or symptoms only warns there may be another problem — it does not tell you what the problem may be. If signs of other problems are noted, you should recommend a comprehensive evaluation by a professional trained in this type of assessment (e.g., a clinical psychologist, psychiatrist, or mental health professional with similar skills) if you do not feel ready to make that assessment yourself. That way you will know for sure what your client needs help with.

CASE STUDY

Rebecca Is Restless!

Rebecca is a 13-year-old student who began to have problems in school recently. Her teacher is convinced that her falling grades show that something is wrong, but she is not sure what. She tells you that Rebecca has been increasingly restless in class, and seems to have difficulty sitting still. In addition, she has noticed that Rebecca is more irritable and does not want to be around others. The teacher also has noted that Rebecca has more acne now than she did a few weeks ago.

So what is wrong with Rebecca? Is she on drugs? Does she have Attention Deficit Disorder? Was she exposed to alcohol or drugs as a fetus, and now the symptoms are beginning to be noticeable? Does she exhibit early symptoms of a major mental disorder? Is she abused or neglected at home? How would you find out?

Co-occurring Mental Health Symptoms

Psychotic behavior is the most obvious cluster of mental health symptoms to identify. *Psychotic* means that the person has a mental disorder that contributes to sensations or beliefs that are not real. Sensations that are not real are referred to as *hallucinations,* and they can be perceived by means of any of the senses. For example, auditory hallucinations often are perceived as voices or noises that in reality have not occurred, and sometimes these voices command the person to do things he or she does not want to do. Visual hallucinations, sometimes experienced as visions, amount to seeing things that are not real. Hallucinations also can be tactile (touch related), including the perception of feeling something in the body that in reality is not happening; or olfactory, which involves smelling things that are not there. Sometimes people even perceive tastes that are not really experienced.

Delusions, on the other hand, are persistent beliefs or belief systems that are not based in reality and often cause the person experiencing them to be anxious or paranoid. Many of these delusions have a theme (a common thread), which frequently involves feelings of threat, concerns about being personally targeted by a conspiracy, obsessive thoughts, or inordinate concerns about ill health. If a person has both hallucinations and delusions, these experiences tend to feed off one another and confirm one another's content. Hallucinations tend to support the delusional beliefs, and the delusions usually are related to the hallucinations. However, you can have the experience of one without the experience of the other, meaning that some people have delusions without hallucinations and some have hallucinations without delusions.

Although hallucinations and delusions are common symptoms of *schizophrenia,* psychotic mood disorders (depressive or bipolar), and a few other disorders, it must be noted that these symptoms can be experienced by anyone under stress. For example, if you are tired enough, you may believe you saw something run out in front of your car in the middle of the night when in fact it was simply a shadow. Or perhaps you think you hear someone calling your name, and when you turn around, no one is waving to you or even looking your way. Hallucinations can happen to anyone if the circumstances are right, and sometimes we may even engage in delusional thinking for brief periods of time. So it is critical not to determine a diagnosis on the basis of one symptom, but rather on the basis of a pattern of symptoms.

Psychotic disorders can be effectively treated with medicines if properly diagnosed and if the person is referred to appropriate treatment. Antipsychotic medication has been found to control symptoms, and a new generation of atypical antipsychotic medications has fewer side effects for users. However, after the psychotic symptoms are controlled, it is strongly advised that you include cognitive behavioral skills training as part of therapy to teach the person to care for him- or herself appropriately (see Chapter 5). A sizeable percentage of people with psychotic disorders also misuse drugs, but in relative terms, the occurrence of psychotic behavior in society is small. When these symptoms occur, the most challenging task is to try to determine their source — which may be related to a psychotic disorder, but also can be related to drug use, since many substances (such as methamphetamine and hallucinogens) can cause psychotic symptoms and even lead to psychotic breaks (referred to as *drug-induced psychosis*) in clients.

Unlike psychosis, depressive symptoms do commonly occur among people with drug problems. *Depression* can include psychotic symptoms, but that tends to happen very rarely and only in extremely severe cases. Depressive symptoms that may be observed include dysphoria (sadness), inertia (lack of energy or movement), *suicidal ideations* and behavior, psychomotor retardation (sluggishness) or restlessness, anhedonia (not experiencing pleasure, even from things that may have given great joy in the past), significant weight change (excluding that from active dieting), problems concentrating or thinking, insomnia or hypersomnia (sleeping a lot more than usual), thoughts about death, and dark thoughts toward the self, including self-denigration. Another key factor to consider is whether these symptoms are noted to be interfering with a person's life in a noticeable way. There are two general types or patterns of depression that are most commonly observed. One is called *Dysthymia*. Dysthymia is the kind of depression in which a person seems to have the blues generally all the time. In Dysthymia, sometimes the blues become full-blown depression and debilitate the person, but at other times the person simply seems constantly down in the dumps, and perhaps irritable and difficult to be around because of his or her negativity or cynicism. The other type of depressive pattern is called *Major Depression*, which is debilitating for a person and tends to be more acute than Dysthymia. (People with Dysthymia often do experience Major Depression from time to time, however.)

Some people have a seasonal pattern to their depression, meaning that the degree of depression changes throughout the year. The pattern of depression revolves around the relative amount of sunlight available, so that depression onset may occur in the fall, worsen in the winter, diminish with the return of spring, and subside completely in the summer. This type of condition is called *Seasonal Affective Disorder (SAD),* and it is much more commonly seen in northern latitudes in this hemisphere (or in far southern latitudes in the southern hemisphere). Researchers have tracked changes in substance use among people who have SAD, and have found a profound increase in use during the depressive cycle (winter) for a great many people. Many clients with SAD told me they were using more during the darker months to self-medicate their symptoms (recall the discussion about self-medicating in Chapter 1). Professionals should be aware that a cyclical pattern of substance use that seems to mirror changes in seasons may suggest underlying SAD, even if this condition has not been previously diagnosed. This would be especially true for people who live in the northernmost areas of the United States. SAD may be missed if a professional is not actively looking for a seasonal pattern to drug use.

If a family member notices any of the symptoms previously mentioned in a loved one, then it may be that the loved one is depressed and should be evaluated by a mental health professional. If a loved one is expressing suicidal thoughts, or it is discovered that he or she has put his or her affairs in order (has sold or given away significant amounts of personal property, written a will, settled debts, etc.), then it would be critical to get help for that person as quickly as possible. Suicide is a major concern with people who abuse drugs, since a majority of suicides in the United States are attempted under the influence of drugs or alcohol.

Mental health professionals are legally bound in many states to assess for possible harm to self. Because of the high comorbidity of depression and suicidal behavior with drug use, clinicians working with drug users need to be aware of the particular laws and procedures for reporting possible harm to self within the states in which they are practicing. Generally speaking, it is important to assess *all* clients with drug problems for possible depression and suicidal ideations, as well as for a history of suicidal behavior (see Chapter 4 for more details on assessing depression). The treatment of choice for depression is usually a combination of psychotherapy (like cognitive behavioral therapy or interpersonal therapy — see Chapter 5) and pharmacotherapy (antidepressants). In addition, another difficult task is determining which came first, the depression or the drug use. Depression can be a natural consequence of rebound effects and withdrawal processes that occur after chronic and acute substance abuse, so it is very commonly seen in drug-using clients. However, some clients I have worked with have told me that they remember being blue or depressed long before they ever touched a drink or a drug, so depression is not always a consequence but instead may be an antecedent.

Another type of mood disorder that commonly co-occurs with drug problems is *Bipolar Affective Disorder*. Bipolar disorders include depression as a symptom (one of two emotional poles — hence, *bipolar*), but they also include mania or hypomania, which is a period of high energy and potentially other problematic and high-energy symptoms. Loved ones may observe symptoms like sleeplessness (for days on end), irritability, and excitability; extreme behavior related to, and obsession with, religiosity, sex, spending, and pleasure seeking; grandiosity (beliefs of exaggerated self-worth, superhuman power, strength, etc.); very rapid, constant, and sometimes incoherent speech; poor judgment; or racing thoughts (as described by the person experiencing them). Again, a key factor to consider is whether more than one of these symptoms are occurring at once and whether these symptoms are interfering with the person's life. A manic episode is frequently followed by a down cycle of depression and a physical crash, during which the person may sleep a lot and be very de-energized. Anyone who observes these symptoms in a friend or loved one should be advised to seek an assessment of the person by a mental health professional.

However, one difficulty is that many drugs cause behaviors that mimic mania. In some cases, the person may not be manic per se, but rather may be intoxicated on a stimulant drug. It is up to professionals to determine whether the symptoms are drug induced or whether there is something more than drug effects contributing to the behavior. Professionals also need to be aware that the risks of suicide among people with bipolar disorders are quite high even during the manic or hypomanic phases (which actually may provide them with the energy to carry out the act), so care should be taken to assess for suicide risks. Bipolar disorders are very treatable, by using mood-stabilizing drugs and sometimes antipsychotics to treat the symptoms, and cognitive behavioral skills training to change dysfunctional coping styles (see Chapter 5).

RESEARCH FRONTIERS

Treating Co-occuring Disorders

For years, psychiatric and drug abuse disorders were not even treated together. Now we know they commonly co-occur, which means for many years clients were getting only partial treatment. Even today we are still not sure how to treat these co-occurring conditions simultaneously in a consistently effective way with both psychotherapy and pharmacotherapy (see Chapter 5). The next century is likely to see many advances in both pharmacotherapy and psychotherapy to treat co-occurring conditions. There are effective methods to treat drug abuse and to treat other co-occurring psychiatric disorders. The next frontier in research is to learn how to combine these approaches in a way that can treat multiple disorders at once!

Another set of symptoms commonly observed among people with drug problems revolves around anxiety. Besides observing the more obvious symptoms of worry and restlessness, loved ones might notice exaggerated and extended fight-or-flight (sympathetic nervous system) responses, in which the person appears high-strung, uptight, and on edge; expressions of extreme fearfulness or exaggerated concerns about something bad happening to the person or to his or her family; or panic attacks, in which the loved one feels like he or she may die and worries that there may be some physical problem (like a heart attack, stroke, cancer, etc.) even though a medical doctor finds nothing wrong. In addition, the person may be very afraid of certain objects, experiences, or situations, and may do everything possible to avoid them. People who have experienced trauma in the past may sometimes feel like they are reliving the traumatic event, and may have anxiety and worry resulting from that trauma, including problems with nightmares while sleeping and possibly flashbacks of the experience while awake. People with drug problems may be at greater risk for experiencing trauma, since drug use leaves them vulnerable to victimization and can lead them into certain situations where violence can occur to them.

There is a wide variety of disorders with *anxiety* as a principle feature. One specific one is Generalized Anxiety Disorder, and its major feature typically involves being constantly worried, with particular themes of worry in specific areas of the person's life (e.g., a theme of exaggerated worry about a loved one getting hurt or sick). Another expression of anxiety is Panic Disorder, which is typified by multiple panic attacks that sometimes seem to come out of the blue. Obsessive-Compulsive Disorder is another form of anxiety and is typified by repetitive behaviors that are debilitating, such as repeated hand washings that cause skin damage, extreme concern about germs or health, and other extreme habits that may involve checking and rechecking, obsessive counting, or even ritualistic behavior patterns that are repeated over and over again. Yet another anxiety disorder related to the experience of trauma is Posttraumatic Stress Disorder (PTSD), and it may occur after a person has been confronted with a horrible disaster or an event that threatened death.

Having *phobias* (fears about objects, experiences, or situations) is a common experience for people with drug problems. For instance, Social Phobia or anxiety is frequently observed. Some of my clients have told me that their drug use started as a way to cope with anxiety and fears related to social situations. People with Social Phobia tend to get embarrassed very easily, often are perfectionists (which sets them up to judge themselves and others harshly), usually have performance-related anxiety in social situations, and try to avoid social situations as much as possible because of concerns about embarrassment and failure. Agoraphobia also is a commonly experienced disorder among people who have drug problems. Agoraphobia often leads to an avoidance of places (like an elevator, bridge, or crowded supermarket) where the person may feel trapped. Because of fears of being trapped, the person often stays at home a great deal and will avoid certain places at all costs. Agoraphobia can develop as a result of Social Phobia and Panic Disorder because the person is afraid of being embarrassed in a place where she or he cannot escape public observation.

Professionals should be aware that anxiety often co-occurs with depression, so it is reasonable that if you determine one is present in a client, you should assess for the other. Again, one of the challenges of assessing anxiety among people with drug problems is that many substances can induce anxiety by withdrawal symptoms, by overwhelming life consequences that may occur because of drug use, or by long-term neurochemical changes (similar to depression) that some substances cause in the brain. The client presentation can be complicated since anxiety tends to increase *after* a person quits using the substances, which means that for some time after a change in drug use, it will be difficult to sort out whether the anxiety is a result of physiological rebound or an underlying anxiety disorder.

Finally, benzodiazepines (tranquilizers) are the most commonly abused drugs by people with anxiety disorders. Even though researchers have found that benzodiazepines actually contribute to making anxiety worse in the long run (even though they may provide some short-term reductions in anxiety) because of their rebound effects, many physicians are still routinely prescribing these *anxiolytic drugs* to treat anxiety. Anxiety patients often carry spare amounts of these drugs (called *safety signals*) in their pockets for security purposes and tend to overuse and even abuse benzodiazepines in an effort to control anxiety symptoms. Professionals who suspect comorbid anxiety with drug abuse also should assess the client's use of benzodiazepines, and professionals working with anxiety patients should routinely assess for abuse of tranquilizers. The treatment of choice for anxiety disorders is cognitive behavioral therapy (see Chapter 5), which is highly successful in treating them, and in some cases the use of antidepressant medications may be helpful to control symptoms.

Sometimes *personality disorders* may co-occur with drug abuse. There are three commonly found among people who have drug problems: Antisocial, Narcissistic, and Borderline Personality Disorders. Antisocial personalities are defined by lack of concern about rules, disdain for authority, and sometimes utter lack of regard for the welfare of other people. Antisocial Personality Disorder often is defined by its behavior, including manipulation of others for personal gain, cruelty to others (and animals), criminal behavior, and a desire to take risks and seek thrills. Again, identifying these qualities as a pattern of behavior rather than a single or isolated incident is important before making a judgment that your client has this problem. As mentioned in Chapter 1, Antisocial Personality Disorder is likely overdiagnosed among drug users because drug use often includes illegal activities to support the drug use behavior.

However, if a person who has a drug problem is consistently breaking rules, defying authority, manipulating people, and seemingly acting without a heart or without a conscience toward others, then you may wish to consider whether

Antisocial Personality Disorder may be co-occurring with the drug use. Many more men meet criteria for this disorder than women, but there are women who do meet these criteria. Sometimes borderline (described later in this section) behavior can be mistaken for antisocial, and certainly there can be overlap between the two disorders. However, clients with whom I've worked who have borderline features generally have the capacity to care about other people, whereas people who are antisocial may not have this capacity.

If the client is an adolescent or child and engaging in antisocial behavior, then comorbid *Conduct Disorder* should be considered, although such behavior also may indicate an *Oppositional-Defiant Disorder* if there is little *deviant behavior* but lots of arguing and defying the wishes of authorities such as parents and teachers. Adult antisocial behavior is difficult to treat but usually involves use of behavior modification (see Chapter 5) through the use of incentives. *Conduct Disorder* and *Oppositional-Defiant Disorder* can be successfully treated with behavior modification and by modifying the youth's environment (e.g., using multisystemic therapy or the community reinforcement model — see Chapter 5).

In some cases, *Narcissistic Personality Disorder* can cluster with both drug abuse and antisocial behavior. People with this disorder typically display grandiosity, selfishness/self-centeredness, exploitation of others, beliefs about being gifted and special, arrogance, an excessive preoccupation with self and personal appearances, and the need to have others affirm how special they are. Sometimes these qualities are difficult to separate from antisocial behavior, but key differences center around the criminal behavior and the ability to inflict physical cruelty found in antisocial behavior. Effective treatment for Narcissistic Personality Disorder includes cognitive behavioral therapy as well.

Finally, people with *Borderline Personality Disorder* often use drugs and alcohol. Borderline Personality Disorder is defined by acts of self-harm, including self-mutilation behavior such as cutting, burning, and picking behavior; and by poor judgment and impulsive acts that may place the person at high risk for being victimized and for other adverse consequences. Emotional dysregulation is common among people with this disorder. For example, you may witness emotional lability, over- or underreacting emotionally to certain situations, rage and out-of-control behavior, and an avoidance of emotional situations or intimacy. Borderline clients often engage in black-and-white thinking and behave in an all-or-nothing fashion. They can appear quite competent at one level even when they are utterly confused, and can appear quite needy one moment and completely rejecting of social support in the next moment.

As Marsha Linehan (1993) has noted, this personality disorder is typified by *dialectical behavior* (extremes, like love-hate, at either end of a particular behavioral spectrum, sometimes within the space of a few moments). Some professionals have great difficulty working with people who have this disorder. This is primarily because they do not set personal limits in professional interactions and because borderline clients sometimes have very unpredictable behavior, including significant numbers of suicidal and *parasuicidal* acts that keep professionals always on their toes. The treatment of choice for this disorder is dialectical behavior therapy (also see Chapter 5).

Professionals working with a suicidal drug client may wish to determine whether the person meets criteria for Borderline Personality Disorder. Borderline clients often have a history of suicidal behavior and high utilization of health and mental health care services. Most people who meet criteria for Borderline Personality Disorder are women, but not all. As mentioned, some professionals find it difficult to work with borderline clients without becoming very upset or cynical. If you cannot work with such a client respectfully, then it is recommended that a *referral* be made to someone who can (see Chapter 3). Treating the client with dignity is important if trust and a solid therapeutic alliance are to develop.

Remember that it is important to assess for suicidality when working with any client with a history of suicidal and parasuicidal behavior. Not only ideations should be assessed, but also plans, lethality of plans, means to carry out those plans, and proximity of means. You would surprised at how often such clients carry lethal doses of pills, razor blades, or even guns in their purses, pockets, or backpacks during such an assessment interview with intentions to use these items. (Please see the extended discussion about suicide assessment in Chapter 3.)

Co-occurring Physical Health Symptoms

Other commonly co-occurring conditions are not necessarily related to mental health disorders. For example, co-occurring health problems such as chronic pain or a neurocognitive dysfunction related to a head injury or other insult (both mentioned previously) can accompany a drug problem. Impulsive behavior by a person with a drug problem can be a sign of an unrecognized head injury. Even if a person has an accident and seeks medical attention, he or she may not be adequately assessed for a head injury. If the injury occurs when the person is intoxicated, it is difficult to make such an assessment due to the drug or alcohol impairment. Sometimes the results of such an injury do not become obvious until much later. Since the risk for falls, auto accidents, victimization, and other sources of head injuries is elevated for people when intoxicated, and because many of those accidents may not be adequately cared for (the person may not even have a memory of the injury or accident), it is critical for professionals to remember that an undiagnosed head injury could be an explanation for certain patterns of irrational behavior they may observe.

In addition, pain often is used as an excuse for drug-seeking behavior in health care clinics, dental offices, emergency departments in hospitals, and other primary care clinics. I have heard about some people seeking and receiving unnecessary surgical and dental procedures in order to obtain pain medicines.

The abuse of prescribed medicines is one of the fastest growing drug problems in the United States, and a great deal of this behavior is related to pain behavior (although some of it begins as an attempt to reduce anxiety symptoms, as mentioned). Certainly, repeated visits for different ailments or injuries should be treated with suspicion by physicians, nurses, and dentists, especially if the presentation of the problem does not fit the description of the pain.

When Professionals May Be Impaired

Professionals are certainly not immune to drug problems of their own, which can be problematic when the professional has direct client contact and is coming to work impaired. Even if not impaired at work, though, impaired health care workers certainly may not be cognitively sharp during work if abusing drugs during nonwork hours. Here are some tips for identifying colleagues or coworkers who may be experiencing drug problems. First, signs observed in the workplace, as described earlier, may include tardiness, long lunches and multiple breaks, absenteeism, and a noticeable reduction in the quality and quantity of work. In addition, health care professionals with access to medications may divert those medicines for their own use and then cover the *diversion* by fraudulent records and chart notes. If chart notes seem odd and there is a pattern to this oddness that points to one employee, or if a patient seems to be unresponsive to a particular medicine, try to determine whether the medications are actually being received by the patient. Diversion is most often done among patients who have been prescribed pain medications. Another sign may be an excessive wasting of medications by an employee, which may suggest that the medicines are not being wasted at all. In some cases, health care professionals who have drug problems gravitate toward particular units or clinics where they have access to the desired drugs — for instance, units (e.g., oncology) that treat conditions for which there may be a great amount of pain tend to be attractive places to work if your goal is to obtain opioid pain medications.

THINGS TO REMEMBER

Disorders Commonly Co-occurring With Drug Problems

- Mood disorders, such as depression, Bipolar Disorder, and suicidal behaviors
- Anxiety disorders such as Panic Disorder, PTSD, and phobias such as Social Phobia and Agoraphobia
- Personality disorders, such as Antisocial, Borderline, and Narcissistic
- Chronic pain related to accidents and medical conditions
- ADHD, Conduct Disorder, and Oppositional-Defiant Disorder in youth

Physicians who have drug problems sometimes use a process called *harvesting* in order to obtain the medications for their own personal use. Harvesting occurs when a physician (seemingly innocently) asks a patient to return any unused pain or other type of mood-altering medications to the physician. The physician will tell a patient that this is for his or her protection to take away the threat of accidental use of the medicines by someone in the household. The physician will offer to dispose of the medicine properly so that it is out of the household. However, the medicines will likely be used by the physician instead of being wasted. Patients should understand that since they have paid for (or their insurance has paid for) those medicines, it is unethical for a physician to ask for them in the first place, and such a request should warn of a problem.

All of the tips mentioned in this section may serve to aid in the identification of a drug problem, but please remember that these symptoms and signs are simply warning flags for some type of problem. Many of them are associated with several different types of problems, and having a symptom does not necessarily mean that the problem is related to drugs. A thorough assessment conducted by a professional is truly the only way to know for certain whether a loved one, friend, colleague, or client has a drug problem. As mentioned in Chapter 1, remember that all drug problems are not the same and can vary in presentation, in severity, and in the way they should be treated. Furthermore, even if the symptoms or signs observed are related to a drug problem, there is always the possibility that other, co-occurring problems needing attention may lurk in the background.

How Attitudes Influence Drug Problems

Certain attitudes associated with drug use can interfere with behavior change and may be cause for concern. One such attitude is the belief that it's acceptable to use drugs to cope with life problems (or, more correctly, *instead* of coping with problems). Obviously, using a drug to cope with problems does little to solve them, and in many cases will make those problems worse. Usually the drug use represents a way to avoid problems rather than solve them. Using drugs to cope does not enhance the client's abilities to respond thoughtfully to problems, nor does it aid in developing appropriate plans of action. Instead, skillfully coping with problems requires new, non–drug-using skills in order to avoid developing new problems.

Another worrisome notion clients may have is the idea of using drugs to compensate for something they feel is missing from their lives. Drugs obviously have the capacity to induce pleasure, relaxation, and other positive effects, depending on their chemical compositions. However, drug use cannot fill holes in people's lives. Once the effects of the drugs have dissipated, the holes remain. Working on personal growth and development to fill holes rather than using drugs to compensate for them makes more sense in the long run.

Attempts at self-medicating symptoms can be problematic because they often lead to habitual behavior patterns of drug use even when the drug is not working to reduce the symptoms (as mentioned in Chapter 1). Beliefs that self-medication is an effective way to treat symptoms are quite powerful and difficult to change, even when the physical evidence suggests that self-medication is not working very well. Furthermore, self-medicating with *psychoactive* substances often causes other problems, such as new symptoms or exacerbation of old symptoms through rebound effects, which in turn can complicate the original disorders and symptoms.

Finally, attitudes about the power of certain drugs (drug myths and positive expectancies) can cause problems for some people. Usually these myths are completely false and not supported by research. Other myths may have some kernel of truth to them, but usually those beliefs do not tell the whole story about drug effects. Often, beliefs in these myths create misperceptions about the power of drug use that are difficult for professionals to intervene upon. Usually these myths proclaim the drug's ability to make a person more likeable and sociable, more physically powerful, more intellectually capable, more energetic, and more sexually potent and attractive.

Clients are not the only ones who can have problematic attitudes that may interfere with changing drug problems. Family members and friends can have problematic attitudes toward the drug-using loved one or friend as well. The most potent attitudes are those that influence how a family member acts toward the person using drugs. In the past, many people believed that it was a good idea to heavily confront a person using drugs to break through his or her denial. However, we now know that confrontation rarely is helpful and has the potential to actually make things worse by straining relationships with the person who has a drug problem. Since good social support is a strong predictor of success in treatment and recovery, it does not make sense to strain such relationships unnecessarily.

In addition, there is no research that supports the attitude that tough love helps people with drug problems, and in fact, there are incidences in which tough-love interventions by family and friends backfire and are followed by tragic endings. Again, the reason that tough-love interventions can backfire is related to the importance of solid social support if a person is ultimately going to succeed in changing a drug problem. Since there are much better strategies available now for getting a person interested in behavior change (see Chapter 3), I would not recommend organized interventions to coerce treatment, nor so-called tough-love approaches in general. Family members and friends certainly do not want to reinforce drug-using behavior unnecessarily, but they also do not want to shun the person who will need their help to change (even if the person doesn't act like it now, he or she will need the help of family and friends in the future). Burning bridges is rarely a good idea in life, and this is especially true when addressing a drug problem in someone you care about.

POINTS OF CONTROVERSY

Interventions

Interventions have been widely used by families, coworkers, and loved ones to encourage people with drug problems to go into treatment, but do they work? An intervention often is directed by a counselor, who coordinates an effort by participants to share their observations and feelings about the drug use and to describe negative consequences they are willing to endure if the person with a drug problem does not seek help. Often these consequences include ending contact with the person if he or she does not get help. However, there is no research to support that these interventions work well enough to justify their use. In addition, we do know from research that confrontation and loss of social support are linked to poorer outcomes in people with drug problems over time, and often leave the drug user embittered toward treatment professionals. At best, the research suggests that using an intervention to coerce a loved one or friend into seeking help is a gamble.

Finally, professionals also can have problematic attitudes that can hurt the therapeutic process. One problematic attitude is that the person with a drug problem is uneducated, naïve, or in any manner less knowledgeable about his or her life and his or her drug problem than the professional is. As it is said in *Motivational Interviewing* (Miller & Rollnick, 2002, see Chapters 3 and 5), the client *is* the expert on him- or herself, and professionals can learn a lot by acknowledging this simple truism. Remembering that professional-client relationships represent extreme power imbalances, professionals have the capacity to use their extraordinary power in these relationships for good or for harm. Anything less than a collaborative effort in a therapeutic relationship is likely to end in failure. Similarly, treating a client with disrespect is certain to destroy the therapeutic relationship, sometimes before a therapeutic alliance has an opportunity to develop.

Another problematic attitude among professionals is the belief that adolescents and youth should be treated in the same way as adults are treated for a drug problem. The research is very clear about this: Adolescent substance abuse appears to be much different than adult substance abuse in a number of ways, from the beliefs and behaviors of the users to the courses and patterns of their drug abuse. Most youthful drug users mature out of their drug use behavior naturally, as discussed in Chapter 1. In addition, interventions based on fear are ineffective motivators (again, as mentioned in Chapter 1); adolescent problems seem to be influenced more strongly by their environments than adult problems are; adolescent brains are still developing, and research suggests that novelty seeking (sometimes through risk taking) is related to this natural process of brain development; and young people do not understand the concepts of powerlessness and personal identity in the same way as adults. Adolescents are not little adults, so it does not make sense to treat them that way.

With this in mind, natural novelty seeking for some adolescents may include experimentation with drugs, whether we like it or not. It is important not to overreact to these moments of teen curiosity. How a parent responds to the discovery that his or her child is using drugs may be critical for a credible and continued parental dialogue with the youth. Thoughtful and respectful responses are recommended. In an instance like this, it may be useful to examine the youth's attitudes with regard to the choice to use drugs to understand whether it is cause for concern. Was it curiosity, which is typical for the age group? This attitude does not concern me as a professional. However, if the reason for the drug use by the youth was associated with one or more of the problematic attitudes discussed earlier (using the drugs to cope, to be different or whole, or to self-medicate something), then further investigation may be warranted to determine whether a drug problem exists.

Another attitude held by professionals that can be problematic is the idea of treating all drug problems similarly. The belief in a cookie-cutter approach to treating drug problems limits the professional's ability to find creative, individualized strategies to help clients. This severely limits the ability of a therapist or counselor to respond effectively in treatment to a person's drug problem. As was mentioned in Chapter 1, not all drug problems look the same, therefore they cannot all be treated in the same way. Using a one-size-fits-all approach to therapy or treatment will likely hinder the development of a strong therapeutic alliance with a client who feels like the therapist has no understanding of her or his individuality or autonomy.

Professional Collaboration

Many programs include a variety of professionals who function as an interdisciplinary unit, using the strengths of several different disciplines to provide for a comprehensive treatment experience. Often such interdisciplinary teams include physicians to provide medical care and, in some cases, pharmacotherapy; nurses to provide other medical services; psychologists to conduct neuropsychological and other types of assessment, provide interpretations of those results, and consult with the team regarding psychotherapy; and counselors who lead groups and conduct individual sessions. A wide variety of counselors and therapists can be included in the counseling team. For instance, besides drug abuse counselors, there also can be family, occupational, recreational, physical, and even spiritual therapists on a treatment team. Professionals from each of these specialties work together to provide a comprehensive treatment plan for a client (see Chapter 4).

Unfortunately, not every treatment center has access to unlimited resources, so some of the previously mentioned positions may be absent from the team, or in some cases a professional may be asked to fulfill more than one role, perhaps a role outside his or her discipline, because no one else is available to handle it.

It is highly recommended that the professionals who wear hats other than those of their own profession seek out some formal training and supervision in the new areas. For instance, some college and graduate nursing programs provide training and clinical supervision in group therapy skills because nurses may be asked to fill that role in a clinical setting someday. Treatment programs should make sure, for ethical reasons, that a person asked to perform a specialized role in treatment is trained effectively for that role, and consumers may want to check on the qualifications of the treatment staff before a loved one is admitted to such a program. With that being said, I know that in some areas of the country people have few choices regarding treatment, and that choices are often limited by finances. I also know that many treatment programs are doing the best they can with very few resources of their own.

In areas that suffer from few resources, treatment professionals should consider pooling their limited resources with other local professionals. In rural areas, it makes sense to work more closely together, perhaps through professional organizations at a county or regional level. Continuing education training may be offered through those organizations in order to help the smaller treatment facilities where a very few dedicated professionals have to wear multiple hats in caring for clients. Also, it is worth noting that many resources are available online (which will be discussed more fully in subsequent chapters).

For example, when assessing for a drug problem, it makes sense to get a comprehensive assessment by professionals in different disciplines. Since drug problems are biological, psychological, and social/environmental, it makes sense to assess for a drug problem in each of these life domains. Certainly conducting medical assessment would be useful to identify a drug problem, but so would psychological, family, vocational, and recreational assessments for how drugs may be affecting a person in those domains. It makes sense to have professionals trained in these specific areas to conduct these specialized assessments, if possible. Larger treatment facilities with interdisciplinary teams available for such assessments have an advantage, but smaller facilities can collaborate in conducting assessments and can share interdisciplinary resources in this way.

On the other hand, sometimes these specialized assessments are conducted simultaneously in a clinical setting, but professionals miss the opportunity for sharing this information because they are not talking among themselves. It is important in such settings that time is provided for consultation or treatment-team meetings so that such information can be shared freely across the staff. In some cases, if a professional is concerned about the possibility of a drug problem, the clues may exist in previous chart notes. In clinics and hospitals, for example, sometimes medication-seeking patterns can be determined by reading previous chart notes and determining a pattern of clinical visitation by a patient. Many times, documentation exists that would suggest that a person may have a drug problem, but the little bits of evidence are not put together systematically in a way that clarifies the picture.

Professional Obligations to Intervene

In some instances, it may seem easier to ignore a suspected drug problem than to take the time to evaluate it and possibly intervene upon it. Certainly, time demands on professionals make it difficult to attend to every suspected problem, especially when there is the sense that such an evaluation or intervention may be a waste of time. I have seen professionals become jaded while working with people who have suspected drug problems. Under these conditions, professionals may find it easier to dismiss helping clients out of hand because previous experience has taught them that a drug user may not be interested in receiving help. However, the research suggests that many people with drug problems are highly ambivalent about their drug use (Miller & Rollnick, 2002), which means they often are keenly aware of the downside of their drug use as well as the upside.

What this means, of course, is that drug-using clients are not necessarily unreachable. In some cases the problem is that people who use drugs feel as if professionals have reached out to help in disrespectful ways, which diminishes their desire to accept the help. So, in the eyes of many drug users I've worked with, what is needed is a fresh approach by health care professionals to offering help that is less judgmental. This would work to everyone's advantage. If professionals were consistently patient and compassionate in their handling of people suspected of drug problems, then people with drug problems might be less likely to act like difficult clients. In turn, working with less difficult clients would help professionals stay focused on helping them.

In addition, the professional may have had multiple contacts with the client over a period of weeks, months, and perhaps even years, and because of these chronic contacts has given up on the idea of helping a chronic utilizer of the system who has a drug problem. Over the years, it has been interesting to observe how easily some professionals give up on a drug-using client, when I suspect they would not have given up so easily if the same client had cancer instead. Rightly or wrongly, some people continue to believe deep in their hearts (even if they say otherwise) that having a drug problem is qualitatively different than having another type of health problem such as cancer. This belief by professionals that drug problems *are* different frequently seeps out as an emotional response when the client has failed to make changes, in spite of an admonition from the professional and in spite of the evidence that making a change would be helpful to the client.

Some people tend to fall back into a moral perspective on what a drug problem is (sometimes without even knowing it) when a client does not change or does not seem to get better, believing that the person is at fault for not changing the problem. Anger toward a person with a drug problem who is not visibly changing is common, and blaming the victim may be a response. But how common is it to feel the same way toward a cancer patient who is not changing his or her condition? For the one health condition (drug problems), some professionals act as if it says something about a person's character that he or she is not changing, while for the other health condition (cancer) the lack of change is linked to issues beyond the person's control. If you believe that drug abuse is a disease, then anger is not a rational response toward someone who is not changing drug use. If you believe that a drug problem is a reflection of poor skills and reinforcement history (a behavioral disorder), then anger is not congruent with the understanding that the person is doing the best he or she can with the skills he or she currently has. If you are feeling anger about lack of progress, then you may wish to examine your assumptions about the client and about the cause of his or her problem.

A major reason that professionals get burned out surrounds circumstances in which clients do not seem to get better as quickly as hoped (or maybe not at all). Most professionals, if not all, want their clients to get better and most would give 120% of themselves in order to help a client. Sometimes there are certain assumptions on the part of professionals about themselves and about their clients that may cause difficulties. One such assumption is that if clients wanted to get better, then they would do what we tell them to do. The reality is that, across a variety of health conditions, compliance rates with professional advice are not great, so why should we expect it to be different when treating a drug problem? Asthma patients rarely take their medicines as advised by their physicians, diabetic patients often are noncompliant regarding their diets and forget to check their blood sugar, cardiac patients may not exercise as recommended, and the person with a sinus infection may not finish his or her course of antibiotics as requested. Even competent health care professionals sometimes do not act consistently with what they preach. But in spite of this noncompliance with medical advice, people often do get better and many times maintain positive health changes over the long term.

Expecting a person with a drug problem to be compliant with professional recommendations is unrealistic, given what we know about patient compliance across all health conditions. Does that mean we should give up on providing recommendations? By no means; but we should become more realistic in our expectations about how closely our clients will follow them. Having unrealistic expectations of our clients is *our* problem, not theirs, and we need to moderate such views so that we do not expect too much from our clients. Lowering our expectations for compliance will probably reduce the likelihood that we will be disappointed in our clients. Our clients can pick up on our anger and disappointment in session (just as we can on theirs), and their course of treatment can be influenced by it, so we have to be careful with our feelings toward them — especially if those feelings are the result of unrealistic expectations.

Another problem with expecting total compliance is that sometimes we do not know what is best for the client. We would like to believe that we are wise sages in our respective professions, but that does not mean we are infallible. Sometimes we make mistakes when working with clients, and frequently our clients forgive us for those errors and stick with us. In other cases, we may not totally understand the situations of our clients, so that the solutions we offer them may not fit well with their circumstances. Many times our clients have the capacity to determine their own courses better than we do, since we have not walked in their shoes for any length of time. That is why it is a good idea to offer a range of options for help and recovery, and then allow the clients to choose the best path for themselves (Miller & Rollnick, 2002). This allows therapists to avoid disappointment with noncompliance and, in turn, respectfully validate the autonomy (and intelligence) of clients.

Another assumption that we professionals sometimes make is that we should be able to help our clients get better, when the reality is that they must help themselves. We can show them the door, but ultimately it is the clients who must walk through it to better health. When a person does not walk through the door, it is easy to personalize our responsibility for the lack of progress and get frustrated because we could not help him or her. Long-term frustration in working with clients can lead to apathy or disillusionment, stepping stones toward what some have called *professional burnout*. In my opinion, burnout occurs as a result of unrealistic expectations by professionals about their own abilities to help others and of unrealistic expectations for their clients to get better. The truth is that behavior change is completely up to the client. We can motivate and teach but we cannot force people to act.

Finally, it is worth noting again that the pervasiveness of drug problems in American culture contributes to their being taken very personally. Many professionals have loved ones or friends who have had substance use disorders. Many of those experiences have no doubt been emotionally charged, and those emotions can crop up in professional situations when cued by encountering a person with similar problems in daily work. It is important to be aware of our feelings and biases toward drug problems and to deal with these reactions in such a way that we do not poison the waters of caring for another person who we do not know. One rule of thumb is to use that emotional energy to work as hard as you can to help, but not to allow that energy to interfere with your capacity to care respectfully for another person. Objectivity is always a difficult thing to maintain when caring for people, and complete objectivity is probably unrealistic and unobtainable. However, personal feelings should not creep into a session, assessment, or intervention and affect our abilities to deliver quality care for a stranger.

Obligations Toward Other Professionals

When professionals suspect that fellow professionals may have drug problems, they are obligated to speak up. The situation described is complicated by the fact that careers may be at stake if the person is found to be diverting drugs at work, forging documentation, or making other types of errors in judgment that may not be forgiven by a professional board or employer. My recommendation would be to use treatment options first before punitive options, perhaps using punitive options as an alternative if the person refuses treatment. Formal punishment, as

SELF IMPROVEMENT TECHNIQUE

How to Challenge Six Unrealistic Assumptions About Clients

The following six assumptions that professionals have about clients may cause distress in the therapeutic relationship if not challenged. After each commonly held belief is a realistic way to view the concern. When you notice yourself holding one of these errant assumptions about your client, follow this exercise to remind you of the reality of the situation, using the statement of reality to challenge the related errant expectation. See Chapter 5 for more information on challenging errant thoughts and assumptions.

Errant assumption #1: Clients and patients with drug problems should want to change.

Reality: Clients and patients are ambivalent about drug use and whether to change it.

Errant assumption #2: High utilizers of the system never change.

Reality: Many do change, but not on our time line, and you cannot predict when.

Errant assumption #3: They should do better or know better.

Reality: If they are ill or if they have skill deficits, then they are doing the best they can.

Errant assumption #4: Clients or patients will choose to comply with recommendations.

Reality: Clients rarely follow professional advice to the letter — for any health problem.

Errant assumption #5: If they did follow my recommendations, they would get better.

Reality: Some do follow our recommendations and do not get better, while some do not follow our recommendations and do get better

Errant assumption #6: We always know what is best for our clients and patients.

Reality: We do not always know what is best for ourselves, so how can we always know this for others?

mentioned in Chapter 1, has not been found to be a particularly helpful strategy to encourage successful behavior change.

Professionals also have to be concerned about client or patient care, and impaired professionals threaten that care. Health care workers are obligated to protect their patients, so they are obligated to make a report when they suspect that a coworker is impaired. If the health care organization and the professional guild placed priority on treatment before punishment, colleagues would likely report more frequently, since they would know clearly that they were helping rather than harming a coworker. However, even if the organization or professional body does not see fit to deal with impairment in this fashion, professionals still are obligated to place patient care above any obligation to protect coworkers. Fortunately, many professional health care organizations understand the value of suggesting treatment instead of punishment when a professional is deemed to be impaired. Clearly there are circumstances, though, where punishment is necessary and warranted.

When reports of impairment have been made, an investigation is usually directed by a human-resources official who has been trained in assessing and making referrals for drug problems. Although sometimes it would be appropriate for direct supervisors to be involved in this process, typically they have not been trained how to conduct such an assessment and referral, and perhaps may not be objective enough to do such an assessment. Many organizations have employee assistance programs (EAPs) that are available to help employees with problems, including those related to drug use. In some cases, EAP personnel have been trained to conduct such assessments and usually have the authority and means to make appropriate referrals. *Motivational interviewing* would be a useful therapeutic strategy to use in these assessments (see Chapters 3 and 5), since it would reduce the likelihood of a defensive reaction by a worker who may be mandated to seek an assessment against her or his will.

Of course, it would be best if a worker voluntary sought help. However, many times the threat of punitive measures by the organization or guild make the professional very reluctant to admit having a drug problem or to seek help. Voluntarily seeking help, in my opinion, should be reinforced rather than punished. Obviously there are instances in which laws have been broken, and that complicates the picture, but clearly more people would seek help if they were certain they could get it *and* not be punished for seeking it.

> "If we burn ourselves out with drugs or alcohol, we won't have long to go in this business."
>
> —JOHN BELUSHI

Professional Referrals

Professionals sometimes have to make choices about whether to treat the person with a drug problem or whether it would better if someone else treated that person. In some cases, a professional may not provide treatment at all, which makes referrals to another professional for treatment or therapy necessary. There are many advantages to referrals if they are made for the right reasons, but there also can be a few disadvantages.

Referrals should be made if one of the following conditions is present. First, *a referral should be considered if the client would be better served by working with another therapist than working with you.* There are a number of reasons this may be the case. For one, it may be a matter of *finances*. Perhaps the client does not have the resources available to afford the therapy you offer. Therapists should consider

CLIENT HANDOUT

Problems Can Be Changed

If you think you may have a drug problem, you may wish to allow your therapist or counselor to do a thorough evaluation. It is certainly better to seek help early if you do have concerns about your drug use. Most of my clients have told me that they knew they had drug problems long before they sought help, and many expressed regret at not having sought help sooner. We know for certain that changing behavior is easier when you are younger than when you are older. Old dogs can learn new tricks, but it often takes a little longer to unlearn the old tricks. There are several reasons for this; for one, mental flexibility needed for new learning seems to reduce gradually as people age. Another reason is that habitual behavior is increasingly difficult to change over time because such behavior often occurs automatically and sometimes without the awareness needed to stop the behavior before it starts. Yet another reason is that the effects of chronic drug use seem to multiply as we age, including negative effects on the body and brain that can make it more difficult to change behavior in the future.

For some people I have worked with, changing drug use later in life was really difficult for them because drug use had reduced their ability to think clearly enough to solve problems and make wise decisions.[1] Others were physically battered and just plain tired, which made the resolve to change difficult in the context of physical discomfort. However, people who decide to change drug use later in life do have experience on their side. Remember, it is never too late to change, but changing now will always be easier than changing later.

Change can take many forms. Some people with drug problems are able to change habits on their own without professional help and support. If you think you are one of these people, you should set a goal for yourself to have a period of trial abstinence for a certain length of time to bring the habitual behavior under control. Some people I have worked with have set trial abstinence goals of anywhere from 2 weeks to as long as 6 months. Others have decided to "never use again," and as far as I know they have not. A period of trial abstinence buys you some time to allow your body to heal, which of course will aid you in your efforts to change your behavior. Some of you may decide to return to using drugs again, hopefully at a reduced level; others will decide that abstinence is good. My recommendation is to abstain if you can, because you will be kinder to your body that way. There are self-help books available that may be useful to you as you work toward kicking your habits; one of these is Changing for Good, by J. O. Prochaska, J. C. Norcross, and C. C. DiClemente (New York: Avon Books, 1994). This book is very helpful for teaching you how to make progress toward behavior change, based on where you are in the change cycle. It considers your levels of both motivation and commitment when suggesting scientifically tested ways to help the change process.

Others of you may decide that you want support while changing your drug use. For some, it can be helpful to associate with a self-help group that may or may not be in the 12-step tradition.[2] Still others of you may opt for individual counseling or psychotherapy with an addictions psychologist, counselor, social worker, or psychiatrist. Some of you may decide that you need formal treatment. One rule of thumb is that it is always a good idea to have at least one backup plan just in case the original plan that you set for yourself is not working as well as you would like. So perhaps your Plan A is to stop on your own, but you might want a Plan B or even Plan C if the other plans fall short. In addition, some people like the stepped-up care model of changing behavior, in which you can gradually increase the amount of help you are getting if the previous level of help was not working for you. An example of a stepped-up care plan may begin with trying to quit on your own; as the plan evolves over time, you may wish to add increasing elements of services to ensure your success in reaching your personal goals for changing your drug use.

[1] *Therapist: Chapter 4 provides information about cognitive assessment that you can discuss with the client.*

[2] *Therapist: See the Useful Resources box on page 84.*

the impact of financial debt after treatment when deciding whether to treat the person in the first place. It is not ethical to treat a person's problems only to create new ones with a large treatment debt. In other cases, third-party reimbursement might cover more of treatment if it is conducted within another treatment system. The financial considerations for a client should be considered when deciding whether a therapist-client match is a good one; and if there is a financial mismatch, a referral should be made. In addition, *location* should be considered. Is the client far from home, and would that client be better served by being matched with services closer to where he or she will live after completion of treatment? If the answer is yes, then a referral to treatment services closer to home should be considered.

A second reason for referral is the determination that you and the client do not match up well as a therapeutic team. One example of this is the client's having a very different worldview than yours, such that your philosophy or model of therapy is not a good match for the client. Perhaps you are working with a very religious person and you are not religious at all. Maybe the person you are working with does not believe in the disease model of addictions and you do. Or maybe there are racial, ethnic, or cultural differences or language barriers between you and your client that impede the relationship and would make it difficult to understand each other. Often the level of *acculturation* (how much a person has adapted to and accepted the ways of the majority culture) of both therapist and client is more important than racial-ethnic differences per se in determining the goodness of fit of a therapist-client relationship.

CLIENT HANDOUT

Benefits of Therapy

Therapy works extraordinarily well when the therapist and client act as a team. It can change your life for the better, so I would highly recommend it. The type of therapy that you should choose depends on your values and worldview, and you should determine whether a particular style of therapy fits you and your needs.[1] You also will want to make sure that you match up well with your primary therapist (the one who will be directly working with you most often).

For some people, therapy will begin with a detoxification period. Detoxification is the period of time where your body begins to heal itself after you stop using drugs. This period of time can be uncomfortable, because some people will experience withdrawal symptoms. Detoxification therapy can occur in two different forms. The first is social detox, in which a person goes through the detoxification period without the aid of other medicines. Discomfort is treated in other ways, so this is not as scary as it sounds. Social detox works well if you would like to stay away from drugs completely and if you have not been a very heavy user of drugs.

If you have been a very heavy user of drugs, you may wish to go through medical detox, which medicates (or "covers") your withdrawal symptoms with other drugs that minimize discomfort. After withdrawal symptoms subside, you will be tapered slowly off of those drugs as well. In either type of detox, physicians generally will monitor your withdrawal symptoms and provide an overall checkup on your health. If you have already quit drugs and have finished the withdrawal period, you may not need detoxification at all, but for those who have been using for a while it is generally a good idea to be detoxified safely. After detoxification, your body will slowly but surely begin to return to normal and your health will return to you. Most people notice a remarkable difference in their body comfort, appetite, skin and eye color, energy level, and other areas of health within a few days to a few weeks of being detoxified.

Psychotherapy usually begins late in the detoxification period or even after it has been completed. The reason it begins later is to allow your body some healing before you begin to learn new material. In that way you will not be unduly distracted from meeting your goals for therapy.

Treatment can make a major difference in your life. The treatment process often includes components of psychoeducation (learning new information about changing your behavior) and psychotherapy (learning new skills to reach your goals and learning new information about yourself). The duration of these sessions varies and often is completed on an outpatient basis (although some people may opt for inpatient services if they feel they need extra structure and support). Psychoeducation and psychotherapy provide new opportunities to improve your life in very significant ways.

Many clients find a gradual improvement in their physical health as they move through treatment. Not only does treatment allow for further healing in the body, but it also teaches new ways to care for yourself physically. This period of healing and of learning new skills often leads to a marked improvement in appearance. People tend to look healthier at the same time they are feeling healthier. Some of my clients looked physically younger at the end of treatment than they did upon intake. In addition, you will begin to notice improvements in the way you are thinking as your mind clears from the effects of the drugs. Memory begins to improve and will continue to improve for some time. The problems with attention and concentration tend to subside with time for most people. If they do not, it may suggest that other treatment is required, but at least you will know that the extra help is needed (when you might not have known it before treatment).

People in treatment often begin to notice improvement in quality-of-life issues as well. You may begin to notice that you are not as irritable, and that your patience is returning. You also may notice that your positive emotions come back if they have been blunted over time, or you may notice that you are not feeling like you are on an emotional rollercoaster as often. Most people notice after successful treatment that emotions begin to stabilize. And if they do not, then it may be a sign that other types of therapy may be needed, perhaps related to another condition that escaped diagnosis before.

It is worth noting that experiencing a depressed mood may be common in early recovery from a drug problem. Often, a number of issues contribute to these blues. For one, it may be that personal regrets arise related to the period of drug use. In other cases, depression may be a result of a rebound effect from the chemical properties of the drug. Even if this happens to you, it is important to know there is relief. Many people feel less depressed over time after changing a drug problem, and new antidepressant drugs and psychotherapy can help relieve the acute symptoms you may experience. However, many people also experience true joy in recovery, a joy they have not felt in a long time, so mood improvement can be expected, too.

Related to this joy, people often notice interest in life returning, as well as renewed interest in the future. Many of my clients have described improvement in their spiritual lives. Personal values, goals, directions, and even identity become clarified and people often feel a renewal in personal meaning and purpose. Some people may find or return to spiritual communities, and others find spirituality through service work and self-improvement. Some of the great joy I was describing seems related to a re-engaging in the world that commonly occurs after a drug problem has ended.

For many, these improvements are seen at work, where you will likely have greater energy and enthusiasm. Some people find they do not have the same enthusiasm for their jobs as they used to, though, and some change jobs or return to school to learn a new trade or profession. Relationships will likely improve over time with family, partners, children, and friends. Money problems may begin to subside with less expenditure on drugs. Obviously, some of the problems will not disappear just because you have sought treatment. These problems may take time before they can be resolved, but you will be able to solve them more effectively with a clear mind.

Perhaps the greatest gift of therapy is the freedom to choose. You will find that even if you have problems to solve, you will have the ability to choose your own path again without the ball-and-chain of drug use to slow you down. Most drug users I've worked with have been impressed (after quitting or changing their use) with how much time they used to spend on drug use behavior. This time will be returned to you in recovery, and you will be amazed at what you will be able to do for yourself with that extra time. You may still make mistakes in your choices, but at least you will not be piling on the extra mistakes you make when your judgment is impaired by drugs. Freedom to choose is a gift that most people rediscover after they change their drug problems.

These benefits tend to multiply for those who are able to maintain their behavior change for a year or more. The research suggests that people's lives become increasingly more stable the longer their drug problems remain changed. Improvements in health, cognitive abilities, finances, and relationships should continue to be noticed with long-term behavior change. The research suggests that physical healing may occur for up to 2 years after stopping the use of substances, so patience is a virtue after treatment. That patience is likely to be rewarded with remarkable and enjoyable changes in your life.

So, it is up to you what kinds of goals for drug use change you would like to set for yourself. I usually recommend abstinence, at least for a trial period, to allow the maximum amount of healing in the early stages of change. Some of you may decide to stay abstinent if it works well for you. However, some of you may decide that abstinence is not for you. Regardless of your choice of goals, any change will likely result in noticeable improvements in your quality of life, which is why change is good in this instance. Changing a drug problem not only is possible, but can lead to new and challenging life adventures that you may never have dreamed about.

Note: The remainder of this book presents many ideas that may be useful to share with your client, including suggestions for how the client can choose the right services (in Chapters 3 and 5), how the client can help develop a treatment plan that will serve him or her well in therapy (Chapter 4), steps the client can take to succeed in reaching his or her goals after treatment or therapy, and how the client can move forward into a new life free from drug problems (Chapters 6–8).

[1] *Therapist: Chapter 5 provides details on therapy styles you can discuss with your client.*

USEFUL RESOURCES

National Contact Information for Support Groups

Cocaine Anonymous (CA)	Phone: (310) 559-5833 Web link: http://www.ca.org/
Harm Reduction Coalition	East Coast Phone: (212) 213-6376 West Coast Phone: (510) 444-6969 Web link: http://www.harmreduction.org/links.html
Marijuana Anonymous (MA)	Phone: 1-800-766-6779 Web link: http://www.marijuana-anonymous.org/
Narcotics Anonymous (NA)	Phone: (818) 773-9999 Web link: http://www.na.org/
Rational Recovery	Phone: (530) 621-2667 Web link: http://www.rational.org/
SMART Recovery	Phone: (440) 951-5357 Web link: http://www.smartrecovery.org/
SOS	Phone: (323) 666-4295 Web link: http://www.cfiwest.org/sos/index.htm

Third, *a referral should be considered if you find working with the client to be intolerable for you.* Therapists and counselors would like to believe that they are flexible enough to work with all people, but of course therapists bring their biases, rules, and limits into the session just like clients do. Sometimes when working with a client we discover that the client is rubbing us the wrong way or seems to be pushing all the buttons that make a relationship uncomfortable. This, of course, can happen at times even with a client with whom we generally work well; therapeutic relationships can have their bad days. However, if we as therapists find ourselves dreading to work with a particular client, it is worth considering a referral. Obviously it is difficult to mask dread when working in close proximity with someone.

Our dread should be examined closely to see if it can be overcome. Dread may allow therapists to learn more about their own personal limits or even about previously unexplored biases. Sometimes this dread can be replaced with a new resolve to make the client-therapist relationship work. Dread does not mean the relationship is doomed, but it is a warning sign that it must change. Frequently, that means the therapist must make the changes.

However, as with any relationship, *the potential for harm* should be the principle factor in deciding whether a referral should occur. If your sense of dread of working with the client is harming that client, with no change possible, then the referral needs to be made. On the other hand, if the client is threatening or harming you in the relationship, then by all means make a referral. You are therapeutically obligated to model to the client that abuse is not acceptable interpersonal behavior. In making these types of referrals, care must be taken as to how the subject is broached. For example, it is important to protect the client when suggesting the referral. You should make it clear that the referral has to do with protecting the best interests of the client. More importantly, make a point to let the client know that there is nothing wrong with him or her, but rather that it is your own limits or expectations that are at issue. Tell the client that it is a mismatch in values or styles rather than there is something wrong with the client. The exception, of course, would be if the client is being threatening or abusive. For those circumstances, you may wish to use the referral as a teachable moment about appropriate interpersonal behavior.

Fourth, you should consider a collaborative referral for an adjunct therapist if you meet the needs of the client in most areas, but find that the client would benefit from specialized treatment in another area. An example of a reason for this type of referral would be the discovery that your client may need a psychiatric evaluation and perhaps medication management after you have been working with her or him for a period of time. You are not relinquishing your relationship with the client, but it may be necessary to bring in an outside expert in another area of care to help the client reach her or his goals for treatment.

Finally, if you have worked with a client for a significant amount of time (which may be defined in different ways, depending upon your model) and she or he is not getting better with your help, then it may be time to consider a referral. This may be the hardest referral of all, for both therapists and clients. We therapists would like to believe we can help most people, but certainly we cannot help everyone. Sometimes it is hard not to be upset when you cannot help a

CLIENT HANDOUT

Referrals Can Help You Change Your Drug Problem

If you are a person with a drug problem, referrals can be very helpful for you because they allow you to receive appropriate services that fit your needs. There is no need to take offense at a referral; sometimes therapeutic matches are not ideal, and in other instances new issues arise during therapy that were not considered at the start. Sometimes a referral represents a necessary midcourse correction in treatment. If your therapist is recommending a referral, then it is likely being done to help you help yourself. Good referrals usually make winners of both clients and therapists.

particular client. However, the best help you can provide may be to refer the person elsewhere in hopes of a better match. Similarly, the client may have feelings about the relationship's ending, and some I have worked with have expressed that they felt the referral was a punishment for not getting better. Obviously it is important to be careful and thoughtful about the referral process in these situations. One strategy that I have used is to set regular goals ahead of time for when therapy should be jointly reevaluated. The idea that a referral might at some point be necessary is discussed, with the idea that progress will be evaluated in a certain number of sessions, at which time you will revisit whether a referral is optimal. This strategy allows the client time to consider the issues and the possible change in therapists or counselors that lie ahead, and it also gives the therapist time to examine the therapeutic relationship more closely. In this way, the idea of referral because of lack of progress is not suddenly sprung upon a client who may have difficulties adjusting to change.

In spite of the advantages of matching professional skills with the clinical needs of clients through referrals, there are some disadvantages as well. One disadvantage can be the loss of opportunity to help a person. For example, maybe you as a therapist have decided that the person presenting with a drug problem may be better served working with a specialist. You make the referral. However, there may be a lag time between your last contact with the client and the client's first appointment with the referral contact. Some research has found that this in-between time allows for a lapse of services that can discourage help-seeking by clients. Some clients will not show for the next referral appointment and the opportunity may be lost. The research suggests it is better to strike while the iron is hot and make certain to treat the client when he or she is ready to accept help.

Another disadvantage to a referral is that a budding therapeutic alliance is lost and therapeutic continuity is broken. The client has already (one hopes) developed a relationship of some sort with you, which will be broken by the referral; and then you are asking her or him to form a new relationship with another therapist. Some clients find developing new relationships difficult to do and may drop out of therapy entirely because of this challenge. One solution is to attempt to pass a client from you to the other therapist in person, meaning that the referral therapist and you meet together with the client for a brief period to ease the transition. Another idea might be to physically go with the client to the referral appointment to make sure it happens and to make sure that the referral turns out to be a good fit for the client. Referral of clients is a fine art form, to be sure. Care should be taken not to make referrals too soon, and care should be taken not to make them too late. Referrals are a complicated process but highly effective when done well. Part of making them effective is to thoroughly orient the client to the reason the referral is being made; to take your time helping the client understand and be comfortable with the process if you can; and to be respectful and supportive. See Chapter 3 for more information on the dos and don'ts of referrals.

CASE STUDY

An Unexpected Invitation

Jordan was a 24-year-old man who was in early recovery from methamphetamine dependence and marijuana abuse. Jordan is a very pleasant but rather quiet young man. He had done well in outpatient treatment and was about two months abstinent from drug use when he came in one day to my office. This was unexpected in and of itself, since he was supposedly working during the day and was receiving his outpatient services in the evenings. He asked the receptionist if he could see me, and although he was obviously not on my schedule that day, I had time. He stepped into my office with a very bright smile on his face, and proceeded to announce to me that he was on his way to Jerusalem. I was a bit taken aback by this, and asked what was up with these travel plans. He then told me that Jerusalem was his home, and that he wanted to go see his temple. However, he had come by this morning to invite me to come with him as one of his disciples.

If you were working with Jordan, what else would you want to know about him at this moment? What would you ask him? What would you do next? Do you know what laws in your state would apply to such a situation?

Summing Up

There are many signs and symptom that could suggest that a person has a drug problem. However, many of these signs and symptoms are also markers for other types of problems that may not be drug related. A professional assessment is really the only way to determine what kind of problem may be related to the signs and symptoms being observed. A drug problem can be observed in many different arenas of life, including in the home or in the workplace. The suggested signs and symptoms in this chapter can help you sort through whether there is cause for concern and whether you should professionally intervene.

In addition, when clients do ask for help, they may arrive with many other problems besides those related to drugs. In some cases, you may not be able to address the problems on your own and may need help. Referrals for care can be very helpful for clients when their problems do not match up well with your expertise.

Key Terms

Anxiety disorders. Disorders that involve sensitivity to physiological changes linked to the sympathetic (fight-or-flight) nervous system and fears related to those changes.

Anxiolytic drugs. Medications that treat anxiety, usually tranquilizers.

Bipolar Affective Disorder. A class of disorders that features mood swings from great highs (mania) to great lows (depression).

Collateral. A clinical term used to denote a significant other to a client or patient.
Conduct Disorder. An adolescent disorder that features deviant and antisocial behavior.
Depression. A class of mood disorders that feature low energy, sadness, hopelessness, and sometimes suicidal behavior.
Deviant behavior. Behavior that is antisocial and violates social norms.
Diversion. Professionals' taking drugs from patients or clients in the workplace for their own use.
False positive. A signal that a problem exists when in fact it really does not.
Oppositional-Defiant Disorder. Adolescent disorder featuring defiance toward authority.
Parasuicidal. Behavior that involves self-harm without necessarily the intent to die.
Personality disorders. Disorders in which people have problems with social interactions.
Psychoactive. Substances that have mood- or reality-altering properties.
Referral. A process of sending your client to another professional for care.
Schizophrenia. A debilitating class of mental disorders that involve psychosis.
Suicidal ideations. Thoughts about self-harm or suicide.
Toxicology. The study of the harmful effects of drugs on physiology.

Recommended Reading

If your client would like an additional resource when changing, the following book (mentioned previously in the Client Handout on pages 79–80) may be helpful: *Changing for Good,* by J. O. Prochaska, J. C. Norcross, and C. C. DiClemente (New York: Avon Books, 1994). This book is very helpful for teaching a person how to make progress toward behavior change, based on where he or she is in the change cycle. It considers the person's levels of both motivation and commitment when suggesting scientifically tested ways to help the change process.

TRUTH OR FICTION

QUIZ ANSWERS

1. False; 2. False; 3. True; 4. True; 5. True; 6. True; 7. False

CHAPTER 3

Utilizing Optimal Professional Resources

TRUTH OR FICTION QUIZ

After reading this chapter, you should be able to answer the following questions:

1. Professionals should attempt to match clients with service models that fit their worldviews. True or False?
2. Client resistance is a sure sign of denial about drug use. True or False?
3. Confrontation is effective for increasing motivation to change. True or False?
4. Developing a plan of action is appropriate when working with a pre-contemplator. True or False?
5. Clients with suicidal ideations should always be referred elsewhere. True or False?
6. You always have an ethical obligation to continue to work with clients who threaten you. True or False?
7. Finances represent a major barrier to many seeking help for a drug problem. True or False?

Answers on p. 134.

Treating drug problems requires a collaborative effort. Clients with drug problems generally have wide-ranging needs that may require service from several professionals in order to ensure a positive outcome from therapy or treatment. Because of these needs, savvy professionals develop resource networks so their clients have the best options of treatment and services available. In some cases, quality care may require a referral for services or treatment outside your clinic. A good referral can be one of the best interventions that a professional can provide while caring for a client with a drug problem. Developing professional networks also can be very helpful when dealing with clients amid difficult circumstances, in order to protect the well-being of both client and professional. This chapter will provide a review of how to develop healthy professional networks, along with ideas for how to provide the best available resources to your clients.

Developing a Professional Network

Counselors and therapists find strength in numbers. Developing a professional network is a way to increase your effectiveness as a provider through collaboration, even if you practice alone or live in a small community. A *professional network* usually starts as a group of professionals who share an interest in treating and intervening upon drug problems, and can include people from a wide variety of clinical settings, many of those mentioned in Chapter 2. Typically the purpose of a network is twofold: to help clients, and to help professionals as they work with clients. Networking can provide avenues for seeking out therapist education, client services, and therapist support. Network groups provide opportunities to consult (seek advice, suggestions, and support) with other professionals about clients on a regular basis. Therapeutic networks often cross disciplines, so that counselors, psychologists, social workers, physicians, and other professionals all interested in treating drug problems can meet and work with each other.

Many professionals develop their professional networks through group meetings of addiction-treatment professionals that vary in focus. One such forum to develop relationships with other professionals is at *continuing education* events. Continuing education is required for many professional organizations, and these events allow the opportunity to learn about recent research findings and new therapeutic techniques, as well as meet and establish new connections with like-minded professionals. In addition, many larger communities have weekly or monthly luncheons at which professionals can gather to discuss particular community issues surrounding treatment, socialize, and perhaps even to listen to an invited speaker. Membership in community professional treatment organizations generally facilitates development of a network.

Another way to develop a local professional network is to get involved with a *consultation group*. Consultation groups are common in large collaborative clinics and hospitals where multidisciplinary care occurs. Consultation groups are forums where clients' care can be jointly discussed by the treatment team, with the goal of improving care by having all professionals on the same page with regard to treatment. Generally, consultation groups meet weekly in clinics. This model for networking has been extended out into the community is some places, so that professionals from different clinics might participate in a central consultation group. This arrangement offers the chance for interested professionals to discuss cases (in a confidential fashion) with other skilled professionals. The advantage to these groups is clear: A professional has an opportunity to receive input from multiple clinically oriented minds into treating clients, which allows even therapists and counselors in a solo private practice to have a community of resources available for treatment. A community consultation group also is a great way to develop a *referral system* (as discussed in Chapter 2).

Many times, consultation groups develop around a specific treatment model so as to include like-minded professionals operating under the same basic premises about the nature and treatment of a drug problem. This type of network offers an advantage of being able to make collaborative referrals, if needed, to professionals who hold similar views. Members of consultation groups developed in this manner operate with very similar goals in mind for client care, and these more homogeneous groups tend to be on the same page about how treatment should progress. An example might be a consultation group oriented toward the disease model, or perhaps another toward a cognitive behavioral model (models will be discussed in Chapter 5). This type of consultation group may feel more supportive to you and will potentially provide consistency of care for clients.

However, I also have been part of consultation groups in which members span the spectrum of models concerning the nature and treatment of drug problems. This type of consultation group offers the advantage of providing fresh ideas and suggesting multiple directions for understanding and carrying out treatment. Diverse-model consultation groups work quite well when their members are tolerant of other views. In many cases, the care of the client can be enhanced in such a group if therapy seems to have hit a wall, or if treatment progress is marginal. If your model of therapy does not seem to be working for a client, a referral might be made to a consultation-group member operating under a different treatment model who may have some familiarity with the case.

Consultation groups help clients when they are functioning well. But the true strength of consultation groups is that they provide social support for the therapist. This support is especially critical when providing services in small communities, working with difficult cases, or working alone in a practice. Consultation groups provide fresh perspectives and offer new suggestions for strategies of intervention. Furthermore, being part of such a group is a great way to avoid burnout as a therapist. Having a network of other professionals to provide perspective is a valuable resource in improving care for people with drug problems.

Many professional networks extend beyond the local community. Although local networks provide accessible and personalized resources in ways state, regional, or national networks cannot, there are some advantages to larger networks. Many of these larger networks happen within large professional organizations, although some networks occur within governmental entities. In terms of advantages, a larger network often has greater access to resources, including access to education about recent research findings and best practices in therapy. *Best practices* is a phrase used to delineate which techniques have been scientifically shown to work. State and federal agencies encourage the use of best practices in order to offer the best known care for clients with drug problems.

Many larger professional organizations have state, regional, and national special interest groups that include like-minded members. These groups offer resources to their members, often including manuals for treatment, fliers of psychoeducation for clients and their families, magazines or journals with the latest in research and information about best practices, and sponsored Internet lists and Web-based resources. Attending state, regional, and national meetings of these organizations is a great way to develop a very large network that can be instantly accessed over the Internet. Some professionals now take full advantage of Internet access, including engaging in consultation groups online, or downloading helpful resources for clients.

Many governmental agencies offer similar types of services to professionals. For example, states agencies that oversee drug treatment and its providers also provide Web-based information and support Internet lists. National agencies have a wide variety of resources available online, with a great number of them being free of cost for users. Governmental boards that regulate professional ethics and licenses sometimes have these services as well. The Internet allows networking to rise to a new, more global level. The breadth of your professional network may span the globe if you want it to in this technological age.

Involvement in networks also helps you determine who are the talented, dependable, and knowledgeable professionals you can count on to treat a drug problem. Networks allow you see a microcosm of the styles and skills of another counselor or therapist so you can determine whether you would feel comfortable referring a client to that professional. Networks also clue you in to the reputations of other professionals, as well as to their professional orientations (methods and models). Sometimes information provided by direct contact or word of mouth within a network can be quite helpful in determining whether a client would be a good fit with another professional. This information pipeline may extend beyond the local community, which can aid in an appropriate referral in another geographic area. Often state, regional, and national organizations and agencies can provide referral lists and information about professionals in other locales if you need to refer a client who is moving away or lives elsewhere. In some instances these lists include information about the model orientation of the professional (if you are interested in determining how well he or she will match up with the client).

Highly organized and experienced professionals keep all the information they learn from networking over the years until they have developed substantial databases to help their clients. Many skilled therapists keep this information on file, in their personal digital assistant (PDA), or on the computer. Many have handy card files of names, model orientations, and contact information on their desks. Since many network groups cross disciplines, networking provides wise professionals with numerous contacts who can provide a wide range of services to clients. The savvy professional even keeps the names of those skilled individuals who operate from different orientations just in case a referral is needed for a client who requires a different approach to treating a drug problem. Over the course of years, networking provides a substantial and growing number of resources that the best professionals are able use over and over again in matching services to clients.

CLIENT HANDOUT

Matching Clients to Therapists

As mentioned in Chapter 1, matching the needs of a client to an appropriate therapist is crucial for treatment success. If you are a consumer of treatment (namely, a person with a drug problem or a family member of that person), you should carefully consider whether the particular treatment center or professional of interest will match up well with your worldview, cultural values, goals and needs for therapy, model for understanding a drug problem, and methods for treating that problem. Ask many questions of service providers to determine whether a good match exists, just as if you were buying a house or seeking a physician for important surgery. The research suggests that a strong therapeutic alliance (the ability to work together as a team) between client and therapist is essential for a positive outcome in treating a drug problem.

The following are specific questions that you may wish to ask before saying yes to treatment:

1. What is the therapeutic model that the professional operates under, and how does that model determine the course of treatment?
2. What exactly should the you expect as therapy unfolds — that is, what input would you as a client have in the development and implementation of your treatment?
3. How often would you meet with the therapist, and for how long during each session; and, more generally, what would be the expected duration of treatment or therapy?
4. How would your confidentiality be protected while you were in therapy?
5. How much would treatment cost, what would be included, and how would payment for therapy be expected to be completed?

In addition, before going for help, you should compile a list of individualized questions that account for your own special needs, writing them down so they can be easily remembered and taking notes on how the therapist answers each question. It is important for you to remember how important this decision may be for your health. You wouldn't necessarily buy the first house you see, or have your surgery at the first hospital you pass. Check out several treatment programs or therapists to ensure that you are making the best selection for your needs.

Remember, too, that treatment is a business enterprise, and because of this many treatment centers are concerned about the bottom line. Some treatment centers provide high-quality programs, but in other instances the concern about economics overrides concern about client care. This is not a knock on the treatment industry, because the balancing act among economic solvency, profit, and quality of services is true across all other types of health care as well. As a matter of self-protection, try to judge for yourself whether the program you are contemplating has your best interests at heart.

Matching Clients to Therapists

The Client Handout on page 93 gives some suggestions for potential clients who haven't yet settled on a therapist or counselor. Professionals should make similar considerations when referring a client for other services. As mentioned in Chapter 2, balancing quality care with economics is important to ensure a good match for the client. In addition, make sure that you as a professional are considering other client needs when trying to determine such a match. Frequently, professionals and clients do not agree on what constitutes the best match for a client. In other instances, therapist and client may not agree on the best course of action for reaching client goals, or may even disagree on goals with regard to treatment or therapy. In such situations, professionals can be tempted to overrule what the client would like to see happen. Remembering the power imbalances in therapy, the importance of the therapeutic alliance, and the inability of professionals to actually change a client's behavior, it makes little sense to overrule the client in such disagreements. Instead, we can and should make our recommendations to clients, but ultimately we need to determine referral matches based upon the clients' wishes and goals rather than our own. To develop a match at odds with a client's wishes or needs invites hard feelings on the part of the client and may ultimately delay his or her progress. The client is not likely to comply with such a referral if it does not have his or her interests in mind.

If you are very uncomfortable with a match that is provided, one strategy is to develop a backup plan to offer the client in the event that the match he or she desires does not work out. Here is an example. Suppose you as a therapist have worked with a client who is not getting better with your help. You believe strongly that the client needs to be matched with a therapist who will demand abstinence in the client as a precondition for therapy. The client insists that he or she wants a therapist who will not demand abstinence immediately upon entry into the program. What do you do?

Obviously you feel very strongly, but so does the client. Also obviously, the client will not seek further help if he or she is mismatched (by his or her standards) with a therapist who demands abstinence as a precondition to therapy. In this instance, I would recommend holding your opinions as best you can, and focusing on developing ways to help the client determine whether his or her choice is working well. You might say, "I want to make sure this will be the best match for you. So how will you know if it is working well?" The client responds, and then you might ask, "How will you know if it is *not* working well for you?" After the client responds, you may wish to suggest developing a backup referral if the first match does not work for the client. This strategy takes care to balance several competing interests in therapy. First, it addresses your concerns as a therapist about the choice of therapy or treatment for the client. Second, it acknowledges that the client is the expert on his or her life, which keeps the alliance intact. Third, if the first choice for treatment or therapy does not work, and you have given the client a personal yardstick for measuring success by asking how he or she will know if it is not working well, then this strategy provides for a backup plan of action so that the client has options. In one diplomatic move, you as a therapist have affirmed a client's right to choose her or his own therapeutic path, preserved the client's interest in therapy, and yet protected the client just in case the best choice was not made.

The example presented also illustrates another important concept in matching the client to another professional, which is that the client should be an equal partner in making treatment decisions if at all possible to protect the therapeutic alliance, including decisions about match and referral. I say "if at all possible" because there are some circumstances in which court-ordered treatment may not allow for such participation. However, in my opinion, court-ordered therapy might work better if it did allow for more direct client participation. Many clients have told me about lying and complying to get through such programs. Obviously such behavior limits what will be learned in court-ordered therapy. So, in general, if it is possible, matching works best when it is a collaborative effort.

Finally, when making collaborative matches or referrals for treatment of a co-occurring physical or mental health disorder, professionals must know what the best practices are for treating that particular disorder. Treatment professionals need to stay abreast of research concerning best practices for treating commonly co-occurring disorders. As a rule, you cannot presuppose that all therapy models work well to treat a particular disorder. There are clearly best practices that should be selected in the treatment of specific disorders, and matching a client to the best practices for treating that disorder is critical for changing a drug problem. (Best practices for different disorders are reviewed in Chapter 5. It is not necessarily an exhaustive list, but it does provide some background on what kind of therapy you may wish to consider when matching a client to enhanced health or mental health services for co-occurring disorders.) Keeping abreast of the most recent research is very important when treating a drug problem, because new developments are being routinely reported that increase your ability to help the person in your office.

Referral Dos and Don'ts

Making a proper referral is an art form, one part of which — the when and why to make a referral — was discussed in the previous chapter. Another part of that artistry involves making the referral in an appropriate way. For the sake of simplicity, there are certain dos and don'ts related to making an appropriate referral. For example, do make referrals in a timely fashion. Our clients often need help quickly when a referral is necessary. Delay can harm progress. Related to this, do make sure that you have your client sign a release so that you can talk with another professional about the client, and do make sure there is little to no lapse in treatment services between referral to appointment.

Do thank another professional who has accepted your referral, because showing your appreciation will help develop your professional network. And do follow up to make sure that the referral led to contact. We have an ethical responsibility to determine whether the client made it to his or her appointment. Many times this may require the treatment professional to whom the referral was made to sign a release in order to talk with you.

Do make sure that the client is safe before referring him or her to another professional. A client should be stable before such a referral if possible, unless the goal of the referral is for more intensive care to stabilize the client. Care should be taken to make sure that the client is not at high risk to harm him- or herself, or someone else for that matter, between referral and appointment. If the person is at risk, then the referral should be postponed until that risk has diminished (again, *unless the goal is for stabilization*).

Do refer only for services that are necessary for the well-being of the client. I have witnessed unnecessary referrals for clients. Sometimes professionals overdo promoting special services that may swamp their clients with trivia. Using the *stepped-up care* model to guide whether a referral is overkill, I would advocate a minimalist approach: Suggest only what you think is absolutely necessary for the well-being of the client. If circumstances change, then you can add new services, but too many services may hamper the client's autonomy. The client does not need to be overwhelmed by treatment. Being overwhelmed hinders the learning of new behavior.

Don't violate confidentiality during a referral. Be careful not to allow information about your client to be accessible to people who have no business with that information. One way to inadvertently violate confidentiality is to leave a phone message that may be picked up by a secretary rather than by the professional for which it was intended. Another way is to informally contact an insurance provider to check on benefits. Yet another way is to discuss the case in public places. Consider whether the information being shared has the capacity to find its way to unintended hands, eyes, or ears. If so, then modify the way you are sharing the information.

Motivating Change

Perhaps the most important consideration for helping a person with a drug problem is how to motivate that person to take the next step toward change. To begin with, as mentioned in Chapter 1, motivating behavior change can be affected by the level of awareness of a drug problem. In addition, motivating behavior change can be influenced by personal beliefs about the drug problem and about the solution to that problem.

Effectively enhancing the change-motivation of a person who has a drug problem is perhaps the most important skill a professional can have. Usually such skill takes a great deal of experience and training to develop. Enhancing the motivation

DOS AND DON'TS

Referrals

- Do refer if the client would be better served by working with another therapist.
- Do refer if you find working with a client to be intolerable.
- Do refer if the client would benefit from specialized adjunct treatment.
- Do refer if you have worked with a client for a significant amount of time and she or he is not getting better.
- Do make referrals in a timely fashion.
- Do thank another professional who has accepted your referral.
- Do follow up to make sure that the referral led to contact.
- Do make sure that the client is safe between referral and appointment.
- Do refer only for services that are necessary for the well-being of the client.

On the other hand...

- Don't refer if there will be a lengthy lapse between services.
- Don't refer if you think the client may drop out of therapy instead of accept the change.
- Don't make referrals too soon or too late.
- Don't violate confidentiality during a referral.

of another person is very similar to two people paddling a canoe: If one person is doing all the paddling, the canoe goes around in circles. However, if both people in the canoe are sharing the work and making the necessary strokes to adjust the course of the canoe, then progress is made. The highly skilled therapist who has been trained how to effectively motivate change has the advantage of being in the stern of the canoe. Those skills allow the therapist to very subtly keel the canoe of motivation so that the course can be adjusted without the client in the bow being aware of the subtle changes in movement.

Motivation can be misunderstood if a professional has a preconceived notion of what motivation should look like. Sometimes defining and recognizing motivation to change is tricky. The definition of *motivation* tends to vary across treatment models (see Chapter 5). For example, motivation to change may mean a desire to become abstinent in one model, whereas it may mean a desire to be safe within another model. So it is possible that the same client can be deemed motivated within the latter model while being considered unmotivated in the former. Because of this, it may be more important to determine a client's level of motivation as it relates to her or his goals for therapy rather than by our own understanding of the term. This, of course, may cause us as therapists or counselors some discomfort, since our definition of motivated may not fit with the client's view. Ultimately, giving the benefit of the doubt may help the client, as you will see.

The importance of giving this benefit of the doubt is illustrated by the research. For example, one very interesting body of research concerning therapy found that therapists treat clients differently depending upon what they know about the clients' motivations. If a therapist believes that the client is motivated, then the therapist actually does better therapy with the client than if she or he believes the client is unmotivated. Clients benefit when therapists believe they are motivated to change and may be harmed when therapists do not believe they are motivated. From my perspective, we as professionals have an ethical obligation to evaluate motivation on the client's terms rather than our own because the research suggests that our own perceptions of motivation have the capacity to hinder a client's progress. When in doubt, it is better to assume the client is motivated to change a drug problem.

One way to overcome our own biases about motivation to change is to consider change as a continuum, not just as an either-or proposition. Behavior change can happen in a wide variety of ways, perhaps in ways that may not even occur to us. I have worked with some clients who solved their problems in very creative ways that would not have occurred to me. Sometimes those pathways to change varied from what I had recommended, but ultimately worked well for the client in a manner that surprised me. Since changing a drug problem can happen in multiple ways, as illustrated in Chapter 1, it also is safe to assume that motivation can occur in different ways. The fact that clients are not motivated to change in the way you think they should be does not mean that they are not motivated to change in another way. Our task as professionals is to help the client find a path toward behavior change that interests the client. This interest in the path sparks the motivation necessary to change the drug problem.

"Ability is what you're capable of doing. Motivation determines what you do. Attitude determines how well you do it."

— LOU HOLTZ

There are several different ways to encourage motivation to change behavior that may be useful to a professional. Just as with matching the client to the appropriate referral, it pays to match the client to the appropriate style for encouraging motivation. The following section discusses different strategies to encourage motivation in clients in work and under different conditions.

Motivational Strategies

There are several strategies, derived from the different components of the biopsychosocial model, for encouraging motivation to change a drug problem. The first method that works with some people is to present data about changes in health. Using health care professionals to identify and intervene upon drug problems can be highly effective, but there is evidence that many professionals are missing drug problems in patients when they present for services. In one recent study conducted by the National Center on Addiction and Substance Abuse at Columbia University, 90% of primary care physicians failed to diagnose a drug problem when it existed in an adult patient and 41% of pediatricians missed a drug problem when it existed in an adolescent patient.

Medical professionals have the advantage of *laboratory measures* that can be used as data to be presented to the client. The key, though, is to present the data without being perceived as judgmental, condescending, or lecturing the client. The client will likely be looking for the lecture, as mentioned before, so medical professionals have to be extra careful to avoid that trap. One strategy for presenting medical data is to do so by highlighting how the client's lab values compare to national norms, and to explain what the lab values mean. I would then leave it up to the client to initiate a discussion about what the values mean to him or her, and what he or she would like to do when confronted by these health data. Answering questions is permissible as long as the answer is not followed by a lecture. For example, making suggestions to the patient is okay if you do it like this: "With other people who have had similar labs, I have recommended they do (blank)." In that way, the professional is not telling the patient what to do directly, but providing advice nevertheless. When we present recommendations in this way, the client is not threatened.

Strategies from *operant psychology* also can be very effective in helping to shape motivation. A therapist using this strategy will give full attention to any client statements that show motivation or movement toward behavior change, while ignoring client statements that work against motivation or change (or statements that may be considered unmotivated). This strategy may work well with people who are less able to reflect on behavior change in a rational fashion. Operant strategies also are quite successful when a well-developed therapeutic alliance has been established and the client values your attention (finds it rewarding) in session and abhors your neglect. The power of this strategy is to use attention and praise to shape the behavior. Care must be taken not to be obvious in what you are doing, however.

In some cases, motivation may be encouraged by the use of *commitment strategies* (Linehan, 1993). Three very effective strategies, foot-in-the-door, door-in-the-face, and devil's advocate, are described in great detail in Linehan's book. To begin with, door-in-the-face and foot-in-the-door are techniques used by salespeople. As a therapist, when using *door-in-the-face,* you ask the client for an outrageously large commitment with the goal of negotiating for a smaller commitment. When you start big, clients feel they have won when you settle for less. In reality, clients will likely agree to do what you as a professional wanted all along. Everyone is happy. *Foot-in-the-door* is the opposite approach, in which you start small and try to negotiate for more. Many times you use these two strategies together: start big, go to small, and then try for more again.

Here is an example of how to use this with a client who has a drug problem. Suppose this client is beginning to show some signs of acknowledging a drug problem and you want to see what he is willing to do about it. In your mind, getting this client into therapy for any length of time would be fabulous, but you want to test how far the client may be willing to go. You may decide to use these two strategies together. First, you may recommend to the client that he seek treatment for no less than 6 months (arbitrarily chosen for this example). The client, who is not committed to such a course, tells you, "That's impossible. I can't do that." You respond by saying, "Well, I think six months would be good. Okay, if you won't go for six months, then how about three months?" If the client balks, you negotiate downward again. If your client agrees, then you might choose to try for more. In effect, by using foot-in-the-door and door-in-the-face together, you are negotiating commitment with the client.

The other strategy, playing the *devil's advocate,* must be done with great care because it includes irreverence at its heart. In this instance, you are challenging the client toward motivation by highlighting the difficulties of change. In effect, you are taking on the argument *against* change, which forces an ambivalent client to argue *for* change. Being the devil's advocate might include statements by you such as, "Well, I understand why you would not want to change. You have little reason for changing your drug use." Another statement might be, "Well, it would be incredibly hard to change, so you may be right that change is not for you." Part of the skill involved in using the devil's-advocate strategy is to appear very serious about what you are saying, rather than irreverent or sarcastic, using both clinical acumen and a clinical face to achieve this seriousness. The goal of using this strategy is to light a fire under a client who may be defiant or complacent, who may thrive on challenges, or who seems to be competitive. Using this skill effectively requires training and practice, so I would not recommend using it unless you feel confident in your ability to do it in a very skilled way.

Problem-solving skills also motivate if used effectively (again, see Chapter 5). One of the techniques of problem solving is to have the client *brainstorm* solutions to the problem. If your client has acknowledged a problem with drugs, then this strategy may work to get him or her to change behavior. The first step is to have your client identify the problem in very specific terms so that it can be worked on. "Defined in specific terms" means described completely and succinctly so that it can be solved, so defining drug use as a global problem is not specific enough. Rather, an example of a specific definition is the following: "Drugs have caused problems in X, Y, and Z areas of my life because of A, B, and C behaviors." When the problem is defined this specifically, it provides a number of different options for how to change the behavior, which increases the odds that the client will find one to his or her liking.

After the problem is specifically defined, then you can have the client brainstorm a variety of solutions for the problem. You may have to suggest a couple of ideas in the beginning to get the client used to the style of brainstorming. Tell the client, "All alternatives should be considered, so throw everything that occurs to you out on the table, and later we can sort through the alternatives to find the best options. Don't worry about how feasible the idea is while brainstorming, just keep generating the ideas and I'll write down the options as we come up with them." Again, these options should be directly linked to the specific problem as defined. So, as an example, the brainstorming of a solution should be more specific than "get treatment." Examples of specific solutions include, "Get anger management therapy to treat how I lose my temper with my partner while using drugs," "Learn to structure my time with non-using friends or activities so I will not be tempted to use," or "Seek help for my social anxiety that often triggers my drug use." Your role as the professional is to suggest specific courses of action to reach these goals (where to go to get the best help given the solutions chosen by the client). After the client has brainstormed solutions, the solutions are ranked according to feasibility, likelihood of success, and preferences of the client.

Problem-solving techniques presume that the person has the cognitive abilities to reason out a course of action to solve the problem. If you have doubts about this, or if the person has not yet acknowledged a problem with drugs, this may not work to motivate him or her to seek treatment or change behavior. However, if you are working with a person who has awareness of a drug problem and is able to think rationally about his or her circumstances, problem-solving techniques may work well to motivate him or her to take the next step toward behavior change.

Other cognitive strategies that may be useful to motivate change include challenging *errant assumptions* (see more on cognitive therapy in Chapter 5) and expectancies related to treatment or therapy. Frequently, clients are not favorably predisposed toward therapy because they have misconceptions about what may transpire. Sometimes these misconceptions are completely in error and easy to challenge. However, sometimes these misconceptions have some basis in fact. The client may have heard a horror story about treatment from a friend, or may have heard something about the way treatment was 20 years ago when confrontation was sometimes fierce in group therapy.

Checking out the assumptions and expectations of clients about treatment can be very helpful. You may find that the client has some funny ideas about what will happen in a therapeutic relationship. In order to challenge these thoughts, you may wish to have the client do some homework to find out more about specific practices at certain treatment facilities, maybe assign the client to call those facilities or therapists anonymously and ask if they really do "blank" in therapy, or have the client read a book on therapy or treatment. The results of that informal survey can be reviewed and discussed in a later session. Or you may wish to present your own evidence to challenge the errant assumptions or expectancies that the client has concerning therapy or treatment in a nonjudgmental and nonlecturing fashion.

Challenging assumptions or expectancies works well when a client is aware of a drug problem but is having difficulty committing to treatment or therapy because of misinformation. This technique will not work as well if the person is unaware of a drug problem, or if the assumptions or expectations are true — in which case, you can use another cognitive therapy technique that can be called *imagining the worst that can happen,* which challenges the person to face his or her worst fears about the dreaded event. Then you ask the client to determine the probability that the worst possible outcome will actually occur. This provides some perspective regarding the belief about treatment or therapy that prevents the client from taking the next step toward behavior change. The best solution, of course, would be if treatment professionals and therapists would not do things to scare clients away from seeking services in the first place!

Another approach to encourage motivation to change is both cognitive and behavioral, and involves setting benchmarks for assessing progress and then attaching contingencies for stepped-up care if those benchmarks are not reached. The motivation for change is enhanced by having the client establish points of reference for determining whether her or his way is working well. If not, then a

CLIENT HANDOUT

Trial Abstinence

You can improve your chances for changing a drug problem by giving yourself a breather from using drugs for awhile. *Trial abstinence* involves setting a goal for not using drugs for a brief period of time, such as one month or two weeks. Not using drugs for a short time will allow you to regain some control over your behavior while giving your body some time to heal. You will be able to make a more reasoned decision about your goals for changing a drug problem if your mind is clearer.

1. Trial abstinence begins by making an agreement with yourself and your therapist or counselor not to use drugs for a limited time period.
2. Committing to do this in the presence of another person sometimes makes it more likely that you will follow through.
3. Decide when you will stop and for how long.
4. Make sure to use your therapist or counselor, your new skills, and any other support that you have to meet your goal for this period of abstinence.
5. Finally, before you start using drugs again, discuss the experience with your therapist or counselor and decide what your next step toward behavior change will be.

Trial abstinence may not be easy, but it will be a healthy start toward overcoming your drug problem.

new path is established for trying a different way, which is often developed ahead of time. Usually this works in the form of an agreement between client and therapist as a contract of sorts. For example, say your client has awareness of a drug problem, but no willingness to seek treatment. In this instance, the client agrees to try abstinence on her own for a specific period of time. You ask her to identify specific ways to document that the *trial abstinence* is working for her, and perhaps specific ways to know it is *not* working, as well; you explain that these benchmarks are to be used after a certain period of time to identify whether it is time to try something else. You may even make notes of the answers and the benchmarks being suggested by the client to assess progress, which constitutes the *contract*. Finally, you gain commitment from the client to evaluate the period of trial abstinence at a specified time in the future to determine whether it is working, according to her standards. Finally, when that time arrives, progress is evaluated jointly. If it has worked, fabulous! If the client has not succeeded, the therapist uses the client's own contractual benchmarks to suggest a *stepped-up care* approach, which may be in the form of some type of therapy or treatment.

Stepped-up care with client-developed benchmarks for assessing progress and reevaluating change strategies can be quite effective when the person is ready to change. This strategy also is useful when the change strategy may not succeed in the estimation of the professional. Rather than leave the client jumping into the abyss of change without a parachute, it provides a more intensive change option available if the first plan does not succeed. And it works because it is the client who determines the benchmarks for whether more intensive change strategies are needed, and, because of this, he or she is more willing to agree to a different plan if the previous one falls flat. Obviously, a client has to be motivated to make some change for this to work. If the client does not have awareness of a drug problem, this change strategy will not work well. Furthermore, this strategy presupposes a well-developed therapeutic alliance, so it may not be as effective if used early in a professional relationship.

Many of the strategies discussed presume that a person has some awareness of a drug problem. But what can you do to motivate someone who has little awareness of a problem, or who may be very ambivalent about behavior change? Do not despair, because there are strategies that may work with unaware or ambivalent clients, too.

Motivational Interviewing

Motivational interviewing was developed by William Miller and Stephen Rollnick (2002) to address the need for strategies to work with people who had substance-related problems and were not necessarily ready to change their substance use. Motivational interviewing operates on basic principles that encourage rapid development of a therapeutic alliance and that enhance motivation to change through therapeutic strategies designed to help clients resolve their ambivalence about change. Its basic principles include expressing empathy for the client by

CASE STUDY

Ed the EAP Caseworker

Ed is a 38-year-old EAP caseworker and this Wednesday afternoon is visited by George, who tells Ed that his wife is tired of his smoking marijuana. George makes it clear that he does not smoke at work or on the premises, but admitted that he may smoke too much from time to time on the weekends and with friends after hours during the week. George tells Ed he just wants to get his wife off his back and does not know what the big deal is; after all, he works hard for the family and she should appreciate his efforts rather than complaining about how he relaxes. However, he promised his wife that he would stop by and see an EAP representative.

Ed tells George about the options for outpatient treatment; then he reaches into his files and pulls out schedules of Marijuana Anonymous (MA) and Narcotics Anonymous (NA), and suggests that George try one or more of these meetings. At the end of the session, Ed makes an appointment with George next week to check up on his progress. George quietly takes the appointment card, shakes Ed's hand, and briskly walks out of the office. Next week, Ed waits and waits, but George never shows. Ed is a little mystified by this. . . . Are you?

hearing and validating what the client says to the therapist, and by showing respectfulness at all times; developing discrepancy by using the words of the client to highlight contradictory and ambivalent statements about the problem; avoiding arguing with the client for any reason, and at the same time rolling with a client's resistance rather than confronting it (remember that resistance is escalated by confrontation); and supporting the *self-efficacy* of the client by increasing the competence and confidence of the client for changing the drug use behavior.

Motivational interviewing focuses on the verbal and nonverbal language of clients, and uses their own language to allow them to examine their natural ambivalence about behavior change, including both the positive and negative aspects of drug use. However, the ambivalence is highlighted in a very strategic way in order to enhance the client's motivation to change. Critical components of motivational interviewing include providing feedback to a client about what she or he tells you about her or his drug use, leaving the responsibility for change with the client, providing advice when appropriate and asked for by the client, providing a menu of options when she or he is ready for behavior change, expressing empathy for her or his situation, and supporting her or his self-efficacy to carry out a plan for behavior change. For example, providing feedback to a client usually means repeating or rephrasing the client's words in a skillful way to enhance motivation, rather than telling the client in an unsolicited fashion what you think about his or her situation. Even if your opinion is requested, care is taken to avoid falling into a role of being the expert; often it's best to defer back to the client's best judgment about the situation (with the therapist saying, e.g., "Well, I am not the expert on your situation; what do you think?"). Leaving the responsibility for change to the client is simply acknowledging the powerlessness of a therapist to make a client do anything without his or her consent. Accepting this powerlessness is liberating to a therapist and allows the process to be viewed less personally if it does not go according to what the therapist would like to see happen.

Note that there is an opportunity to provide advice to the client, but it is contingent upon two things: whether the client is at a point in the change cycle at which advice would be accepted (i.e., whether he or she is less ambivalent about and more committed to change), and whether the client would welcome the advice. If you are uncertain whether the client would like your advice, ask, perhaps saying something disarming like, "Would you like to hear what others in situations like yours have done?" Similarly, if a person is ready to develop a plan for change, it is important to suggest a range of options rather than just one, asking the client to choose the one that seems to best fit him or her. If you provide only one or two options, it is easy for the client to dismiss them out of hand. However, if you provide a menu of options, and ask the client to choose the best one, it will empower rather than restrict the client. This strategy also allows you to build in a backup plan if the first choice did not work for the client.

Finally, expressing empathy does not necessarily mean a "touchy-feely" response to the client. *Expressing empathy* simply means respecting the client by listening to what he or she says, regarding the client in high esteem, and taking very seriously the concerns of the client and his or her stated goals for treatment. Related to this, it is important to support the competence and confidence of the client in his or her ability to carry out any plan chosen to change drug use, and to reinforce motivation to change when it is recognized in session.

To carry out these strategies, motivational interviewing relies on a specific style of verbal interaction in the session by the professional. The first verbal stylistic component is to reflect clients' statements back to them so they can listen to and sort through their own ambivalence. Such *reflective statements* by the professional can mirror or paraphrase clients' words in a way that enhances motivation to change, or can be used to illustrate personal ambivalence about drug use exposed in verbal statements by the client. The second verbal stylistic component is the use of *open-ended questions* in order to avoid yes/no–type answers that provide little information about the client. One goal of motivational interviewing is to have clients talk themselves into change (rather than our talking them into change), so obviously we have to get clients talking to us. Open-ended questions, commonly beginning with the words *what* or *how,* encourage the client to tell us his or her story.

In addition, professionals should use affirmational statements liberally in order to reinforce movement toward increased motivation and change, as well as to support self-efficacy. *Affirmations* use praise and reinforcement to support movement toward progress, and may include remarks that highlight the client's past successes. In addition, summary statements are another useful verbal stylistic component that provide a transition between what the client has told you about the past and determining where the client wants to go next with his or her drug use behavior. *Summary statements* repeat the client's verbal narrative in such a way as to illustrate that you have heard and understood what the client has told you, and then provide a transition in the therapy session by setting up key questions about what the client may wish to do next. Miller and Rollnick (2002) provide great detail on these strategies and how to conduct motivational interviewing in a variety of settings, if you are interested in learning more.

Motivational interviewing can work very well to encourage a client to seek help or change drug use behavior on his or her own. If the client is considering treatment, the professional can use motivational interviewing to explore the ambivalence about treatment and about drug use in an empathetic way while providing feedback and advice when requested. When the client expresses a desire to change, the professional can provide a menu of treatment options, and then support the client's self-efficacy to seek treatment of the client's choice. If the client expresses a desire to change on his or her own, the professional can again provide a menu of options (strategies) and support the client's self-efficacy to carry out his or her plan. Motivational interviewing also can be used as an adjunct to other treatment strategies, and is a key component of motivational enhancement therapy (see Chapter 5).

As mentioned, motivational interviewing is only one option for increasing motivation in clients. There are ways to motivate some clients through assessment and feedback about the assessment, as well as using previously mentioned cognitive and behavioral strategies. In addition, other therapies that have not been mentioned here have been developed to increase clients' motivation, so you may wish to browse the research literature if you are interested in learning about other options.

The Transtheoretical Model

A very useful model for understanding a client's relative level of motivation to change is called the *transtheoretical stages of change model* (Prochaska, DiClemente, & Norcross, 1992). Prochaska and colleagues spent a number of years researching the common cognitive and behavioral processes that people use while on the road to health behavior change, and found that they often pass through similar stages on that journey. Although the model is still theoretical and research is still being conducted to test its efficacy, I find it quite helpful in conceptualizing clinical cases.

According to the transtheoretical model, people tend to move through different stages on the road to recovery. The beginning of the journey is the *precontemplation* stage, which exists prior to awareness of a drug problem. The lack of awareness can be due to several factors, as mentioned in Chapter 1. It could be as simple as the fact that the person has not experienced consequences that have raised awareness, or as complex as the fact that the client may have perceptual problems that distort reality. In any case, it is important not to automatically assume that precontemplation is being in denial.

Because people in the precontemplation stage do not have awareness of a drug problem, it does not make sense to treat them the same way as someone who is aware of problems and asking for help. One of the most common mistakes that professionals make in working with people with drug problems is assuming they are aware they need help. This is simply not the case with someone who is in precontemplation. If you as a professional make this assumption, and begin discussing treatment alternatives with a person in precontemplation, he or she will probably look at you like you are from Pluto, and may get angry and seem resistant.

To motivate a person who is in precontemplation to seek help, you first have to increase awareness of a drug problem. One strategy is to use motivational interviewing to get the client talking and telling his or her story, and then to highlight the contradictions (or discrepancies) inherent in what he or she may tell you. Another strategy is to use assessment to present objective data to the client, comparing his or her drug behavior to normative behavior across society (or perhaps with normative behavior of a population with drug problems). Again, this has to be done skillfully, disarmingly, and in a motivational interviewing style. The key to motivating a precontemplator is to use therapy to increase awareness, but you have to be very careful in how you do this to avoid alienating your client.

Clients who are court-ordered or deferred from prosecution generally are in precontemplation (although not always!). Other clients who are pressured by others in their lives to seek help can be in precontemplation (or at least appear to be, since they are usually angry about being pressured into treatment and may act defiantly). Adolescents tend to fall into this category. In addition, people in treatment involuntarily (due to a mental health commitment procedure) or in treatment for the first time may be precontemplators. Clients in precontemplation often say things like, "I don't have a problem. It's (fill in the person's name) who has the problems. I use drugs — yeah, so what? A lot of people use drugs. And drugs are not a problem for me!" Professionals often misinterpret this behavior as problematic, but it is not. In fact, it is normal for people at the beginning of behavior change to feel this way.

People in precontemplation learn to comply quickly if forced to do so by the circumstances of treatment. Many of my clients have told me they learned to talk the talk, so to speak, in order to get through a previous treatment that had been coerced. Precontemplators often learn to become dishonest because they are not allowed by the circumstances to be sincere in coerced treatment. An alternative is to make treatment a safe place for a person in precontemplation to express doubts about a drug problem, and to discuss the joys of drug use as well as the not-so-good things. The client is forced into a corner when coerced into treatment, and tends to lie rather than engage in order to just get by. I would much rather work with an honest precontemplator who seems unready to change than with one who complies to get by, because then you have a chance to at least discuss issues honestly.

The second stage of the transtheoretical model is called *contemplation.* As opposed to people in precontemplation, those in contemplation are aware of a drug problem, but very ambivalent about what to do about it. In the contemplation stage, people are caught on the fence, aware of both the joys and sorrows of drug use. The client may have some awareness of drug-related consequences that are unpleasant, but these tend to balanced by the pleasant reinforcing properties and positive outcome expectancies of drug use. One common mistake that a professional will make with someone in contemplation is to assume that awareness of a drug problem means motivation to change when in fact the client is quite ambivalent about such change. One minute a client in contemplation may be discussing the advantages of changing drug use and then the next minute reflecting on the fun associated with it. If a professional assumes too quickly that awareness of a problem is the same as committing to change that problem, it can cause friction.

One concept used by transtheoretical researchers to understand contemplation is the idea of a *decisional balance.* A graphic representation of a decisional balance (see Figure 3.1) looks very much like a teeter-totter on which is balanced the opposing tendencies of an ambivalent client in contemplation, as well as the reasons *for* changing (pros in the figure) and *against* changing (cons in the figure) drug use. In contemplation, the client's teeter-totter for motivation to change is generally in balance (i.e., he or she is sitting on the fence). The goal of a professional is to resolve the ambivalence in favor of commitment to change. However, this process is not easy, and the strategies to achieve this end require great skill.

For a moment, reflect on the meaning of a teeter-totter in balance. Both sides must be equally matched in weight and pressure. This image represents the balance between the reasons for changing versus not changing in contemplation — an accurate representation of how ambivalence results in lack of movement. Now, what happens if the pressure increases on one side of the teeter-totter? In order to remain in balance, the other person on the board has to lean farther backward. This is what generally happens when a therapist argues one side of the ambivalence about change: The client often will take the opposite side of the argument. One common mistake on the professional's part is arguing for change — which leads to quite a surprise when the client in contemplation responds by arguing against change. As mentioned previously, it is important that the *client* make the argument for change rather than the professional.

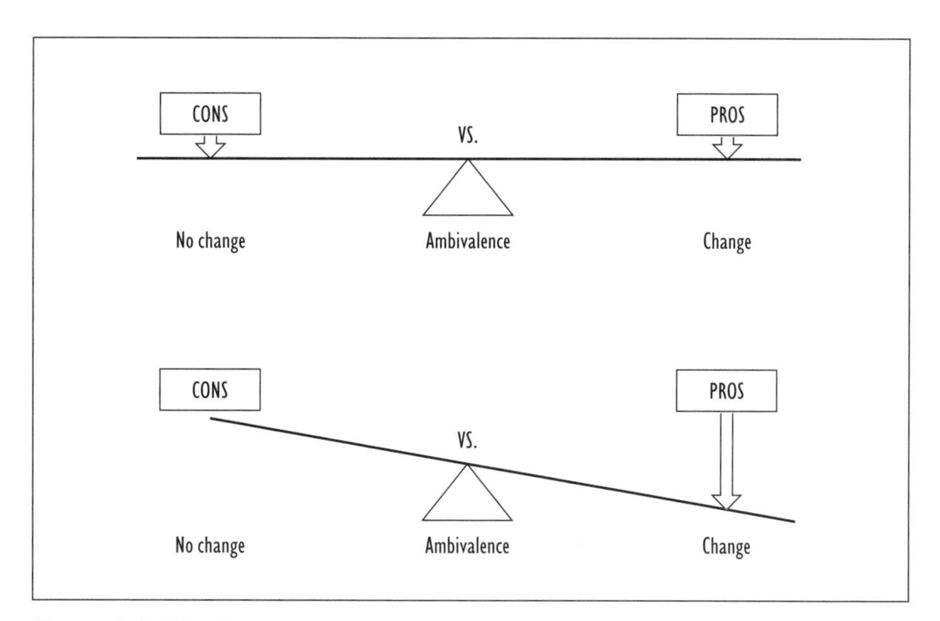

Figure 3.1: The decisional balance.

Changing the client's behavior on the teeter-totter is more important than a therapist's or counselor's pressuring the person toward change. Only the client has the capacity to change the decisional balance. You as a professional can use motivational interviewing to aid the client in shifting the weight, but ultimately the client is the only one who can decide whether change is better than no change. If someone else decides for the client, the client will not be committed to the plan. The best strategy is for the professional to use motivational interviewing to highlight the ambivalence of the client and to enhance motivation.

At first contact, professionals generally are working with clients in the precontemplation or contemplation stages. However, sometimes clients who come in for help, referrals, or advice are already preparing — or even taking action — to change drug use. If a person does resolve her or his ambivalence and begins to plan how to take steps to change, she or he has entered into the *preparation stage*. The preparation stage is typified by less ambivalence about changing drug use, by more commitment to making changes or seeking help, and by a willingness to plan the next steps toward taking these actions. The preparation stage is not yet a time of action, but instead is a time of planning and preparing for action. Preparation is a good time for a professional to provide directions and suggest advice for a client on what strategies to use to meet her or his goals for behavior change. Professionals assume the role of guide on the road to changing a drug problem among clients in the preparation stage. At this stage, clients ask for suggestions and directions, and are not liable to react angrily to discussions about problems and solutions. Professionals often refer to clients in this stage as being willing to seek and receive help.

Sometimes a client will be taking action to change a drug problem when you first meet. Your role as a professional is to support these efforts by reinforcing progress, suggesting course corrections if problems or setbacks are noted as the client tries to change his or her drug use, and to match the client to services that will increase his or her ability to reach his or her goals. Motivation is no longer the most pressing concern if the client is already changing, but supporting self-efficacy and developing skills are of great concern at this stage. When assessing the client's situation, is it important to ask how the client's action strategies for change are working, including what is working well and what is not working so well. In the event of shortcomings, backup plans may be developed and offered, and other resources and services may be suggested. Additional referrals may be warranted if there are some roadblocks preventing the client from reaching his or her goals.

Behavior change does not simply end when action is taken. The transtheoretical stages of change model refers to the period after making successful changes in drug use behavior as the *maintenance stage*. Maintenance is a time for sustaining change over the long term, making successful action steps into long-term, healthy habits, and working on quality-of-life changes that may be attainable after the client successfully overcomes a drug problem. Related to this, a client may relapse rather than maintain changes continuously. *Relapse* is recognized as a natural part of the change cycle because it is a very common phenomenon. Since maintenance (and relapse prevention) are long-term concerns and the result of extensive self-change efforts, therapy, and treatment, professionals usually do not need to be concerned about these issues during initial contacts or in early efforts to motivate change. Maintenance strategies become salient after the person becomes more committed to long-term change, although addressing relapse early in therapy or treatment is generally recommended. Action- and maintenance-stage issues, as well as relapse prevention, are discussed more completely in Chapters 5 and 7.

The professional working with a client for the first time or with a client who is presenting for therapy prior to changing behavior may wish to consider using the transtheoretical model to determine where the client is on the motivation and commitment continua, and also to determine what might be an appropriate way to encourage movement toward the next stage of change. Related to assessing motivation, therapists and counselors will want to determine which obstacles are preventing clients from being more highly motivated to change. In the next section, many of these potential obstacles will be described so you can remember to keep your eyes open for them in session.

Overcoming Client Obstacles

Obstacles that interfere with client motivation and behavior change can arise from a variety of sources. Some obstacles arise from the behavior of the client, but others may arise as a result of interpersonal relationships and environmental factors outside the session that may be beyond the client's control. Moreover, not all obstacles in session are from the client. The professional can sometimes unwittingly place obstacles in the way of client progress.

Resistance to change is one common obstacle. Clients in the precontemplation or contemplation stages of change may balk at moving toward change as mentioned, and because of this may actively resist any efforts that they perceive are pushing them toward change. If this obstacle arises in session, it alerts you that you have pushed too much. Motivational interviewing, for instance, has strategies for avoiding such pitfalls by using a type of therapeutic judo (so to speak) to dodge client resistance. Resistance in a client is generally a sign that our motivational strategies are not working, so it is time to use a different strategy!

If a client is showing signs of resistance, back off. You can back off in a number of different ways. If the resistance arises because the client perceives you do not understand what he or she is saying, then offer an apology, admit to the misunderstanding, and ask for clarification. If the resistance is apparent because you used a wrong strategy, and the client backpedals, then try another, less aggressive strategy. If the client goes silent on you, try to summarize what you have heard and then ask if you have missed anything. If the silence continues, go silent as well and use nonverbal language to communicate. Sometimes resistance arises if you misjudge how motivated the client is to change, or how committed a client is to a particular plan. If the client begins to act with compliance rather than willingness, then you may assume you overestimated the stage of change and levels of motivation and commitment. If the client is determined by you to be motivated, then the resistance may be related to not accepting the plan of action. Under this circumstance, it may be helpful to review and reformulate the plan with more attention to the client's wishes. If ambivalence about behavior change in general becomes more apparent, then it is not yet time to develop a plan. Rather, you will need to step back and work on enhancing motivation some more. As mentioned in Chapter 1, resistance is a function of therapist behavior toward the client, so it is up to professionals to take steps to lower client resistance in session.

Denial is another obstacle that many professionals encounter. However, just like resistance, denial is misunderstood by many professionals. As mentioned in Chapter 1, denial can be many things besides dishonesty — for example, increasing as a function of trust (or distrust). Professionals who are working with clients under circumstances in which discussing drug use could be potentially harmful (or even dangerous) to a client should recognize the awkwardness of the client's situation. To begin with, the client may be placed into your care without consent or under duress, which influences a person's attitude about therapy or treatment. In addition, the client may be afraid that any information he or she shares will be used against him or her (at work, in court, etc.). To top it off, the client likely has not explored his or her ambivalence about drug use prior to treatment in the same way that someone who voluntarily turns for help would. Under these circumstances, the client may know very little about treatment or therapy, and be highly suspicious of it.

Professionals will have to honestly address all of these issues and concerns (and probably much more) in order to gain the trust of clients who are being assessed and treated under coercive conditions. If information provided to you is confidential (not provided to others), then tell the client up front that whatever is said in the office stays in the office. Then validate the awkward position the client is in by acknowledging the difficulty of his or her situation. I usually say something like, "I understand that you aren't here because you want to be. Since we have to meet together regardless of whether you want to or not, I'm wondering if there is something we can work on together that would help you. So, how can we use this time together in a way that will benefit you?"

If the client is correct in assuming that information provided to you can be used against him or her, then you have an obligation to tell the client. If your role as a professional is to represent an agency that has some control or power over the client, then acknowledge the power imbalance. The client will likely be aware of this anyway, and the best way to develop trust is to be totally honest about this with the client. Ask the client if he or she would like to discuss issues related to drug use under these conditions. If the client is unwilling, then find ways to discuss drug use in general without discussing the client's drug use directly. Sometimes I will use a motivational interviewing style, and say things like, "Others I have met with have talked about enjoying X, Y, and Z about their drug use. At the same time, they also told me about some less enjoyable things about drug use, such as A, B, and C." In this way you are exploring the decisional balance without the client's having to share potentially damaging personal information. Similarly, you may want to discuss a menu of options for change that others have chosen (again in a motivational interviewing style) by saying something like, "Others I have talked with who had a drug problem have chosen to do things like D, E, and F. If you had a drug problem, which of those options might you choose?" In this way, you may be able to develop a plan for a client with some chance for success (not simply compliance), again without forcing the client to discuss the drug problem. This is particularly effective if the client does not want to share personal information and you have an obligation to place him or her in mandated services. This indirect approach also can gain the trust of clients who find themselves in a personally awkward situation. Some of these clients may actually want help but are not at liberty to discuss their situations, so it is not always safe to assume low motivation under these conditions.

In other situations what appears to be denial may be due to the client's not having experienced many negative consequences. If this is the case, then the professional can use the decisional balance to explore the good and not-so-good things about a person's drug use. Sometimes developing a list of pros (good things) and cons (not-so-good things) is an effective way to increase the client's awareness about ambivalence toward drug use even if very few consequences are being experienced. If the client does not seem to have many "not-so-good" items, then you may wish to work with him or her to develop benchmarks for what *would* constitute a problem in his or her mind, and what he or she would do if *that* happened. One way to start this process is to say the following: "It seems like you feel that using drugs is a good thing for you now. Is there something that might happen to you related to your drug use in the future that would cause you concern, that might cause you to consider changing your drug use?" The client answers, and you ask, "If that were to happen to you in the future, what would you do to help yourself?"

Remember that denial-type behavior can be related to other cognitive and perceptual problems as well. If you see signs that the person is not tracking well cognitively or is acting dangerously and impulsively, perhaps showing little common sense or judgment, having extreme difficulty maintaining focus, and having problems with attention and concentration, it may be worth referring the person for a neuropsychological evaluation. If the person shows symptoms of other mental problems, perhaps even behavior that suggests a possible psychosis or other severe mental disorder, then he or she may need to be referred for a psychiatric consult and possible medication management to stabilize before treating the drug use. Assessing these conditions is described in greater detail in Chapter 4 and treating comorbid disorders is discussed in greater detail in Chapter 5. Any of these conditions can cause a person to appear as if he or she is in denial, when in fact a physiological problem may be interfering with the person's ability to make accurate judgments about his or her personal situation.

Another obstacle that can hinder motivation or behavior change develops when the client normalizes his or her behavior by comparing him- or herself with peers who use drugs. Researchers have found that people who use alcohol tend to overestimate how much peers are using while underestimating their own use. By engaging in this flawed social comparison, some people justify their drinking behavior because it seems that they are using less than their peers. Presumably this type of social comparison occurs among people who use drugs as well.

Two different strategies can work to remove this particular obstacle. The first is to have the client monitor his or her drug use behavior between sessions to gather accurate data on the quantity or variety of drugs being used. Such *self-monitoring* allows the client, sometimes for the first time, to see exactly how much and when he or she is using drugs. Often the client is surprised at what and how much he or she is using, and in some instances, the monitoring alone can be enough to motivate the person to modify his or her behavior. The second strategy often is used in conjunction with the first. The data gathered by the client from self-monitoring can be compared to the *social norms* of a well-matched comparison group so that the client can get an objective view (perhaps for the first time) of normative drug use for his or her peers. The skillful professional will then have the client compare his or her use to the norms for his or her age group, so that the client can draw conclusions about how normative his or her drug use is when compared to that of others. Using self-monitoring together with social norms strategies may allow the client to experience a moment of pause to consider whether personal drug use is abnormal. Even if the client continues to use drug-using friends as a comparison group to argue that he or she does not have a problem, you can show the client that those friends may be using drugs at an abnormal level when compared to societal norms.

Another common obstacle is *inertia,* or lack of energy to initiate movement. Inertia is a common feature of depression. A person with depression often feels de-energized and demoralized, and finds it difficult to do anything. People with depression often have to force themselves to do even the smallest tasks, finding little enjoyment in those tasks that used to bring about pleasure. People with depression are literally immobilized because of inertia. To use the language of physical science, an object at rest remains at rest until another force puts it into motion (law of inertia). Your role as a professional is to put inactive clients into motion, and you may wish to assign homework that involves movement and taking action. Assign them to engage in pleasurable activities (without drug use) that have slipped out of their daily lives because of inertia (e.g., going to a movie, taking a long shower or bath, or engaging in a hobby or recreation). You assign them to do this (or any) activity even if they argue that it will not help. Consider completing an assignment in session if you think there is a possibility that the client will not comply. The solution to inertia is to engage the client in activity, or what some researchers and therapists call *behavioral activation.*

Sometimes inertia is related to fear of making a mistake. If so, then perfectionism may need to be addressed. Making a mistake can be reframed as an opportunity to learn more about how to succeed next time. In other instances, inertia may be a reaction to past failures and discouragement. Supporting self-efficacy and reinforcing baby steps toward progress (behavioral researchers call this strategy *reinforcing successive approximations toward the goal*) can be effective in restoring the client's confidence in succeeding. Other times inertia is related to sadness and grief. For some clients, grieving may be necessary, but behavioral activation and socialization assignments should be given in order to avoid isolation. Inertia also can occur because the person finds little pleasure in daily life. The professional's responsibility is to restore this pleasure in creative ways. Finally, the depressive disorder may have sapped the person of the physical energy needed to carry out a plan of action. In some instances, antidepressant medication may be needed to jump-start the person's energy level, but these medications often take a few weeks to reach a therapeutic dose. *Cognitive behavioral therapy* for depression may help while the medication reaches therapeutic level, and ultimately cognitive behavioral therapy seems to work quite well to reduce depression relapse over the long term (see Chapter 5).

Another common roadblock to changing a drug problem is *social anxiety.* Many people use drugs and alcohol to alleviate anxiety in social situations.

However, when you take away the drugs and alcohol, the person still has the social anxiety that needs to be treated. It is worth determining whether your client fears social situations. Social anxiety can be a tremendous obstacle to recovery, since many sources of help and support involve social contact and groups. In some instances social anxiety may have to be treated before a person is able to seek help, so alleviating the condition may be one way to increase motivation to seek further treatment. In other cases, social anxiety may make treatment out of the question for a client, so using more impersonal strategies for treating a drug problem may have to be considered. For instance, some therapy can be conducted online, and many support groups now have groups that meet online. However, the best solution would be to get the client out into the world to socialize, so treating the social anxiety is preferred. Treatment for social anxiety will be discussed in Chapter 5 as well.

Another common obstacle is dislike of the *12-step philosophy,* or of support groups in general. The use of support groups and the 12-step traditions does not work well for everyone, as mentioned previously. Some people have worldviews that do not agree with the basic tenets of 12-step philosophy. Other people are not comfortable in support groups or in groups in general. Still others have had negative experiences associated with traditional treatment or while participating in support groups. Regardless of the reasons, there are many people who do not fit well into 12-step or other support groups; the research suggest maybe a majority of people with drug problems never find a home in groups like NA.

If the client you are working with expresses these views or concerns, then you should refer her or him into an alternative type of treatment or group. The alternatives for traditional treatment usually take the form of individualized psychotherapy. Some larger cities have *harm-reduction treatment centers* that focus on alternative types of treatment, and generally accept anyone into treatment even if he or she is still using substances. If the client has problems with the 12-step philosophy but not with support groups in general, alternative support groups such as Rational, Smart Recovery, and SOS are available. There are even groups (such as Moderation Management) that seek moderation as a goal rather than abstinence. Finally, some religious organizations, Christian and non-Christian, have their own programs to help clients with drug problems. Many of the groups listed previously have online programs just like NA does. See Chapter 4 for more details on contact information for some of the groups mentioned here.

Twenty years ago the dislike of traditional treatment may have presented some real challenges. Today, however, there are many more treatment alternatives to which a client can be referred to if she or he would not match well with a traditional treatment facility. A good referral might be to a psychologist or other therapist who practices cognitive behavioral therapy for individuals. In addition, the advent of the Internet era allows for new and creative treatment alternatives even for people in small communities.

Finally, another obstacle is that some clients will not seek help out of fear that others will discover that they have drug problems and use that information against them. One solution is to educate the client about *federal confidentiality laws* that protect against disclosure while in treatment, or state laws that protect client confidentiality in therapy. However, you also should be very honest that there are ways in which confidentiality can be suspended, or when outside institutions can access personal health information. For example, make sure to explain that state confidentiality laws can and will be suspended if the client expresses thoughts about harming him- or herself or others, and in some states, if he or she damages property. Additionally, if a client is mandated to services, he or she should be told that those officials who mandated the treatment may have access to treatment records and reports. Finally, tell clients that insurance carriers and their representatives also may have the right to access that information. Clients should be made aware that there are a number of protections in place to protect them, but also told frankly that some of the protections have limits.

In addition to obstacles brought into the therapy by clients, environmental and social factors may place pressures on clients that can influence changing a drug problem. One important factor has to do with *family and family obligations*. If the client believes that seeking help will interfere with family obligations, she or he may be less motivated to seek help. Research has found that for women with substance-related problems, an inability to care for children often prevents their seeking help. Some treatment facilities recognize this obstacle and provide child care services, but this option is still quite rare.

Clients from ethnic-minority groups that have relational worldviews with strong bonds to extended families and prescribed social roles also may have difficulties seeking help if treatment interferes with family relationships and social roles. Many therapists and other professionals make the mistake of believing that the value of treatment should be so evident that the client would be willing to forgo family obligations for a brief period of time in order to obtain long-term gain. This is a critical error when working across cultures. For many clients from non-majority cultures, there is little distinction between self and family, so to talk about separation is completely unacceptable. Professionals need to consider family obligations and cultural values when making referrals. The rule of thumb is to make the referral that is the least intrusive and the most helpful to a person (see Figure 3.2). Making such a referral may help motivate a client worried about family responsibilities.

Another potential obstacle is *work-related obligations*. Fortunately, many outpatient services are now offered in the evenings for working professionals. These options diminish, though, when a client works in the evenings or through the night. Again, it may be that individual psychotherapy would be a reasonable (and time-flexible) option for clients whose work schedules may preclude attendance in outpatient groups. Professionals should try to refer the client to services that do not interfere with work. It is generally unthinkable to ask clients to risk jobs by going into treatment. The research, as mentioned in Chapter 1, suggests that

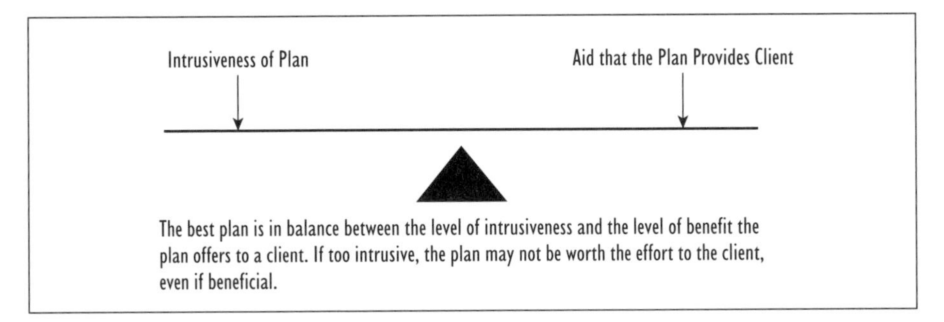

Figure 3.2: Plans should balance helpfulness vs. intrusiveness for a client.

unemployment is a high risk factor for drug problems, and data suggest that people who are unemployed have poorer outcomes after treatment. Again, matching the client with a treatment or therapy option that does not interfere with a job will likely enhance motivation to seek such services.

For many people, *finances* may represent the largest obstacle to treatment services. Although some insurance policies have substantial coverage for such services, many do not, and many people with drug problems have no coverage at all. As mentioned previously, professionals need to consider finances when making referrals. Some communities have publicly funded treatment centers that may ease financial burdens on cash-strapped clients. If the professional is working with the client in an effort to minimize the financial burden while maximizing the treatment services, then the client is likely to be more motivated to seek the recommended services. Burdening a drug-using client with heavy debt is not a particularly effective way to help him or her begin a new way of life.

For others, the main obstacle to seeking help is finding *transportation*. In many cases, suggesting services located close to the home or apartment or close to the client's workplace can help reduce the burden of getting to and from therapy. This strategy also reduces the burden of getting to therapy for someone who may have inertia or time limitations because of work. Other strategies that increase motivation to follow through on a referral include referral to services located on bus or subway lines. For people in more isolated rural areas, one alternative might be to use Internet services as much as possible.

One key factor to enhancing commitment to change is making the plan easy to follow. Confusion is fairly typical in a client early in therapy or treatment. The confusion may result from lingering ambivalence about change. In other instances, the confusion may be the result of cognitive difficulties subsequent to long-term and heavy drug use. Professionals should develop referral plans that are easy to follow to overcome such confusion. The plans should be quite specific and concrete for this very reason. The goal is to make the plan into habit, so there should be structure and routine built into a good plan, at least in the beginning stages of behavior change.

For example, imagine that you are developing a referral plan for your client to attend NA twice a week as part of a self-change plan. You will want to make the plan much more specific than simply suggesting the client go to two meetings a week. Instead, the plan should specify that the client attend NA on, say, Tuesday night at one location (easy access for client) and on Thursday night at another (also easy access for client), and you should consider writing down this plan for your client with specific directions on when and where to be. Lowering the threshold on the difficulty of a plan will make it more likely the plan will be followed, and making the plan structured, routine, and written down will make the plan easy to remember. Some professionals may wish to include a follow-up call to the client to make sure the plan is being implemented, and if it is not, to determine whether the plan was too complex to follow. Of course, if the plan is not being followed, it may be that ambivalence about change has overruled commitment, and the professional may have to return to strategies to enhance motivation.

Overcoming Therapist Obstacles

Clients are not the only ones who can throw roadblocks into the therapeutic path. Therapists have the capacity to hinder client progress in a number of ways, and do so sometimes unwittingly. There are number of bear traps that a professional can walk into that will alienate a client, some that have been discussed earlier in the book. One therapeutic turn-off develops when the client perceives that the professional is lecturing to him or her about drug use or changing drug use. Another occurs when the client feels as though the therapist is being condescending, sarcastic, or ridiculing. These impressions may develop when the client feels like less than an equal partner in the session, or when the client detects verbal or nonverbal signs of arrogance or of distance in the therapeutic process. Finally, another therapeutic turn-off is a professional's arguing with the client, or aggressively pushing the client toward change. The common element to all of these therapeutic turn-offs is that the client does not feel validated by the professional, and therefore has trust in neither the professional nor the therapeutic process.

One solution to preventing these turn-offs in session is to build trust in the client by treating him or her with dignity and respect. A golden rule in therapy is to treat your client as you would want to be treated yourself. Building a therapeutic alliance takes some time, but the process can be enhanced if the professional is truly listening to the client, and responding in such a way in session that lets the client know that she or he is being heard, loud and clear.

By using the client's own words when summarizing what you have heard, you can let the client know she or he is being heard. By showing you understand what the client is saying to you in your own body language, you show your respect and interest, and the client will feel that you understand her or his story. By illustrating that you understand that drug use can be enjoyable as well as troubling for a client, you develop credibility as an objective resource for the client to draw upon

CASE STUDY

Robyn Flies the Coop

Robyn is a 31-year-old mother of three who began working with a therapist named Dr. Hart in order to overcome her problem with prescription pain medication. Things went well in therapy for the first month or so; then, suddenly, Robyn did not call or show for her session. Dr. Hart was completely mystified by this turn of events. She attempted to call Robyn several times over the next few weeks before she finally reached her. Dr. Hart asked Robyn why she dropped out of therapy, and at first Robyn dodged the question by saying therapy did not seem to be working for her. Dr. Hart then countered by saying she thought that Robyn had been doing quite well. After this brief exchange, Robyn also mentioned that a bill for services had come in the mail and that her insurance had covered only about half of the charges. She expressed a great deal of embarrassment about this situation. Dr. Hart was very surprised to hear this, since she did not deal with the financial aspects related to the clinic. She suggested that they meet to talk about how they could work around this financial problem, and she insisted that it should not prevent Robyn from getting the help she needed. After all, Dr. Hart is kindhearted and wants therapy to succeed for Robyn, who had been a model client until the bill came in the mail.

when the time is right. *The basics to developing the alliance are to listen, learn, respect, and affirm*. Later, if you have done these things well, the time to teach will present itself.

Professionals also must learn their own personal limits, and share those limits with clients *before* those clients have done something that crosses those limits. Each of us has different limitations that we place on relationships, including professional relationships. When a professional finds him- or herself angry with a client, it often is related to limits' being crossed. The key for a professional is to be aware of his or her limits in therapeutic situations in order to minimize the risk of having those limits crossed.

The crossing of limits is really the professional's problem rather than the client's problem. It is, after all, the professional's limits that are being crossed, and because of this, it is the professional who responds, often with anger or discomfort toward the client. What a professional should realize is that the client likely has no idea that he or she has crossed limits in the relationship. How could a client know a limit has been crossed if she or he has not been told about that particular limit? *Limit violation* by a client usually is out of ignorance rather than out of spite. However, the professional often responds quite humanly to such a violation as if it were a threat and becomes upset at the client.

Here is an example: You as a professional may value punctuality, and in fact, may have firm limits against tardiness. The client shows up late, and you make some judgments (because your limits were crossed) about the client's level of motivation, responsibility, seriousness, and commitment, based on the tardiness, which may or may not be correct. The evaluation you make is done because you are upset about your limits' being crossed, rather than related to any cold, hard facts. Because of this evaluation, you may treat the person differently in session (as mentioned earlier in this chapter). Meanwhile, the client is completely oblivious to having crossed the line, but does perceive being kept at a distance by you in session, and may react accordingly. And the truth is that the client was late because the bus was late rather than as a result of low motivation to change a drug problem.

The interesting thing is that no one is wrong to feel as they do in this scenario, but all the feelings are related to slight misunderstandings of what is really going on. The truth is that the therapist feels crossed by the client, but the client has no idea he or she has crossed the therapist. When therapists are aware of such limits, they should make a point to share them with clients at the beginning of the therapeutic relationship. People deserve to know the rules of the game before they play. If you as a therapist value punctuality, you should share that with the client at first contact, and also set out consequences for those limits' being crossed. It is important for the client and the therapist to play with the same rule book in therapy, and the responsibility is the therapist's to share his or her rules with the client before those rules are crossed. At the same time, the therapist acknowledges that his or her limits are just that, personal limits, and that those limits are not shared by everyone else. However, even though the therapist acknowledges that limitations vary from person to person, the therapist also acknowledges that he or she will be a better therapist if those rules are not crossed in the therapeutic relationship. Most clients will be on board when they understand they will be treated better by you if limits are not crossed!

There are times when professionals learn of new personal limits by having new experiences in therapy. The professional may be unaware of a particular limit until she or he notices her- or himself getting upset, angry, or uncomfortable with a client for no apparent reason. When this happens to me, I know to step back and try to determine what is going on with me, and what behavior in the client triggered such a reaction. Often it is related to recognition of a new limit that had not been tested before. When this happens, it is important to share this information with the client. The appropriate way to share this information is to use "I" language and not "you" language in describing the experience, in order to accept responsibility for recognizing a new limit and avoid blaming the client for the experience. Since it is a therapist limit, albeit a new one, it still is important to understand it as the therapist's problem (not the client's). As the professional shares the recognition of the new limit, he or she must develop new strategies for reducing the likelihood of the limit's being crossed again. A new contract for therapeutic behavior may need to be established in order to avoid the client's crossing the newly recognized limit in the future.

A professional's *distraction* in session represents another obstacle. To be a professional is of course to be human, so there will be times when you are distracted. Maybe you are having one of those days, or maybe there are events outside work that are preoccupying you. Another possibility is that your client is simply dull to listen to today and you are reacting to that. Being distracted happens, but it certainly influences your effectiveness. Clients often notice when you are distracted and that can influence their progress. There are several effective responses professionals can have to being distracted. The first, and perhaps best, solution, is this: If you know before the client shows that you are distracted to the point of being ineffective, postpone the session. If you are not aware of being this distracted until in the middle of a session, then it may be best to end that session early. You should let the client know that you are ending it for your own personal reasons rather than ending it because of anything the client has done. In this way you reduce the likelihood the client will personalize the event.

If you are in the session and notice being distracted, but not to the point of being ineffectual, then concentrate on the client's words, and practice summarizing what he or she has said to you. Many times focusing on what the client says will bring you back into the session. You also may wish to maintain good eye contact if the client is comfortable with that behavior. Another way to regain focus is to turn to a more active task in session. Sometimes role-playing or discussing homework assignments can be effective ways to reengage in therapy when you are feeling distracted. Basically, you want to use the same strategies on yourself that you would use on your client if you noticed his or her attention waning in the middle of a session.

> **"With the gift of listening comes the gift of healing."**
>
> — CATHERINE DE HUECK

As mentioned, sometimes the content of therapy seems irrelevant or dull. If you notice yourself being distracted, ask yourself why. Maybe the client is not using time in session well, or perhaps the client is engaging in behavior that has the effect of putting you to sleep. Observing and identifying this behavior in session provides an opportunity, because if the client behaves this way in session, she or he likely behaves in such a way outside — perhaps contributing to the same response in others. You can point out your distraction to the client, then discuss why it has occurred, discussing the relationship between the client's actions in session and the natural consequences of disinterest. After this discussion, alternative ways of behaving that may be more socially functional can be explored together. In this way, a dysfunctional behavior that may push others away in the real world has been modified in session, all because you noticed yourself taking a siesta in therapy.

Another potential obstacle to therapy and treatment is *lifestyle imbalance* on the part of professionals. As we know, lifestyle imbalance in our clients adversely affects them. The same, of course, is true for us as well. If our lives are out of balance outside session, it will affect our skill level in session. Lifestyle imbalance can cause fatigue, distraction, mistakes, anger, frustration, and impatience. Those problems will likely follow us into session. Lifestyle *balance,* on the other hand, models healthy living for our clients, and provides them hope for the future and interest in behavior change. Lifestyle balance allows us to share personal models for success with our clients so they, too, can seek similar balance after changing drug problems. Obviously we cannot be on top of the world at every moment, and many of us are quite busy and find it difficult to maintain balance. On the other hand, *difficult* does not imply *impossible,* and our skills depend on our health. Clients will not want what we offer if it looks distressing to them!

In addition to our own appearances, our *office spaces* also send a message about happiness and health. If a client feels uncomfortable in your space, then it represents an obstacle to treatment. Remember how hard it is to change a habit, and then multiply that challenge by the difficulty of seeking help in a strange place. If the strange place looks sterile or lacks warmth and comfort, then seeking help seems even more frightening or distressing to a potential client. Try to make your clinic a place where clients feel that hope and peace may abide.

Finally, many clinics have significant *barriers for entry into treatment* that can discourage clients. Some of my clients have told me they would have sought help for their drug problems significantly earlier in their lives if treatment centers did not expect abstinence upon entry. Drug problems are unlike most disorders or health problems, because a person is often expected to stop the behavior in order to receive treatment. Cancer patients are not asked to be in remission upon entry into treatment. Depression patients are not discharged if they are actively depressed and suicidal in treatment. People with schizophrenia are not told they have to be nonpsychotic in order to receive services. But many treatment services tell people with drug problems they have to stop their behavior (leave it at the door) *before* they get services.

The concern, of course, is that it would be difficult to have a treatment center if some of the clients wanted abstinence and had stopped using drugs while others in the same center had not stopped. The traditional answer has been to include those who are abstinent, and to exclude those who are not willing to be abstinent. An alternative would be to provide different types or levels of services, so that people who were seeking abstinence could be among others who were abstinent in one service unit, whereas others who were still using drugs could be placed with clients still using drugs in another service unit. In order to remove this obstacle, treatment centers should consider offering multiple services rather than excluding people who need help.

Europe has had very successful programs, like the one being suggested, for years, so this is not a novel or exotic idea. Not everyone will be interested in providing services to people who are not ready to stop using drugs upon entry into treatment, but for those who may be interested, the change would likely result in their receiving a large number of new clients who are not being served by other centers. Obviously offering such services would help clients, and potentially could save many lives. Treatment facilities that offered different levels of services also would have the competitive advantage of attracting clients who may not be ready to quit at first, who could be treated in the harm-reduction program initially (see Chapter 5 for more details). Later in treatment these same clients may decide for abstinence as a treatment goal. At that time, they can be transferred to an abstinence-based unit, all in house. Consumers love having choices, so I am guessing such a treatment facility would be quite popular and profitable.

Preventing and Dealing With Crises

Another type of obstacle to behavior change is the occurrence of a crisis that threatens to disrupt therapy or threatens the well-being of the client. Frequently, these crises involve extreme emotional responses or mood problems, such as explosive anger and suicidal behavior. In other cases, a crisis might involve a legal situation. The professional will need to respond quickly and effectively to this type of situation in order to defuse it.

Aggression and Anger

There are some rules that will help you under these circumstances. First, with regard to aggressive clients, *do not place yourself at risk under any circumstances*. For example, if you have a client who is potentially explosive, you may want to leave the door wide open so the client can leave if he or she wants, and so colleagues can gauge your safety and whether they will need to intervene. If you are working with a person who is threatening you, get out of the situation. The second rule is related to the first: *You do not have to work with someone who threatens you*. You can refer, or if you believe you are imminent danger, call law enforcement authorities. If the client threatens you, the relationship is broken, so there is little that can be done to repair it at that point. So, protect yourself first, and then refer the client for other help later.

Many of our clients are angry, and sometimes that anger comes out in an uncontrolled fashion. When working with a client who is angry and has a history of losing control, a professional has to be concerned about the escalation of the anger and should avoid responses that might cause this. For example, do not encourage the person to "let it all out" or push the person to express anger in an uncontrolled rage. Although some therapists believe that catharsis is good for explosive anger, the research suggests that catharsis, while it certainly may encourage the client to vent the anger, does not teach the client how to control the explosiveness of its expression. So encouraging the uncontrolled expression of anger is not wise, because it will often lead to explosive behavior without resolution. You also do not want to argue with the client in a situation in which he or she is at risk of losing control of behavior. Escalation on your part will result in escalation on the part of the client. Finally, you will want to avoid physical encroachment or contact. Getting too close to or touching the client may be misinterpreted as aggressiveness on your part and may result in an attack.

However, the professional often can *de-escalate* such a situation if he or she responds appropriately. In addition to avoiding the previously mentioned behaviors, the therapist can respond calmly and rationally to the client. Yelling can be met by a quiet response on your part. As the client gets louder, you respond by lowering your voice even more, maybe to a whisper. By modeling de-escalation in your response, the client may de-escalate with his or her own response. The same can be true for your demeanor and body language. Although it is difficult to relax when being yelled at, this is a response that will likely relax the client. The point is not to provoke a more aggressive response and to buy some time for the client to regain control. After the client regains control, then you will want to discuss the issues related to the outburst of anger in a therapeutic way, including reinforcing what the client did well, and teaching new skills to overcome what the client did not do well.

One of the first things you want to do with such a client is teach alternative ways of dealing with the anger *before* the client gets angry. There are several skillful approaches toward anger management. First, have the client *monitor when he or she gets angry*, and what provokes that anger. This allows you to identify potential triggers for explosive anger with the client in an effort to have awareness of high-risk situations. Eventually you want to teach the client how to control behavior in those situations. Second, teach the client to *do something different when angry* instead of aggressively confronting the cause of the anger. Some ideas include exercising, walking, leaving the situation, or doing a different activity that makes it difficult to remain angry. Third, teach the client *relaxation skills*. This may include progressive muscle relaxation, guided imagery that leads the client to a quiet and peaceful place in his or her imagination, meditation, and breath-control exercises. Fourth, teach *assertiveness skills* so that the client learns to express anger in a controlled fashion. Finally, help the client to develop an *escape plan* in case the client feels he or she is losing control of anger. The escape plan allows the client to determine what he or she will do to disengage from a potentially volatile situation and to rehearse that plan before ever getting in that situation. This will allow the client to engage the plan automatically when the time becomes necessary to do so. Some of these skills are described more fully in Chapter 5.

Suicidal Behavior

Working with clients who engage in suicidal and parasuicidal behavior can be quite stressful for professionals. We care about the health and well-being of our clients, and it often is personally disturbing when a person we are working with engages in self-injurious behavior. The most dreaded situation that many mental health care professionals face is having a client who successfully commits suicide. Many people who use drugs are depressed, and some are actively suicidal.

THINGS TO REMEMBER

How to Work With Angry and Aggressive Clients

- Do not place yourself at risk.
- If being threatened, get out of the situation and seek help if needed.
- Do not encourage venting of anger, which may encourage runaway anger.
- De-escalate the client with rational, quiet, disarming responses (model de-escalation).
- Do not touch the client.
- Teach the client skills to avoid runaway anger before he or she gets to that point, and have the client practice those skills under controlled conditions.

However, there are several things you can do to reduce the likelihood that suicide will happen. The best thing you can do, of course, is help the person to stop using drugs, since many suicides occur while a person is intoxicated.

First, suicidal behaviors include *ideations,* which are thoughts about suicide. Suicidal ideations can range from fleeting thoughts that may immediately be dismissed to total preoccupation with suicide and death in an obsessive fashion. Second, suicidal behaviors may include a *plan* or several plans for carrying out the act of suicide. Included in the plan are ideas about the means of suicide. The means of suicide can range in *lethality* (or potential for a deadly outcome). The plan or plans often have time lines as well. Some plans may happen immediately, and others may be placed well in the future. Finally, suicidal behaviors may include *actual self-harm,* which can range from superficial self-mutilation or self-injurious behavior to death. The outcome of suicidal behavior often is dependent on the lethality of the act of self-harm, and unfortunately, in many cases (especially for less lethal attempts), on the person's being alone and not being discovered in time. Self-mutilation that is not necessarily a conscious attempt at killing oneself is referred to as *parasuicidal behavior,* to differentiate it from suicidal behavior with the intent to die, but sometimes parasuicidal behavior can lead to death even if the intent was not to die.

This discussion brings us to the function of suicidal behavior. For some people, the function of suicidal behavior is to die, but not for everyone. Clearly the most lethal attempts represent a clear intent to die, especially if done in secrecy. However, many other times self-harm behavior is found to have a function besides death after a comprehensive behavioral analysis is completed with a client. For example, some clients have told me that cutting and burning themselves was related to boredom, anger, sadness, shame, uncertainty how to solve a problem, or even revenge toward someone who had hurt them. Parasuicidal behavior is common among people who have Borderline Personality Disorder, and many people with this disorder also abuse drugs and alcohol. Understanding the function of suicidal and parasuicidal behavior is very important in order to help the chronically suicidal client reduce suicidality. However, treating chronically suicidal clients effectively takes a great deal of time and is not something you can do without extensive training (see Chapter 5 for more details).

If you suspect that a client is suicidal, there are certain signs that you can look for. First, people who are chronically suicidal often have multiple scars from past events. These scars are sometimes visible on the arms or legs, but clients may try to cover the scars with long-sleeved shirts or pants. If an opportunity to observe limbs presents itself, then you may notice scars related to cutting or burning behavior. If so, ask about them. Second, clients who are actively suicidal often seem quite withdrawn. The person may sever ties with social support networks, including families and friends. In some people you look for a pattern wherein a client who used to be very socially engaged has cut off ties abruptly, and does not seem to care about those ties any longer. Sometimes there is a complete lack of concern about the future or about the surrounding world. Third, clients serious about suicide often put their affairs in order prior to an attempt. This may include giving away a substantial number of important material items, finalizing a will, and saying good-bye (in sometimes vague and nonspecific ways) to important people. Fourth, people who are serious about suicide often seem preoccupied with death and issues related to dying and death as mentioned.

Professionals should systematically assess for suicidal behavior at first contact with a client. The first part of the assessment is to find out whether the person has ever had any suicidal thoughts or thoughts about hurting themselves. It is fairly common to get a positive response to such a question, so do not be alarmed. The follow-up question is to ask when was the last time that the person had those thoughts. You are looking for recent ideations that might be a tip-off to current suicide risk. For clients who have had suicidal thoughts in the last year or so, you should ask them how frequently they have such thoughts, and ask them to rate on a scale of 1 to 10 how seriously they have entertained carrying out those thoughts in the most recent occurrence. At the same time, you want to assess for any past suicide attempts or self-injurious behavior, and for a history of depression and suicidal behavior in other family members. These factors are associated with increased risks of suicide.

If a person is having suicidal thoughts presently, then you should assess for any plans that he or she may have for carrying out a suicidal act. One way to be attuned to clients' preferred plans is to ask them about *means* used in past suicide attempts or parasuicidal behavior. For example, if a person tells you that he attempted suicide by swallowing a handful of pills in the past, then you can ask if that idea has reoccurred to him recently; or if a client tells you she has burned herself in the past with a cigarette, you can ask if she has been thinking about doing that recently. You also want to look for how specific the plan is to determine its threat to the well-being of the client. For example, "I want to (hurt myself) but I have not decided how yet" is a lot less scary than "I'm going to shoot myself in the head with the loaded gun I have at home." Make sure that you investigate all plans that the client may have; do not assume that the one plan the client has shared is the only plan he or she has. Another thing to consider with regard to a plan for suicide is the impulsiveness of the client. If the client has a history of impulsiveness, you should be concerned about the client's ability to control his or her behavior. The fear, of course, is that the client may look fine one minute, and then impulsively act to harm him- or herself the next.

When you ask the client whether she or he has a specific plan or plans for carrying out a suicidal or parasuicidal act, you also want to find out the time line for the plan (or plans). Ask, "Have you decided when you might carry out this plan? If so, when?" The closer to the present the plan is set to take place, the more concern it represents. In addition, you want to assess the potential lethality of a plan. For example, a plan of "swallowing five or six aspirin in the bathroom of my home while my parents are there" is a lot less scary than a plan to "hang myself in the closet with my belt when no one is around." Part of assessing the lethality includes determining the means, but it also includes determining the proximity of the event to other people who might be able to intervene (or find the person). Since relative lethality of various methods of suicide is sometimes unknown or even runs contrary to popular opinion, it may be helpful to educate yourself on resources based on research into the relative lethality of means (e.g., the Lethality of Suicide Attempt Rating Scales; Berman, Shepherd, & Silverman, 2003; Smith, Conroy, & Ehler, 1984). As an example, swallowing a handful of a selective serotonin reuptake inhibitor (SSRI) antidepressant medication, such as Paxil or Prozac, sounds quite dangerous, especially when compared with the idea of swallowing a handful of Tylenol. However, the truth is that overdosing on Tylenol is much more dangerous. Furthermore, lethality may depend on the very specific method being considered by the client: For example, jumping off a bridge can be extremely lethal, but it depends upon the bridge. Jumping off the Golden Gate is much different than jumping off a 10-foot-high bridge into a lake at a nearby park. Assessing lethality is a skill that comes from experience, but it is an extremely important skill to have when working with people who have problems with drugs.

In addition, the therapist should ask the client whether she or he has access to the instrument of harm (e.g., a gun or razor blade). If the instrument is at home, the therapist should ask the client to call a friend or relative and ask that person to remove that instrument from the client's access. If the client is unwilling to do so, then legal steps may have to be taken to protect him or her (discussed shortly). The therapist also should ask whether the client has the instrument on him or her right now (e.g., in a backpack or purse, in the car out in the parking lot, in a pocket or jacket, etc.). If so, you need to ask the client to give the instrument to you. The exception to this request might be if the instrument is a loaded firearm, in which case you may wish to ask for help from a relative of the client, or get a security guard on site to ask the client to unload and ultimately hand over the weapon. Dealing with a loaded firearm is more complicated than dealing with other means, because of the possibility of accidental discharge of the weapon.

The therapist assures the client that the items will be held in trust (rather than kept permanently by the therapist or counselor), and that these items will be turned over to a family member or friend if the client requests it. If the means involve pills, then the pills should be asked for and kept safe by the therapist for the client. If the pills are not needed by the client (e.g., an unnecessary medicine such as Tylenol), or are a necessary medicine (e.g., a prescribed antidepressant), then the therapist may ask the client to therapeutically dispose of them at a later time in therapy. If the instrument is a car (intended to be driven into a tree, off a bridge, etc.), the therapist must intervene and not allow the client to drive home, and instead have the client call for a ride. When a plan is in place and the means are available, professionals need to throw up as many roadblocks as possible to prevent the client from accessing the planned means of harm.

If a client has suicidal ideations and an immediate and potentially lethal plan, there are certain ethical and legal mandates that must be attended to for the sake of the client. The ethical mandate is to prevent harm to the client, which makes a professional responsible for taking steps to prevent the suicidal behavior. The professional needs to gain a convincing verbal commitment of no harm from the client if possible. If the client commits to no harm until the next meeting, and you are convinced that the crisis has de-escalated to the point that an attempt is not imminent, then a legal intervention may not be necessary; but you should make arrangements to check in on the client by phone, or have the client check in by phone. One way to determine whether the contract of no harm is made in good faith is to assess whether the client is committing to future events, like therapy for example, after the date the suicide had been planned to take place. You may wish to arrange to have another session during the current week instead of waiting until next week (if outpatient). If a client with a potentially lethal plan will not agree to no self-harm, then you should encourage the client to seek inpatient services voluntarily at an appropriate facility. If the person will not seek voluntary admission to such a facility, then you will have legal mandates (they differ across states — know your state commitment laws) that you will have to follow.

There are some cases in which inpatient admission may be contraindicated. For example, the function of the suicidal behavior may not be to die, but to escape or avoid something. The client may have a long history of using inpatient services to escape or avoid responsibilities or problems. If so, an inpatient admission may be precisely what the client is angling for, and by admitting the patient you will reinforce the avoidance or escape behavior. Reinforcing avoidance and escape behavior can make clients into high utilizers of the system. For clients like this, there are other therapeutic strategies (e.g., dialectical behavior therapy has specified strategies to avoid reinforcing this behavior) that are more effective than hospitalizing a client, *but you must have significant training in those strategies in order to be competent enough to attempt these.* I would instead recommend referring such a client, if possible, after the crisis is de-escalated, to a therapist who has that type of training and expertise. If you do not have those skills or access to someone trained in dialectical behavior therapy, then you may have no choice but to hospitalize the client until the crisis is resolved.

Finally, legal mandates for professionals are different in every state, but it is likely that you are a mandated reporter of suicidal behavior if you are counseling a person with a drug problem. When a person has a concrete plan to commit self-harm, you may have to call in the mental health authorities. The authorities in some states will come to your office and make an assessment of risk, then possibly refer your client to involuntary care. In some states, law enforcement officials are involved in the assessment or transport to the commitment center. As a therapist, you warn clients in the beginning of therapy of instances when confidentiality can be legally broken, and this is one example of this (as is threatening violence). If you have correctly discussed this possibility in the beginning of therapy, it will not surprise the client when you respond to your legal obligations. In fact, it may be that the client is expressing these suicidal thoughts knowing fully well that you have to report, perhaps representing some deep desire to live.

Sometimes you can use your legally mandated course of action to leverage a voluntary admission on the part of a client. If you remind the client that you are now bound to report the incident if she or he is not willing to seek help, then frequently the client will acquiesce and voluntarily seek help. Your responsibility is to make certain that the client actually follows through rather than simply feigning compliance. Obviously this outcome is preferred, since it helps to preserve the therapeutic alliance, whereas an involuntary commitment often harms your relationship with a client.

Psychiatric Decomposition

Similar to suicidal behavior, a client may face an imminent threat of harm to self from psychiatric decomposition. *Decomposition* is a term that often is used to describe a psychotic break. Again, you as a professional have both ethical and legal mandates that must be addressed in this situation. Ethically speaking, make sure that the client is directed to appropriate care that will help to stabilize the symptoms. Legally speaking, the issue is whether the client has the capacity to make well-reasoned judgments and decisions about his or her well-being. In many states, psychotic behavior, if proved, is grounds for involuntary treatment under the assumption that being psychotic is synonymous with being unable to care for self. As a professional, it is important you know the laws in your state about how to respond when a client has experienced a psychotic break, and to take appropriate action when this occurs. This can be an issue of genuine concern when working with a client who has a drug problem, since many substances

THINGS TO REMEMBER

Assessment and Intervention for Suicide

Make sure to assess. . .

- for risk factors, such as family history, previous attempts, and major depression.
- for suicidal ideations, and determine how recently they have occurred.
- whether the client has one or more concrete plans for suicide.
- the proximity of the planned suicide event or events to the present moment.
- the lethality of the means of suicide being considered.
- the accessibility of the means.
- whether the client has those means readily available, including whether the means are with him or her in session.

Intervene by. . .

- obtaining the instruments of suicide from the client if possible.
- using collaterals to obtain instruments at home, and checking on the client regularly.
- obtaining a convincing contract of no harm.
- encouraging voluntary admission if the client is not safe.
- calling appropriate authorities if the client is unwilling to seek voluntary admission.

can cause psychosis under certain conditions (although it is rare). A more likely event would be that a client who decomposes may have a co-occurring mood disorder or schizophrenia.

Sometimes clients decompose emotionally. For lack of a better way to say it, clients may simply lose it in session, without necessarily being psychotic, but in a way that may seem disabling and out of control. Sometimes these events are cued by discussing an extremely troubling or painful event in a client's past, such as abuse. Usually this reaction is a result of the client's being overexposed to the event. The client may feel overwhelmed by the intensity of exposure to an emotional event in session, and react by freezing or weeping uncontrollably or by a similarly extreme reaction (sometimes unexpected rage). My recommendation is to avoid intense emotional experiences in early therapy or treatment altogether, because research suggests that discussing or resolving traumatic events in treatment is not necessary for initial recovery. Discussing such volatile issues with a client should be saved, if at all possible, for after he or she has long-term stability with regard to changing drug use, and it should be done under the supervision of someone who has been trained in an empirically validated therapy for that particular issue (see Chapter 5 for more details).

Another crisis that can occur on abstinence-based units is that a client will use drugs on site during a session or in treatment. There are legal complications involved, since the use of most psychoactive drugs is illegal, and many therapists and care centers are concerned about liability and legal issues related to such behavior on their premises. If a unit is abstinence based, it is important to make the ground rules clear at intake (see Chapter 4). Since many clients are intoxicated upon admission, it is worth reiterating the ground rules for no use of substances during therapy or treatment after the person has cleared from the effects of the substance, to make certain the client remembers and understands these rules. If a therapist or a unit has clearly specified this rule and the client shows comprehension of the rule, then if the rule is violated, the client will not be surprised by the consequences — generally, discharge from treatment. If a therapist or a client has specified no use as a condition of care, then the consequences specified for breach of the rule should be enforced as specified in order to be consistent.

Many therapists also are concerned about whether drug use on an abstinence-based unit would endanger other clients. Certainly some clients will be tempted and some may even use if offered the substance by the using client. However, it really depends on your model of what drug problems are and how to care for them as to whether there should be concern about danger to other clients under these circumstances. For example, if you are operating under the assumptions of the disease model, then the powerlessness of other clients makes them at risk to succumbing to the temptations of using happening around them. On the other hand, a cognitive behavioral model may be less concerned about this, since exposure to other people using substances is not viewed as inherently dangerous, and may allow an opportunity to learn how to refuse drugs. Remember that clients are the only ones who have the capacity to make choices about whether to use. Those same choices exist inside and outside treatment, so they will have to learn to make those choices someday. So, does a client using on the unit affect other clients? Yes, it probably does. Does a client using on the unit represent a danger or an opportunity to learn? It really depends upon your model of care as to how you answer this question, but the research suggests exposure to drug-using cues may be helpful rather than hurtful. These issues and treatment models will be discussed more fully in Chapter 5.

Related to this, discharging a client from treatment prematurely can leave some very sour feelings in that client. Researchers have found that clients who felt mistreated in therapy or treatment for substance abuse are very reticent about seeking help again, and some refuse to do so. A discharge for any reason other than successful completion of therapy or treatment should be used only as a last resort since it may adversely affect the possibilities for treatment of the client over the long term. Again, as mentioned previously, one option is to have more than one model of care available at treatment facilities. If a client on an abstinence-based unit uses drugs, then that client could be transferred to another unit where abstinence is not necessarily required (or expected) as a precondition to receiving care. Smart treatment centers that have more than one unit can make such a transfer in-house, and the client is protected from a potential loss of continuity in the care process.

Finally, one of the most difficult types of crises to address is the death of a client. People with drug problems often lead very risky lives, and the threat of death may be ever present with such clients. People who use drugs are at risk from infectious diseases such as hepatitis and AIDS, from suicide and homicide, and from accidents. The saddest events in my professional career have been associated with losing a client. Such losses burden professionals, who may assume some level of responsibility for the death or may feel a sense of loss in not being able to meet with the client any more. Be aware that caregivers sometimes need care themselves, and this is one particular situation in which that may be true. Do not be shy about seeking help if you feel that the death of a client has adversely affected your professional or personal life.

If the client was known by other clients on the unit, then fellow clients may have their own feelings about the death. Clients may need to engage in additional counseling concerning the death. Professionals should not avoid discussing the topic, but also should not spend inordinate amounts of time debriefing or even discussing in group therapy sessions. The professional should check with clients about their feelings, and the best place to do so is in individual sessions (so as not to apply peer pressure to the grieving process). However, if clients are not forthcoming with feelings about the death, professionals should not push the issue. There is evidence that overexposing people to debriefing after critical events (such as trauma and death) is not helpful, and can even harm some people.

Risk Management Strategies

Finally, *risk management* strategies are commonly used during crisis situations. Litigation has made it necessary for professionals to protect themselves. The best way to protect yourself is to closely document crises as they unfold. Save material evidence related to the event and write very detailed *chart notes*. Many professionals learn over time how to document events very closely and in a timely fashion during client crises. Chart notes can be written with great detail and also with sensitivity for protecting the client. Remembering that chart notes can become a public record, it is usually important to walk a fine line in documentation between protecting yourself as a professional and protecting your client if someone outside your office were to read the notes (say, under court order or insurance review). Generally speaking, crises should include much greater documentation than standard chart notes tend to contain.

In larger organizations, there often are risk management committees or departments. Usually there are well-defined protocols for how to address and report a crisis in such organizations. The protocol often specifies contacting a risk management official, whose role it is to assess the risk to the organization and client, early in the process, and to work on protecting those involved at an organizational level. Obviously, risk management officers are biased toward protecting the organization from a legal threat, so it is important as a professional to remember your ethical obligation to your client under those circumstances. Being torn between the obligations to your employer and obligations to your client can be quite difficult, so many professionals under these circumstances consult with other trusted professionals in their community networks for advice and support. Sometimes such a consultation can help to clarify your ethical obligations under such circumstances.

Summing Up

Developing a professional network helps counselors and therapists provide the best care possible to clients. Networks not only work to improve the treatment outcomes of clients, but also can increase the knowledge of therapists and counselors as well as provide for professional support to avoid burnout and poor decisions. Networks can make the process of referring clients much easier as well.

Motivating change requires a good match between clients and therapists. In addition, motivation can be enhanced if therapists and counselors meet the clients at their own level with regard to where they are on the change continuum, use the appropriate change strategies for that level of motivation and commitment, and treat clients with respect and as partners in the therapeutic process. Clients may present with different roadblocks to progress in therapy or treatment, but good therapists and counselors help clients anticipate these roadblocks and develop plans to circumvent them. In addition, therapists and counselors can throw up roadblocks of their own and should be aware of their own potential biases or problems that may interfere with the care of others. Crises may arise in treatment, but can be handled professionally, and if handled well can benefit the client in the long run. Cool heads prevail under these circumstances.

Key Terms

Best practices. Therapies that researchers have found to be effective for a disorder.

Chart notes (or progress notes). Notes in a client's chart that document treatment progress.

Consultation groups. Groups of professionals who gather to discuss cases.

Decomposition. A client's losing control or becoming psychotic.

Federal confidentiality laws. Laws that protect clients from public disclosure.

Lethality of a suicide plan. The likelihood that a plan will lead to a completed suicide.

Operant strategies. Techniques that use reinforcement or punishment to shape behavior.

Risk management. Organizational procedures used to protect clients, staff, and the organization itself.
Self-efficacy. Client mastery that shows both competence and confidence to succeed at reaching a goal or completing a task successfully.
Stepped-up care. Matching the level of intervention to the level of need. Interventions are raised incrementally if needed.
Social norms. Data about what is normal drug use for peers.
Therapeutic alliance. How well client and therapist get along.
Trial abstinence. An agreed-upon period of time to give abstinence a try.

Recommended Reading

I would recommend the following books if you are interested in finding out more about how to motivate clients. First, I would highly recommend to anyone interested in treating drug problems to read *Motivational Interviewing,* by Miller and Rollnick (New York: Guilford Press, 2002), which not only can provide the basics of that therapy, but also includes a great deal of information about what therapists and counselors can do right (and wrong) while trying to motivate clients. To get another perspective on how to motivate clients, I also highly recommend the *Handbook of Motivational Counseling,* edited by Miles Cox and Eric Klinger (Hoboken, NJ: John Wiley & Sons, 2004). In addition, there is a section on motivating clients in Robert Coombs' book *Addiction Recovery Tools* (Thousand Oaks, CA: Sage Press, 2001). The advantage to having this book in your library is that it teaches you how to use a wide variety of other tools for treating clients (some mentioned in Chapter 5 of the present text).

To learn more about suicidal behaviors, and about treating borderline clients, I recommend reading Marsha Linehan's *Cognitive-Behavioral Treatment of Borderline Personality Disorder* (New York: Guilford Press, 1993). Although this book specifically addresses treating a particular disorder, it also has wonderful information and treatment suggestions for dealing with clients in crises and difficult clients.

TRUTH OR FICTION

QUIZ ANSWERS

1. True; 2. False; 3. False; 4. False; 5. False; 6. False; 7. True

CHAPTER 4

Developing an Effective Treatment Plan

TRUTH OR FICTION QUIZ

After reading this chapter, you should be able to answer the following questions:

1. Intake interviews can help to develop the therapeutic alliance. True or False?
2. Successful treatment plans are collaborative and may evolve over time. True or False?
3. A well-designed treatment plan will address only client weaknesses and problems. True or False?
4. Function analyses are used to understand the patterns, goals, and outcomes of drug use for a client. True or False?
5. Cognitive problems in drug-using clients are easily detected. True or False?
6. Family involvement may improve the chances for successful treatment if family members are supportive of the client. True or False?
7. Assessment instruments may have cultural biases that overpathologize ethnic-minority clients. True or False?

Answers on p. 177.

When a client shows up for treatment, a screening process usually precedes actual client care. The goal of the screening process is to determine the needs of the client and compare those needs to the type of care provided at the center. First, the center determines whether it can adequately treat the person's physical symptoms. If a potential client is determined to be too ill to be treated by the facility, then that person may be referred elsewhere for more intensive medical care.

Second, the center determines whether the potential client matches well with the therapeutic services provided at the center. Many treatment facilities have restrictions on who they will take into therapy. Usually these restrictions are related to available resources, so if a client needs resources not available at that particular center, then they may choose to refer the person to another treatment center that offers those services. For example, some treatment centers cannot adequately care for people with severe mental disorders, and therefore may refer to a facility that specializes in treating such disorders.

Third, the center determines during the screening process whether the client is a threat to self or others. Suicidal behavior should be routinely assessed in a screening interview. Some care facilities do not have the resources to treat an actively suicidal client, so if the person expresses suicidal ideations and plans, then a referral may be made elsewhere. The treatment center also wants to protect clients and staff from someone who is extremely aggressive and hostile and may represent a threat to the safety of people in the unit. In some cases, treatment facilities may refer such people elsewhere if the threat cannot be adequately contained within that facility.

Finally, treatment centers determine whether the client's financial situation will allow him or her to enter into the program offered by the treatment center without hardship. Insurance benefits are checked, after consent has been obtained, in order to determine whether the treatment costs will excessively burden the client. Information about insurance benefits is generally shared with the potential client so that he or she can make an informed decision about whether to engage in therapy, given financial considerations.

Potential clients should know that some insurance carriers require a referral from a primary care physician for treatment or therapy, require preauthorization for treatment prior to a screening, or have a list of preferred treatment providers from which the client will have to select in order to obtain maximum insurance benefits. Sometimes remembering this information is difficult when a person is ready to seek admission into therapy, so it is important for family members and referring professionals to remind potential clients to check on insurance benefits before seeking help. Family or friends may wish to aid the client in contacting the insurer and asking the appropriate questions for determining the maximum benefits allowed for treating a drug problem (and any restrictions on reimbursement).

Once a client is screened, determined to be a good match with the type of care offered, and officially admitted into care, the next important step on the road to behavior change is to develop a well-constructed treatment plan. Therapists begin by conducting an in-depth intake interview to gather important biographical information relevant to treating a person's drug problem. After the intake, the therapist uses the information gathered to develop a *treatment plan,* a written plan that guides how treatment will be conducted. Most therapists wait until the client clears from intoxication and withdrawal symptoms and is medically stable before conducting an intake interview. This delay allows the client to be more physically and cognitively capable to provide accurate and complete answers to questions.

Intake Interview

Intake interviews are critical for effective therapy. Intake interviews represent the first formal and prolonged contact that a therapist or counselor has with a client. As such, the intake often is the first step toward developing a strong therapeutic alliance. Since the goal of the intake is to gather information, the client does most of the talking. By default, the therapist does a great deal of respectful listening with the occasional use of open-ended questions to guide the interview.

Some therapists like to introduce themselves and then break the ice by asking the client, "What prompted you to seek help at our center?" or a similar type of question. Somewhere very early in this interview you might briefly interrupt the process by asking the client if it is okay for you to take notes of what is being said, in order to remember the details. Usually the client is quite amenable to allowing you to do this and will understand the value of taking notes. Asking for permission to take notes validates the rights of the client in the therapeutic process. The client will appreciate that you respect her or his rights in session by asking for permission to take notes, and she or he is usually more likely to trust your motives after your being respectful in this way.

After a person begins talking, use of a motivational interviewing style can be quite helpful to keep him or her talking so you can glean more information. A motivational interviewing style gives the client evidence that you are listening carefully and are genuinely interested in learning more. One motivational interviewing strategy that can be quite helpful is to ask a client about a typical day in his or her life, and how drug use is a part of such a day. Frequently such a question can break the ice while providing a large amount of information about the client. I like to let the client talk freely about his or her life at first, to hear his or her story, in order to reduce any nervousness or anxiety the client may have about therapy. Later, I can go back and ask more detailed questions to fill in the biographical holes in the interview.

Many treatment centers have standardized intake interview templates that prompt you to ask about different domains of a person's life to provide a comprehensive *psychosocial history*. Some of these templates can be quite detailed, with numerous, very specific questions designed to gather a wide range of information. However, using only the intake template risks making the interview seem quite impersonal to the client. I would recommend a balance between asking the standardized questions as needed and encouraging the client share her or his story as it occurs to her or him. This style might be thought of as *guided interviewing* rather than *structured interviewing*.

Structured written summaries of intake interviews (see Figure 4.1 as an example) are placed into the client's chart. As you can see by this example, there are certain areas of information that you will want to investigate with the client during the intake. First, you want to document basic identifying information, as well

Intake Summary
Confidential

CLIENT'S NAME:
DATE SEEN FOR INTAKE:
IF MINOR, PARENT'S NAME:
LEGAL CUSTODY: PHYSICAL CUSTODY:
THERAPIST'S NAME: FILE NUMBER:
SUPERVISOR'S NAME:

I. IDENTIFICATION AND BEHAVIORAL OBSERVATIONS:

II. PRESENTING PROBLEM AND HISTORY OF PRESENTING PROBLEM:

III. SOCIAL AND FAMILY HISTORY:

IV. MENTAL HEALTH HISTORY OF CLIENT AND FAMILY:

V. MEDICAL HISTORY OF CLIENT AND FAMILY:

VI. MENTAL STATUS EXAMINATION:

VII. DIAGNOSTIC IMPRESSION—DSM-IV:

Axis I: ____________________

Axis II: ____________________

Axis III: ____________________

Axis IV: ____________________

Axis V GAF: ____________________

Figure 4.1: A condensed example of an intake interview template.

as describe behavioral observations that you make during the intake interview. Documenting behavioral observations usually includes describing body language and posture, affect, speech patterns, eye contact, interpersonal interactions with you, and other information you deem important to developing a roadmap for treatment.

Next, document the presenting problem and its history. Sometimes you retrieve that information rather quickly when asking why the client is seeking help, then use the motivational interviewing style to encourage the person to tell the rest of the story. As you document the presenting problem, you will want to describe how drug use is associating with seeking help, and to identify how drug use has affected other areas of the client's life. Record what the client tells you about personal likes and dislikes about drug use, outcome expectancies related to drug use, and the client's perceived function for drug use. In this section of the intake, develop a clear picture of what drug use means to the client, and how that drug use has affected her or his life.

In addition, if family involvement appears useful for the client and she or he consents to their involvement, try to include family members in the intake interview. Using family members during intake interviews may allow you to fill in gaps of information that the client is not able to provide about consequences of drug use behavior. However, as mentioned, clients may be better historians than family members about their drug use simply because a great deal of the drug use was hidden from their families. Including family members in an intake interview also makes them active participants in treatment at the earliest stages. Family participation represents a real advantage to clients when clients and their families are on good terms. Family involvement in treatment planning also can be helpful, and this is discussed later in this chapter.

Treatment Planning

A successful *treatment plan* is developed with three important factors in mind. The first two factors must be balanced. First, a successful treatment plan must be comprehensive in order to address important variables that will enhance or hinder behavior change. Second, a well-devised treatment plan must not be so complicated or overbearing as to overwhelm a client. Therefore, a skillful therapist

DOS AND DON'TS

Developing a Treatment Plan

- Do make the treatment plan comprehensive enough to ensure success.
- Do make the treatment plan a collaborative effort on the part of client and therapist.

On the other hand . . .

- Don't make the treatment plan so complex that it overwhelms the client.

must develop a balanced treatment plan that is comprehensive yet not overwhelming in order to guide the client on the road to behavior change.

Third, the treatment plan must be a collaborative effort. Effective treatment planning represents a dialogue between the client and the therapist. The client tells the therapist about problem areas that need attention but also shares his or her vision for what goals he or she has for therapy or treatment. At the same time, the therapist provides feedback on the goals that the client shares, advising the client on the best approaches toward achieving those goals. The therapist or counselor also encourages and instills confidence in reaching those goals, which in turn motivates client commitment to work on the plan. Treatment plans are signed jointly by the client and therapist or counselor as a symbol of this collaborative agreement, and placed in the client's chart. A copy of the plan should be given to the client for his or her own use. A signed agreement symbolizes that the client is a full partner in the treatment plan. Signed plans guarantee there are no surprises to the client since informed consent is involved. The client also will feel more heavily invested in the plan and therefore more likely to carry it out.

Many therapists develop an initial treatment plan to cover the very early stages of therapy (the *intake period*). Eventually the initial treatment plan is replaced by a more comprehensive treatment plan. Although the comprehensive treatment plan is meant to guide the course of therapy, it is not set in stone and can be modified as treatment progresses. For example, a new problem area may be identified by either the therapist/counselor or client after the treatment plan has been developed. However, any revisions to the treatment plan should be developed collaboratively, noted in the client's chart, and signed by both parties as a symbol of consensus for modifying the plan. See Figure 4.2 for a sample of an evolving treatment-plan document.

A well-designed treatment plan identifies both client strengths and weaknesses (or problem areas). Identifying strengths in the treatment plan is critical. The strengths will be an important foundation for the development of new skills necessary to carry out behavior change. All clients have strengths and it is up to the therapist or counselor to help the client identify those strengths. Strengths also represent important areas where client self-esteem and self-efficacy to succeed can be nurtured. Clients may feel a little beaten down when coming to treatment, so identifying strengths can regenerate a client's resolve and hope, as well as promote the personal persistence needed to succeed in changing drug use behavior.

On the other hand, identifying problem areas allows for interventions to be devised to reduce or remove roadblocks to recovery. In a well-designed treatment plan, a problem area and its specific links with the drug use are identified and described. After the descriptive portion of the problem area, the treatment plan prescribes specific courses of action on the part of the client, with therapist or counselor support, to change the problem behavior. Problems areas may be biological, environmental, behavioral, cognitive, or emotional domains, or in some cases may represent complex combinations in more than one of these areas.

MASTER TREATMENT PLAN:

TARGETED PROBLEMS:	GOALS:	PLAN:

Treatment Review Date:	Targeted Problems:	Progress and Changes in Plan:

SIGNATURE OF CLIENT: ______________________ DATE: __________

SIGNATURE OF THERAPIST: ______________________ DATE: __________

Figure 4.2: A condensed example of a treatment plan template.

Depending on the type of problem, the therapist or counselor should treat with *empirically validated therapies* if they have been developed and tested for that problem. *Empirically validated* means that researchers have tested the strategies under experimentally controlled conditions to find out whether they really work to change the targeted problem. Generally speaking, empirically validated therapies have treatment manuals, which are like cookbooks for conducting precise and consistent therapy. Treatment manuals developed for a specific problem tell you exactly what to do (and in what order) when treating that problem. Using empirically validated strategies ensures that the client is getting the best care known to treat a specific problem, and using a treatment manual allows for the strategies to be done consistently and correctly. A greater discussion on this topic follows in Chapter 5.

Sometimes there are problems for which no empirically validated strategies exist. These situations challenge therapists and counselors to develop creative approaches to addressing unusual problems. On the one hand, it is very important to use an empirically validated approach to correct a problem if such an approach exists, because it makes little sense to reinvent the wheel when a radial tire may already be available to you. However, if the wheel has not been invented or tested, therapists and counselors still have to do something.

I was told this story once by a colleague, and I am not entirely sure whether it really happened. However, it is a good story with a very good point. It seems that a heart surgeon was in consult group with her residents and medical students. They were discussing a patient under their care who had a rare condition, one for which no known cure or treatment had been established. The surgeon quizzed her students about what the options for therapy were, to which the students responded correctly that there were no known options. The surgeon then asked her students, "So what should we do?" The students responded by saying they did not know, because there seemed to be no known options. Without pausing even a moment, the surgeon rose, ended the consultation meeting, and invited her students to come along. The senior resident on the team asked the surgeon what she was doing, to which she responded, "We have discussed all available options and there appear to be none. Now we have to take action anyway." The moral of the story, of course, is that health care professionals may not always have knowledge on their side when caring for people, but they are obligated to do anything they can to help even if the path toward helping is not yet known.

Even when the path is unknown, there may be many clues about what may help. Novel problems may have some similarities to other, more well-known problems for which empirically validated interventions have been tested and developed. In such cases, those validated strategies may be modified to treat the problem at hand. In some instances, you may not have to reinvent the wheel so much as adjust it so it fits a different cart. In other cases, perhaps someone in your professional network has worked with a similar problem and can provide consultation regarding what she or he did, and whether it worked.

My advice is to use empirically validated approaches to treating problems as much as you can so you can provide the best care available for your client. This will protect your client, but also may protect you as a professional from litigation. Using empirically validated strategies also helps instill confidence in your client that the care she or he receives will be the best available, which of course makes it more likely that the client will commit to the treatment plan. If there is a unique or unusual problem for which no known empirically validated strategy has been developed, then you may have to create a novel and creative approach for intervening upon the problem. In those cases, it is important to share this information up front with the client so she or he has informed consent about the experimental nature of the intervention. Also let her or him know how you arrived at the proposed solution to the problem so that the client does not feel you just conjured up some strategy up out of the blue.

Prioritizing Items on the Treatment Plan

A well-developed treatment plan also prioritizes the problems to target in therapy. The priority of targets usually is developed with consideration for how critical behavior change is for the well-being of the client, how much time is available in therapy to work on the targeted behaviors, and whether it is necessary to change one problem area before another area can be changed. Developing a prioritized problem list in a treatment plan can be similar to *triage,* in which the highest priority items represent those essential for treatment success, the middle-priority items are important but not necessarily essential, and the lowest priority items are like icing on the cake if resolved — that is, they are not terribly important but would boost the quality of life for the client. In this way, time is spent on changes deemed essential first and foremost, then whatever time remains can be spent targeting less important problem areas. This formula aids the therapist in determining how to structure therapy in order to efficiently use limited time and resources.

A logical ranking for targeting problems follows from this triage-like formula. The most essential problems to target on a treatment plan are those that are life threatening to the client. The therapist in conjunction with the client determines those problems that may represent a real threat to the client and develops a plan to use whatever time is necessary to intervene upon them until the imminent threat is reduced. Examples of these first-tier types of problems would include life-threatening health problems or suicidal behavior. When these problems arise in session, they should take precedent over any other topic. The second tier of problems needing attention is those that threaten treatment or therapy. Examples of these problems include financial crises related to insurance coverage, or behaviors that place the client at risk for leaving treatment prematurely or at risk for being discharged from treatment. These first two tiers of problems must be addressed and resolved before any progress can be made in therapy. Risk of death (Tier 1) or of being distracted during therapy or even leaving treatment (Tier 2) adversely affects all other life problems, and those other problems cannot be treated until the first two tiers of problems are resolved.

After the client is safe and committed to treatment, other important problems may be addressed effectively. For a client with a drug problem, the next priority is to address problems directly related to drug use behavior. These problems in the third tier may include consequences of drug use in all the domains that have been discussed in this book, or may include behaviors that contribute to drug use. Many of those behaviors that contribute to drug use may be associated with other health or mental health problems. In such instances, a treatment plan will

THINGS TO REMEMBER

Prioritizing Problem Lists

Problems can be categorized by their relative threat to client progress, with more-threatening problems needing attention immediately and less-threatening problems attended to later in treatment/therapy or in aftercare. Quality-of-life problems may be tackled once the threatening problems have been resolved. The following is a list of the four tiers of problems that will help you prioritize the amount of time spent working on them in therapy.

Tier-1 Problems: Life-threatening problems, which must be addressed first.

Tier-2 Problems: Treatment-threatening problems, which should be addressed second.

Tier-3 Problems: Problems related to drug use and not linked to problems in Tiers 1 or 2, which should be addressed third.

Tier-4 Problems: Quality-of-life issues, which are addressed after Tiers 1–3 have been addressed.

need to prescribe help for those co-occurring problems (see Chapter 5). Generally speaking, treating these problems takes precedent over what I call quality-of-life problems (the fourth tier), because issues directly related to drug use may prevent improvement in quality of life. As when one is walking up a staircase and must logically climb the lower steps before climbing the ones above it, many of the problems associated with drug use must be tackled before progress can be made on quality-of-life issues not directly related to drug use.

Finally, addressing these quality-of-life issues is the icing on the cake, and therefore should be prioritized low on the treatment plan. An example of such a targeted behavior in the fourth tier might be something like vocational retraining if the client is already employed but dissatisfied, or perhaps something related to changing personal values or reaching for dreams. Quality-of-life changes are more like a wish list: problems that are not critical to address in the short term but are important long-term goals for the client. Addressing these types of problems often occurs much later in therapy or perhaps even in aftercare (see Chapter 6). The therapist may suggest resources later in treatment to reach those goals, but achieving them during the scope of treatment is unlikely. The hope is that the client can take the lead on tackling these types of problems since they may represent a slow, long-term personal journey toward change.

You might have noticed that the ranking of these problems moves along three different continua. The first continuum represents the level of threat to the client, with threats to life and treatment being the most severe and therefore the most important to address, and quality-of-life concerns not being necessarily threatening but more desirable to achieve. The second continuum represents the

CLIENT HANDOUT

The Advantage of Treatment Plans

Treatment planning benefits the therapist in developing a road map for helping the client. However, treatment planning also is meant to benefit you, the client. People with drug problems who seek help should view the development of a treatment plan as an opportunity. First, your active participation is needed in developing this road map for how your treatment will be conducted. You have a right to have your goals met in therapy or treatment, and the collaborative development of a treatment plan is one way to ensure that treatment is relevant for you. Second, treatment planning allows you to educate your counselor or therapist about yourself. If the therapist knows you in a more personal way, he or she will be a stronger advocate for your well-being.

Third, treatment plans usually evolve over time, which means your plan is open to negotiation. Since treatment depends upon your commitment, you ultimately have the last word in how your treatment progresses. Therapy and treatment can feel very intimidating if it seems that therapists or counselors hold all the therapeutic cards, but your treatment plan is one way to ensure you will be an equal partner throughout the therapeutic process. Finally, you are the expert on your own life; that in and of itself gives you great power in therapy. Therapists or counselors may be the experts on change strategies, but they need your expertise on *you* in order to recommend the appropriate change strategies. Although excellent change plans developed by competent therapists are very important for your well-being, so too is the expertise that you bring into therapy about yourself. Success in treatment and therapy depends upon the skills of your therapist or counselor *and* your expertise on yourself.

The treatment plans protects you and assures that you are an equal partner in the process. However, being equal partner also brings some responsibilities. For example, it is critical that you level with your therapist or counselor as you develop a treatment plan. In addition, a treatment plan will not be effective without your commitment to do your part in implementing the plan. Finally, you need to be forthcoming on your own sense of progress while using the plan, and if the plan is not working for you, actively participate with your therapist to adjust the plan as needed while in treatment. Treatment plans are helpful road maps for getting to where you want to go, but they will not do the driving for you. In treatment, your counselor or therapist is your navigator, using the treatment plan to get you to the right place — but you are the driver.

ability of clients to work on the problems on their own. Overcoming problems that threaten the health and well-being of the client require more therapeutic support (strength in numbers), whereas overcoming quality-of-life issues may require little to no therapeutic support. Finally, the third continuum represents the ability of therapists or counselors to help clients reach their goals related to these problems during the time they are in therapy. Acute and drug-related problems are our specialty to treat as professionals, but quality-of-life issues generally are problems that people have to tackle mostly on their own terms. In a real sense, getting our clients to a place where they are tackling quality-of-life problems means that we have taken them about as far as we can in therapy.

The Importance of Assessment in Treatment

Conducting a thorough assessment of your client is a crucial part of effective therapy and treatment. Therapists will want to learn several important facts about the clients' drug use in order to better understand how to treat those clients effectively. To begin with, you obviously want to know what kinds of drugs they are using, how much is being used per occasion, when they are being used, and whether there is a specific pattern to the use. You also want to know what types of consequences clients have experienced related to drug use. As you gather this information, you will want to assess for whether major life events or changes may have occurred recently that could be related to drug use. In addition, you will want to understand what kinds of expectancies (both positive and negative) clients have about drug use, the level of self-efficacy clients have about controlling drug use across different situations, their levels of motivation to change drug use behaviors, and whether they have the skills necessary to change drug use behaviors and maintain those changes over the long term.

> "If I could kick the person in the tail that causes me the most problems I could not sit down for a week."
>
> —WILL ROGERS

A thorough assessment also will identify problem areas, strengths and supports clients may have to help them reach treatment goals, and what kinds of treatment strategies may be the best match for them. In addition, assessment throughout treatment is truly the only way that you have to document progress toward treatment goals.

Assessing History and Diagnosis

The intake interview is usually the first assessment that a counselor or therapist conducts with a client. The intake is usually a semistructured and subjective form of assessment, meaning that it gathers personal information about the client and his or her drug use. Assessing the personal history of a drug problem is quite helpful to understand the context of the drug problem, and to understand how the client interprets drug use. However, there are other ways to assess drug use behavior besides gathering autobiographical information.

For example, *function analyses* are a typical form of assessment conducted by therapists and counselors. Function analyses are used to determine the relationship of one behavior to another, and to ascertain which behavior patterns may help the client change behavior and which patterns may hinder progress. Function analyses are used to understand the patterns, goals, and outcomes of drug use for a client, and they can be used to understand behavioral patterns associated with other problems that may not be linked to drug use at all. Function analyses are conducted early in therapy or treatment to identify problem areas and the behaviors that contribute to them. In addition, function analyses can be conducted as a matter of course in therapy to fine-tune skills and behavioral responses for a successful outcome.

Determining the function of the drug use in the client's life is essential to understand what behaviors need to be targeted for change in treatment. One strategy to determine the function of the drug use is to analyze a client's drug use during a typical day or typical week. First, you want to ask the client to describe a typical day (or week) in great detail and how drug use is a part of that day. Next, have the client tell you what he or she thinks is the goal of the drug use for him or her at different times when he or she is using during the day. For example, maybe the client tells you that she uses in the morning to "get going," but later in the day to "relax." Function analyses can be conducted as part of the intake assessment while you are gathering other biopsychosocial data about your client, or these analyses can be conducted in a regular therapy session. Understanding what the client believes about the function (or goals) of the drug use can help illuminate how to challenge those beliefs and ultimately change the drug use behavior.

During a function analysis, I also want the client to talk about both the positive and negative consequences associated with the drug use. I encourage the client to talk about all the behavior preceding the use of the substance, including what he or she was doing, thinking, and feeling in the moments before use of the drug. Part of this analysis is to ascertain exactly what the client expected that drug would do for him or her. Then I ask the client to tell me what happened after the use, and to link the expectations for the use of the drug (before using) with the actual consequences (after using) to determine whether there are any discrepancies between the two. By determining the function of the drug use in this way you are using a strategy known as *behavior chain analysis*. You may want the person to go backward in time from the moment of first drug use and describe all the steps that preceded the actual use of drugs. This type of chain analysis is called *backward chaining*. If you ask the client to start with the first thing he or she did that day, then talk about successive steps along the way that eventually lead to drug use, this is referred to as *forward chaining*.

Determining the function of the drug use in this fashion also allows you to closely examine the series of events or steps that immediately lead up to drug use by the client, as well as understand the consequences after drug use. Identifying each link in the drug use chain allows you gain valuable information about steps or triggers leading up to the use of drugs. This, in turn, helps you to determine different intervention points along the way so that the behavior pattern that leads to drug use behavior can be stopped early in the chain. A behavior chain analysis allows you to determine dysfunctional behavioral patterns that place the client at risk for drug use. Since behavior patterns are often habits, a person may not even be aware of the connection between the links in the behavior chain and the eventual drug use at the end of the chain.

As you might imagine, function analyses raise awareness of drug problems if done skillfully. When working with clients who do not believe they have a problem, using a function analysis can help you increase awareness without increasing resistance by having the client link successive events with drug use verbally. You may wish to ask a client about a typical day and how drug use enters into that day, as part of the function analysis. In this instance, though, the function analysis is being used to engage clients in a thoughtful look at their drug use in a disarming fashion by using a motivational interviewing style.

As you are discussing drug use with the client in this type of function analysis, you may wish to interject something like this: "Many of my clients have told me that they have enjoyed using drugs during a typical day for various reasons. So, what would you say are the good things about using drugs for you during a typical day?" The client may respond by telling you about what he or she enjoys about drug use. After the person has finished you may want to follow up by saying, "My clients also have told me that there were some not-so-good things about using drugs on a typical day. Are there any not-so-good things about using for you, and if so, what are they?" Notice that the last question is phrased in a way to minimize the risk of defensiveness on the client. The client is not being placed in a position such that she or he has to defend drug use, since the behavior is being normalized by the suggestion that other clients have said this and that. In addition, asking about the good things about drug use has the effect of increasing the therapeutic alliance since you are acknowledging that not everything about drug use is aversive for the client; moreover, you are not judging the client by asking about the "bad" things that happen after drug use, but rather the "not-so-good things" (which is a softer way to say it).

In addition to intakes and function analyses, *diagnostic assessments* often are completed with drug-using clients early in treatment. Diagnostic assessments are generally conducted for practical purposes, such as to determine whether the client meets *DSM-IV* criteria for substance abuse or dependence, and to document the need for a specific level of treatment or care to an insurance carrier so that the services will be reimbursed. Probably the most widely used instrument for diagnostic purposes is the Structured Clinical Interview for *DSM-IV,* or SCID (First, Gibbon, Spitzer, & Williams, 1995). The SCID is a highly structured interview that asks specifically about different criteria necessary to meet specific *DSM-IV* diagnoses. Since there are many different such diagnoses, administering a full SCID can take a great deal of time. However, some professionals, in the interest of time, opt to administer only selected portions, such as the Substance Use Disorders section. Administering the SCID requires specialized training since it is a structured interview, and trainees should be checked for adherence by a seasoned administrator before being allowed to complete the interview with clients. There are computerized versions of the SCID that can be administered much more quickly, and even a computerized version that clients can complete themselves. The advantage of computerized SCIDs is that they automatically provide diagnoses for you in print-out form. However, when the client self-administers the SCID on a computer, it may prevent the therapist or counselor from observing and interacting with the client during the assessment. Sometimes observation of assessment sessions can generally yield a great deal of information about the client's behavior. Another potential disadvantage of these software programs is their price.

There are other diagnostic interviews available as well. For example, there is the Diagnostic Interview Schedule (DIS; Robins, Helzer, Croughan, & Ratcliff, 1981) for adults, which many professionals use; and there is the Diagnostic Interview Schedule for Children (DISC; Shaffer, Fisher, Lucas, Dulcan, & Schwab-Stone, 2000) for youth and adolescents. These interview schedules are similar to the SCID and each is now in its fourth edition. Computerized versions for administration and scoring have been developed, but these, like the SCID software, can be pricey for small and solo practices. There are other diagnostic interviews not mentioned here that may work for you as well.

Diagnostic assessment represents a very powerful tool since these interviews may pin a label on a client. How therapists use this label can have some potentially important consequences for treatment and, in some cases, for what happens after treatment. Researchers have found that diagnostic labels can be *helpful* if they provide clients with useful information on how to successfully treat their

CASE STUDY

Good Catch, Carl!

Carl is a highly skilled substance abuse counselor at Starbright Treatment Center who firmly believes that you can never do too much assessment of clients. Maria, his newest client, looks very depressed, and he is worried about her mood and general well-being. Carl discovered through his intake interview that Maria has been using methamphetamines, so he wonders if the depressive symptoms may be related to withdrawal or rebound effects. Just to be on the safe side, he completes a comprehensive diagnostic interview with Maria to determine whether there may be more to the depression than meets the eye. He is evaluating whether she may have Major Depression or another type of mood disorder. In addition, he wants to determine whether the depression preceded the drug use. As he is conducting the interview, he finds out from Maria that sometimes she is not depressed at all; in fact, her mood seems to be quite manic at times, and she seems to cycle between depression and mania. Carl is certainly glad that he conducted this diagnostic interview, because the depression he'd been seeing in treatment was only half the story!

conditions. If the diagnosis allows the client for the first time to understand what the solution to the problem is, as with a diagnosis of Bipolar Disorder that is followed by education about how to successfully treat the disorder with a mood stabilizer, then the diagnostic label is helpful.

However, diagnostic labels also can be *harmful* if they stigmatize clients or leave them feeling isolated or without hope. Counselors and therapists have to be judicious about how they use the diagnostic information. For example, therapists should determine whether sharing diagnostic information with clients will serve their best interests. In order to make this determination, the therapist must determine whether the value of sharing the information will outweigh the potential harm that labeling may do to the client. Personally, I prefer to avoid sharing diagnoses with a client simply because the potential for harm often is greater than the helpfulness such a label can provide. As you may remember, many clients do not find it important to believe that they are addicted or powerless over a drug, but may find it more important to think of the drug use as a problem that can be solved. If a client wants to label him- or herself, and feels that labeling is helpful for solving the problem, that is great. But being labeled by a counselor or therapist is not a necessary or important precondition for changing a drug problem, and such a label does have the capacity to hinder progress for some clients. Therefore, I choose to side with caution with regard to diagnostic labels.

As a researcher and therapist, I also do not like the use of colloquial terms such as *addict* or *junkie.* These terms, although potentially helpful for some who find recovery in self-help programs, are not useful for everyone with a drug problem, and can be demeaning to some. In fact, some of my clients have been put off by such labels in treatment, and found them stigmatizing, and therefore potentially harmful. Besides, such terms are highly pejorative and uncomplimentary descriptions of behavior and are not diagnostically accurate terms (i.e., are not defined in the *DSM-IV*). I choose not to use these terms with my own clients for these reasons.

In addition to conducting a diagnostic assessment, performing a thorough health assessment may provide critical information about the client's physical well-being. Some treatment facilities have a physician on site to do such an evaluation. Some clients may not have the financial resources to seek out a physical evaluation on their own, so providing this service as part of treatment may the only way that such an evaluation will occur. Given the physical stress that drug use places on the body, conducting a thorough physical examination when a person enters into treatment is recommended. Many clients with drug problems have not had recent routine physical examinations, so it is imperative to check up on their health if possible.

A clean bill of health can be a relief for many clients who have not taken care of themselves physically. On the other hand, sometimes abnormal results in an examination can motivate some people to change their behavior. For some clients, however, health concerns are not as important as we would hope they would be. In other cases, the physical examination may reveal a chronic and perhaps potentially debilitating health condition. Drug abuse often contributes to risky behaviors, such as sharing unclean needles or having unprotected sex, that can leave drug users vulnerable to infectious diseases. I have witnessed reactions of hopelessness in some clients when they received unexpectedly bad news regarding their health. When some clients are informed that they are positive for HIV or for hepatitis, they have the tendency to give up in treatment. In those cases, counselors and therapists must encourage hopefulness in clients, not in a naïve fashion, but in a realistic way that validates the genuine concerns for prognosis but also recognizes significant medical advances. In addition, the research suggests that medical treatment for such diseases is enhanced if the client ceases drug abuse. Research evidence suggests that drug use may lower immune function and may interfere with the active properties of the medicines used to treat these conditions. Encouraging clients to take care of themselves by remaining abstinent may buy them time for a medical breakthrough to occur.

If a physical examination is not possible, then a therapist or counselor will have to assess physical health in an interview format. The therapist can ask specific questions about health conditions and symptoms in the intake interview, and then can address specific health concerns through referrals as part of the treatment plan. It may be that a particular non–life-threatening health problem cannot be addressed during the course of therapy or treatment, but can be listed as a quality-of-life problem in the treatment plan to be addressed at a later date. In that way, the therapist and client can brainstorm ideas about treating the problem while in therapy and develop a plan of action for addressing the health concern after therapy is completed.

There also are several brief measures that assess symptoms of drug use to detect possible drug problems. Usually these *brief screens* are used when assessment time is limited; for example, in locations where large numbers of people are served (medical centers, hospitals, clinics, and sometimes treatment centers), a full assessment is virtually impossible. These brief measures cannot always reliably determine a drug problem, nor are they comprehensive enough to assign a diagnosis. However, cut-off scores have been normed on these instruments that can suggest a high likelihood of drug problems. The best known screening instrument for drug problems is the Drug Abuse Screening Test (Skinner, 1982). There also is the CRAFFT (Knight et al., 1999), which is a more recent brief measure developed specifically to detect potential drug problems in adolescents and youth.

These screening measures provide the advantage of rapidly assessing for a drug problem with some accuracy. However, screening instruments can produce *false positives* (scores above the cut-off point for individuals who do not have a drug problem) as well as *false negatives* (scores below the cut-off point for individuals who do have a drug problem). Because these measures are prone to errors, they cannot be used as the only source for determining whether a client has a drug problem. Generally, these instruments are useful for detecting possible problems and identifying when a more comprehensive assessment for a drug problem is needed. If a client scores above a cut-off point on one of these screening instruments, I recommend conducting a SCID or other diagnostic interview to confirm whether a drug problem is indeed present. I also strongly recommend that treatment facilities use diagnostic interviews rather than screening measures whenever possible, because diagnostic measures are more accurate and provide much more clinical information than a screen.

Assessing Substance Use Patterns, Consequences, and Contexts

Diagnostic interviews are useful to determine what kind of problems a client may have, and whether those problems may be related to drug use. However, diagnostic interviews do not provide detailed information about quantity, frequency, and peak periods of use, nor do they provide great details about the pattern and consequences of drug use. For obtaining that information, the therapist or counselor may wish to turn to a wide variety of measures available that can be used for understanding consumption patterns, consequences of those patterns, and the context for drug use in greater depth.

Some of these measures are part of larger, semistructured interviews administered by the therapist. The most commonly used assessments in this category are a family of instruments developed mainly in the Veterans Administration (VA) hospital system. The first instrument in this family is known as the Addiction Severity Index (ASI; McLellan et al., 1985). The ASI assesses for a wide variety of biographical data, so it has the advantage of potentially being used as part of an intake interview. The ASI asks about consequences in a wide variety of life domains, and determines recent and lifetime patterns of drug and alcohol use. The ASI also detects recent and lifetime occurrence of problems in these different life domains (e.g., work). Each domain can be scored for the severity of the problems based upon the responses of the client and the clinical judgment of the interviewer. The ASI can be administered by computer to provide for rapid interpretation of answers.

In addition to the ASI, there also are other instruments in this family that have been developed for adolescent clients. These interviews include the Adolescent Drug Abuse Diagnosis (Friedman & Utada, 1989), the Comprehensive Adolescent Severity Inventory for Adolescents (Meyers, McLellan, Jaeger, & Pettinati, 1995), and the Teen Addiction Severity Inventory (Kaminer, Bukstein, & Tarter, 1989), all of which begin by asking about biographical data. These instruments, like the ASI, assess recent and lifetime problems in several life domains that are more relevant for this age group (e.g., school), as well as recent and lifetime occurrences of drug and alcohol problems. All of these ASI-type interviews can take at least an hour or more to administer, but they do provide a wealth of information about the client if you can spare the time. Each of these interviews requires specific training in order to be able to administer and score the responses appropriately.

However, since instruments like the ASI do cover a breadth of material, they are not likely to give you as many details about a specific problem area as you may want when working with a client. The questions on these interviews are somewhat limited for each domain and sometimes the details are not fully assessed by the limited questions. For example, consumption-pattern questions on the ASI ask how many days a person may use or whether the person has problems with a particular substance, but do not assess how much is used each day and when, or what a particular pattern of use may be during a typical week.

There are instruments specifically designed to assess recent substance use patterns, such as the Steady Pattern Chart and Other Drug Use Questionnaire from the Form 90 (Miller, 1996), as well as an interview style known as a timeline follow-back interview (e.g., Cervantes, Miller, & Tonigan, 1994). These interviews provide the advantage of identifying how much is being used per occasion, as well as determining typical weekly drug use and binge drug events. The method of asking the questions on these interviews allows the therapist or counselor to determine very clearly whether there is a specific pattern to a client's drug use over time. These measures help a therapist or counselor determine frequency of use, peak amounts used during typical drug use weeks or during special occasions (binge events), and total consumption over a specific period of time.

Several instruments can be used to assess consequences related to drug use. For example, the Inventory of Drug Using Consequences (InDuC; Miller, Tonigan, & Longabaugh, 1995) assesses both lifetime and recent drug-related consequences in a variety of life areas. The InDuC also can determine how frequently the consequences were experienced by a client, and this measure includes scale scores for particular life domains, such as Interpersonal, Intrapersonal, or Physical Health Consequences. There also are instruments that measure specific types of consequences. For example, one measure called the Losses of Significance Self-Report Questionnaire–Revised (LOSS-QR; Blume & Marlatt, 2000) assesses the frequency and importance of particular losses that may have been associated with a client's substance use. For adolescent clients, the Problem Oriented Screening Instrument for Teenagers (Rahdert, 1991) assesses consequences that are more specific to that age group. In addition, the Personal Experience Inventory (PEI; Stinchfield & Winters, 1997) and the Customary Drinking/Drug Use Record (Brown et al., 1998) also assess consequences for youthful and adolescent drug users, but include questions that help to determine consumption patterns as well.

Beyond using measures that assess patterns and consequences of drug use, therapists and counselors may want to consider assessing other psychosocial factors that have been shown to be important in predicting successful (or unsuccessful) therapy and treatment outcomes (as discussed in Chapter 1). There are well-established measures for measuring psychosocial factors such as expectancies, mood and emotions, self-efficacy, the ability to problem solve and use coping skills, and motivation to change drug use. There also are clinical approaches to conducting observational assessments of behavior in session that do not involve paper-and-pencil assessment tools. Psychosocial assessments provide useful information about the context of a drug problem and, in some cases, can help determine the prognosis of clients.

For example, assessing expectancies can tell you a great deal about clients' beliefs about their drug use. Measures of expectancies can help to identify those beliefs that may interfere with successful treatment outcomes. Understanding a client's expectancies also can help with developing appropriate relapse-prevention strategies for use in the treatment plan or in aftercare (see also Chapter 7). Positive expectancies about substance use may perpetuate it. Furthermore, a client's positive expectancies about drug use provide clues about high-risk situations and roadblocks to successful drug-use behavior change after treatment. There is a wide variety of adult measures of expectancies, many of which assess positive and negative expectancies simultaneously. Some of these measures of expectancies are specific to the effects of a single type of substance, while others assess expectancies across a wide variety of psychoactive substances. In addition, there are expectancy measures designed specifically for use with young adults and youth.

Therapists and counselors also may wish to use one of several brief instruments that assess moods and emotions. These measures identify extreme emotional states that place the client at risk for drug use. A couple of the more well-known assessments include the Profile of Mood States (McNair, Lorr, & Droppleman, 1992) and the Multiple Affect Adjective Check List (Herron, Bernstein, & Rosen, 1968), which ask clients about various moods and emotions that they are experiencing at the moment. Furthermore, examining how the client socially interacts in therapy and treatment can identify strengths and weaknesses in the way a client is able to express emotions. If there are problems with identifying or expressing emotions, then the therapist or counselor can assess whether those problems are related to skill deficits.

Assessment of patterns, consequences, expectancies, and the emotional context of drug use can aid the therapist or counselor in conducting a thorough function analysis of the use of the drugs by the client. You will be able to see the total picture of the clients' drug use through their eyes — from the vulnerabilities of emotional experiences to beliefs about the outcomes of drug use to the consequences of drug use — and then you can link those beliefs and behaviors with the pattern of drug use described by the clients. A savvy therapist and counselor also will help clients see the big picture of drug use in a disarming fashion. While conducting these assessments, the therapist or counselor can use reflective and summary statements to reframe and restate in therapeutically helpful ways the information that clients have provided in these assessments that will connect the dots among mood, behavior, expectancies, patterns, and consequences.

Assessing Client Potential for Behavior Change

To understand whether the client is able to change behavior, you must assess several factors, including coping skills, self-efficacy, and motivation to change. Appropriate use of skills is critical for success after therapy or treatment. If the client is unable to use the appropriate coping skill at the appropriate time after treatment, then he or she may not successfully negotiate risky circumstances without reliance upon drug use. Also, as mentioned in Chapter 1, self-efficacy is crucial for competently using skills in specific high-risk situations, and for having the confidence to succeed without drug use under those conditions. Finally, a client's motivation, as mentioned, directly influences her or his ability to learn new skills or apply old skills when needed, and directly influences the client's self-efficacy to succeed without drug use. You also may remember that client motivation dictates what kinds of therapeutic strategies should be used by a therapist in order to successfully match interventions with stages of change. Because it is essential to understand these client factors for successful treatment to occur, assessing these variables is a must.

> **"The significant problems we have cannot be solved at the same level of thinking with which we created them."**
>
> — ALBERT EINSTEIN

Observational methods in sessions can be used to identify skill deficits or inappropriately used skills. Observation of skills can be conducted in a more structured fashion by use of a devised test of skills. One such test is called the Situational Competence Test (SCT), and using this to assess use of skills in imaginal, or simulated, situations in session can yield useful information about the client's skill level or use of skills. In the SCT, which was initially developed for use among people with alcohol problems (Chaney, O'Leary, & Marlatt, 1978), the therapist describes a problem or stressful situation that could place the client at high risk for drug use, and then asks the client what she or he would do to solve the problem if in this situation. What the client says about solving these problems can provide you with a great deal of information about whether the client has the ability to skillfully cope without losing control in these high-risk circumstances.

The SCT is scored in terms of how effectively the client solves the imaginal problem. In addition, responses are timed to discover how long it takes for the client to begin to answer (solve the problem) after you have described the problem, and slower response times for solving a problem have been found by researchers to be related to poorer outcomes after treatment. Slow responses likely mean that the client has not considered how to respond skillfully to a particular situation (i.e., shows inappropriate use of skills) or does not know how to respond (i.e., shows lack of skills). In any case, a slow response or a poor response suggests that further skills training may be needed to prepare a client to cope rapidly and appropriately with crisis situations without resorting to drug use.

The SCT has been developed with a predetermined set of specific situations and questions, but there is nothing that prevents you from developing your own set of high-risk situations to ask your client about that are specifically adapted to situations he or she will face after treatment. You may want to develop your own, tailored SCT by using situations from the treatment-plan problem list (identified high-risk areas), or develop this tailored test from what you have learned about a client's drug use patterns from other assessments. Then, using relevant situations from a client's own personal life, you can assess the client's ability to refrain from drug use when negotiating high-risk situations she or he will likely encounter.

Another method to assess skills is to observe how the client works with others in group sessions, how the client interacts with others during nontherapy situations at your center, or even to observe client interaction with you in and out of session. Observation of this social behavior provides insight into how the client may interact with others outside treatment, and whether that style of interaction is appropriate. Finally, role-playing in session gives you an opportunity to observe the client in action. For example, you may want a client to role-play with you in session how he or she will deal with specific relationship problems in order to observe how the client might interact outside of session. This provides an opportunity to correct inappropriate or dysfunctional behavior in a safe situation, as well as practice new skills. In addition, you get to observe the client under some pressure if the role-play is done realistically, and that will provide you a great deal of information that can help you help your client.

In addition to assessing skills, you also may want to determine a client's level of self-efficacy to use those skills across a wide variety of situations. Conducting this type of assessment provides clues about the high-risk situations in which the client believes he or she has little control over her or his drug use. Since assessing self-efficacy exposes areas where the client may not feel able to cope without drug use, you can use that information to develop a treatment plan that enhances the client's self-efficacy in those areas. The Drug-Taking Confidence Questionnaire (Sklar, Annis, & Turner, 1997) is probably the most well-known instrument to assess self-efficacy to avoid drug use in various high-risk situations. This questionnaire measures relative confidence to avoid drug use across many different situations in which drug use may be an option.

Understanding your client's skill level and self-efficacy can help guide you in planning what needs to be taught and rehearsed in therapy or treatment. Assessing the skills that clients possess and their self-efficacy to use those skills across a wide variety of situations will be helpful to ascertain a prognosis for a client. If a client is identified as a high risk for a poor treatment outcome by use of these assessments, it may be prudent to step up the care and consider adding adjunct specialized care that increases the client's ability to succeed.

Finally, when assessing motivation to change drug use, you may wish to use one of several instruments developed to measure levels of motivation through the transtheoretical stages of change model. By determining the stage of change of your client, you will be able to match stage-appropriate therapeutic strategies to help your client make progress. Assessing the client's motivation to change will provide you with information about the level of awareness about the drug problem that your client has, as well as a sense of how ready to change he or she might be. Some of the more useful assessments of stages of change include the University of Rhode Island Change Assessment (URICA; DiClemente & Hughes, 1990), Stages of Change Readiness and Treatment Eagerness Scale (SOCRATES; Miller & Tonigan, 1996), and the Brief Readiness to Change Questionnaire (Rollnick, Heather, Gold, & Hall, 1992). These questionnaires also provide the client another opportunity to examine how she or he feels about her or his use of drugs, and whether there are reasons to consider behavior change.

There are other methods to assess readiness to change drug use besides these paper-and-pencil-type questionnaires. For example, you may want to use what is called a *decisional balance inventory* with a client who is early in the change process. Decisional balance inventories were first developed for treating alcohol use among adolescents (e.g., Migneault, Pallonen, & Velicer, 1997), but should work as well when discussing other types of drugs. They allow clients to explore their ambivalence about changing drug use. These inventories provide counselors and therapists a lot of information about what clients perceive to be the pros and con of changing their drug problems. Decisional balance inventories are especially useful when working with a client who is in the contemplation stage of change.

Another useful assessment of motivation was developed by Stephen Rollnick, who also helped to develop motivational interviewing. This tool is called Rollnick's Ruler (e.g., Stott, Rollnick, & Pill, 1995) and it assesses motivation by the use of a rulerlike scale of numbers from 0 to 10. The measure is actually shaped like a ruler, and the numbers are evenly spaced from left to right. Under each number is a comment like "not thinking about change" (under 0), "thinking about change" (under the middle of the ruler), or "am actually changing" (under the number 10). After explaining the ruler to the client, you can ask him or her to point to how ready, on this informal scale of 0 to10, he or she is to change drug use. This will provide you with a rapid assessment of readiness to change. This ruler works especially well with clients who are in the precontemplation or early contemplation stage. When a client points to a low number, say, a 2, you can ask, "What would have to happen in your life for you to point to a 5?" Having the client establish this benchmark for when to consider behavior change can be used to motivate change at a later date if he or she is not ready for change at present.

If you are interested in learning more about assessment tools for drug problems, there are several great resources to find them. I recommend several books at the end of this chapter that may help. In addition, many assessment tools can be found on the Internet. The best places to look include Web sites for the National Institute on Drug Abuse (NIDA; http://www.drugabuse.gov) and the Substance Abuse and Mental Health Services Administration (SAMHSA; http://www.samhsa.gov).

Assessing Cognitive Function

Since both chronic and acute drug use have been associated with cognitive changes, such as memory problems and executive cognitive function (ECF) deficits that can cause problems with judgment, planning and problem solving, remembering new information, awareness, abstraction abilities, and self-regulating and controlling behavior, it is a very good idea to do a comprehensive *neuropsychological assessment* if possible. There are several standardized neuropsychological tests that assess memory, including verbal and visual/spatial memory, short-term and long-term memory, recall and recognition memory, and working memory (memory used for reasoning in the present moment). Most of these tests have manuals with age-corrected norms. Sometimes the manuals provide specific score profiles of people who have drug-related memory problems so you can compare those profiles to your client's. Probably the most well-known memory test is the Wechsler Memory Scale (WMS; Wechsler, 1997), which is now in its third edition.

There also are numerous highly regarded, creative, and sophisticated tests to assess attention, concentration, and ECF, and these tests usually have manuals with age-corrected norms and sometimes provide sample test profiles of people with drug problems to compare with your client's profile. The WMS, for example, has a section that assesses attention and concentration in addition to memory functions. Another well-known attention and concentration test is the Symbol-Digit Modalities Test (Smith, 1991). Some of the more well-known measures of ECF and related cognitive functions include the Wisconsin Card Sorting

CASE STUDY

Impulsive Ima

Ima is a 27-year-old client who is being treated by you for abusing cocaine and alcohol. Ima had an auto accident just prior to seeking help with you several weeks ago; he lost consciousness at the scene momentarily, and was treated in an emergency department and released. He had been intoxicated when he had the accident and does not remember much about the incident. Ima seems to be doing well in therapy sessions, but you hear reports from family members that he has really poor judgment and is making lots of mistakes at work and at home. These family members told you that he has not been the same since the accident, that even his personality is somewhat different and that he acts even more impulsive than when he was using cocaine. You do not see this behavior at all in session, and in fact he seems to be saying and doing all the right things. Last night, Ima forgot to turn off his stove and set off the smoke detector because a pan got so hot. What is going on with Ima? How would you find out?

Test (WCST; Heaton, Chelune, Talley, Kay, & Curtiss, 1993), Category Test and Trail Making Tests (Reitan & Wolfson, 1985), Stroop Test (Stroop, 1935), and other tests developed by R. M. Ruff that bear his name. There are many newer ones that may be appropriate to use as well, depending upon the suspected problem you want to assess. Some of these neuropsychological tests can be self-administered, either on a computer or by paper and pencil. However, many of these tests must be administered and results interpreted by a highly trained therapist, usually a clinical psychologist.

Here is a warning of sorts for those who work with people who have drug problems: Identifying clients who have neuropsychological deficits or problems is not very easy to do without a comprehensive assessment battery. For instance, I have worked with clients who appear quite normal in session. However, their loved ones, friends, and acquaintances reported very different behavior outside therapy — bizarre and impulsive behavior that I did not necessarily see in session. People with ECF problems can mask those problems in short-term social interactions and in casual conversations. However, others who observe the person with ECF deficits over the long term will notice that the person has impaired judgment, which causes strange and often destructive behavior. Many times people with ECF problems have difficulties negotiating complex situations and may not be able carry out important life tasks without major problems and difficulties.

The covert nature of some of these cognitive problems is another reason I would highly recommend that clients with drug problems get a comprehensive neuropsychological exam to seek out those subtle deficits that are not easily identified even by highly trained therapists. I begin to suspect such problems in my clients who are highly motivated to change but are still having problems controlling behavior in order to achieve their goals for therapy, or if they forget important information needed to change behavior at critical and stressful times. If you are working with a client who is exceedingly impulsive or perhaps relapses frequently, and a psychiatric condition has been ruled out, it may be a good idea to have the client assessed for cognitive problems, including ECF difficulties.

Many treatment professionals may not have adequate resources to obtain comprehensive neuropsychological evaluations. However, there are some brief assessments available that can be used to spot-screen for cognitive problems and that are administered relatively easily and rapidly. The most commonly used cognitive screening assessment is the Mini Mental Status Examination (MMSE; Folstein, Robins, & Helzer, 1983). The MMSE often is used in clinical settings to determine whether a person is having difficulties with orientation to the present moment and with memory. The MMSE is a screening measure and not designed to be diagnostic for specific categories or types of cognitive problems. Moreover, since it is a screening tool, the MMSE is not particularly sensitive to identifying more subtle cognitive problems, such as ECF. Another cognitive screening tool that is relatively easy to administer and can be done in about 30 minutes is called the Neurobehavioral Cognitive Status Exam (COGNISTAT;

Engelhart et al., 1999). This instrument assesses many more areas of cognitive function than does the MMSE. However, as a screening tool, it too has limits to what it can tell you. My recommendation is that if a client of yours screens positive for a cognitive problem on one of these measures, you refer that client for a comprehensive neuropsychological workup as part of the treatment plan. Note that sometimes a person will screen positive during detoxification, but will clear cognitively after that period is finished. You should probably retest after detox has been completed if the client screens positive while in detox.

Assessing Psychiatric Symptoms

Psychiatric symptoms should be evaluated as a matter of course in treatment, given the high rates of comorbidity with drug problems. There are many ways to assess symptoms. The first way to assess psychiatric problems is to administer a full SCID (meaning assessment of *all DSM-IV* diagnostic categories). If you are using the SCID to diagnose a drug problem, you may wish to consider administering other sections of the SCID to determine comorbid psychiatric conditions. Some people opt to assess for Axis I (severe, non–personality-type) disorders only. Others prefer also to assess for Cluster B–type Axis II personality disorders (like antisocial and borderline) since many clients with these diagnoses use drugs. In addition, the SCID does having screening questions that can tell you whether a person has a certain type of disorder (e.g., anxiety), but will not tell you what kind of anxiety disorder it may be. If you have the time and the resources, it is a very good idea to administer the full SCID to your clients.

Another way that professionals assess for psychiatric disorders is to use an inventory that assesses for personality characteristics. The most famous of these inventories is the Minnesota Multiphasic Personality Inventory (MMPI), which is now in its second edition as an instrument. Although the MMPI is actually a personality inventory, as it names suggests, many professionals will use it to spot suspected psychiatric disorders, such as depression, Bipolar Disorder, Schizophrenia, and Anxiety Disorder. The MMPI has several scales to assess common personality traits, such as depression, mania, psychopathic deviance, and even alcohol and drug use (Weed, Butcher, McKenna, & Ben-Porath, 1992).

Many treatment centers administer the MMPI as part of standard care to clients. However, interpreting MMPI results takes a great deal of training. Computerized administration and scoring versions are available, and the scoring version can provide a printed-out interpretation of the results to help you understand them. These scoring programs can be quite expensive, though, probably prohibitively so for small clinics and for counselors in solo practices. In addition, sometimes the computerized interpretations do not give as much detail as you might get from an interpretation by a highly trained professional. This computerized option can be helpful, however, if you have the resources to afford this service and you do not have a trained professional on staff who can interpret MMPIs for you.

There also is a similar type of measure called the Millon Clinical Multiaxial Inventory (MCMI; Millon, 1994), which assesses for psychopathology. Like the MMPI, the MCMI has several dimension scores, but the dimensions are somewhat different. The MCMI has the advantage of assessing for Axis II disorders (personality-type disorders), which is not a strength of the MMPI. Again, the MCMI, like the MMPI, requires extensive training in order to properly administer and score it. There are computerized administration and scoring versions, but they may be expensive for small agencies and professionals in small practices.

Beyond personality-type inventories, there are measures that assess for psychopathology by asking about types of symptoms. The most commonly used instruments for these purposes are the Symptom Checklist–90 (SCL-90; Derogatis, Lipman, & Covi, 1973) and its cousin, the Brief Symptom Inventory (BSI; Derogatis & Melisaratos, 1983). These two measures take significantly less time to administer than diagnostic interviews or personality inventories do. However, symptom inventories do not assess for as many psychiatric dimensions, precisely because of this brevity. The SCL-90 has 90 questions, as the name implies, and the BSI is a shortened version of the SCL-90. They assess for psychiatric symptoms such as anxiety and psychosis, but these assessments cannot produce a definite diagnosis like the SCID can. Their brevity makes them quite popular in treatment settings, however, and these measures can be self-administered by clients and scored very easily by treatment professionals without a great deal of training. If your resources are limited, these measures can be quite helpful in identifying symptoms that may indicate a clinically relevant psychiatric problem.

Finally, there are a number of measures that assess symptoms within one specific diagnostic category (e.g., depression or anxiety, but maybe not both). The advantage to these instruments is they can tell you rapidly the kinds of symptoms your client is experiencing now, and can be used at regular intervals to track changes over time. The disadvantage of these measures is that they do not help very much with making a definitive diagnosis. A large number of these instruments were developed by Aaron Beck as part of his cognitive therapy protocols for different disorders (see Chapter 5 for more details). For example, the Beck Depression Inventory (BDI; now in its second edition) to assess depressive symptoms, the Beck Hopelessness Scale (BHS) to assess hopelessness as it relates to suicide risk and depression, and the Beck Scale for Suicide Ideation were all developed as part of Cognitive Therapy for Depression (Beck, Rush, Shaw, & Emery, 1979). The Beck Anxiety Inventory (BAI) was developed to assess symptoms as part of the cognitive therapy protocol for treating anxiety disorders (Beck & Emery, 1995). These measures are designed to be completed by clients prior to the beginning of each session. Using these measures at regular intervals can be quite useful for therapists and counselors because they provide documentation of progress from session to session.

Other therapists and researchers have developed similar questionnaires to assess symptoms common to other disorders. For example, there are a number of measures to assess trauma and PTSD symptoms and others that assess social anxiety. For PTSD I would recommend using the PTSD Symptom Scale–Self-Report (PSS-SR; Foa & Tolin, 2000) because of its brevity, and, for social anxiety, the Social Phobia and Anxiety Inventory (Beidel, Turner, & Cooley, 1993) because of its established track record.

Assessing Interpersonal Relations

Some of the greatest stressors for people trying to overcome drug problems are strained interpersonal relationships. Determining and intervening upon relationship stressors during treatment will help the client negotiate these high-risk situations successfully after discharge from treatment. Relationship stress has been found to be an important determinant of relapse for people with drug problems (see Chapter 7), so assessing the quality of, and behavior within, relationships is recommended in order to address these issues in the treatment plan.

Besides the intake interview, which can help gather information, there are a number of assessment measures for determining the quality of an important interpersonal relationship. The questions on these measures generally ask about things like communication styles, satisfaction in the relationship, joint decision making, and in some cases, abusive behavior. Two of the most well-known measures are the Dyadic Adjustment Scale (Spanier, 1976) and the Marital Satisfaction Inventory (Snyder, 1979). Therapists and counselors also may choose to interview couples together (with the consent of client and partner), and some therapists may recommend couples therapy (see Chapter 5) as part of the overall approach to treatment if deemed appropriate to help the client. Relationship assessments can yield important information that may be useful when working with couples.

Assessment as Intervention

Finally, research suggests that assessment can act as an intervention, prompting some people to change their behavior. Assessment is a powerful tool to increase self-knowledge and perhaps to promote change during that process. If a client is not cognitively impaired, then he or she may be swayed to act by new data about his or her drug use. Assessment provides an opportunity for clients to analyze their own behavior as they answer the questions. As mentioned in the last chapter, sometimes looking at data about health or other negative consequences can increase the client's awareness of drug-related problems, and may make changing drug use a more attractive option. Assessment may be one way to enhance client awareness of these consequences.

One very interesting research study used what was called a *marijuana check-up* to encourage people in the community to seek an assessment of their marijuana use (Stephens, Roffman, & Curtin, 2000). The study was advertised as a way for marijuana users to get a check-up to make sure their marijuana use was not causing any unseen problems. When the person arrived at the center, he or she would meet with a therapist, who would use motivational interviewing styles to gather more information about the research subject and his or her marijuana use. At the end of the first session the client was encouraged to complete a wide-ranging battery of assessments in many of the areas mentioned earlier in the chapter. This study used the model of an earlier study called the *drinker's check-up* (Miller, Sovereign, & Krege, 1988).

After the assessments were completed and scored, the results were presented in such a way (as mentioned in the last chapter) as to avoid argumentation, lecturing, or increasing resistance on the part of research subjects. Results were compared to peer norms, so that subjects could see whether their scores were normal or abnormal for their age groups. After the results were presented, the therapists continued to use motivational interviewing strategies in an effort to enhance the research subjects' motivation to change. The results of the study found that the intervention worked quite well in encouraging less marijuana use in the check-up condition. Although motivational interviewing was the means by which the therapy was conducted, the assessment battery was likely part of the mechanism that increased awareness of the need for changing the marijuana use.

Other research studies have used methods that encourage self-assessment and impersonal methods of providing feedback about the results of the assessment to encourage drug use change. In other words, these studies used assessment but not any therapy per se. Some of these studies have been conducted on Web sites, which then provide computerized feedback to the respondent immediately after assessment. Other studies used mailed feedback rather than in-person feedback. These studies show promise in changing substance use behavior, which suggests that assessment and feedback on that assessment may be useful for encouraging behavior change. This, however, should not be a great surprise, given what we know about behavior. After all, many people with drug problems can and do change on their own, without therapeutic intervention, when confronted with the facts about the problem. In those instances of self-change, it is likely that some type of self-assessment played a role in convincing people that it was time to do something about their drug problems. Assessment may be a useful intervention for helping those people who will never darken the doors of a treatment center. Studies like these remind us all how incredibly powerful assessment and objective feedback can be in helping to treat drug problems.

Problems With Assessment Across Cultures

In spite of the numerous strengths that assessment brings to the treatment of a drug problem, many measures are culturally limited. *Cultural bias* of measures may be one of the most poorly understood concepts in the treatment community. Researchers have discovered over time that assessment can be culturally biased in a number of ways, some that are quite obvious and others that are much more subtle. These biases can negatively affect the treatment of minority clients by producing false information about the clients and their drug problems, which in turn adversely affects the development of effective treatment plans. Because of cultural biases in many measures, including diagnostic interviews, minority clients have been found to be *overpathologized* by counselors and therapists. What this means, simply speaking, is that culturally biased assessment tends to overestimate problems among minority clients, since minority clients seeking mental health services have been found to have artificially inflated scores on many mental health measures.

There are a number of ways that assessment becomes culturally biased. First, most assessment instruments are developed in populations where White Anglos are the majority, and where the majority American cultural worldview is most prominent. However, the worldviews in ethnic-minority communities may be quite different than that of the larger majority culture. Because these worldviews are quite different, it is not safe to assume that questions can be asked in the same as they can in majority culture with White Americans. Members of ethnic-minority communities with little acculturation into the larger majority society may not understand the content of questions in the same way, and therefore will respond differently than majority members of the culture might respond. These responses produce distorted answers to questions. If you then add a language barrier to the mix — and many assessments are given in English — it complicates the results even further. If the client's first language is not English, then the potential for misunderstanding questions increases dramatically. The net result is that an assessment measure that may produce accurate information among White Anglos may not produce accurate information in another population.

Although many questionnaires have been translated into Spanish, those questionnaires may use a style of Spanish not compatible with the client you are working with in session. Many Spanish translations use formal instead of slang Spanish, and often use vocabulary that clients with limited education may not understand. Some English words simply do not have vocabulary equivalents in Spanish, so questions may lose part of their meaning as they are translated. As an example, the idea of "craving" is not well understood in Mexican culture, and so is not easily translated. In addition, there are many Spanish-speaking groups in the United States from different places of origin, and because of that there are many different nuances to the Spanish language being written and spoken in America. An instrument written for a Mexican-origin population may not be well understood by your Cuban American client.

And these difficulties don't even account for all the minority groups in the United States. Most instruments to assess drug problems have not been translated into African, Asian, Pacific Islander, American Indian, or Alaskan Native languages, for example. Sometimes counselors and therapists have opted to use interpreters when conducting assessments with non–English-speaking clients. Anyone who has done this before is likely aware of the shortcomings of this approach. Language problems are encountered when words do not translate well from one language to the other, so frequently the interpreter has to make a judgment call on how to ask your question to a client in order for that client to understand it. By definition, the interpretation will be different than the original question, which suggests a high likelihood that the response will not be to the question you asked in English in the first place. In addition, in many small, closed communities, an interpreter may know the client or the client's family, which could inadvertently lead to reluctance to disclose personal information because of concerns about shame to family and self.

Finally, measurement across cultures is complicated because behavioral norms may be different. As an example, some behavior that may be viewed as extremely dependent or perhaps extremely passive by majority-culture standards may be normative and even proscribed within some minority communities. To compare these behaviors apart from their cultural contexts is not going to provide you with useful information to help your minority client get better. Because of these measurement difficulties, what is an abnormal score on a measure for a White Anglo client may not be abnormal at all for a client from a minority community. You cannot make the assumption that measurement of a particular behavior across cultures yields the same results. Similarly, what you are measuring may not be or look the same in another culture. As an example, self-efficacy has been found to be an important construct in the majority U.S. culture for predicting successful treatment outcome. However, there is some research that suggests that self-efficacy is not important in cultures where the construct of self is not important. In these cultures, efficacy is a collectivistic construct in which competence and confidence is thought of in group terms rather than individual terms. So for a Chinese American client who has acculturated very little into mainstream American society, it might be more useful to assess for collective efficacy rather than self-efficacy with regard to changing drug use.

As you probably have guessed, these are very complicated subjects and researchers still do not have a great handle on how to adequately address measurement concerns across cultures. In the meantime, professionals in clinical settings are left with the challenge of conducting accurate assessment with limited options among the context of a rapidly changing society. Most of the instruments available are culturally biased, but since there are few alternatives, professionals may have to use them anyway. Because we know that they may be flawed in gathering the information wanted, we have to be extra careful in how we interpret and use the data they provide to us, especially when developing a treatment plan. A good rule of thumb (although not always true) is to assume that the assessment may overly pathologize your client, so you may anticipate a higher score than what may be true in reality. In other instances, like the heart surgeon mentioned earlier in this chapter, you will be forced to act even though your assessment may not be entirely accurate. Under these circumstances, it is important to use collateral resources to help you understand the true picture of a minority client's behavior, including diagnostic features and drug use. Use of collaterals (or people close to the client, such as family members or close friends) to aid in the development of treatment plans is discussed in the next section.

RESEARCH FRONTIERS

Assessing and Treating Ethnic-Minority Clients

Assessing and treating ethnic-minority clients can be quite challenging because traditional practices often do not work very well with them. The problem is that most therapies and treatments have been developed and tested among White populations of European descent. There are many ethnic-minority clients who do not share the majority worldview, so traditional practices in treatment and therapy may not be meaningful or interesting to them. In addition, language barriers make it difficult to adequately assess ethnic-minority clients, which in turn makes it hard to effectively diagnose and treat their drug problems. Researchers are beginning to understand and respond to these problems, but the development of new, culturally relevant assessment and treatment methods is slow. However, developing culturally relevant methods to treat ethnic-minority clients is critical, since ethnic-minority groups are projected to outnumber White Americans within the next 50 years. Treatment should look remarkably different then than it does today, given these radical demographic changes in American society!

Involving Family and Friends in Treatment

Family and friends can be incredibly helpful resources in treatment if the client has a good relationship with them. As mentioned in Chapter 1, if the client has strained relationships with a certain family member or friend, it may not be wise to include that person if his or her participation threatens the client. In other instances, the client simply may not want the person to be involved. Therapists and clients should make certain that the client does want family members and friends involved prior to a therapist's or counselor's contacting them. Ethically speaking, it is important to respect the wishes of your client with regard to collateral involvement in therapy or treatment. Legally speaking, it is important for consent to be provided by the client for a therapist or counselor to speak with collaterals or to involve them in the therapy process.

If the client consents to involvement of family or friends, they can be good sources for information that can help you devise a thoughtful treatment plan. As mentioned earlier in this chapter, people with drug problems may have relationship stressors that need to be addressed in order to promote a successful treatment outcome. Being able to gather information from partners or friends about the nature of these stressors adds another dimension to understanding the source and treatment for the problems. Sometimes a family member or friend has a different view on the nature of a problem or on the behavior pattern related to a problem that may help you better understand how to treat it.

Furthermore, if family involvement is important for the client, then family input and commitment to the treatment plan may help make treatment a success.

Family involvement may be essential when conducting therapy or treatment with a minority client. If the family members have aided in the development of a treatment plan by providing helpful information, and understand the rationale behind the treatment plan, then they are more likely to support treatment as it unfolds. Again, this should be done only with the consent of the client, but it can be incredibly helpful to have collateral support for the treatment plan if the client consents to their active involvement.

Treatment plans are a first step toward getting collaterals interested in treatment. One problem that I have seen while working with some clients is that although they would like their families involved, their family members feel somewhat excluded by the way treatment works. In many cases, what happens in therapy and treatment is more of a mystery to family and friends than it is to a client. Family and friends feel left out if not actively invited to participate by therapists or counselors (when the client assents to such participation), and if not adequately educated about what treatment entails. Family and close friends should be oriented to treatment in the same way as are clients. Involvement in treatment planning can be a way to orient family and close friends as well as to gather helpful information about the client and his or her world. If collaterals understand treatment better, then they will be more likely to support it.

As you may remember from Chapter 1, social support predicts successful treatment outcome. Because of this factor, collaterals who are important allies to the client in her or his efforts to overcome a drug problem should be strongly encouraged and welcomed throughout the treatment process. Therapists and counselors should maintain regular contact with supporters of the client when appropriate. Obviously, client confidentiality should be protected under these circumstances, but being friendly, helpful, and respectful to collaterals and keeping them in the treatment loop, so to speak, will ultimately help the client.

Another way to include collaterals is to offer treatment services to them as well. Many treatment facilities offer such services, which may include family support groups or even individual therapy for family members of clients. Some treatment centers include family therapists specifically for these purposes. Sometimes counselors and therapists will refer family members to outside support groups, which may include Al-Anon or Alateen 12-step programs for family and friends. Family therapy may include assessment, sometimes using similar measures discussed earlier for assessing client needs, in order to more adequately help family members with their needs. In some cases, these assessments may be used to develop a family treatment plan or an individualized treatment plan for a family member.

Family therapy in treatment centers occurs in a variety of ways. Some centers provide opportunities for weekly individual counseling or therapy for partners, or even couples therapy sessions (see Chapter 5 for more details). Many treatment programs offer group counseling or therapy sessions for family members that are similar to group sessions for clients. Some of the groups are therapeutic in nature, with a goal of behavior change for family members. These groups may include skills training and rehearsing new skills through role-playing, among other things, and may even assign homework between sessions in order to encourage behavior change outside the session. Other groups are meant to be supportive rather than therapeutic. Treatment centers sometimes sponsor family weekends, which may include psychoeducation and therapy events throughout the day, and sometimes include family recreational events and meals together. Many facilities offer weekly family-evening programs as well.

One touchy issue in working with families is the idea that family members are *codependent* on the drug-using client. There has been a great deal made of this alleged condition in the popular press and culture, including popular movies and books. Myths have developed about the behavior patterns of family members of people with drug problems, and from these myths have been suggestions about appropriate and inappropriate ways to act toward clients during and after treatment. A multimillion dollar industry has sprung up based on these ideas. However, researchers have found no support for codependency as a condition or for a codependent personality or set of behaviors. In addition, worries about family members' *enabling* the loved one to continue using drugs seem secondary to the importance of social support for successfully changing drug use. There may be times when the family member covers for the person with a drug problem, or perhaps reinforces the drug use behavior. But on the other hand, social support is crucial for a successful outcome to treatment, so it may be that any inadvertent reinforcement of drug use is more than compensated for by the value that positive social support has for the client's well-being.

Related to this is that so-called *tough love* from family members and friends is important for the client to succeed, which is another myth (as mentioned in

POINTS OF CONTROVERSY

Codependency

Codependency, which is defined loosely as emotional dependence upon the person with a drug problem, has received a lot of press in popular culture, and literally dozens of self-help books have been written on the subject. Some have gone so far as to suggest that codependency is a chronic and progressive disease, and that loved ones experience powerlessness and loss of control related to their attachment to people with drug problems. However, research has not supported the existence of codependency as a condition, which prompted Hazelden Treatment Center to state publicly they had found no evidence that such a condition exists, and there is no *DSM-IV* diagnostic category for codependency. In spite of the complete lack of any research to support its existence, there remains a persistent belief in the popular culture that codependency is a legitimate mental health condition.

Chapter 1). Tough love is confused with punishing the client for drug use, which often leads to withdrawal of social support through ultimatums (an "if-you-don't-get-help-I'm-leaving" type of attitude). Withdrawal of social support is not helpful for a person with a drug problem. There is no research that shows that leaving a love one ultimately helps him or her. It may help the family member if that (the end of the relationship) is the goal, but it does not necessarily help the loved one, and may actually harm his or her chances for help later. If family members want to help loved ones, leaving them is not a great idea.

There is a huge difference between *not reinforcing* drug use and *punishing* drug use. Tough love opts for punishment, using the relationship as a weapon to coerce compliance, which often means that social support for the client is withdrawn if the person does not do this or that. However, one need not withdraw social support in order to avoid reinforcing drug use behavior. Maintaining a close relationship will be much more important to the client when help is sought than threatening to shun the client if behavior change does not occur. Shunning the client often is done out of anger and frustration, which is obvious to everyone including the client. Withdrawing reinforcement of drug use behavior does not involve a threat at all, and can be done without the person's even telling the client that he or she is doing it simply by changing the way he or she interacts with the client when the client is using drugs. The family relationship can be used to encourage change only so long as the relationship exists.

There are a number of important issues to address with clients and their family members during therapy that may become issues after treatment is completed. The first factor that may affect family relationships and treatment success concerns expressed emotion by family members. As you may remember, negative emotion expressed by family members toward clients may hinder the clients' recovery. Family members may be angry or hurt over the client's drug use, and may express those feelings inappropriately. Those emotional expressions may take the form of passive-aggressive comments, blame, or even aggressiveness toward the person with a drug problem. Family members may need to undergo assertiveness training to reduce the risk of expressed negative emotion. Such a risk can be determined from assessment of past emotional interactions between family members and the client, as well as assessment of current angry feelings in family members toward the client and how those are expressed in therapy sessions. Assertiveness training is discussed more fully in Chapter 5.

A second factor that may affect family relationships and long-term treatment success is the likelihood that a client may experience depression after changing drug use. The client's depressive symptoms may be directly related to rebound effects after stopping drug use, or to life changes and losses associated with leaving behind drug-using situations or friends. The depressive behavior may show up as lethargy, inactivity, disinterest in life or in family, sadness, withdrawal from social events, or changes in sleep patterns (it is not unusual at all to have sleep problems early in recovery, however, apart from depression). Fortunately, professionals now understand that this is a common problem, and many treatment facilities will treat for depression by use of psycho- and pharmacotherapy (see Chapter 5).

Finally, sometimes for the same reasons that depression may develop, sexual disinterest by the client often is another posttreatment factor that can affect couples' relationships. Sometimes sexual problems occur before the client enters treatment, but they tend to be blamed on the drug use (probably appropriately so). However, when these problems persist after treatment, and the loved one no longer uses drugs, then a partner may tend to personalize the behavior even though this interpretation usually is not true. Instead, the lack of interest may be related to drug-rebound effects and sometimes to side effects of prescribed medicines (e.g., antidepressants have very high rates for sexual side effects, such as reduced interest and ability to perform). In other cases, the problems with sexual relations may occur after therapy. Sometimes these problems are but a symptom of a larger problem, which generally means that partners are having problems communicating with each other, or cannot resolve issues of conflict. Many couples find that once other communication problems and conflicts are resolved, sexuality becomes easier. It may be that couples will want to continue with therapy after treatment in order to enhance their posttreatment relationship.

Some of my clients also have expressed fears about sexual performance while not using drugs. Some have confided in me that they had not had sex without drugs in their systems for so long they were apprehensive about what it might be like. A few have told me they were not sure if they had ever had sex while clean. In some cases, clients would avoid sex with partners because of these fears. Couples should be aware of these potential problems with sexual behavior and of possible fears related to sex after treatment, and discuss them openly. Sometimes simply discussing these issues openly is enough to help clients generate their own solutions for how to overcome these concerns as a couple. If discussing these issues seems difficult to facilitate on your own, then seek a couples therapist to aid in this process. There also are now widely publicized pharmacotherapy agents that may help if sexual performance is hindered by past drug use or by prescribed medicines, especially for depression. Discuss these options with a physician, since these medicines have some possible side effects of their own.

> **"All marriages are happy. It's trying to live together afterwards that causes all the problems."**
>
> — SHELLEY WINTERS

Assessing Progress

Treatment plans are effective only if they help clients and families improve. To be able to determine progress, you need to review treatment plans periodically. Usually treatment teams will conduct weekly interdisciplinary staff reviews of a client's progress, and the staff's recommendations for improving care will be documented in the chart. These interdisciplinary staff meetings are quite useful,

CLIENT HANDOUT

A Word to Family and Friends About the Advantage of Being Involved

Family members and friends may wonder why it is important for them to participate in therapy or in treatment. After all, it seems as if the problem all along has been drug use by the client. However, treatment provides a unique opportunity for family members and close friends to learn more about how to effectively help their loved one and friend to succeed. Remember all the times that you had wished that he or she would stop using drugs? Now he or she is in treatment, so there is a very good chance that your wish is coming true, but it is not going to be easy process for anyone involved. Feel good about participating in the process of treatment, because research suggests that your participation improves your friend's or loved one's chances of succeeding.

Part of participating in treatment is to educate yourself about drug problems and their treatments. You will be called upon to be a source of support by the client after treatment, just as you always have been. Therapy or treatment may teach you new ways to show your support, ways that perhaps neither you nor your loved one (or friend) have considered before. You may learn new ways to encourage and reinforce your loved one's efforts toward recovery.

Treatment and therapy also will help you sort out your own feelings about your friend or loved one and his or her drug use, and therapy will prepare you to express or cope with those feelings in a way that is healthy for you and the person you care about. Reflecting upon your own thoughts and feelings may help you decide how to improve your relationship, or perhaps even how to improve yourself. Times of crises are major opportunities for personal growth, and therapy may be able to help you in this regard. Your participation in your loved one's therapy does not mean that you have a problem — but you may find along the way that your participation in therapy can be as liberating for you as for your loved one. Many family members and friends I know who have participated in the therapeutic process because a loved one or friend entered into treatment for a drug problem have told me that they felt personally enriched by the experience themselves. It is my hope that you have a similar experience.

since they offer an opportunity for all important players in treatment to discuss progress that they see in clients, problems they may have noted that may be interfering with progress, and options for how to make midcourse corrections in treatment that may benefit clients. Sometimes these staff meetings also will discuss family therapy, if those services are offered by the center, and then discuss the progress, problems, and midcourse corrections in family relationships as well.

Progress should be reviewed routinely with the client. Many therapists like to make a brief review of progress with the client during each session, and perhaps include a more comprehensive and formal review weekly or perhaps monthly, depending upon how often therapy occurs with the client. Many professionals like to use the interdisciplinary reviews as part of the feedback they provide to their clients, so these regular reviews of progress often occur after the staff reviews take place. This provides for a large amount of professional feedback that may benefit the client. During these reviews, I find it very important to mention client successes prominently, as well as any areas that may need more attention. The client's self-efficacy has to be considered in these feedback sessions, so it is important to make them as positive as possible, and to make sure that midcourse corrections are attainable for the client and that problems mentioned can be resolved. It has been my experience that it is not useful to confront a client in therapy with new problems that have no solutions, or to expect too much from them in areas where they may be at risk for not succeeding.

Assessments that measure changes in symptoms from one session to the next can be quite helpful in documenting progress on reducing anxiety or depression. The therapist or counselor can use those data when discussing progress with other staff, or can even share such data with the client if it is deemed to be useful for the client. I would not share those data in order to confront lack of progress, however, because that would place a client on the defensive.

You do not need a large treatment facility with a multidisciplinary staff to review progress with a client. Reviewing progress regularly is highly recommended even if you are in a solo practice. Many clients have lived in environmental situations that provided inconsistent or nonexistent messages about behavior. Some of our clients' problems can be directly linked to this historic lack of feedback on how to behave appropriately with others. The last thing we want to do as treatment professionals is continue the pattern of inconsistent or nonexistent feedback about the behavior of our clients. By conducting a regular review of progress, we are not only providing feedback needed for behavior change, we are also modeling honesty, consistency, and predictability in social interactions for our clients.

Documenting progress is also important for determining when to terminate therapy or treatment. Most therapists want to be able to document diagnosis and prognosis at discharge. Without documentation throughout treatment, it is difficult to determine discharge diagnoses or prognoses, and certainly difficult to justify them. Some insurance companies do not look favorably on discharge summaries that are not justified with documented reviews of progress made throughout treatment; this may jeopardize third-party reimbursement. In addition, some clients may need treatment summaries to return to work or to provide to the court that referred them for treatment; again, reviews of progress throughout treatment will support what you write in such summaries.

Some treatment-plan problem lists are written in such a way that progress on individual items can be documented on the treatment plan itself (please refer back to Figure 4.2 for an example). These documents include space to write notes related to the regular reviews of clients' progress, and also may include space for notes discussing recommendations for altering the treatment plans in order to better serve clients' needs. Providing space for notes on the treatment plan itself offers the therapist a structured way to document progress, as well as includes midcourse corrections adjacent to the original treatment plan itself in order to have these resources together in the chart. Regular progress notes can be used for recording greater details if space does not allow such details on the actual treatment-plan document. If an evolving treatment plan is used, then the therapist or counselor may want to provide copies of adjusted treatment plans to clients regularly, and then consider having the client sign off on the modifications as well. Again, the advantage of having the client sign off on modifications is that it provides some level of participation in and commitment to the revised treatment plan. A treatment plan signed by both the client and the therapist can serve as a contract to work collaboratively toward meeting the client's goals for treatment.

Finally, the treatment plan must be developed with an eye toward *aftercare* as well, and should include relapse-prevention strategies (see Chapter 7) as well as behavioral strategies the client plans to use to maintain changes after treatment. These plans for maintaining changes can become a contract for a long-term recovery plan, again developed collaboratively. Many treatment professionals like to work during treatment on developing an after-treatment plan to fine-tune over time. The plan may start as a basic agreement of what the client plans to do while in treatment to avoid drug problems, then evolve over time into a document that addresses posttreatment activities. The plan generally means structuring the client's time when not in therapy toward outside activities that encourage personal growth and support behavior change while minimizing opportunities to use drugs.

Sometimes *time schedules* are used to help the client structure his or her week around these activities that encourage progress toward treatment goals. Figure 4.3 illustrates what a time schedule may look like. As you can see, it looks like the weekly calendar or day-planner that many people use for work. The goal is to structure time in such a way as to avoid opportunities to slip back into old drug-using behavior. The catch is to structure time in such a way that it protects but does not exhaust the client. A balance has to be made between structure and overwork in order to prevent fatigue and frustration, which — as has been mentioned — are potential high-risk triggers for drug use. Note also that the time schedule in Figure 4.3 includes prompts to encourage adherence to the schedule, as well as alternative activities that can be used by the client in case of emergency.

Day of the week: ______________________

Hour of the day:	Activity planned	How will you get to this activity?	Why is this activity important for you?
6 am			
7 am			
8 am			
9 am			
10 am			
11 am			
12 pm			
1 pm			
2 pm			
3 pm			
4 pm			
5 pm			
6 pm			
7 pm			
8 pm			
9 pm			
10 pm			

Activities I can do if I get stressed or bored that will help me feel better:

____

Figure 4.3: A sample planner for structuring a client's time.

The priority is to structure the times when the client is at the highest risk to use drugs. You can determine these high-risk times from the information the client has given to you on the consumption-pattern assessments and functional analyses of drug use. Use this information to determine the client's high-risk times to use or overuse drugs. For some, the pattern may be using on break and at lunch during work hours; for others it may be using after work. Depending on the pattern of the client, you should structure that time of greatest risk with activities that make it difficult to use drugs. The plan for structured activities is written on the time schedule, which also can be signed (a copy made for the client and a copy made for the chart) and used as a beginning recovery contract while the client is still in therapy.

Time can be structured in very creative ways. For some people it will involve recovery self-help group meetings, if they are comfortable with those groups. Structuring time may involve interesting and challenging recreational activities that have not been linked to prior drug use, or perhaps family activities. For some it might involve attending classes. The point is to develop a weekly plan to structure a client's time so he or she is not bored or tempted.

This plan will slowly evolve into an after-treatment plan that is adjusted regularly. A regular review of how well this plan is working to structure the client's time should be made. At the review, the client shares which activities are interesting and engaging for her or him, which activities are not challenging or not working to meet goals for treatment, and whether the plan is too ambitious or not ambitious enough. The therapist or counselor reflects upon these reports, and then may suggest adjustments to the plan based on the recommendations. Then client and therapist discuss and negotiate potential changes to the contract and reiterate commitment to the contract by signing the revised document, and copies are made once again.

Eventually, the contract will require less adjustment over time, and the client will begin to convert the plan into habit. By the end of treatment, a new contract for recovery after treatment (the *after-treatment plan*) will be developed in a similar fashion. However, since the plan was developed at the beginning of treatment and adjusted throughout its course, the after-treatment recovery contract will not be something new to learn and practice just as the client is entering a new phase of behavior change without treatment support. Instead, the client will have been practicing the plan for some time, and the plan will have been tried and tweaked to meet the needs of the client over time. A few adjustments may be made as treatment ends, but the after-treatment recovery plan will likely be only slightly different than what the client has been practicing all along. This process should minimize some of the stress on the client related to ending treatment. An important aspect of the after-treatment plan, just like the treatment plan, is to make it simple enough to follow so that the client can succeed.

Summing Up

A well-constructed plan is ultimately designed to do the greatest amount of good with the least amount of intervention. You can tell when you have devised a well-constructed treatment plan because it makes your job easier and because you can observe your client succeeding in treatment. A well-constructed treatment plan is also a blueprint for deciding the appropriate treatment model and strategies to use in therapy and how session time is best spent. Using a wide range of assessments helps you determine what to address in the plan and how to address it. Assessment tools are not without shortcomings, but they can provide a great deal of information about your client if used appropriately. Family members also can be great sources of information about the client and, if supportive of the client, make for tremendous allies in the treatment process. Finally, a well-constructed treatment plan leads to a well-developed after-treatment plan. Taking the time necessary to develop a well-constructed treatment plan will pay dividends for both you and your client.

Key Terms

Affect. Visible mood and emotion.

Aftercare. A treatment modality that comes after and is less intensive than outpatient or inpatient therapy. The focus is usually on relapse prevention.

Behavior chain analysis. Assessing how one behavior leads to another, which leads to another, and so on.

Codependency. A notion, which is not scientifically supported, that family members become dependent on the problems of drug-using loved ones.

Cultural bias. The concept that assessment is biased, either overtly or covertly, by the cultural values and language in which it is developed.

Empirically validated. Supported and tested by scientific methods.

Enabling. The idea that family members can unwittingly make it easier for the client to use drugs because they rescue the client with safety nets.

Function analyses. Determining the goals of behavior within specific contexts.

Intake interview. Usually the first lengthy interview between therapist and client.

Neuropsychological assessment. Assessment of cognitive function and problems.

Passive-aggressive. Usually behind-the-back behavior, such as gossiping about, complaining about, or blaming others.

Psychosocial history. A systematic biographical assessment.

Treatment plan. A document developed to guide the progress of treatment.

Recommended Reading

First, I would recommend a book called *Assessment of Addictive Behaviors,* edited by Dennis Donovan and Alan Marlatt (New York: Guilford Press, 1988). This is a very comprehensive book on how to assess for drug problems. A newly revised edition of this book is due to be released in 2005.

Second, I would recommend the handbook put out by NIDA called *Assessing Drug Abuse Among Adolescents and Adults: Standardized Instruments* (Rockville, MD: NIDA, 1994). This handbook can be easily obtained from

NIDA and has a wide variety of measures assessing psychological predictors of drug use for both adults and teens.

Third, I recommend two handbooks put out by SAMHSA. The first is called *Screening and Assessment of Alcohol- and Other Drug-Abusing Adolescents* (Rockville, MD: SAMHSA, 1993). This handbook can be easily obtained from SAMHSA and is specifically geared toward assessing drug problems among youth. The second one is called *Alcohol and Other Drug Screening of Hospitalized Trauma Patients* (Rockville, MD: SAMHSA, 1995). This SAMHSA manual is good because is provides ways to assess drug abuse among patients hospitalized for traumatic accidents.

The last three recommended resources are federally produced manuals that are relatively inexpensive or free.

TRUTH OR FICTION

QUIZ ANSWERS

1. True; 2. True; 3. False; 4. True; 5. False; 6. True; 7. True

CHAPTER 5

Recovery Tools, Programs, and Theories

TRUTH OR FICTION QUIZ

After reading this chapter, you should be able to answer the following questions:

1. Naltrexone is used to make people sick when they use drugs. True or False?
2. Insomnia among newly recovered drug users can be treated only by medicines. True or False?
3. Rule-governed behavior may cause clients to feel guilty or resentful. True or False?
4. Distress-tolerance skills always accompany cue exposure. True or False?
5. Twelve-step groups were first developed within the philosophy of the disease model for treating a drug problem. True or False?
6. The most effective treatment for anxiety disorders is the use of anxiolytic drugs. True or False?
7. Treatment centers in ethnic-minority communities often use different treatment models than those in suburban communities. True or False?

Answers on p. 230.

Treating drug problems requires a great deal of skill. Generally other problems accompany the drug problems, increasing the complexity of treating them. A therapist or counselor treating a drug problem must have many tools available in the therapeutic toolbox in order to aid clients in reaching their goals for treatment or therapy. In this chapter, these therapeutic tools will be reviewed, as will the theoretical models that support their use. In addition, suggestions for empirically validated treatments for other psychological disorders will be discussed. The therapeutic tools will be described within the context of the biopsychosocial model in the following sections.

Tools for Motivating Change and Promoting Commitment

Many suggestions for how to motivate change were made in Chapter 3, so they will not be repeated here. Those strategies suggested for motivating a person to seek help also work well for a motivating a person when in treatment. Remember, even a person who has sought help is not necessarily committed to change or even completely motivated to follow your suggestions in therapy. There may be many times during therapy when you have to use motivational strategies to encourage compliance with a suggested course of action or even with carrying out the treatment plans. The methods for encouraging motivation to change, such as using motivational interviewing, and for testing and promoting commitment to change, such as devil's advocate or foot-in-the-door/door-in-the-face techniques, can be used throughout therapy to help clients follow treatment plans. In addition, self-monitoring of behavior (described more fully later in this chapter) between sessions can potentially increase motivation by increasing awareness of behavioral patterns and consequences.

Finally, treatment plans can be used to motivate clients to reach their personal goals for therapy or treatment. Remind the client of what he or she wants from treatment in order to reinstill a sense of commitment to the plans. However, do so in a disarming and nonjudgmental fashion so as not to risk a defensive response. Questions as simple as, "What are your reasons for continuing with treatment?" or "What do you want from therapy?" may be enough to remind the client of the reasons she or he committed to this course.

Tools for Treating the Biological/Physiological Aspects of a Drug Problem

Drug problems take a great toll on the human body, so therapists and counselors need to be aware of how the physical effects of drug use can be treated. As recommended in Chapter 4, clients with drug problems should receive physical examinations by a physician as part of the routine care of treatment, if possible. Since drug use can adversely affect a client's diet, it also may be important to refer the client to a nutritionist who can determine whether there are any dietary deficits and perhaps develop meal plans to aid the client in restoring her or his health.

Detoxification, as mentioned in Chapter 2, may involve the use of certain medications to prevent severe discomfort or even possible medical side effects related to withdrawal symptoms. These medicines can range from tranquilizers (often benzodiazepines) and antidepressants to anticonvulsives and antihypertensives, and the medical protocol for detox will depend on the drug or drugs being abused, the client's vital signs and other symptoms, and the known risk for certain withdrawal symptoms associated with the drugs being used. The duration of use of these pharmacological agents to control or cover withdrawal symptoms are determined by monitoring the client's symptoms, and these medicines are slowly tapered as the signs of withdrawal dissipate.

In addition, medicines may be prescribed to control cravings. As mentioned in Chapter 1, cravings can be both physiological and psychological. For physiological cravings, certain medicines have been found to provide some relief for the cravings associated with certain types of drugs. The most promising drugs, such as naltrexone and acamprosate, seem useful for deterring cravings for opioid drugs. There is a great deal of research currently being conducted in the pharmacological treatment of substance abuse, so more craving-reducing drugs will likely be developed in the coming years. Some research studies have looked at using these medicines in conjunction with psychotherapy to provide a one-two punch at treating a drug problem. The idea is that the craving-reducing drugs help the client remain in treatment during the early stages when withdrawal discomfort is common so that he or she has an opportunity to learn new skills for changing behavior in psychotherapy.

Tools for Treating the Psychological Aspects of a Drug Problem

Many tools have been developed for treating the psychological aspects of a drug problem. I mentioned some of these tools earlier but did not discuss their use in great detail. Psychological tools focus principally on helping the client learn how to take charge of behavior change. Initially, the therapist aids the client in the process of learning and using these tools in session, but eventually the goal is for the client to be able to use the tools on his or her own outside session. This represents a process known as the *generalization of the use of skills.* Simply put, generalization of skills means the client is able to use the newly learned skills successfully across a wide variety of life situations outside therapy. Obviously, the generalization of treatment skills is critical for successfully overcoming a drug problem.

In the following sections, different types of change strategies that you may wish to use with your clients will be discussed. The first section will be dedicated to behavior-modification strategies used to target patterns of behavior related to drug use. The second section will review cognitive-modification strategies that can be used to address thoughts and emotions related to drug use. The third section will review skills training and psychoeducational strategies you can use to teach your clients how to behave and respond differently than they have in the past, with the goal of coping successfully without resorting to drug use.

Behavior-Modification Strategies

Therapy must address the drug habit before a client with a drug problem can change the behavior. *Habit* implies a pattern of behavior that may be rote and automatic. Your role as a counselor or therapist is to increase clients' awareness about these rote and perhaps automatic behaviors by teaching them how to identify the pattern. After the pattern is identified its components, from the way it is reinforced to the way a client responds to its particular cues and situations, must be altered. These behavioral changes can be addressed in therapy by the use of self-monitoring, shaping and contingency management, cue exposure and response prevention, and skills training and psychoeducation. Each of these therapeutic techniques is described in detail here. Skills training and psychoeducation will be discussed in a later section because these strategies often represent a merging of both behavioral and cognitive interventions.

Teaching Your Client to Monitor and Change Drug-Use Behavior Chains

To begin with, the therapist or counselor helps the client understand the context, function, and reinforcement history of his or her drug use behavior. This is done by use of behavioral analyses, which are helpful for identifying relationships between different behaviors and situations to the use of drugs. The therapist or counselor will want to identify how behaviors, thoughts, and emotions link together (or interact) in the client's pattern of drug use. As the therapist discusses the behavior chains leading to drug use with the client, effort is made to identify each link in the chain and how it leads the client one step closer to using drugs. At each point in the chain a client learns what he or she can do to stop the forward progress. In the effort to generalize skills learned in treatment, the client first learns how to intervene upon each link of the chain in session with your guidance, but eventually must be able to use those interventions on her or his own in the real world.

For example, imagine that your client tells you about the following behavior chain for her drug use. She tells you that she uses Xanax (alprazolam) right before her partner arrives home from work. You ask her about that, and discover that she feels anxious about her partner's arrival because the partner tends to yell at her about something immediately upon arrival home. So she looks at the clock to see what time it is, and at around 5:00 p.m., when her partner gets off work, she takes her first Xanax, followed by another one when she hears the garage door opening a bit later, signaling the arrival of the partner. Her behavior chain includes the links of a behavior (looking at the clock) and of an emotional response (anxiety about being yelled at), and particular cues (5:00 p.m. and the garage door's going up, as well as the partner's presence) that lead to the use of Xanax. By raising the awareness of the client to this chain of events, you have armed her with knowledge that may allow her to circumvent the use of drugs in this situation, if you teach her how to respond differently at each link in the chain. For example, changing her behavior (not looking at the clock or not being available to be yelled at), changing her response to her anxiety, or changing her beliefs that Xanax somehow manages her anxiety or diminishes the bad feelings about being yelled at, will allow her many different ways and points of opportunity to respond in other ways rather than using drugs.

In order to understand the details about these behavior chains, the client will need to monitor her behavior, including what she does, when and why she may do it, what she thinks, how she feels, and, eventually, how she can respond differently. This requires the ability to *self-monitor,* which you as a therapist will want to teach to her. Figure 5.1 represents a form that may help your client self-monitor behavior, thoughts, and emotions. The form presented here is meant only as an example. You may wish to devise your own form to include the specific items you wish for your client to track related to his or her individual needs. The goal is to generate as much information as possible for your client to use in order to understand how his or her behavior patterns lead to drug use, and what the client can do at each step along the chain to reduce the likelihood that drugs will be used.

Related to the idea of self-monitoring, you may need to educate your client on identifying how one behavior links to emotional responses and vice versa. Some

Weekly Drug Use Diary

Date and time you started using:	What kind of drug(s)?—(list time you used each type)	What happened right before you used (the situation, your thoughts, and your feelings)?
Day 1		
Day 2		
Day 3		
Day 4		
Day 5		
Day 6		
Day 7		

Other notes about drug use this week (other observations you made):

Figure 5.1: A sample self-monitoring form.

clients will have difficulty identifying how emotions relate to the behavior, and may confuse thoughts with emotions. Other clients may have difficulty identifying alternative ways to solve problems or understanding how to respond to a particular situation in a different way. You may wish to help your client by suggesting a number of examples of how to respond differently at each particular link in a chain. Use a motivational interviewing style when suggesting these options. For example, you may want to suggest to your client that "other people in a situation similar to yours have found it useful to respond in this way." In this way you are presenting options in a disarming way instead of appearing as if you are imposing your own agenda on the client.

Shaping Behavior

Shaping client behavior in session can be a powerful tool to promote behavior change. Especially in the beginning of therapy, you may want to shape your client's behavior by the use of reinforcement and sometimes by use of punishment. *Reinforcement* makes it more likely that the client will repeat a certain behavior in the future. Generally speaking, client movements toward changing a drug problem should be rewarded. The rewards may include giving the client more attention or time in a session, or perhaps giving praise or offering a compliment. The point is to make sure that you reward (positively reinforce) the client when she or he is making progress toward changing drug use.

On the other hand, there may be times when you will want to use punishment with a client. Punishment can be misunderstood, since in some cases it is linked with authoritarian behavior and used in an attempt to control others rather than with the goal of changing behavior. It goes without saying that the use of an authoritarian kind of punishment is not a wise idea for developing a therapeutic alliance, and the research suggests it may be harmful for clients. So when discussing punishment in the context of psychotherapy, I am not talking about control or harshness.

In therapy, *punishment* can be accomplished simply by ignoring what the client is doing or saying (*therapeutic neglect*), or by expressing disapproval about the behavior. If the therapeutic alliance is well developed, the client will care about the relationship with the therapist or counselor, and will be dismayed if you disapprove of or ignore what he or she is doing in session. Another good example of punishment involves spending time discussing things in session that the client has been actively trying to avoid. For example, if the client has not completed his or her homework from the last session, and you see this behavior as avoidant, then the punishment might be to use the whole session completing the homework together. You will know whether this use of session time is punishing to the client if she or he hesitates about complying or complains about the use of time.

Using reinforcement and punishment with in-session material can do a great deal to modify your client's behavior, if done skillfully and respectfully. After shaping the behavior in session, the next step is to have your client practice those in-session behavioral changes outside therapy.

Teaching Your Client How to Shape Personal Behavior and Seek Alternative Activities

Eventually, you will want to train clients to take charge of shaping their own behavior as part of generalizing the new behaviors to real-world situations. At the same time you're shaping behavior in session, you should be encouraging clients to find ways to reinforce themselves for changes they are making so that they will find it rewarding to act differently. At least in the beginning stages of this process, you may need to suggest specific types of rewards to your clients that represent alternatives to drug use or drug-using situations.

Since the goal is to change the behavior patterns that contribute to drug use, it will be important to incorporate new behavior patterns, or activities, into the life of your client to replace the old. Helping the client develop alternative activities that do not involve the possibility of drug use is one recommended way of doing this. *Alternative activities* simply means that the behavior is new and provides an alternative to old behavior that may be linked in some way with past drug use. Alternative activities should be interesting, stimulating, and relevant in order to fully engage the client — for example, career and vocational training, new-hobby development, exercise routines or challenging and vigorous recreational activity, spiritual or traditional cultural practices, or development of new social support networks and involvement in new social activities. Alternative activities also structure your client's time in order to prevent the risk of boredom and fill up the time voids left when drug-using patterns are extinguished.

Moving From Extrinsic Reinforcement to Intrinsic Reinforcement

Therapists and counselors should remember that permanent change is more likely to occur if the client finds the new behavior reinforcing inside *and* outside session. Although learning a new behavior in therapy relies a great deal upon reinforcement (e.g., praise or shaping) by you, eventually the client will need to rely less on your reinforcement and more on his or her own. After all, you will not be around to encourage the new behaviors in your clients after treatment or therapy has ended.

Part of encouraging a movement from *extrinsic* (coming from outside) to *intrinsic* (arising from within the client) reinforcement is to gradually taper the amount of reinforcement you do over time. Tapering is referred to as *fading,* and fading encourages the client to gradually become less reliant upon your imposed reinforcement in session. In the beginning of training a new skill, it is important to heap lots of reinforcement upon your client to encourage progress. But later, when the new behavior becomes more habitual, fade the amount of reinforcement you supply and point out to the client how the behavior changes seems to be improving his or her quality of life. This will encourage the client to seek reinforcement through increased personal satisfaction and real-world experiences rather than from you as counselor or therapist. Eventually the client will find personal reasons to maintain those changes over the long term. The movement from reliance on extrinsic reinforcement to reliance on intrinsic reinforcement validates that you have done your job well as a therapist or counselor.

Cue Exposure and Response Prevention

Exposure to reduce sensitivity to cues that may trigger cravings or that may even be linked to a pattern of behavior associated with drug use can be highly effective. Exposing clients under controlled conditions to the stimuli that trigger specific drug use behaviors can modify their reactions to those cues. The exposure technique was first developed in order to treat clients with anxiety, but has a wide variety of applications now, including with people who have drug problems. In the case of treating someone with a drug problem, the stimuli (or cues or triggers) being exposed are those that are directly associated with drug use. To effectively expose a client to a cue or trigger, you must require him or her to face the cue in session to the point of discomfort and stay in the presence of the cue until the discomfort fades. The discomfort will rise and fall away like an ocean wave, and when the discomfort falls to zero the cue will no longer trigger an unhealthy response in the client.

The second part of exposure is what is called *response prevention,* in which you as the therapist prevent the client from engaging in the old behavior while exposing him or her to the drug-using cue or trigger. Exposure to a cue followed

CASE STUDY

Mason's Musical Nightmare

Mason is a 34-year-old client who has been trying to overcome a cocaine problem. A particular Eric Clapton song about his drug of choice has caused him some grief; for a long time, when he heard this song it triggered cravings to use the drug. In his first treatment several years ago, his counselor told him to avoid listening to the song in order to avoid the cravings. However, a few weeks after treatment was finished he was stuck in gridlock when he heard the song blaring loudly in the car next to him. He felt the cravings coming on, and later that day relapsed. However, now he has a therapist who understands how to use cue-exposure techniques to reduce the power of triggers such as this song. He has been assigned to listen to the song constantly while in therapy. At the same time, he has learned to use relaxation techniques, new skills, and relapse-prevention methods while he is listening to the song in order to practice using these techniques in real life. As the end of treatment approaches, Mason's nightmare song seems to have lost its power to trigger cravings, maybe because he has heard it so many times in a drug-free context.

by response prevention allows the client to learn how to break the old behavior pattern by tolerating the cue without responding with drug use. Eventually the cue no longer links to drug use, which means the cue no longer will trigger a drug-using response.

There are different ways to use exposure with clients. The first method, called *in vivo exposure,* means that you expose the client under real-life conditions. In vivo exposure allows clients to practice for experiences they will likely face regularly in the real world under the controlled conditions of therapy. Let me present an example of how in vivo exposure would work with a client. Suppose your client has chronic pain and a history of abusing prescription pain-controlling medicines. Chronic pain in this instance represents a cue for drug use. You would most certainly want your client to learn how to confront his or her chronic pain directly without resorting to use of the pain medicines. In vivo cue exposure to pain in session would encourage the client to face his or her pain in real life without responding in the old way.

However, some exposure experiences cannot or should not be done in vivo (or in real life). Sometimes this is because the conditions are difficult to recreate and in other cases in vivo exposure might be risky for a client. Under these conditions, counselors or therapists may opt for using *imaginal exposure* to cues or triggers related to drug use. In imaginal exposure, you expose the client to cues under simulated rather than real-life conditions. Imaginal exposure might involve role-playing particular high-risk situations related to drug use during a session, or having the client imagine being exposed to those situations. The goal for imaginal exposure remains the same as for in vivo exposure: to lessen the potency of a cue to trigger a drug use response in your client. Imaginal exposure targets cues indirectly, whereas the in vivo method targets cues directly.

Cue exposure with clients who have drug problems can be particularly effective to diminish the power of cues or triggers that will likely be encountered by clients outside treatment. For example, if the client will be exposed to variety of drug-related cues or triggers in the home or in the neighborhood, then it will be important to try to reduce the client's sensitivity to those cues. In the past, some treatment professionals have been wary of exposing clients to such cues while in treatment, worried that their clients might be too weak to resist the temptation. However, the only way to break the bonds between the cues and the old behavior is to practice new responses when faced with the cues. Therapy is the best and safest place to do this. Avoiding exposure in therapy of a cue that your client will likely encounter will not help your client prepare for the moment when she or he comes face to face with that cue outside treatment or therapy. It makes sense to reduce the power of the cue during therapy in order to inoculate your client from its effects. The research suggests that cue exposure is a highly effective technique for curbing drug use cravings and habits.

In addition, exposure can be varied in terms of its dose. For example, you may want to start exposure with a mildly uncomfortable cue to begin with, and when the client experiences no more cravings or temptations when facing that cue, then you may wish to move up to a little more uncomfortable trigger. Graduated cue exposure like this often is referred to as *systematic desensitization*. With systematic desensitization, you begin with less threatening cues, and then after the client loses temptation to use in the face of such cues, move on to more potent cues that cause greater levels of temptation. This process requires developing what is called a *hierarchy of cues* or triggers, which means that you ask the client to rank-order cues from least to most powerful in terms of their ability to produce cravings or temptations. After the client completes the ranking, you start by exposing the client to the lowest ranked cue until the discomfort subsides permanently, and slowly work your way up through the hierarchy as the client masters facing the cues with no experience of craving or desire for drug use. Remember to prevent the drug-related behavioral responses that have been linked in the past with such cues as you conduct the exposure. In addition, counselors and therapists need to make sure that clients succeed in the exposure experience, which is why you want to start with less threatening cues in the beginning of this type of therapy. Only after your client has mastered one cue should you move on to the next in the hierarchy.

Exposure is a highly technical therapeutic skill to master. I would strongly recommend that new therapists get structured clinical training and supervision when learning how to conduct this type of behavior-modification technique. However, learning how to conduct exposure will add a highly effective tool to your therapeutic tool chest, so I strongly recommend taking the time to get trained.

Cognitive-Modification Strategies

Therapy also needs to address client beliefs that contribute to drug use behavior if a client is going to successfully change that behavior. Because of the power of thoughts and beliefs to influence future behavior, cognitive modification strategies should be used to address thoughts, perceptions, and emotions related to drug use. This would include modifying positive expectancies by use of expectancy challenges; thinking about the natural consequences of drug use behavior before actually engaging in it; learning how to problem solve and plan ahead; and altering distorted perceptions and thoughts through the use of other strategies such as imagery, meditation, urge surfing, and thought stopping, all of which will be discussed in the following sections.

Expectancy Challenges

Your clients' positive expectancies about drug use could present a roadblock to behavior change. It will be crucial to teach your clients how to challenge these expectancies in a variety of ways. One method involves simply presenting information to your clients that may contradict or refute the existing beliefs they have about the effects of drugs. When doing this, though, you must be very careful not to lecture or preach. Use a motivational interviewing style in order to present these facts in a disarming way. Try not to put the client on the defensive by saying "you" or "your" beliefs, but instead make the presentation more impersonal by saying "some people believe that drugs have this effect, but the research has shown that is not true." You may wish to assign readings to your clients that present these facts in an objective and nonjudgmental way, so that the assigned readings, rather than you, are disputing the clients' views.

Additionally, other types of cognitive-modification strategies can effectively challenge expectancies. One strategy, called *hypothesis testing,* teaches your client to view his or her belief as a hypothesis that needs to be examined rather than an unquestionable fact. A related modification strategy, called *data collection,* teaches your client to gather evidence to support and refute his or her beliefs about drug use. For example, if your client has a certain belief about drug use, ask him or her to find a way to test whether that belief is really true. Sometimes you can do this by having the client walk through past experiences to see whether those experiences support the belief. Frequently they do not, which is exactly the point of this exercise. Another way to gather data and test a hypothesis involves having the client discuss all the evidence in favor of the targeted belief, but then to turn around and have the client discuss all the evidence that refutes the belief as well. This strategy allows the client to see both sides of the argument about the belief to determine its truthfulness. Finally, you may want to ask your client to determine how frequently what he or she believes to be true actually happens in real life. In this way, you get the client to see that a belief about drug use may be partially true, but not always. This is an especially good one to use when addressing beliefs about the positive effects of drug use (e.g., the high may be good sometimes but not all the time).

Examining Consequences

A second important cognitive-modification technique involves examining consequences. One way to do this is to ask your client to examine the consequences of believing certain things or behaving in a certain way. For example, have your client examine how her or his beliefs about drug use lead her or him to act in certain ways. In addition, the therapist or counselor may ask the client to imagine how her or his behavior would be different if she or he thought differently about this situation. This exercise can illustrate to the client how her or his behavior is being governed to a large degree by what she or he believes about drug use, and that, if the client simply changes the way she or he thinks, then the behavioral outcomes may become radically different. Some clients find great hope in such an exercise, as well as a sense that they can liberate themselves simply by changing their thoughts.

Another helpful exercise asks the client to walk through a behavior chain to its natural consequences. Many times a client will act without thinking about what the eventual outcome of such an act might be. For example, a client may tell you that he wants to visit a friend at the friend's home. You remember this is one of the client's friends that he used to smoke marijuana with. The behavior itself may seem very harmless to the client on the surface, and the perception of risk very low. You may want to ask the client to walk down this path so that he can see what eventualities may be ahead — consequences he may not perceive when first thinking about the visit. By walking down the path ("So what happens after you step inside your friend's house?") and then continuing down it ("Then what may happen, and what may happen after that. . . ?"), the client may eventually see that the friend may act in ways that could tempt him to smoke, events that he had not considered when simply thinking about "stopping by to see my friend." Having the client walk down the full length of the behavior chain allows her or him to see a likely risky outcome to what initially seemed like an innocent act.

Problem Solving and Planning Ahead

In my experience, one of the most difficult things to learn for clients who have drug problems is how to effectively solve problems and plan ahead. Therapists and counselors must not assume that clients have these abilities when entering into treatment, and may want to assess problem-solving and planning abilities as a part of therapy. If these abilities are not apparent, you will want to teach your client how to do these things. The inability to solve a problem places a person at risk for coping ineffectively, which may lead to drug use as an escape from the problem. As you may remember, in Chapter 3 I described a strategy for teaching clients how to problem solve by specifically defining the problem, brainstorming solutions, and selecting the most appropriate solution to solve the problem. Make sure that your client knows how to conceptualize and solve problems in this very systematic way.

> "We are continually faced with a series of great opportunities brilliantly disguised as insoluble problems."
>
> — JOHN W. GARDNER

In addition, train your client to think ahead by setting goals and mapping strategies for how to reach those goals. Have your clients learn to outline plans for how to get from the present to where they want to be in the future with regard to these goals, and what logical sequence of events needs to happen to reach the goal. Many clients are uncertain how to plan ahead and find it very difficult to know where and how to start to reach a goal. Teaching your client how to outline a plan for reaching a particular goal will be critical. You can use the treatment plan as a model with the client to illustrate how to develop such an outline, but also use it to teach the client how to systematically and periodically evaluate progress and make midcourse corrections needed to reach desired long-term outcomes.

Imagery

Another cognitive-modification technique, called *imagery,* is used primarily to improve self-efficacy or to relax. Imagery allows the client to imagine situations in session. Imagery differs from imaginal exposure since the goal of imagery is not to be exposed to an uncomfortable situation. In fact, imagery has virtually the opposite goal, as you will discover. Imagery can be guided in session by a counselor or therapist, who instructs the client to close his or her eyes, and then tells the client to concentrate on a particular situation or setting being described by the counselor or therapist. However, eventually the counselor or therapist will want to teach the client to guide his or her own imagery, so that the client can use this tool in real-world situations.

Imagery can be used to effectively increase the client's self-efficacy. Imagery used in this manner focuses on imagining situations in which the client is able to perform a specific task or solve a problem successfully, or negotiate a high-risk situation without using drugs. This type of imagery allows clients to imagine succeeding at tasks and experience how that feels, so that they begin to develop confidence in their ability to succeed at these tasks under real-world conditions. The counselor or therapist reinforces the imagined success, which encourages the client to use the behavior successfully in real life. Imagery used in this way can be a great confidence-builder for a client.

Another important use for imagery in session involves teaching your client how to relax. Imagery can be used to take your client to a quiet and peaceful place in her or his mind whenever she or he feels stressed. Counselors and therapists teach their clients to create such safe places to which they can return when they need stress relief . In other situations clients can be taught how to take minivacations by imagining they are in different places, such as in Hawaii on a beach, or in a place that may have special meaning to them. Developing the imagery may require imagining sounds, smells, and other sensations beyond merely imagining a scene. Sometimes the imagery can be done in conjunction with various types of meditation. Using imagery in this way helps the client develop the ability to check out of stress in a healthy way, a skill she or he likely will use many times outside your office.

One particular type of imagery, called *urge surfing,* is a technique used for distress tolerance and relapse prevention. Urge surfing encourages the client to imagine drug cravings like an ocean wave that may swell up but eventually will subsides This imagery allows clients to see cravings as temporary discomfort rather than as an insurmountable and intolerable condition. More will be said about this technique in Chapter 7.

Meditative Practices Including Mindfulness

Meditation can be used effectively as a cognitive-modification technique to aid in changing drug problems. Meditation generally includes a strong *mindfulness* component, which teaches clients how to stay focused on the present moment rather than worrying about the future or fretting about the past. Meditation hones concentration skills that may benefit the client greatly in solving problems and making plans. In addition, the client can use meditation to alter his or her perception of reality without resorting to chemicals; and because of this change of perception, it may allow the client to view problems as not insurmountable or situations as being not so intolerable as first imagined. Meditation can help clients place things in perspective, an important skill for people who are changing drug problems.

Sometimes therapists practice meditation themselves and can instruct clients on the basics. However, it may be more desirable that the client find a teacher in a nontherapeutic setting so that the meditation training can continue uninterrupted after therapy has ended. In some cases a recommendation to attend an intensive meditation retreat may be a good way to help the client to start learning these skills.

Thought Stopping

Sometimes the client faces ruminative or obsessive thought processes that hinder progress. The client may find his or her mind wandering, spinning, or racing out of control with negative thoughts that are not helpful. Sometimes the thoughts may be related to regrets or past shortcomings, and in other instances the thoughts may be related to self-inflicted put-downs or doubts. Counselors and therapists should teach clients how to stop such destructive thoughts in their tracks.

Teaching thought stopping represents one way to help clients freeze those harmful thoughts before their toxicity can harm progress. In thought stopping, the client learns to literally stop the thoughts right then and there in a dramatic fashion. One way to do so involves saying the word *stop!* out loud when she or he notices rumination or obsession in action. Sometimes the client may have to say *stop!* in a dramatic way to break the chain of thoughts. Sometimes it will be sufficient for the client to simply imagine the letters S-T-O-P, or to imagine seeing a stop sign or stoplight in his or her mind that breaks the cycle of negative thoughts. Instruct the client to throw up a cue to stop the cycle of thoughts when she or he is obsessing or ruminating and to do something different after the stop has been thrown into place.

An example might be when a client ruminates about a regret she has about past drug use. You teach her that once she catches herself engaging in this type of thinking, she must say *stop!* out loud (if she is at home) and, if the thoughts are potent, maybe even slam a book down on a table as she does so in order to distract her from the chain of thoughts. (You can teach her to imagine the S-T-O-P silently if she is out in public.) After the stop is thrown into place, teach her to go do something else. So, for instance, she might want to take a walk outside if she is in the house. The point is to break the thought pattern by whatever means necessary, including use of distraction, and to engage in a new activity.

Modifying Other Kinds of Thinking Errors

Other kinds of misperceptions and errant beliefs cause trouble for people with drug problems. Since drug use often involves behavior that would naturally hinder a person's ability to think clearly about life circumstances, it likely is no

THINGS TO REMEMBER

Psychological Tools for Changing a Drug Problem

- Self-monitoring
- Shaping and contingency management
- Cue exposure and response prevention
- Expectancy challenges
- Hypothesis testing and data collection
- Previewing the natural consequences to the behavior chain
- Problem solving and planning ahead
- Imagery
- Meditation
- Urge surfing
- Thought stopping
- Challenging thinking errors
- Accurate estimation of threat
- Assessing the realistic outcome
- Alternative ways of thinking
- Skills training
- Psychoeducation
- Alternative activities
- Support groups

surprise that many people with drug problems make errors in the way they interpret reality and their places in it. This kind of distorted thinking can become habitual and presents a challenge that can interfere with successful treatment outcomes. Therapists and counselors will likely want to assess for and intervene upon the following errors in thinking if their clients are engaging in them.

All-or-Nothing Thinking

The first type of thinking error involves engaging in what is called *all-or-nothing thinking* but also can be thought of as black-and-white or rigid thinking patterns. This type of cognitive pattern is problematic because it limits the client's choice to only one or two options, both which are generally unpleasant. People with drug problems in particular may have problems with this type of thinking error because psychoactive substances can reduce the capacity for abstraction. The reduced ability to abstract may cause the client to see fewer options when placed in situations in which she or he may have to solve problems or make choices. As you can imagine, all-or-nothing thinking errors, which narrow options in life, can cause the client to feel trapped in a problem or even to dig in his or her heels when confronted with change and uncertainty.

As a therapist or counselor, you will need to assess for any evidence that your client is thinking in this way. The client's language generally will expose this type of thinking error: using words and phrases such as *all, every, always, never, nothing ever, no other choice,* or *only one way* is one clue to such an error. Your job as a therapist or counselor is to increase client awareness of the number of choices that are available. There are different strategies for doing this. As a first strategy, you could ask your client to consider what other people might see as an option, or how other people might view the problem or situation. This strategy increases options by inviting the client to see another point of view. A second strategy encourages the client to describe what kind of advice he or she would give to a friend in a similar situation. This strategy has the advantage of taking away the perception of personal limits by focusing the problem or situation on someone else. If the client provides new solutions for another person, you can use that information to challenge the client to consider that those options might work for him or her, too.

Anticipating a Negative or Poor Outcome

A second type of thinking error that can hinder progress is *anticipating a negative outcome.* When engaging in this thinking error, people believe that an event will likely have a lousy outcome most of the time. If something nice does happen instead, then the person believes it must have been a fluke or else fully expects the other shoe to fall soon. Anticipating a negative outcome causes a client to be pessimistic about chances for changing drug use, or may even set the client up for relapse because of a belief in a poor outcome. This kind of thinking error commonly occurs with people who are depressed or anxious, disorders that commonly co-occur with a drug problem.

Anticipating a negative outcome can be expressed in three different ways. First, clients may engage in what cognitive therapists call *fortunetelling,* which means that they believe they know for certain what the outcome of an event will be (and it is usually not good). This type of error leads clients toward inertia, because it seems fruitless to try to cope since the outcome appears to be failure. You may wish to use the following strategies to modify this type of error. First, you can ask the client to determine how often he or she has been in the situation in the past, and then how often the outcome has been negative. Frequently the client will discover that the odds are not as bad as they anticipate for a poor outcome, and that in fact the odds may favor a neutral or even positive outcome. Second, you may wish to challenge the client to tell you *how* she or he knows the outcome (the future), then perhaps have the client test the assumption of a poor outcome. This may have the effect of challenging him or her to move forward in spite of the prediction of doom by collecting personal data on a real-life outcome rather than simply guessing that the future will be unpleasant. Some cognitive therapists call this *hypothesis testing,* which means teaching clients to test their assumptions about outcomes just as scientists do.

Second, the client can expect a negative outcome by engaging in what cognitive therapists call *catastrophizing,* which means expecting that the worst possible thing that can happen, will happen. To combat catastrophizing, therapists and counselors want to ask clients what they imagine is the worst thing that can happen, in order to get the worst possible outcome on the table. That question should be followed by, "What is the best possible outcome?" This question allows clients to view a range of outcomes for perspective, rather than merely focusing on the negative. Finally, ask the client, "What is the most *realistic* outcome?" which of course usually falls somewhere in the middle.

Third, related to catastrophizing, another form of anticipating a negative outcome is called *overestimation of threat,* which occurs when clients assume that the likelihood of a bad outcome is much greater than reality would suggest. In addition to the questions previously suggested to challenge catastrophizing, you will want to have the client determine how frequently this anticipated negative outcome has happened in the past versus when it did not occur. For example, the client may believe that the probability for a poor outcome in this particular situation may be somewhere in the neighborhood of 80–90% at first. But if you challenge the client to consider how many times in the past he or she has been in the situation, then determine how many times the predicted negative outcome has occurred in the past, you will likely end up with a much smaller ratio than 80–90% of the time. Frequently the realistic probability dwarfs what the client initially believes because he or she has exaggerated the threat of the poor outcome in his or her mind.

Discounting the Positive

A third type of thinking error that may interfere with changing a drug problem is called *discounting the positive.* When clients engage in this type of thinking error, they generally ignore or refute evidence that supports the idea that positive events or changes are happening to them. Frequently this type of thinking error can be detected in a client's language. You as a therapist may point out something positive to your client in session, but a client engaging in this thinking error may respond by saying, "Yes, but. . . ." At other times the client may have problems accepting a compliment or may express suspicion when one is given, or may verbally diminish the impact or importance of a positive event. This behavior may cause the client to discount positive or reinforcing experiences related to drug behavior change, which can adversely influence motivation and commitment to continue making changes over time.

To counter this thinking error, ask the client to come up with alternative explanations (other than one discounting the experience) for how he or she could interpret the compliment or the event. If the client has trouble doing this, ask how another person might interpret the compliment, the positive outcome, or the reinforcer being discounted. Another strategy involves having clients examine the consequences of believing the way they do (discussed earlier this chapter), and then following the suggested strategy for altering perceptions in order to alter outcomes. Finally, the therapist or counselor may want to play the devil's advocate if the therapeutic alliance seems strong (see Chapter 3) and agree with the client that the negative interpretation probably is the correct one, and maybe extend or exaggerate that negative interpretation to the point that it sounds ridiculous. In using the devil's-advocate strategy, you hope that you will nudge an ambivalent client toward taking the positive side of the argument (since you are taking the negative side). In effect, by discounting the positive more than your client is, you may find your client discounting the negative just to spite you!

Emotional Reasoning

Emotional reasoning, a fourth thinking error that may hinder changing a drug problem, occurs when a person decides something must be true simply because it feels like it must be true. Emotional reasoning places intuition above evidence, and the client often uses circular reasoning to perpetuate these types of errors. Sometimes a client's language will be a tip-off. For example, your client may share with you a particular perception or belief she has that seems to come out of left field, in your opinion. You ask your client why she believes that, and she responds, "Because, I just know it is true." This type of reasoning, based more upon gut feelings rather than real-world information, can cause clients problems if the misinformation makes them vulnerable to a risky drug use situation, to making an error in an interpersonal relationship, or to underestimating the risk involved with behaving in a certain way. Again, hypothesis testing and data collection can be important strategies to get the client to consider whether the ideas really have some validity. In addition, you may wish to ask the client to consider alternative interpretations or ways of thinking about the situation by asking how someone else might interpret the event.

Labels That Trap Clients

Labeling, a fifth thinking error that causes problems for someone trying to change a drug problem, occurs when the client labels him- or herself in a way that stigmatizes or suggests little hope for change. One example of such a label would be calling oneself a black sheep. Recall from Chapter 1 that labels can be helpful or harmful, and that the difference depends on whether the label helps identify solutions to the problem. Considering oneself a black sheep can help make sense of past behavior and interpret past relationships with others, but continuing to think of oneself as a black sheep may lead to continuing to act like a black sheep.

It would be better if the person would reframe such a label from *black sheep* to *black sheep no longer.* This example illustrates one way a therapist or counselor can help a client with this type of thinking error, by prompting him or her to reframe labels in a way that provides for a more positive interpretation of behavior and potentially suggests a more positive outcome in the future. Labeling can contribute to following *life scripts* that may lead to poor outcomes for clients. In other people, the label may suggest a fatalistic attitude that change is unlikely, and that fate (the label) controls the outcomes. The label may contribute to a self-fulfilling prophecy that does not bode well for the client. Other great examples of labels that may need to be modified include *junkie* or *drug addict.* The reframes for these labels that would help your client are *junkie no more* or *drug addict no longer.*

Negative-Thinking Filter

Negative-thinking filters are a sixth type of thinking error that can hinder progress in treatment or therapy. This type of thinking problem commonly occurs among people who are depressed and anxious, but also is frequently seen among people with drug problems. With negative-thinking filters, the client actively looks for bad things to happen to her or him, rather than actively looking for the good or even for a balance between good and not so good. People engaging in this type of thinking error often scan the environment for negatives, meaning they selectively attend to cues in the environment that support the view that bad things are happening to them, that they are cursed, or that life has dealt them an unfair hand, rather than looking for the positive. Among drug users, you may see the client actively ignoring signs of progress or even overlooking evidence of new joy or successes occurring as a result of therapy. The counselor or therapist working with such a client will want to make assignments so that the client focuses on the positive, gathers evidence to support the idea that good things are occurring, and learns to challenge the thinking error with evidence that disputes the perception that only negative things are happening to her or him. The therapist or counselor may assign observational homework to collect real-life data to work toward this end, as well as develop lists that focus on gathering evidence that positive things are happening to the client.

Perfectionism can be one result of such a thinking error, since perfectionists often scan for negatives in other people. Perfectionism makes intimacy difficult, since the other person never quite stacks up to the expectations of the perfectionist. In clients, perfectionism can cause problems with interpersonal relationships. Perfectionism often harms the client, as well, since life and other people are doomed to fall short of such lofty expectations. Cognitive exercises for treating perfectionism include hypothesis testing and data collecting to test whether the assumptions held by the client are reasonable, and probability testing to assess whether the expectations are likely to occur as the client predicts. In addition, an interesting behavior-modification strategy would be to assign a client to intentionally make public mistakes (that will not harm the client or others) for a certain period of time. The client records or monitors emotions and thoughts related to this exercise of making mistakes, and then those observations are discussed in session. The goal of this exercise is to moderate the high expectations on others and the personal need to aspire to perfection.

Mind Reading

A seventh type of thinking error that adversely affect the course of therapy is referred to as a *mind-reading error.* Clients commit this type of error when they believe that they know what others are thinking or feeling in the absence of any hard data. People with drug problems often use this type of thinking error to perpetuate thoughts about feeling unwanted, excluded, or isolated from others, including family, friends, and even the larger society. Mind reading leads to many unspoken assumptions on the part of clients, assumptions that often translate into sometimes erratic and unpredictable responses in social situations. Frequently a mind-reading error is speculative and without any data to support it. Therapists and counselors can teach clients to challenge these errant assumptions by testing them. Clients can be taught to treat such assumptions as hypotheses that need to be tested, and to collect data that either support or refute these hypotheses. The weight of evidence can be examined in session to determine what it suggests about the truth of the assumptions. In addition, the therapist may wish to ask the client, "What is another way to interpret this situation?" or "What is an alternative way of thinking about this issue?" or perhaps "How do you think another person such as (insert a name or role) might interpret this same situation?" The idea is to open the client's mind by indicating that his or her interpretation is but one of several that can be made. Especially if the client with a drug problem uses mind reading to self-isolate, it will be very important for his or her counselor to teach the client to challenge these thoughts.

Overgeneralization

Overgeneralization, the eighth type of thinking error that can cause problems for a person attempting to change a drug problem, involves making sweeping conclusions drawn from scant evidence. The person making this type of error usually makes a sweeping negative conclusion as a result of inductive rather than deductive reasoning about situations or circumstances. Something small may happen to the person, who then takes that event and draws universal conclusions. For example, a person with a drug problem may try once to get a job, not get it, and then decide that he or she cannot or will not get a job, ever. Such a sweeping generalization contributes to a sense of hopelessness that can thwart progress in treatment or therapy.

Counselors and therapists must contain overgeneralizations from their clients when they engage in this type of thinking process. Many times a sweeping generalization can take on a life of its own, like a runaway freight train. The goal is to slow and calm the person, and then get him or her to focus on the very specific situation (rather than the generalization) by asking him or her to describe the event in very specific terms and descriptors. So rather than letting the client jump to the conclusion that no job is possible, get the client to focus on the interview and what happened only in this event, with the idea that there may be other explanations (e.g., the job was already filled, or the client sought a job outside of his or her area of vocational skill, or perhaps the client interviewed poorly or had a poorly designed résumé in hand). Another method to address an overgeneralization error would be to ask whether there may be an alternative way to interpret or think about the event.

Overgeneralization thinking errors are commonly observed among people who have phobias. Since drug users may have co-occurring Social Phobia, Agoraphobia, or other types of fears, this type of thinking error may be one to assess for when working with a new client who you suspect has a co-occurring phobia.

Maladaptive Thoughts

A ninth type of thinking error is not necessary an error at all, but represents a way of thinking that may be true (or partially true) but not helpful. These thoughts are called *maladaptive.* Maladaptive thoughts often contribute to rumination or to obsessive thoughts. *Rumination,* generally associated with depression or anxiety, can be defined as an endless stream of negative thoughts that spin around in a person's mind like hamsters on a treadmill. *Obsessive thoughts,* usually associated with anxiety, represent persistent worry or unwanted thoughts related about a very specific item or area of one's life. Among people with drug problems,

CASE STUDY

What Are You Thinking, Theresa?

Theresa is meeting with her therapist. One of her homework assignments was to seek out and interview for a job during the last week. Her therapist, Janice, is asking her how it went. Theresa begins with, "It's useless. I went on this interview and it's clear to me that I'm not going to get a job."

Janice replies, "So what makes you say that?"

Theresa continues, "I could tell by the way that she was looking at me when I entered the room for the interview that she didn't like me. In fact, I'm sure that will be true at other interviews, too. People just don't like me."

Janice asks, "What *did* go well during the interview?"

Theresa says, "Well, she said that I had the right skills for the job, but they didn't have any openings right now. But, you know, she was just saying that. I can tell this just isn't going to work. Face it; I will never get a job at this rate."

Can you identify Theresa's thinking errors? What would you do to challenge those errors?

rumination generally presents through regrets about past mistakes or lost opportunities, and obsessive thoughts usually are associated with drug use behavior.

The challenge with changing maladaptive thoughts is that they may be partially true. The problem is that the client spends an inordinate amount of time and energy focusing on things that may be true but likely cannot be changed. Under these circumstances, it is useful for the client to learn the "Serenity Prayer" to remind him or her that there are some things that cannot be changed, and for unchangeable things the solution is acceptance of the situation. However, acceptance is not the final step, because it must be followed with behavioral activation to cope in spite of the unchangeable events or facts. In essence, you want to teach the client to accept the things that cannot be changed, but not to use acceptance as an excuse for inertia or to avoid progress in other related areas. Teaching a client distress-tolerance skills (see the Skills Training section later in this chapter) also can be helpful under these circumstances, but again the goal should be behavior change in spite of these unchangeable circumstances.

In addition, a client engaging in maladaptive thinking usually blows the threat out of proportion. As an example, the client may have concerns about certain situations that may cause him to freeze in therapy. In order to get the client moving again, you must challenge him to consider, "What is the most likely outcome?" and "What is the realistic probability that this maladaptive way of thinking will harm me permanently?" As another example, the client may have serious concerns about the survival of a relationship, and there is evidence that supports those concerns. A client may be tempted to check out of therapy at that point. You as the counselor or therapist will have to refocus the client. One way to do so is to have the client determine likely outcomes. One assumption by the client is that he or she will be unable to survive the broken relationship, which gives you a place to intervene as a therapist. The broken relationship may be a probable outcome, but it does not mean that the client's life will be over (as she or he may believe). Under these circumstances, focusing excessively on the possibility of the breakup hinders therapy, so the client needs to be directed toward acceptance, and then towards behavior change in spite of the distress.

Shoulds Versus Wants: Rule-Governed Behavior

A tenth type of thinking error involves the content behind *should* or *must* statements. Should or must statements are detected in a client when she or he acts in a certain way because of a personal rule about life. Personal rules often develop as a result of personal experiences; in some cases, rules about life are taught to or indoctrinated into the client by others. The problem is not necessarily the rules so much as their rigidity of application. A rule may have been functional (or helpful to the client) in the past, but no longer functions well in the present; or a rule may be functional in some situations but not if applied universally, as some clients will do. Some examples of rules might include "I have to be perfect" or "I have to take care of (fill in the name or role)" or perhaps "It is my obligation to do this." The language is usually a tip-off for such a rule, and you can spot such rules when a client uses the words *should* or *must*. Problems arise when these rules cause clients to be miserable under their bonds, when the rules are viewed as valid without exceptions, or when the rules set the client up to fall short or fail.

Many cognitive therapists have found that when clients confuse *shoulds* in life with *wants* they are contributing to their own misery. Clients may be operating with a wide variety of assumptions, or rules about life, that may cause personal hardship and life problems because the rules being used to guide behavior do not lead to healthy choices. Help your clients to sort through their personal rules. Have them examine the rules not as absolute truths about life but rather as options or choices, so that clients have the capacity to alter the rules to make them reasonable and attainable. The goal may be not to replace the rule, but rather to make it less binding or rigid. Helping clients see that personal rules can be modified may help them see the world in less rigid ways.

Another way to change a rule is to make it into an ideal rather than an absolute should. You can help your client reformulate a rule so that it is not so rigidly binding on the person, so that he or she can see it as an ideal goal for a situation but not an absolute demand. For someone who is a perfectionist, the goal may be to use cognitive-modification strategies to encourage the client to change the rule from an absolute "I should not make mistakes" to an ideal goal of "I will try to do my best."

The shoulds in life often contribute to what is called *rule-governed behavior,* meaning simply that the person acts a certain way because of the rules, not because he or she necessarily wants to act that way. Rule-governed behavior can cause difficulties since behavior is perceived as an obligation rather than a choice. People with drug problems who feel obligated to act a certain way can get into trouble when the rule-governed behavior results in strong negative emotions (remembering Chapter 1). Rule-governed behavior can cause a person to feel resentful (abiding by shoulds rather than what the person wants out of life), guilty (if the obligations are not met), or unhappy (if the obligations are unfulfilling). Any of these strong negative emotions may be potential triggers for drug use.

The first step is to identify the rules that are causing the resentment, guilt, or unhappiness. When these have been labeled, therapy can focus on modifying the rules in a way that liberates the client from the obligations and converts the shoulds to wants. In some cases, the obligation cannot be realistically replaced, but it can be modified to be less restrictive and rigid — to be an ideal goal. In these instances, obligation can be balanced by realistic expectations and by restoring some of the client's freedom to choose. Sometimes examining the rule that governs the behavior in therapy will reveal that the rule may have developed from another type of thinking error, such as all-or-nothing thinking. Maybe the rule has been distorted, and by using a combination of the cognitive-modification strategies mentioned earlier in this chapter, the therapist or counselor can allow clients to see other alternative ways of thinking and acting that may leave parts of their rules intact and functioning better for them.

Skills Training

Of course, behavior and cognitive modification are not meant to be mutually exclusive endeavors in therapy. Behavior- and cognitive-modification strategies can be combined as a one-two punch to aid your clients in changing drug problems. Many times, behavior patterns and thought patterns cannot be easily separated, and often behavior and thoughts seem to interact in complex ways. Using various combinations of behavior- and cognitive-modification strategies to change drug use patterns helps you develop sophisticated and relevant individualized treatment plans for your clients.

The most common intersection of behavior modification with cognitive modification occurs in the area of training new skills. *Skills training* begins with assessing the current level of client skills to determine whether he or she has the skills necessary to successfully cope with a particular situation or successfully complete a particular task without drug use. Obvious clues that a client may not have good skills in a particular area may include evidence that your client may have failed in the past under similar conditions, or that the client may have avoided coping with such a situation in the past. A second set of clues may be within-session evidence, failure to cope well in session with you during a role-play, or problems in interpersonal behavior while interacting with other treatment clients. Finally, as mentioned in Chapter 4, the client may show signs of skill deficits during an assessment, such as the Situational Competence Test, or may respond slowly and vaguely when attempting to solve a particular problem in session.

If the skills are present but the client still is not succeeding, then a second consideration is whether the problem may be a misapplication of skills. Sometimes clients may have the skills necessary to succeed, but fail at applying those skills at the appropriate moment or in the appropriate way. If your client knows how to cope successfully with a particular situation in session but still shows signs of not being able to respond successfully outside session, then you should suspect a problem not with lack of skills but with their application.

The answers that you uncover via these two sets of assessments will dictate what you should do with your client. If the skills are absent, then you teach the skills. If the skills are present but not being used appropriately in the situation being analyzed, you must train the client to understand how to use the already present skills under the conditions being analyzed. Perhaps your client misfires by not picking up on cues that suggest it is time to use these skills. In this case, you teach your client how to identify these cues. Perhaps the client misfires because he or she does not understand that this situation is similar to another that he or she would know automatically how to respond to effectively. Under these circumstances, show your client how this particular situation is similar to the other situation, so the client understands that she or he should respond in the same way. Perhaps your client misfires because risk is misperceived. In this instance, you must elevate the client's awareness of risk in this particular situation.

Finally, generalization of skills will help to circumvent the problem of misapplication of skills. The client may learn a set of skills in session, but there is no guarantee that the client can generate those skills once outside of session, and especially under stressful conditions in the real world outside of therapy. In order to ensure that the client learns how to use these skills outside therapy, the counselor or therapist must make sure the client practices using the skills in different situations in and outside sessions.

Homework assignments are the best way to generalize skills learned in session to situations outside therapy. Assign your client to practice what she or he learned today with you in session in various situations outside therapy. Check on homework progress during the next session, first thing. Evaluate whether the client puts these skills into practice across a wide variety of real-world conditions, and whether he or she succeeds when using the skills. Finally, use the reinforcement principles discussed earlier in this chapter, and encourage the movement from extrinsic reinforcement for successfully using these skills to intrinsic reinforcement. Helping the client see the benefits of the new behavioral skills outside therapy will aid in this process. If the client can see the personal benefits for practicing these new skills, then it is likely that she or he will use them more often and in more diverse real-world situations over time.

Clients may have difficulties with one or multiple types of skill set. The type of coping problem the client experiences can suggest what kind of skill set that you may need to teach. First, clients who cannot care for themselves or cannot do basic tasks in their lives may have deficits in *average daily living skills (ADLs)*. ADLs are the basic skill sets that most of us take for granted, but we should not take it for granted that they exist in our clients. Some examples include whether your client knows how to shower, keep and balance a checkbook register, read and write, take medicines as prescribed, prepare and cook food, go shopping, drive, and other basic skills like these that may be important to know in order to cope with our society on a daily basis. A second and related type of skill set involves the ability to reach vocational goals, which of course concerns whether the client has the skills necessary to get and keep a job. Does your client know how to create a résumé, to interview well, and to dress appropriately for work? Finally, a third and related skill set concerns whether a client knows how to stay healthy by exercising or eating right. Each of these basic skill sets is often assumed to be present but may not be in some of our clients.

In addition to these ADLs, there are many other types of skill sets that may be missing among our clients that we may need to teach to them. First, clients may not have the skill sets necessary to tolerate distressing situations that cannot be avoided or changed. Skills used to negotiate these difficult situations are referred to as *distress-tolerance skills*. Meditation and imagery are examples of distress-tolerance skills, but there are others. For example, you may want to teach your client how to pamper her- or himself under distressing conditions, perhaps by taking a warm shower or bath. One distressing situation that may be helped by the use of alternative pleasurable activities such as these is the need to tolerate cravings. In other instances, you may wish to teach the client how to use *distraction* as a means to tolerating a distressing situation. You might want to teach a client how to self-distract while in the middle of an argument or while having a negative thought, or when experiencing a craving or chronic pain. Distraction techniques often involve engaging in activities such as complex puzzles and problem-solving activities, counting things, doing something different, thought stopping, or even inflicting a different kind of discomfort to forget the current one. For example, one distraction technique that can be quite effective is to have clients hold ice in their hands until cravings go away (it usually does not take very long before the ice begins to hurt the hand, which of course is the point!).

An important exception is that you do not want to teach your client to use distraction skills when engaging in cue-exposure experiences. As mentioned earlier, exposure requires experiencing some discomfort in order for the client to become desensitized to the drug-related cues. Since some distress-tolerance skills may involve distraction, they should not be used during cue exposure or used by clients to avoid exposure exercises.

Relaxation training can be very helpful to clients. There are a variety of techniques that can be used to help clients relax. The first is called *progressive muscle relaxation*. In this technique, a client is taught how to tell the difference between when her or his muscles are tensed and when the muscles are relaxed. The method for doing this procedure is to have the client contract each individual set of muscle groups for 10 to 15 seconds to feel tension, then to relax those muscle groups for the same amount of time to sense relaxation. In some cases you may wish to repeat this contraction and relaxation phase a second time before moving to the next muscle group. Teach the client to begin by contracting fingers, and then progressively work up the different muscle groups in the arms, then the shoulders, neck, and face, then down through the trunk, legs, feet, and toes. The idea is to tense and relax each muscle group in the body so that the client learns to relax muscle groups automatically on command. Eventually, a client can be given a verbal command (such as "relax") and the client will be able to relax all muscle groups without going through the contract-and-relax procedure. Your clients may even be able to generate this relaxation on their own without your prompting if you have done your work well.

Breathing retraining represents another highly effective way to relax. Anxiety and stress cause many people to breathe improperly, experiencing rapid and shallow breathing, having inconsistent respiration cycles, or even holding their breath for a period of time when stressed. This irregular breathing pattern can cause physiological changes that can increase anxiety. In addition, many times poor breathing habits cause misuse of muscles not meant to be involved in breathing at all, and therefore may contribute to chest and back pain. So the benefits to breathing retraining involve not only relaxation, but also reduction of tension and possibly reduction of muscle pain.

In breathing retraining, you want to teach your client how to breathe at a regular, adult resting respiration rate by counting the length of the breath and consciously controlling how the breath is drawn. In the counting portion of this exercise, you instruct your client to draw a breath smoothly in over a 1-2-3 count, then exhale smoothly over a 1-2-3 count. The counting regulates the number of breaths per minute to around the resting respiration target number for adults. The counting can be quite meditative and relaxing for many people.

Controlling the way the breath is drawn can reduce muscle pain and promote the use of the proper muscles for breathing. Have your client put a hand on his or her chest and show how his or her breathing causes the chest to move. Then instruct your client that proper breathing involves very little movement of the chest. The stomach muscles (diaphragm) should be drawing the air in and moving it out instead of the chest muscles. Have your client put a hand on the stomach, and teach him or her to breathe by moving the stomach and not the chest area. Watch to make sure he or she is breathing with minimal movement of the chest area. One analogy that can be helpful for some clients is to think of the diaphragm as a vacuum that sucks the air down into the stomach area without any movement of chest muscles at all. Have your client practice drawing breath without moving the chest together with the meditative counting, and then assign this technique as homework so that the client can practice using this outside session.

In addition, many clients find that alternative activities such as walking and exercising can increase relaxation and reduce stress. Similarly, some clients may find yoga to be relaxing, and you may want to suggest this option to a client. Others find relaxation through engaging in a new hobby or returning to one that they may have let get away because of drug use. As a counselor or therapist, you want to make sure that the client has skills to reduce stress and increase relaxation before treatment or therapy ends. Some larger treatment facilities offer recreational therapy as part of the treatment experience, and may even have a recreational therapist on staff. A recreational therapist serves as a great resource, because such a therapist can assess the client for recreational skills, and make recommendations for changes to the client that will enhance the client's fitness level while providing outlets for stress release.

> "The foolish man lies awake all night
> Thinking of his many problems;
> When the morning comes he is worn out
> And his trouble is just as it was."
>
> — NORSE PROVERB

Insomnia can be a common problem for people when first changing a drug problem. Sleeping problems can be related to the rebound effects of the drugs, or may be related to rumination and regret. Since insomnia is common, therapists and counselors will likely want to teach their clients how they can reduce the duration of this potentially uncomfortable problem. To orient the client, the counselor or therapist will want to emphasize to the client that insomnia is not life threatening, and that eventually he or she will sleep. This orientation is meant to put the client at ease about the condition, because anxiety about not sleeping breeds greater anxiety (which of course makes it even more difficult to sleep!). Next, the therapist or counselor will want to teach different techniques the client can use when having problems sleeping at night.

First, behavior modification can help some people, so you may ask the client to monitor her or his behavior, especially in the evening, so you can determine whether your client is doing something before going to bed that might making sleeping difficult. For example, have the client monitor eating and drinking behavior in the evening to see whether food or drink (caffeinated, especially) is being consumed in close proximity to bedtime. Does she or he get up several times to use the bathroom? This activity makes it hard to relax! Also have clients monitor other behaviors prior to bedtime. Do they watch television action shows immediately prior to bed, or do they engage in some form of vigorous activity that would elevate heart rates and make it difficult to relax immediately? With this information, you may determine that the client's evening activities need to be altered in order to promote relaxation prior to bedtime.

Second, you may want to encourage clients to engage in an activity that is utterly relaxing right before going to bed. An example might be something like a warm, soaking bath. Relaxation will tend to promote sleep. Doing something stimulating before going to bed tends to work against being able to relax when preparing to sleep.

Third, speaking behaviorally, the bed must be associated with rest rather than restlessness. You will want to teach your client how, through conditioning, being in bed can become paired with the outcome of not being able to sleep, so that eventually the bed loses is ability to cue relaxation. For example, sometimes a person ends up worrying in bed, and then cannot sleep because of the worrying behavior. For some people, getting into bed eventually can become a cue to worry, and this is an unfortunate situation. At this point, behavior-modification strategies must be used to break the association between worrying and the bed itself. Under these circumstances, behavioral therapists and counselors instruct their clients that when they start to worry, they must immediately get out of bed to break that association (or behavior chain) and do something else. Some therapists recommend that worriers should keep notepads available to write down all their worried thoughts before returning to bed. Others might want to use thought-stopping techniques before returning to bed. For some clients, a long, soaking bath might be recommended. Regardless of the chosen strategy, the client should be instructed not return to bed until the worrying has stopped.

For some clients, reading in bed prevents sleeping behavior. Under these circumstances, reading may be stimulating, and being in bed gets paired with the stimulating activity of reading a book or magazine. In this case, if reading in bed is found to precede insomnia (or to occur concurrently), then the client should be instructed to read elsewhere. The same also may be true for people who watch television in bed. The goal is to make the bed a place for sleep, not a place for activities that may contribute to sleeplessness.

Fourth, distraction techniques can help clients who are doing all the right things before bed but still are having problems with insomnia. The distraction activity assigned ideally would be both complicated (to get the person's mind off other things) and boring (to put the person to sleep). One of the best forms of distraction that I have heard about is a counting strategy (not necessarily involving sheep). In using this strategy, teach your client to count backward starting at 1,000, by serial sevens. To illustrate, have your client count (not out loud) as follows: 1,000, 993, 986, 979, 972, and so on, with her or his eyes closed. As you can imagine, this counting task is complicated and boring, which provides the perfect conditions needed to encourage lights-out.

Another area in which you may need to teach clients new skills is the domain of social skills. Many of our clients have large deficits in their social skills that often contribute to their seeking socialization among drug-using peers or having problems in interpersonal relationships. For example, people with drug problems

CLIENT HANDOUT

Overcoming Insomnia

Insomnia can be overcome by using behavior- and cognitive-modification techniques.

Behavioral strategies to overcome insomnia include the following:

- Modifying your evening activities — avoiding beverages, stimulating activities, and caffeine in the evening.
- Doing something relaxing before heading to bed.
- Making sure not to make your bed a place of worry.
- Leaving a pad of paper next to your bed to write down all worrying thoughts before lying down.
- Using complex counting strategies to bore yourself to sleep.

Cognitive strategies to overcome insomnia include:

- Challenging thinking errors related to worries; evaluating the likelihood that worry will solve the problem.
- Problem solving well before bedtime; setting aside time to do so earlier in the day.
- Remembering that insomnia is not life threatening and is commonly experienced after changing a drug problem.

often have problems understanding how to communicate with others in an assertive way. Your clients may be too aggressive or too passive in social interactions, and perhaps not even realize it, which can cause all sorts of problems, including social marginalization. Aggressiveness and passivity can be huge social turn-offs. You may have to teach your clients how to be more assertive in order to circumvent relationship problems after treatment. Some clients may be shy or experience social anxiety. You can train these clients how to interact more effectively in social situations. In addition, some clients may have problems understanding, identifying, or expressing their emotions. The teaching of anger management skills is often included on the treatment plans for many clients working to overcome a drug problem.

Finally, mindfulness skills can teach clients how to concentrate or focus. The goal is to teach the client to use these techniques, which often are meditative, to learn how to focus on the present moment. Since many people with drug problems have difficulty focusing on the moment, these skills can be extremely helpful ones to learn. For example, when clients have comorbid depression or anxiety, they often find it difficult to stay in the moment. Clients with depression tend to focus on the past whereas clients with anxiety tend to focus on the future. Teaching these clients how to focus on the present can be quite useful for treating a drug problem, depression, and anxiety simultaneously. You can teach your clients how to practice mindfulness by focusing on breath or breathing, or by concentrating completely on a single object. If you have not engaged in these practices or feel uncomfortable teaching them, you may wish to encourage clients to seek out formal training in meditative techniques.

Support Groups

Many therapists and counselors like to refer their clients to *support groups* outside therapy in order to maximize the amount of social support available to a client as he or she tries to change a drug problem. In addition to the social support mentioned, support groups often will include program activities intended to prevent or reduce drug use, including psychoeducation to help their members. Support groups also may sponsor events such as dances, picnics, or other drug-free entertainment or recreational events that can help to structure clients' out-of-session time with enjoyable social activities with peers.

There are many different types of groups available to help people who may have a drug or related kind of problem. Support groups span the ideological spectrum in terms of their philosophies of recovery. The most commonly known are from the 12-step tradition, including Cocaine Anonymous (CA), Marijuana Anonymous (MA), and the already-mentioned Narcotics Anonymous (NA), although there are others that are less well known. Larger communities have multiple meetings, and their schedules can be found by calling the local community offices of these groups or by looking at their Web sites in some cases (usually in very large urban communities). Some of these groups have gone online, as a matter of fact, and you may be able to join such a group by accessing the national Web sites. The 12-step support groups tend to philosophically align themselves with the disease and spiritual models for treating a drug problem (described in the next section), but some clients who are being treated by therapists operating in other models have found help in these groups.

In addition, there are alternative support groups generally more aligned with other models for treating a drug problem. The mere fact that these groups are called "alternative" shows how pervasive traditional disease- and spirituality-based support groups have been historically, but alternatives have grown rapidly in the last few years as consumers have become more educated about different models for treating drug problems. Support groups that would fall into these categories would include Rational Recovery and SMART Recovery, and even some groups that espouse harm reduction or moderation types of goals (rather than abstinence goals). The support-group contacts are listed in Useful Resources (chapter 2, p. 84).

Helping Your Client Choose a Support Group

If you feel a support group is important to the successful treatment of your client, make sure to explain this to him or her and why you think it is important. Remember how difficult it is for anyone to go into a meeting of strangers, especially when a personal problem is involved. Inspire the client to want to attend by showing how it is in her or his best interest. Explain ahead of time what the client will likely see and experience at this meeting so it will not be a total surprise. Try to make the transition to a new group as familiar as possible. And make sure that you know the quality of the group that you are referring your client to: I have observed clients being sent into some very dysfunctional groups over the years.

In addition, make sure that the group matches well with your client's needs. Any old group does not necessarily work (remember that treatment match is very important, which likely would be true for support groups as well). Any old group might actually cause the client not to want to go to a group ever again! Matches should be made with consideration for the client's worldview and for the client's understanding of his or her drug problem. In some cases, this may be a match that will not agree with your own understanding or model. However, remember that the goal is to get the client to agree to go to a support group, and if you try to coerce a client into attending a group that will be offensive to him or her, then your client may decide not to use any support group at all. In many instances it would likely be better if he or she went to an alternative group even if it were not the one you would prefer, rather than attend no group at all.

> **"It would be naïve to think that the problems plaguing mankind today can be solved with means and methods which were applied or seemed to work in the past."**
>
> — MIKHAIL GORBACHEV

CLIENT HANDOUT

Choosing a Support Group

Choosing to attend a support group will add another weapon to your recovery arsenal for overcoming a drug problem. Support groups have helped people like you maintain changes in drug use over the long term, especially when times were tough. An important consideration is how to choose a group that is right for you. Sometimes you can determine the best fit with a group by listening to what others say about it, and then deciding whether the members of that group (and its philosophy) are a good match for you. In other cases it may be that the meeting times and proximity to your workplace or home or to public transportation may be the deciding factor as to whether a group is a good fit.

With regard to 12-step groups, there are different kinds of meetings. *Open* meetings are just that: They are open to anyone who would like to attend, including people who may not have a drug problem. *Closed* meetings, on the other hand, are limited to people who believe they have a drug problem. In addition, some groups have *speaker* meetings, meaning that one person gives a talk that may last an entire meeting. Many of these talks are meant to be inspirational about recovery. Other groups may have some restriction in membership, such as men only or women only. Usually the type of meeting will be noted the on schedule, which you can obtain from the local office of the group, from your treatment facility, or from your counselor or therapist.

Traditional 12-step groups suggest that you eventually find a *sponsor,* a peer who also is recovering from a drug problem, to help guide your recovery. Usually a sponsor agrees to have an interactive relationship with you so you can contact her or him when you want to talk, or the two of you may even decide to socialize. The sponsor is a mentor of sorts (*therapist:* see also Chapter 8) who serves as a resource as you learn how to overcome your drug problem by working the 12 steps. It is recommended that this person be of the same gender as you, have extensive time without drug use, and be working a healthy program (meaning that she or he is stable). It is not necessary to have a sponsor right away, and in fact you may wish to take your time. But it will not hurt to get phone numbers from other members if you want someone to talk with before you have a sponsor.

There are other support groups that do not use the 12-step program but utilize other techniques that can help you overcome a drug problem. Some of these groups seem to work very well for people who find it difficult to agree with the 12-step philosophy or model. In addition, a few groups are available for those of you who may not be ready to quit drug use today but may want to reduce how much you are using.

Your therapist or counselor can provide you with information from this book and other sources about different recovery theories and models. This information may help you decide which support group, if any, would benefit you. Try to match the support-group model to your conceptualization of your drug problem and how to treat it effectively. You will feel much more committed to going to a support group if you find that you agree with the basic premises of the philosophy of that group. Do not despair if the first group you attend uses ideas foreign to your way of thinking about a drug problem. There are many different groups out there with very different ideas about what to do to overcome a drug problem. I would urge you to shop for the group that best fits your needs.

Recovery Theories and Models

There are several different ways to conceive of a drug problem; how you define a drug problem will likely determine which model for recovery most appeals to you. However, highly effective and interesting techniques have been developed within each of these models, so even if a particular model does not fit your understanding of a drug problem, that model may have produced a strategy that can help your client. So I would encourage you to be open-minded as you read through the following sections.

The first and perhaps most common way to conceive of a drug problem is as a *biological condition* or *disease* that needs to be treated. Most traditional treatment centers operate using this model and teach clients that they have a disease that needs to be treated each and every day for the rest of their lives. The disease model emphasizes abstinence as the ideal goal of treatment, and treatment in this model attempts to persuade clients to remain abstinent and teaches them how to do so, primarily by confronting and breaking through denial, by psychoeducation on treating the problem, and by suggesting attendance and participation in a 12-step support group like NA (see also Chapter 2).

Disease treatment has been commonly referred to as the *Minnesota model,* in reference to being principally developed in that state. The Minnesota model typically has a highly structured format centered upon group activities and individual sessions with a treatment counselor. There can be many other types of therapists (e.g., family therapists or recreational therapists) on the units available as resources for clients. Originally the model developed as intensive inpatient services for approximately 28 days, followed by an outpatient program and/or an aftercare program (see Chapter 6 for more information on aftercare), but changes in third-party reimbursement policies have severely limited insurance coverage for inpatient treatment. This policy change contributed in no small way to the rise of the current model of intensive and long-term outpatient therapy followed by aftercare.

After treatment, clients work in groups on issues that hinder recovery. The groups also offer forums for denial to be confronted by counselors and peers, as well as a place to practice and receive feedback on the use of new skills. In group therapy and in psychoeducation groups (explained later in this chapter), clients will likely work with other counselors besides their primary counselors. Individual sessions involve teaching, rehearsing, and confronting denial, and in some cases provide a place for discussing and venting on emotionally charged issues. Counselors in individual sessions may take on the role of teachers-of-recovery to clients, sometimes confronting what they see as dishonesty on the part of clients, and other times serving as role models for a drug-free life. In groups, counselors can play different roles from group facilitator to teacher and even to referee. Counselors working in the Minnesota model must have a good grasp of the 12 steps and how they work. They also must understand other aspects of a strong recovery program, such as the importance of finding a good sponsor and of knowing which support-group meetings may be appropriate for each client. Often counselors in this model are in recovery as well.

One of the problems with the Minnesota-model treatment is that the product varies widely from treatment center to treatment center, so you are never quite sure what you will get. In addition, counselors tend to have greatly different approaches to how they conduct the therapy, even within the same treatment center. However, progress has been made to tighten the quality of the treatment being delivered. In a recent research study funded by the government (Project MATCH; National Institute on Alcohol Abuse and Alcoholism [NIAAA]), the researchers developed and tested a 12-step treatment manual called *Twelve Step Facilitation Therapy* (Nowinski, Baker, & Carroll, 1995), which was found to be effective for many clients in this study. Using a treatment manual like this one helps to ensure adherence to a treatment protocol, which prevents drift from the treatment protocol. *Drift* occurs when therapists stray away from what they are supposed to be doing in therapy, and a treatment manual such as this one makes drift less likely if it is followed like a cookbook. The manual can be ordered from the government at the NIAAA Web site (http://www.niaaa.nih.gov/). If treatment centers and counselors will use this manual, it will ensure much higher quality and consistency of services provided to their clients.

Oddly, in the Minnesota model of treatment, the disease model has been inextricably linked to an entirely different conception of a drug problem: that it is a symptom of a much larger spiritual problem. The *spiritual model* was the first model of recovery to be developed. Within this model, 12-step support groups such as CA, MA, and NA have arisen. These programs offer recovery through the working of the 12 steps, which are highly spiritual in content. Many of the steps directly mention the use of a higher power or a personal understanding of God as a way to overcome the drug problem. The ultimate goal within this approach to overcoming a drug problem is to experience a spiritual awakening that permanently alters the character of the person so that drug use is no longer part of that identity. A *spiritual awakening* seems strikingly similar to what others may call a *spiritual conversion*. The principles behind the 12 steps originally were borrowed from an evangelical Christian organization called the Oxford Movement, which explains some of the religiosity apparent in the steps.

However, even before the existence of 12-step support groups, people were using religious means to overcome drug problems, and some continue successfully to do so today. For some people, spiritual answers work very well to overcome drug problems. The premise is that drug abuse has been used to compensate for a spiritual void in the person, which suggests that drug use represents an existential problem. The solution requires filling the void with spiritual answers or solutions rather than with drugs.

Many urban missions and churches around the country provide faith-based solutions to drug problems. Anecdotal data suggest that some people find recovery from drug problems in this way, but a scientifically controlled study of these approaches has not been completed to see how many people really do benefit from them. The federal government has become more interested recently in some of these approaches, but we still are not sure how effective they are, nor are we sure whether they would be effective with people who do not share the religious model being espoused.

Similarly, some counselors and therapists have used *narrative therapy* to treat ethnic-minority clients with drug problems. Narrative therapy anecdotally seems to work well with people who are from cultures that rely on oral tradition and storytelling to affirm community identity. Very little research concerning the use of narrative therapy for drug use has been conducted, but intuitively it makes sense that using a person's story (autobiography) as a means for determining personal meaning and promoting behavior change could be effective among people for whom stories are very powerful means for healing. Narrative therapy allows clients to rewrite their own stories as therapy progresses, eliminating drug use from the story, so that the person's identity is redefined. Theoretically, the changing of a person's narrative is followed by change in behavior. As you can see, narrative therapy is highly existential in nature as well.

As alluded to at the beginning of this section, traditional Minnesota-model treatment merges the disease model with the spiritual model. Since within this model the disease has no known cure, a spiritual solution has taken on importance. Because of this, disease-model counselors refer people to 12-step support groups for continued recovery. Some treatment centers even have spiritual counselors who work with clients on spiritually related goals listed in the treatment plan. This arrangement provides a great service to the many people with drug problems who have spiritual doubts or problems. However, it has been my experience that not everyone who enters treatment feels he or she has a spiritual problem.

A third way to conceive of a drug problem is as a *family problem* rather than an individual problem. This model draws from the tradition of *family therapy,* which sees client problems as a symptom of a system-wide problem within the family. When a person within the family has a problem, such as one with drugs, that person often is referred to as the *identified patient* (or client) in this model. This label suggests that even though this client is the one seeking help for a drug problem, it will be necessary to treat the entire family unit in order to alleviate the problem. In this model, the problem is the family system and the drug use is merely a symptom of that larger problem.

Many well-known therapists, like Virginia Satir, have come from this understanding of drug problems. Usually professionals who operate within this model are trained in social work or are family therapists. The treatment for a drug problem within this model is to use family therapy to change the relationship dynamics among family members in an effort to find a new, healthy equilibrium in the family system. All family members in the system are considered sick, since the drug problem has caused others in the family to interact dysfunctionally within the family system. The goal becomes to change not only the behavior of the identified patient with a drug problem (including how he or she interacts with family members), but also to change the way that all other family members interact with the patient and with each other.

Some interesting therapy techniques have been developed within the family model. The first technique involves modeling family roles in group therapy sessions by use of *family sculpturing techniques*. This technique capitalizes on the belief that family members assume certain roles within the sick family system in order to compensate for its dysfunction. Some roles that have been described by family therapists include the role of a *family hero,* who is a usually a perfect child and assumes the role of competence in the family; the role of a *mascot,* who distracts a family from the problems by entertaining them; the role of a *scapegoat,* who takes the blame for the family problems; and the role of a *lost child* (or person), who withdraws from the family system. In sculpting, the counselor or therapist has the family members play the parts of these stereotyped roles in a group session in order to simulate the family dynamics. Then the counselor may show the family how to change their roles. The goal is to increase insight among family members into the dysfunctional relationships they have with each other in order to promote change of those roles. Although family sculpturing can be fairly dramatic and interesting, there have not been any controlled trials of this technique to see whether it works well to change behavior.

A fourth way to conceive of a drug problem is to consider it as a *behavioral disorder*. Many psychologists and other mental health professionals operate within this model. The typical treatment within this model involves individualized therapy with a psychotherapist. Three common avenues for treating a drug problem as a behavior disorder include behavior modification, cognitive modification, and skills training; these techniques have been described previously, so I will not describe them again here.

One of the earliest forms of treatment conducted within this model was called *aversion therapy*. The idea was to pair drug use with a really nasty consequence so that the person would not want to use drugs any more. Usually the paired aversive consequence was something that smelled really bad or made a person sick. For example, one pharmacological agent, disulfuram (Antabuse), has an aversive consequence to those who drink alcohol while taking this drug — that is, it can make them really sick. Physicians hoped that the threat would dissuade their patients from drinking alcohol. More commonly, though, aversion therapy relied upon an actual pairing of an aversive consequence (rather than a mere threat) immediately following drug use behavior.

Aversion therapy remains available in some places still, but it is not nearly as common as it was 30 years ago. Aversion therapy seems to work well over the short term, but research suggests that the behavior change does not seem to last over the long term. Some researchers have speculated that booster sessions may be needed periodically to improve the therapy so that the link between the aversive consequence and the drug use remains strong (i.e., is not extinguished) over time. Others have speculated that aversion therapy does not teach the new skills necessary to maintain long-term behavior change.

Today, cognitive and behavioral approaches commonly include behavior modification but will use shaping instead of aversive techniques. In addition, cognitive modification and skills training have been added to the mix, as well as cue exposure and response prevention. Most therapists also include relapse prevention as part of therapy (see Chapter 7). In addition, many cognitive behavioral therapists treating a drug problem now use a motivational interviewing style, especially in the earlier stages of therapy. The goal of combining these therapies is to motivate behavior change and then to teach clients to change drug-use behavior patterns once they are motivated. Those who operate within this model believe that people are capable of overcoming a drug problem without necessarily needing support or therapy the rest of their lives (see more in Chapter 8).

In addition, within this model, goals other than abstinence can be seen as progress. *Successive approximations toward the goal* means that any steps toward progress should be rewarded. Some therapists believe that reducing the harm of the drug use may be an important first step toward changing a drug problem. Many researchers and therapists believe that it may not be realistic to expect abstinence as a goal for some clients. Some therapists believe it is important to work with and protect clients even when they choose to continue to use drugs. For clients who do not desire or cannot maintain abstinence, the behavioral model provides opportunities for improvement.

Treatment manuals within the behavior-disorder model of understanding a drug problem also were developed during Project MATCH. These manuals are the *Motivational Enhancement Therapy Manual* (Miller, Zweben, DiClemente, & Rychtarik, 1999), which uses a 4-session model of motivational interviewing with assessment and feedback to promote drug use change; and the *Cognitive Behavioral Coping Skills Training Manual* (Kadden et al., 1999), which uses a 12-session model to treat drug problems using coping skills and relapse-prevention training for the client. These manuals can be found at the same NIAAA Web address presented earlier in the chapter for the *Twelve Step Facilitation Therapy Manual.*

In addition, cognitive therapy for treating a drug problem has been developed within two different models. The first model is *rational-emotive therapy* (RET; Ellis & Grieger, 1977), originally developed by Albert Ellis; this model focuses on overcoming irrational beliefs that lead to using drugs. In RET, the client learns how to identify and challenge irrational thoughts related to drug use. These challenges are conducted through the use of a systematic approach that identifies how activating events lead to certain irrational beliefs (and emotions related to those beliefs). The client learns how those irrational thoughts lead to acting in ways that produce certain undesirable consequences. Clients learn that changing or modifying their beliefs to become more rational (or more aligned with the reality of their lives) will produce more positive outcomes in their behavior. By taking control of one's beliefs, one is able to change drug use behavior over time. Within this model, alternative support groups have been developed, the most well-known one being Rational Recovery (see Chapter 2). In addition to RET, cognitive therapy to treat a drug problem has been developed (Beck, Wright, Newman, & Liese, 1993). This therapy uses techniques similar to those discussed later in this chapter with regard to treating co-occurring depression.

The fifth way to conceive of a drug problem is as a *response to an aversive environment.* Intervening upon the environment instead of the client has been found to be effective in many instances, even if the client is not present in therapy. Environmental interventions seem to work especially well when directed toward youth and adolescent clients. There are two types of empirically validated interventions developed within this model: the *community reinforcement model* and *multisystemic therapy.* The theory behind these therapies is quite behavioral, although the practice is to shape the client by intervening on as many systems and structures in the environment that touch the client's life as possible. In effect, you are attempting to alter the way that significant others and authority figures interact with the client so that the client is shaped toward behavior change. This method also keeps everyone who interacts with the client on the same page so they are not working at cross-purposes.

For example, such an intervention may be conducted at school and in the family in order to change the client's environment. Teachers and other school authorities may be taught to interact differently with the client when she or he is in school, and family members to do likewise at home. Sometimes new contingencies are created to reward client progress (or even punish old behavior). These important social structures are being targeted for change in an effort to shape the behavior of the client and to reduce the stress on the client. Both the shaping and reducing of stress are meant to make changing drug use more attractive and easier for the client. These interventions seem to work relatively well with adolescents and youth, possibly because that age group is more influenced by environmental changes than adults. The intervention can work well even if the person with a drug problem chooses not to actively participate. Environmental interventions also have been used effectively to shape behavior among clients with severe co-occurring mental disorders such as schizophrenia.

Psychoeducation Within the Different Recovery Models

Teaching clients is an important part of therapy within any treatment model. Teaching often is referred to as *psychoeducation* in therapy and treatment. Psychoeducation can take place in a number of forums, from individual therapy sessions to classroom settings and group therapy. The content and emphasis of psychoeducation varies across the different treatment models, as you will see.

Disease-Model Psychoeducation

Psychoeducation within the disease model of treatment focuses primarily upon teaching the client how to treat his or her disease. Psychoeducation orients the client to the philosophy of the disease model, then teaches how to treat the disease once the person has accepted that she or he has it. Part of the client education will include discussions about the potency of denial to place a person in harm's way. The client is instructed to be totally honest to themselves about their powerlessness over the disease and about the need to seek support from a 12-step support group. Significant amounts of recovery-related reading materials may be assigned in treatment, such as personal accounts of 12-step recoveries by other people and traditional 12-step texts sponsored by support groups such as NA, CA, or MA.

In addition, Minnesota-model treatment centers have over time added other psychoeducational components to treatment, borrowing from the spiritual, family, and behavioral models. Education in 12-step living and other spiritual modifications deemed necessary to promote personality change (discussed shortly) have been borrowed from the spirituality model. Clients are likely to received psychoeducation involving dysfunctional roles they may have played within their family systems, and perhaps even concerning their families of origin (the families in which they were reared), borrowed from the family model. Instruction may be given on how to change these dynamics within a family system. Changes may include learning new ways to interact within the family structure, and may involve a role change for clients within their families.

Borrowed from the behavioral model of treatment are a number of skills-training components that may be used with the psychoeducational components in disease-model treatment. For example, some Minnesota-model treatment centers include psychoeducational components on anger management, assertiveness training, and even drug refusal skills as part of an effort to train clients to retain abstinence over time. In addition, relapse prevention, which was developed within the behavioral model, is routinely taught in treatment and in aftercare within Minnesota-model centers today. Relapse prevention will be discussed is great detail in Chapter 7 and aftercare in Chapter 6.

Spiritual-Model Psychoeducation

Within the spiritual model of treating a drug problem, psychoeducation will be used to orient clients or consumers to a model that sees drug use as an unhealthy response to a spiritual void inside the person. The person will be taught that there is a healthier way to fill that void than using drugs. Psychoeducation within this model may focus on teaching the client the value of humility and surrender with regard to treating the spiritual void. *Humility* is used to counter the pride that is considered inherent in a drug problem, and *surrender* is done in order to fill the void with a higher power that can heal and transform the person. This transformation will theoretically make a drug problem obsolete since the person has been radically changed at his or her very essence.

Psychoeducation may involve teaching a regimen of other spiritual practices that will, in effect, aid the person toward this identity transformation. If the model or treatment is being conducted within a church, mission, or other religious entity, then prayer and holy-book readings may be involved in this process of psychoeducation. If the spiritual model is in the context of a 12-step program, then the readings may be more programmatic to that support group, and the practices more directly related to working the 12 steps. In either religious organizations or support groups, there may be a strong push for the person to become involved in service work, and perhaps even to share recovery efforts with other people who may have drug problems.

Family-Model Psychoeducation

Psychoeducation within a family model, as alluded to under the Minnesota-model discussion, may include orientation to family systems and family roles within those systems, and to how roles and systems can become dysfunctional. Clients will be taught that a drug problem is a symptom of larger family problem, and that, in order for the drug problem to be overcome, the family system will have to change in a way that will alter the dysfunctional roles currently present in that system that make drug use more likely to occur. So, in addition to teaching about systems, roles, and family interactions, the client will be oriented to the therapy, which may include sculpturing or even conjoint therapy with other family members.

Behavioral-Model Psychoeducation

Psychoeducation in the behavioral model consists of orienting clients to the model by teaching that behavior is under personal control and can be modified over time, but that change requires an active effort on the parts of the clients. Clients also will be oriented to each change strategy as necessary with the goal of teaching them why the strategy is important to complete and how it will benefit them. Cognitive behavioral therapies are relatively democratic in nature in that they insist upon informed consent for clients and partnerships in developing and reaching goals in therapy. Many of the tasks asked of clients in cognitive behavioral therapy (e.g., exposure, homework assignments, or learning and practicing new skills) involve high levels of activity and require high levels of commitment. Because of the nature of these tasks, a principle goal of psychoeducation within the behavioral model is to develop client commitment for carrying out the therapy.

In addition, specific nuances of a particular behavioral model may be taught to clients so they understand how to take control of their therapies over the long term. For example, if a client is receiving cognitive therapy, then psychoeducation will be used to teach the specifics of the model, the terms (e.g., *schema* or *core beliefs* — see later in this chapter) used in the therapy, and even how to use the strategies to challenge thoughts or test hypotheses (discussed earlier in this chapter). Clients must eventually become their own therapists in a sense, so that after therapy concludes they can continue to make the changes begun while in therapy. In order to achieve this goal, psychoeducation trains clients how to take control over their own therapy and to learn how to generalize the strategies and techniques being used in session to situations outside session.

Environmental-Model Psychoeducation

Finally, psychoeducation within the environmental model of therapy focuses on teaching the stakeholders for the client (e.g., parents or teachers) how to respond differently to the client in order to change his or her drug use. Psychoeducation will orient the stakeholders to how their behavior influences the behavior of the client, and how changing their behavioral responses will likely cause the client to change as well. The focus also will be to educate the stakeholders to communicate with each other in order to remain on the same page regarding how to respond to the client's drug use.

In addition, psychoeducation will teach those who touch the lives of clients how to use contingency management to shape the behavior of those clients. *Contingency management* uses what is called the Premack principle to shape behavior. The *Premack principle* stipulates that if a client does something, then a particular consequence will occur. The if-then relationship between behavior and consequence is important to define ahead of time so the rules of the relationship are well understood by the client. In the environmental model, contingency management using such if-then rules is used to make it difficult for the client to use drugs. The various stakeholders in the environment are taught how to use such rules to influence the behavior of the client over time by setting up consequences for positive changes (rewards) and for no progress (punishments). For example, teachers, family members, probation officers, employers, or others may be taught how to develop and implement these contingencies with the person who has a drug problem. Psychoeducation is an important component in training those in the environment to interact with the client in a way that may encourage drug use change over time.

CLIENT HANDOUT

Models of Recovery

For those of you who may be potential consumers of treatment or therapy, you can use information on recovery models to decide which type of therapeutic model seems to best fit your worldview and your own ideas about what a drug problem may be. No one model fits all people; each one may work well when matched appropriately with the needs of a client. Considering how you will fit with the treatment center's model before seeking help is important. But some research suggests that how well client and therapist get along may be even more important for your treatment success than a good match on the model. Some counselors and therapists are naturals at helping people regardless of the model in which they operate, and those professionals will do their best to help you.

Helping Your Client Understand the Models of Recovery

There will likely be one model that will appeal to you more than the others. However, each of these models has strengths (and weaknesses, of course), so I would not recommend completely discarding any of these solutions. In fact, you may find that you draw from many models to find solutions for those clients you find difficult to help. So for those clients who are puzzling you, and who do not seem to be getting better using the model that you are most comfortable with, take a look at another model to find out whether there is a solution there that can help this difficult client get better.

Empirically Validated Therapies for Co-occurring Disorders

Remembering that many clients with drug problems also have co-occurring psychiatric or psychological problems, it is useful to know what types of therapy are available to help these clients with their other disorders. Historically, people treating drug problems have been reticent about treating mental disorders, and many addiction counselors have not been trained to do so. In these instances, a referral may be necessary for a dually diagnosed client. However, if you have an opportunity to learn one or more of the therapies listed below, it will enhance your skill set as a therapist (not to mention your marketability in the community!) immensely.

The American Psychological Association (APA) has established stringent criteria for determining whether a therapy is empirically supported or validated. Since those guidelines were developed, the committee researching this area has been working for several years to determine the best practices to use when treating certain disorders, such as depression or anxiety. Insurance companies and health-maintenance organizations (HMOs) have paid attention to these guidelines as well, since they want their clients to be treated with best practices. Sometimes reimbursement is contingent on your being able to demonstrate that you used the best available therapy for the disorder that you have diagnosed. So there are many good reasons to use empirically validated therapies, including providing your client with the best available care.

In this section, I will review what is known about the best practices for treating disorders that commonly co-occur with a drug problem. This discussion is not meant to be an exhaustive list nor an exhaustive description of each therapy, but is meant to point you in the right direction if you want to learn more.

Empirically Validated Therapies for Depression and Bipolar Disorder

There are several therapies for treating depression that have been found to be effective for many people. The first is pharmacotherapy, which may involve use of monoamine oxidase (MAO) inhibitors (which are least likely to be used these days), tricyclic antidepressants, and SSRIs (most likely to be used now). MAO inhibitors may be effective in treating severely depressed clients for whom other antidepressant drugs have not been effective. Use of this class of antidepressant drugs is often thought of as a last resort because of the risks of using them. People who use these medicines cannot have certain kinds of drinks or foods (such as cheese) because they can produce deadly interactions with the medicine. Tricyclic medicines are generally given at night, because their downside is that they

USEFUL RESOURCES

Where to Find Empirically Validated Information on the Web

For Assessment Tools and Therapy Manuals for Treating Substance Abuse:

- National Institute on Drug Abuse (http://www.drugabuse.gov/)
- National Institute on Alcohol Abuse and Alcoholism (http://www.niaaa.nih.gov/)

For Information About Treating Co-occurring Mental Health Disorders:

- National Institute of Mental Health (http://www.nimh.nih.gov/)
- Substance Abuse and Mental Health Services Administration (http://www.samhsa.gov/index.aspx)

For Information About Co-occurring Physical Health Disorders, including HIV:

- Centers for Disease Control and Prevention (http://www.cdc.gov/)

can make people very drowsy and even sluggish into the next day. SSRIs are generally the medicines of choice for depression now, but they also have a very high risk of sexual side effects.

Psychotherapy has been found to be as effective in the short term for the treatment of depression and routinely performs better than medicines over the long term at preventing a depression relapse. There are several kinds of psychotherapy that have been empirically validated, including interpersonal psychotherapy, cognitive therapy, cognitive behavioral therapy, and problem-solving therapy (for more minor depression). The most commonly used of these is cognitive or cognitive behavioral. These therapies have their roots in the work of Aaron Beck, who developed Cognitive Therapy for Depression (Beck, Rush, Shaw, & Emery, 1979).

Cognitive therapy assumes that depression is the result of having core beliefs (or schemas) that cause people problems. *Core beliefs* are basic sets of assumptions or values that people have about life, others, and the world around them. In some cases, the worldview represented by these core beliefs may be distorted and place the person at odds with reality. The thinking errors, mentioned earlier in this chapter, are direct results of these flawed basic assumptions, and these flawed beliefs cause a person to suffer because they are unrealistic. The goal in cognitive therapy is to modify these core beliefs so that clients have worldviews (core beliefs) more in line (less at odds) with the reality of life. Cognitions are changed using the strategies discussed earlier in this chapter. Through the change in beliefs, the behavior changes as well. Cognitive behavioral therapy would use these same strategies, with the addition of behavior-modification strategies discussed earlier, representing more of a hybrid model. These therapies have been tested often and have shown to be effective in treating depression among many clients.

Pharmacotherapy is very important for treating Bipolar Disorder, and the use of *mood stabilizers,* such as lithium, is considered the standard of care. However, after you stabilize a person's mood, you may be left with a person who has not learned a great many life skills over the years precisely because of her or his disorder. Fortunately, cognitive behavioral therapy, including skills training, has been used effectively with bipolar clients after they have been stabilized pharmacologically. Obviously the person must be emotionally stable in order to learn new skills.

Empirically Validated Therapies for Schizophrenia and Other Psychotic Disorders

The same can be said for treating clients who have schizophrenia and other psychotic disorders. They must be stabilized in order to make progress in therapy. As mentioned in Chapter 2, antipsychotic drugs now allow marked improvement among clients with schizophrenia, and the newer, atypical antipsychotic drugs have fewer side effects so clients are more likely to comply with taking their medications. In addition, cognitive behavioral skills training has been tested successfully among people with a drug problem (cocaine) and co-occurring schizophrenia (Roberts, Shaner, & Eckman, 1999). In the earlier stages, skills training may need to focus on teaching ADLs (discussed earlier in this chapter), but with long-term stabilization clients with schizophrenia may be able to learn additional and more complex skills needed to succeed in society.

Empirically Validated Therapies for Anxiety Disorders

Anxiety disorders can be treated very effectively by cognitive behavioral therapy (see Recommended Reading at the end of this chapter for a very good resource in this area). In this therapy, therapists begin with educating the clients to the model. The first part of the therapy teaches clients that anxiety cues are generated by overinterpreting normal physiological reactions. Clients with anxiety may be more vulnerable than non-anxious people to noticing physiological changes, and tend to misinterpret those changes as a threat. The types of cues that often get misinterpreted are changes in heart rate, muscle pains, sweating, headaches, tingling in the extremities, photosensitivity, and hyperventilation. People with anxiety will assume that these changes are risky, and perhaps will interpret these symptoms to mean that something is physically wrong with them. Of course, if you misinterpret bodily changes in this way, it is likely to make you more anxious!

Therapists also teach clients how fear, in relation to their symptoms and errors in their thinking, leads to worsening anxiety and, to some clients, avoidance of certain situations related to these fears. By being exposed to cues that generate these physiological changes and fears (with avoidance being blocked), clients are taught to circumvent their fears by understanding that the physiological changes are normal and nothing to fear. The most common way to conduct this type of exposure is by the use of *systematic desensitization* (exposure done gradually in small steps), although there are some types of exposure that may require *flooding* or *implosion* (almost the opposite of systematic desensitization — exposure done all at once to the most feared stimulus or cue), not graduated exposure. In addition to exposure, the client is taught to modify and challenge his or her thoughts and fears, using many of the techniques mentioned earlier in the chapter. Rumination and obsessive thinking patterns can be a problem but cognitive-modification techniques help with these as well. Breathing retraining to normalize respiration rates is used to reduce the sympathetic nervous system's fight-or-flight responses, thus naturally lowering anxiety levels. Finally, clients are assigned homework to generalize the new skills being learned in session out into real-world situations. Homework includes exposure exercises to feared cues in the environment and cognitive modification work. If places have been avoided because of the fears, then the homework focuses on the person's reengaging in those places.

Standardized cognitive behavioral therapy manuals, which ensure adherence to a treatment protocol, have been developed for many different anxiety disorders, including phobias, generalized anxiety, panic, social anxiety, Agoraphobia, and PTSD. Many of these therapies can be completed in 12–20 weeks of individual outpatient sessions, but some may be conducted in less time. One exception to using an individualized-therapy format is the treatment of social anxiety, a highly effective treatment for which is cognitive behavioral *group* therapy. The advantage to this method is that the client gets to rehearse social skills among peers who also are socially anxious, as well as get feedback about interpersonal behavior from peers and therapists.

Empirically Validated Therapies for Personality Disorders

Cognitive behavioral therapy seems to be effective in treating many kinds of personality disorders, as well. For example, the innovative cognitive behavioral therapy for Borderline Personality Disorder, dialectical behavior therapy (developed by Marsha Linehan, 1993), has been shown to be very promising in its ability to help clients who have been often described in the past as "untreatable" or "difficult." Linehan's strategies for reducing suicidal and parasuicidal behaviors developed within this therapy are state of the art. However, therapists will require extensive training therapy before they can be expected to use this therapy effectively among suicidal or borderline clients.

Empirically Validated Therapy for Chronic Pain

Cognitive behavioral therapy has been utilized to treat chronic pain for many years. Since the pain is chronic, the person has to learn to live with it in ways that do not debilitate his or her behavior. The goal of the therapy is to stop those pain behaviors that prevent a person from carrying on a normal life, and to encourage those behaviors that promote progress in spite of the pain. The idea is to use behavior modification to shape pain behaviors over time, and ultimately to extinguish such behaviors. In addition, cognitive modification is used to challenge fears and beliefs that prevent the person from engaging in more regular life activities, or to challenge thoughts that suggest that pain can be controlled only by frequent use of medicines. This belief is extremely important to challenge among clients who abuse pain medications.

Cognitive Rehabilitation

Although the research is limited and the techniques relatively new, some hope exists that drug-induced thinking problems may be treated by what some have called *cognitive rehabilitation*. Many of these techniques were developed to help victims of strokes and other brain injuries improve and recover brain functions more rapidly than they would if they were left untreated. Some of these techniques arise from the philosophy that if you exercise it, you will not lose it, meaning exercising brain functions in this instance.

Clients are assigned different cognitive tasks that exercise the specific areas of the brain that seem to have sustained injury. Tasks can run the gamut, but frequently involve engaging in spatial-ability, abstraction, verbal, memory, and

RESEARCH FRONTIERS

Technology and the Future of Therapy

Technology is rapidly changing the face of therapy and treatment. Online technology is being used to intervene upon risky behaviors, and e-mail is being used to facilitate between-session communications between clients and therapists/counselors. In addition, many consumers and their families are searching the Web to find out all they can about treating a drug problem even before they arrive at your office. The future looks even more spectacular, with the possibility of using virtual technology in session to recreate out-of-session situations and conditions that could be faced by clients. The client of the future may get to practice assertiveness or anger management skills and may learn to use relapse-prevention strategies in realistic virtual situations. One down side apparent with these technologies, however, seems to be whether confidentiality can be protected online. Even with these concerns, it seems likely that therapy in the future will involve use of these developments. Someday you may be serving clients a hemisphere away, thanks to these technological developments!

problem-solving tasks, to name a few. New computer programs have been developed to aid in this rehabilitation process. Although these methods have been used primarily with people who may not have drug problems, some of these techniques are currently being used in a few clinical settings for people who seem to have cognitive problems after long-term use of drugs. These techniques are relatively new and untested, but they do provide hope that, in the future, memory and other cognitive problems caused by drug use may be rehabilitated in some way.

How the Technological Revolution Will Change Therapy

As you may have guessed from the discussion about cognitive rehabilitation, technological advances are pushing therapy into new and exciting areas. *Web-based technology* has been used in many research studies and in some prevention programs in an attempt to change people's behavior. With regard to substance use, Web sites provide psychoeducational components in an effort to prevent abuse, as well as providing assessment, feedback, and social normative comparisons for users. Theoretically speaking, the goal is to educate drug users that their substance use deviates significantly from that of peers in an effort to raise concern and hopefully change behavior.

Web access also allows clients to gain knowledge about drug use and behavior from multiple sources all over the globe. Guided Web searches can be highly educational for clients. I say "guided" because therapists and counselors should be aware of what is being retrieved, since there is a great deal of misinformation available on the Web. In addition, Web-based resources tend to make for a much more well-informed consumer, since many potential clients do their homework online before ever darkening the doors of a treatment facility or therapist's office. This easy access to knowledge over time will likely make for much savvier consumers who will not settle for just any kind of care. I see this as a mostly positive development, since it will make for more discriminating consumers, although there is the potential for misinformation when relying upon the Web exclusively.

Many therapists use *e-mail* to interact with clients. The advantages to this process are that e-mail maximizes client access to the therapist while minimizing the intrusion of client contact into the therapist's personal time. Homework assignments can be discussed and clarified between sessions, and between-session questions answered. In addition, e-mail introduces the possibility that a client can access a therapist hundreds or even thousands of miles away. I am a firm believer that face-to-face therapy is ideal for many important reasons (e.g., developing the therapeutic alliance), but in those instances in which clients are isolated from good care, e-mail therapy can be a very attractive option. This option allows the possibility for equal access to the best available treatment and therapy resources even if those resources are not available to the client locally. In addition, as interactive telephones become more standard, therapy by phone may allow distance therapy to become more personalized, and this medium may ultimately supplant e-mail as a way to seek therapy from a distance.

The down side, however, is that many online systems are not secure, so there has been great concern about client privacy's being compromised by using e-mail. Many systems have been working on upgrading their security, so the concern about protecting confidentiality online may eventually be reasonably satisfied. Presumably the same concerns will need to be addressed with regard to interactive phones.

Teleconferencing methods have been used for some time in medicine as a means of consultation with clients and other physicians living in rural areas. These conferences usually are produced at large medical centers with highly sophisticated research programs and are conducted in an effort to provide best-care practices to clients in isolated areas. Presumably, therapy will move toward using this kind of technology as well. It may be that the treatment of the future will take place in the form of a teleconference, including group and individual sessions. At the very least, geographically isolated therapists and counselors may find that consultation or continuing education experiences with cutting-edge researchers or therapy gurus may be more readily available via teleconferences in the future.

Finally, *virtual reality* technology will allow clients to do imaginal exposure virtually. For example, virtual programs can be written that allow the client to face (virtually speaking) all the tough and risky situations in session that they will face outside. They will be able to practice drug refusal skills, alternative ways to act, and new skills in the face of virtually exposed high-risk experiences. Virtual reality will provide a more realistic way to conduct exposure to cues difficult to reproduce in session, which should aid therapists in desensitizing certain drug-related cues and in treating some co-occurring disorders (such as anxiety).

Cultural Pathways to Recovery

The United States is rapidly becoming a country of diversity, with many ethnic-minority groups growing quite rapidly. The net result of this demographic change will be that more clients with drug problems will come from cultural backgrounds that may be much different from mainstream America as it is currently defined. Experiences with mental health services by some of these clients may be quite limited and many of these clients will have opted for traditional cultural healing practices rather than Western types of treatment services. Some clients may be quite suspicious of traditional treatment and therapy, and of mental health professionals in general. In many cases the language differences will complicate these relationships.

Some ethnic-minority communities have opted to create their own culturally relevant models for recovery that incorporate some elements of the treatment models previously mentioned, but that include large numbers of more traditional practices of great relevance to the community. Treatment may look very different when delivered within an ethnic-minority community than it may appear in a suburban treatment facility.

Many ethnic-minority communities want to respect their historic healing cultures and traditions when attempting to help their members with drug problems. So, in many communities, traditional healing practices and healers are highly involved in an effort to circumvent drug problems. In treatment facilities on American Indian reservations, for example, sometimes a shaman will work with clients under the same roof that a psychologist or chemical dependency counselor will. Traditional practices often coexist with newer scientific practices in an effort to provide ethnic-minority clients the best and most culturally relevant care possible. Treatment facilities in ethnic-minority communities may offer clients other traditional activities as part of the regular treatment program. As examples, many reservation-based treatment programs include sweat lodges and other traditional practices as a routine part of care. Some communities include vision quests or sojourns as part of the detoxification and recovery process, or include an elder mentorship model, in which community elders mentor younger community members attempting to change a drug problem, as part of treatment.

Even if an ethnic-minority client works with you in a mainstream clinical setting, this client may be seeking traditional healing care when not with you in your office. You must accept and respect that this may be occurring, and if you want to maintain your relationship with your client, you should discuss, understand, and encourage the traditional care being sought. The research suggests that many first-generation Americans rely heavily upon traditional healing practices, sometimes instead of using Western practices and sometimes in conjunction with them. Ethically speaking, therapists and counselors should respect clients' wishes with regard to how much they want to utilize traditional healers and traditional methods for healing as they overcome drug problems. The only exception to this ethical dictum is if the client is using herbs that may interact with medicines that have been prescribed (although only very savvy physicians usually know about the risks involved with such interactions).

Summing Up

The bottom line: There are many different models and techniques that can help people who want to overcome drug problems. Therapists and counselors who expand their knowledge to tools and techniques outside their preferred treatment models will have the advantage of a multiplicity of tools to help their clients. This will allow you to develop backup strategies to help your clients in case they do not respond well to your primary model and its therapeutic strategies. Therapists and counselors also enhance their abilities to help clients if they know how to treat co-occurring disorders with best practices. Extra training will be required to master new therapies, but the effort will be well rewarded when you are able to serve a client with a co-occurring disorder in a highly effective way.

In addition, regardless of the model and accompanying techniques that are used, the client has a right to know what therapy will look like, and the rationale for the techniques being chosen. Make sure to orient your clients to the model, and to what techniques will be used and why. This does not mean you have to give away all your professional secrets, but you do want to prevent surprises that may interfere with progress. In addition, the client will be more fully committed to working hard in treatment and therapy if he or she understands why it is important to do so.

There is no absolute model of therapy that is right for all occasions. No single model works well for all clients, so it is a matter of trying to match what is known about best practices with what is known about client needs and worldviews. In some cases creativity may be required, especially when operating within an ethnic-minority community. Working with a client of another culture can be complicated, but the task is far from impossible. The key is to find an appropriate model match for your client and gain his or her commitment through orienting to what you are doing and why. If you do this well, commitment to treatment and progress will likely follow.

Key Terms

Anticonvulsives. Drugs used to prevent seizures.
Antihypertensives. Drugs used to lower blood pressure.

Catastrophizing. Beliefs that the worst possible outcome in a situation will happen.
Generalization of the use of skills. Learning to use in-session skills out in the real world.
Hypothesis testing. Testing whether a belief or assumption is really true.
Exposure. Being exposed to a cue that triggers an unhealthy response until it no longer produces that response.
Extrinsic reinforcement. Reinforcement that comes from outside a person.
Fading. The gradual reduction over time (and ultimately the stopping) of reinforcement.
Flooding or implosion. Total exposure all at once.
Fortunetelling. A client's belief that he or she knows the outcome of an event before it happens.
Intrinsic reinforcement. Reinforcement that comes from inside the person.
Mood stabilizers. Drugs that treat disorders with mood cycles, such as Bipolar Disorder.
Overestimation of threat. Overestimating the likelihood of a negative outcome.
Response prevention. Blocking avoidance or escape during exposure.
Scanning the environment for negatives. Looking for evidence to support negative beliefs.
"Serenity Prayer." A prayer by Reinhold Neibuhr often used to close 12-step meetings.
Successive approximations toward the goal. Rewarding small steps toward progress.
Systematic desensitization. Gradual exposure done in small steps over a period of time.
Thinking error. An irrational belief that causes problems for clients.

Recommended Reading

Marsha Linehan's book *Skills Training Manual for Treating Borderline Personality Disorder* (New York: Guilford Press, 1993) is an outstanding resource for learning how to teach skills to clients. As suggested by the title, this book was written for the treatment of a very specific disorder. However, the skills-training exercises suggested in the book are appropriate for use with people with drug problems as well, and the book is a great resource for counselors and therapists alike. In addition, I highly recommend the book *Clinical Handbook of Psychological Disorders, Third Edition*, edited by David Barlow (New York: Guilford Press, 2001). This book has numerous chapters written by experts in the field and dedicated to instruction on cognitive behavioral therapy with anxiety and many other types of disorders. I highly recommend the book *Cognitive Behavior Therapy: Applying Empirically Supported Techniques in Your Practice,* edited by William O'Donohue, Jane Fisher, and Steven Hayes (Hoboken, NJ: John Wiley & Sons,

2003) which has a very practical, cookbook approach to how to use various empirically validated techniques in your practice. Finally, I recommend *Cognitive Therapy: Basics and Beyond,* by Judith Beck (New York: Guilford Press, 1995), as an excellent overview for the basics of cognitive modification and therapy.

TRUTH OR FICTION

QUIZ ANSWERS

1. False; 2. False; 3. True; 4. False; 5. False; 6. True; 7. True

CHAPTER 6

Continuing Care

TRUTH OR FICTION QUIZ

After reading this chapter, you should be able to answer the following questions:

1. Aftercare goals are almost always the same as treatment goals. True or False?
2. In the Minnesota model, aftercare usually meets weekly and in groups. True or False?
3. A client may have a different counselor in aftercare than in treatment. True or False?
4. Booster sessions can help clients after psychotherapy is completed. True or False?
5. Relationships often experience problems after treatment is completed. True or False?
6. It is okay for you to hire your client to do some yard work for you. True or False?
7. It may be okay to share your spiritual beliefs with a client if he or she asks. True or False?

Answers on p. 258.

Treatment obviously cannot last forever. Eventually the client must take what she or he has learned out into the real world and succeed in overcoming her or his drug problem. A key decision for therapists and counselors is determining when therapy or treatment must end. However, ending treatment or therapy abruptly is not recommended. *Termination* or *discharge* from therapy or treatment should occur after a gradual transition period that allows some continued support while encouraging the client to assume greater responsibilities for recovery on her or his own terms without constant professional contact.

Research into behavior change suggests that clients benefit from tapering the frequency of psychotherapy sessions before termination or discharge. Behavioral research has found that new learning can benefit from spacing out sessions more at the end of therapy or treatment, which allows the client to take greater personal responsibility for practicing the newly learned skills under real-world conditions. Allowing clients to assume greater responsibility for their recovery pathways over time allows for generalization of skills and increased self-efficacy in use of skills in real-life situations (see Chapters 1, 3, and 5). Increasing the confidence and competence of the client to succeed using these new recovery skills has the effect of decreasing client dependence on the therapist or counselor. Establishing greater independence from a counselor or therapist toward the end of treatment care is necessary to ensure client success after contact has been ended. Even if a client makes mistakes or misjudgments during this time of tapering sessions, the therapist or counselor is still available to help the client if a serious problem arises.

This period of time when tapering of sessions occurs is called *aftercare* in traditional drug treatment. Individual psychotherapy also tapers sessions, but this process is not referred to as aftercare (see more details later in the chapter). Aftercare represents a much less intensive form of therapy, usually focused on quality-of-life issues in recovery and relapse prevention (see next chapter). Aftercare sessions usually meet once a week for an hour or two, although the model varies from program to program. The idea is to taper the number of formal contacts the client has with a professional while leaving the safety net in place if the client should stumble. The process of learning to walk the tightrope of life alone is important, and aftercare encourages the client to take charge of his or her recovery program but provides a safety net if a mistake is made. Treatment professionals, after all, cannot walk the tightropes for their clients.

Counselors and therapists have to determine when the client has made sufficient progress to move into this next phase of therapy. The decision whether the client is ready to be moved from formal treatment into aftercare is determined by client progress on the treatment plan. The counselor or therapist uses clinical judgment to ascertain whether the client has made sufficient progress on the plan to warrant movement from formal treatment into aftercare and whether the client is sufficiently stable in his or her recovery to take this next step toward autonomous recovery. The next section covers factors that counselors and therapists should consider when making the decision to graduate clients from treatment into aftercare. In addition, this chapter provides an overview of what can be expected during this final phase of treatment and therapy for professionals, and for clients and their families.

Recovery Criteria Used by Therapists

As mentioned in Chapter 1, *treatment success* is defined differently depending on which model of recovery and treatment you believe (also see Chapter 5). For example, in traditional Minnesota-model treatment modalities, treatment success is defined by a period of sustained abstinence. This period of abstinence is described in the *DSM-IV-TR* (APA, 2000) as sustained full remission, which reflects disease-model language, and this period of sustained remission is described as a period of abstinence that last greater than one year. Treatment centers frequently use the *DSM-IV-TR* to diagnose their clients, but generally do not use this strict definition of sustained full remission to determine when treatment should end and aftercare should begin.

Instead, counselors in Minnesota-model treatment facilities often use clinical judgment to determine whether there has been a stable, sustained period of abstinence to decide when a client is ready to graduate from treatment and move into aftercare. In addition, treatment plans are used to ascertain when a client is ready to enter aftercare. Significant progress on a majority of treatment-plan goals and problem areas provides further evidence that the client may be ready for aftercare. Finally, and sometimes unfortunately, financial considerations sometimes weigh into the decision to move a client into aftercare. If the client's insurance company insists, or if the client can no longer afford the cost of formal treatment, then aftercare becomes a logical choice, even if the placement seems premature. Counselors understandably tend to be conservative when making the decision to discharge a client from treatment to aftercare, so a decision like this can seem ill advised. Thankfully, there are many occasions when moving a client into aftercare ends up being helpful over the long term even if it seems premature at the time.

In a behavioral model of recovery, the client's goals for therapy are used to determine whether tapering psychotherapy is recommended. Many times the client's goals will include abstinence, but not always. When the client's goals have been met to the satisfaction of both the therapist and the client, then a recommendation is made to begin to space out the individual psychotherapy sessions gradually. The rationale for this process (to encourage generalization of skills and development of self-efficacy) is explained to the client. If therapy has been conducted weekly, then the therapist may recommend going to biweekly sessions for a month, followed by once-a-month sessions, and maybe eventually extended out to one session three months later, then one last *booster session* 6 months out to check on the client's progress. In psychotherapy, this process of gradually tapering the number of sessions toward extinction is the functional equivalent of an aftercare program.

Suggested Criteria for Discharging From Treatment Into Aftercare

For both counselors and therapists, the treatment plan provides an excellent way to determine when a client is ready for aftercare. As you may remember, the treatment plan includes various types of problems that are prioritized by the relative threat to the recovery and well-being of the client (see Chapter 4, especially Research Frontiers on page 166. Counselors and therapists can also use the tier system to guide their determination of when a client is ready for a taper in treatment or therapy. For example, counselors and therapists will most certainly want clients to be stable before referral to aftercare, which suggests that all Tier 1 and

Tier 2 problems should be resolved before such referrals are made. The resolution of Tier 3 problems becomes more a matter of clinical judgment, but certainly a counselor or therapist will want to determine whether enough progress on Tier 3 problems has been made that the client can begin to direct his or her own treatment out in the real world. I would recommend that significant progress has been made on most, if not all, Tier 3 problem items on the treatment plan prior to discharge into aftercare.

Aftercare represents the ideal forum for addressing Tier 4 problem items, so it is expected that many of these will not have been addressed in treatment. Therefore, it is not necessary to have made progress on Tier 4 problems before a referral to aftercare. Many of these problems, as mentioned in Chapter 4, will require clients to develop their own plans for how to address them in everyday life. The aftercare counselor or therapist can serve as a guide in this effort to find new life pathways, but clients must do the actual walking when the trails are chosen.

Phases of Recovery

Changing the emphasis in aftercare from life-threatening issues to quality-of-life concerns represents a more comprehensive change of focus that is typical in recovery in general. In the beginning phase of overcoming a drug problem, the clients focus primarily on not using drugs. A great deal of time is spent learning to change and control drug-related behavior. Tier 1 and 2 problems are the principal focus for clients in treatment and therapy. In the next phase of overcoming a drug problem, the client begins to develop a new identity apart from the use of drugs, to develop and use new skills more effectively, and to develop self-efficacy in her or his ability to succeed in overcoming the drug problem. Clients still focus a great deal on overcoming the drug problem, but the competence to succeed is greater during this phase, as is the commitment to continue to change. A great deal of time is spent practicing new behavior and skills, and learning how to make changes when mistakes are made. Tier 1 and 2 problems are generally under control and significant progress is made on the Tier 3 problems. Joy begins to return during this second phase of behavior change.

> "Every day you may make progress. Every step may be fruitful. Yet there will stretch out before you an ever-lengthening, ever-ascending, ever-improving path. You know you will never get to the end of the journey. But this, so far from discouraging, only adds to the joy and glory of the climb."
>
> — WINSTON CHURCHILL

The third phase occurs about the time that aftercare would begin. In this phase, there is increased movement toward self-guided therapy and treatment, less reliance on treatment professionals, and increased self-efficacy to sustain behavior change over the long term. Clients continue to develop new identities apart from drug use and to reconstruct their personal lives to reflect these changes. The role of the counselor or therapist changes during this phase of recovery toward more of a mentorship.

The fourth phase occurs toward the end of aftercare, when a client moves behavior change beyond merely a focus on the drug problem. The client's identity becomes no longer defined principally by the drug problem. In fact, the client's identity may be completely different than it was when drugs were a problem. The new behavior patterns have become habit. Tier 4 problems are being tackled as a part of everyday life. The client is no longer a client during this final phase of recovery. In phase four, the person who used to have a drug problem has assumed the role of being his or her own therapist, and in some cases, may have assumed a role in helping others in their recovery. The focus changes from the necessary taking that a person must do when initially learning a new way to live to a balance between taking and giving to others (see Chapter 8 for further explanation). In earlier phases of recovery, the person maintains a strong focus on self, but that focus shifts outward as recovery continues, as you will see.

Spheres of Recovery

Recovery from a drug problem starts with client behavior change. Because of this beginning, personal growth is the primary focus of therapy and treatment in the earliest phases of recovery. Early recovery is necessarily selfish in some respects, since a great deal of the focus is on the client and his or her needs and behavior. This focus on self begins to gradually diminish over time, as suggested in the last section, as the client learns how to make new behaviors become habits.

Recovery can be visualized as the layers of an onion, with each successive layer representing a growth in recovery. The inner core of recovery (or of the onion) is developed early in treatment when the focus is principally on avoiding drug use. When that new behavior becomes habit, a new layer of the onion is added as the client begins to extend these new behaviors into the real world outside treatment. The client begins to extend behavior change into his or her family life, into work or school, and into other institutions in which the client may interact. These middle layers, or *spheres of recovery,* represent a movement of focus from client-only to a focus on how the client interacts with significant others in the environment. This movement represents a change in emphasis from self to social relationships. This shift happens late in treatment and extends into aftercare.

The outer layers of the onion (or the spheres of recovery — see Figure 6.1) are dedicated to yet another subtle shift in focus, in which the client begins to redefine how she or he fits into the larger society. This change in focus occurs when the client has reestablished healthy interpersonal relationships with significant others and stability in those social institutions in which she or he participates. Recovery moves from interpersonal relationships with those close to the client to an understanding of his or her place in the world. Many of the issues involve quality-of-life decisions, and clients may be wrestling with *existential* issues as well. The client establishes a new identity in which drugs no longer define who he or she is, but also realizes that the new identity is a direct result of changing a drug problem. As mentioned, giving becomes as important as receiving during this time.

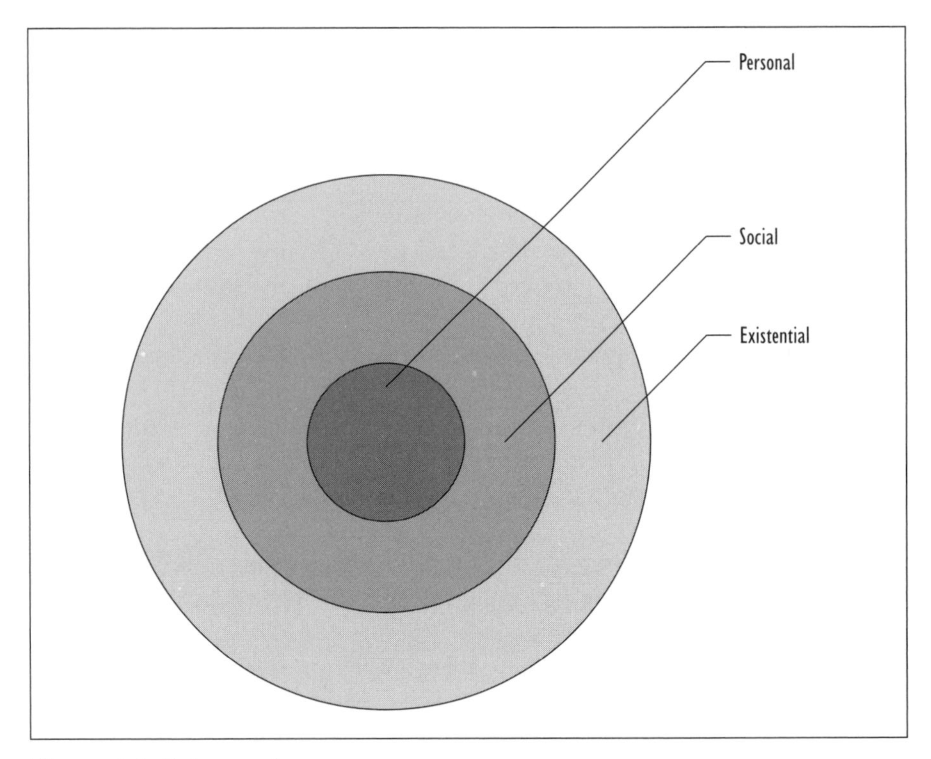

Figure 6.1: Spheres of recovery.

Additionally, a client must tackle different areas of growth, or *zones of recovery,* to develop this concentric growth pattern that occurs as recovery progresses. These zones tend to roughly follow the biopsychosocial model of a drug problem, in that the early sphere of recovery involves mainly physical healing and psychological recovery of the client, and the middle sphere of recovery involves social healing and taking recovery out into the world. The outer sphere is much more personal in nature, even though it involves a broad view of identity in the context of the larger world. This outer sphere, since it involves issues of identity, meaning, purpose, and direction, tends to be very spiritual for many people. *Spirituality* can mean many things in this context, and is not necessarily synonymous with religion. There are many different forums in which people develop this zone of recovery, some of which involve interactions with others (e.g., religious and support groups; social-action and service types of organizations) and some of which are highly personal and private (e.g., meditation or other private endeavors aimed at personal growth). The spiritual zone of recovery usually is the last to develop because it depends upon healing in the other areas before growth can occur in this zone. This does not mean that spirituality is not important in earlier spheres of recovery; it simply means that it becomes more important as time goes along and the client creates a new life.

Continuing Care Plans

The *continuing care plan,* developed prior to discharge from treatment into aftercare, is constructed with the different spheres and zones of recovery in mind. The ultimate goal of the continuing care plan is to help the client move into this new phase of recovery as seamlessly as possible. So, like the treatment plan (remember Chapter 4), the continuing care plan should be comprehensive but not overly intrusive, should be simple enough to follow, and should be developed collaboratively with the client prior to discharge.

Effective continuing care plans integrate community resources with the existing treatment resources that the client will continue to access. One aspect of the plan will be to determine which support-group meetings (if any) the client will attend during the week. The continuing care plan also will link the client to other community resources deemed important to his or her continued success to achieve and maintain behavior changes after discharge from treatment. Referrals may need to be made upon discharge to ensure that the client gets her or his needs met in specialized areas of care. The plan also will include a problem list, just as the treatment plan did, but this list will focus on the uncompleted problem list of treatment with a special emphasis on Tier 4 problem areas. Periodic checkups will be made concerning the other problem areas in Tiers 1–3 to make sure that progress in those areas is maintained.

An important part of the continuing care plan will be to determine how much access the client will have to needed resources upon discharge, especially if the client will be leaving the immediate area in which treatment has been received. Long-distance referral contacts may need to be made by the counselor or therapist to provide for continuity of care. If there appear to be deficits in the resources available to the client, then the counselor or therapist may have to find alternatives. For example, if the client and counselor agree that a 12-step group will be part of the continuing care plan, but the availability of such groups is limited by the client's work schedule or by geographical relocation, then alternatives such as an online group or perhaps an attempt to develop a new group should be examined. Professional networks can help you determine whether the resources necessary for the continuing care of the client are available in a distant location, and then to determine how to access these resources for your client.

> "To accomplish great things, we must dream as well as act."
>
> — ANATOLE FRANCE

If referrals are made in conjunction with the continuing care plan, then the procedures suggested for referrals in Chapters 2 and 3 should be followed. Professional networks can be used to make appropriate referrals. Continuity of care should be provided whenever possible during the referral process, and you should check with your client to make sure that contact with the referral was made within an appropriate amount of time and that the client finds the referral helpful.

THINGS TO REMEMBER

Developing Continuing Care Plans

1. Use the different spheres and zones to guide development of the plan.
2. The plan should be comprehensive but not overly intrusive, and simple enough to follow.
3. Integrate community resources with existing treatment resources.
4. Include family in the plan if possible.
5. Include appropriate referrals in the plan.
6. Include periodic checkup meetings with the client to discuss progress.
7. Include dream goals as part of the plan.

Structuring the Continuing Care Plan

The ideal continuing care plan is a plan of hope. Like a treatment plan, the continuing care plan addresses problem areas and the goals mutually agreed upon by client and therapist within those problem areas. The continuing care plan also allows for dreaming, since it typically addresses Tier 4 problems. Reflecting upon quality-of-life problems invites the client to dream about where he or she would like his or her life to be a year or even 5 years from now. Whereas the treatment plan tends to focus more on the here and now (as a plan for surviving a crisis should), the aftercare plan recognizes that working hard on overcoming a drug problem eventually will yield rewards. The client has passed the crisis stage in overcoming the drug problem for the most part when entering into aftercare, so a little dreaming about the future is in order. This dreaming also provides a great deal of hopefulness about the future, which can carry the client when difficult times arise.

Aftercare Goals Can Lead to a Little Dreaming

Aftercare is the time to address more long-term goals related to life changes. Since these changes typically involve long-term plans, the goals of aftercare can extend well beyond the end of aftercare, and perhaps represent lifelong goals that challenge clients to better themselves. When developing the aftercare plan, you can encourage a little dreaming on your client's part so that she or he feels the future will be interesting, challenging, worth pursuing, and drug-free. As you develop this plan with a client, ask her or him to consider questions like, "If you could do anything with your life, the sky being the limit, what would it be?" and questions that beginning with, "What if — ?"

Brainstorming can be quite helpful in developing this treatment plan. So remembering the process for brainstorming (see Chapter 3), have your client generate a wide range of possible goals related to the future, at first without concern for their feasibility. After the ideas for new life directions are generated, then feasibility of the goals can be discussed. If the goals require major life-direction changes, discuss how to implement those plans. Discussion of these goals and plans is done without concern for the complexity of the process, because the initial goal of this endeavor is to open as many doors as possible for the client. Encourage your client to entertain new directions and goals for improving his or her life over the long term and not to worry for the moment about what the process for achieving those new directions might be.

Next, have the client rank order the dream goals and pick the ones that are most appealing for inclusion on the continuing care plan. I would suggest including perhaps two or three in the plan to make it manageable, but do not discard the other suggestions just because they were not ranked among the top two or three goals. The other ideas that were ranked lower constitute another list of dreams for the client to work on in the future. The fact that they are not top priorities today does not mean they will not be the priorities of tomorrow. You can add a wish list at the bottom of the continuing care plan that simply lists these other dream goals that the client has generated but not ranked at the top for this plan.

The next step is to develop a plan for how to get from point A to point Z with regard to the dream goals. Ascertain what strengths and needs the client has related to achieving a dream goal and list those under the targeted goal. Then develop a roadmap for how to get the client from where he or she is today to where he or she wants to be with regard to this dream goal. Try to work out a skeleton of a plan with the client for how to make steady progress on achieving that goal. Determine what the first step toward achieving the goal is, then the next, and the next, and so forth. Try to develop a plan that allows for weekly measurable and achievable mini-goals related to reaching the greater dream goal. The value of weekly mini-goals is that they provide you with specific benchmarks for evaluating client progress. This method also allows the client to feel as if she or he is making palpable progress toward the long-term dream goal. Visible signs of progress can encourage clients to continue to work toward the dream, especially when the goal is lofty and far into the future.

Good examples of such dream goals include a career change or completing a college degree. Since dream goals usually involve greatly delaying gratification, and since many people with drug problems have limited experiences with delaying gratification, it will be important for you as the counselor or therapist to highlight the mini-payoffs along the way, week to week, for the client. This reinforcement and encouragement will keep your client hooked into seeking the long-term prize. At first, you will have to highlight the little steps of progress and reinforce those for the client. Eventually, the client will find intrinsic reinforcement for making progress on these dream goals as she or he gets each step closer to making the dream come true. Progress on these goals also does wonders for increasing self-efficacy *and* self-esteem.

Dream goals can fall into one or more of several categories. The first category includes vocational and/or educational goals. Your client may desire a change in careers that would lead to a significant improvement in quality of life for her- or himself, and perhaps for family as well. Vocational goals often are linked to educational goals, and the dream goal may prompt your client to seek new training or even pursue a new educational degree. You can help your client as she or he considers how to achieve these goals by directing her or him toward resources to learn more about the directions being considered. Questions that may need to be addressed include what kind of training is involved, how long it will take and what it will cost, whether financial support is available, and where the training can be obtained. Help your client determine how to take the first steps toward reaching the goal, and then define what the weekly goals would look like on the road to the dream.

In addition, make sure that the goal is dreamy but achievable, because you do not want your client to be set up to fail. For example, is your client capable of reaching the goal that is being set? If not, you may wish to suggest a less lofty goal or perhaps an alternative. If the client insists, then develop a backup plan to protect the client. Counselors and therapists have to be careful when evaluating whether clients can realistically achieve what is proposed, because you do not want to unduly hinder pursuing a dream or to underestimate your client. Developing challenging yet achievable dream goals for our clients is one of the more difficult things we do as treatment professionals.

Sometimes vocational and educational goals are inextricably linked to financial goals. Some of my clients have set goals about becoming debt free or developing retirement-savings goals or lofty plans for projects or trips that required financial plans in order to complete them. Help your client identify the first steps and the roadmap to reach these goals, as well as to make appropriate referrals for financial counseling as needed. You may be able to help the client develop a budget if you have those skills and if the goals are simple ones, but a referral should be considered if either the financial needs to fulfill the plans or the client's budgetary concerns are complicated. Avoid giving financial advice to clients, since it could interfere with the therapeutic relationship if the advice proves to be wrong.

In addition to vocational and educational goals, a client may have dream goals related to family and important relationships. Guide the client as she or he develops achievable but challenging goals in these areas. Then match your client with the resources to make those changes possible. Some clients with whom I've worked had lofty goals such as improving interactions with partners and becoming better parents. Others may have goals like increasing the number and quality of friendships, which may be a very lofty goal indeed if the person has comorbid social anxiety. Help the client identify the first steps, and then subsequent incremental steps toward the goal that can be evaluated regularly in conjunction with aftercare meetings. Continuing-care issues for couples and families are discussed in greater detail later in this chapter.

Finally, as alluded to earlier in this chapter, dream goals can be related to issues of personal identity, character, meaning, and spirituality. Again, your role as a counselor or therapist is to provide direction and resources but not to provide answers. The solutions for personal goals like these must be found through personal recovery experiences. You can direct but you cannot determine. Pursuing existential goals such as these is part of developing a new identity apart from drugs, and they can be the most challenging and rewarding goals for your clients to achieve.

Models for Aftercare

Just as with treatment, the appearance of aftercare may vary according to the therapeutic model. For example, Minnesota-model aftercare usually operates in groups that meet weekly. The format of these weekly sessions usually involves psychoeducation around relapse prevention, often related to an issue germane to specific members of the group. Sometimes the psychoeducation topic is predetermined by the outline of a relapse prevention manual (see Chapter 7).

Before aftercare begins, a client will likely meet with the aftercare counselor. This counselor may be different than the one he or she works with in treatment. However, the client likely will know the aftercare counselor from treatment groups even if that person was not her or his primary individual counselor. This first

CASE STUDY

Darien's Dreams

Darien is a 24-year-old finishing treatment and preparing for aftercare. His therapist, Claudia, is meeting with him to develop a continuing care plan. Together they have developed a plan for addressing those problem areas that they did not quite finish in treatment. But Claudia surprises Darien with a question no one has ever asked him before: "Darien, if you could do anything with your life, what would it be? Don't worry right now about how long it will take or how hard it will be. Just dream a little and tell me what you would do." Realizing that Claudia is serious, he eventually replies, "I would love to go to college and become an architect. I have always enjoyed putting things together, and drawing plans for things that could be built." Claudia responds, "I think you can do this. It will take some time, but it is a worthy dream and a good goal for you. Let's put going back to school on your continuing care plan, with the idea that you will become an architect. But of course you may go to school and find something else you want to do instead. Okay, are you ready for some homework related to this goal?"

If you were Claudia, what kind of homework would you assign to Darien related to reaching this goal? What does he need to know to succeed? What are the first steps?

meeting operates much like an intake session and is meant to develop the alliance between the participant and the counselor. The continuing care plan is reviewed and the client is oriented to the aftercare group process prior to the first meeting. Group rules and expectations likely will be reviewed with the client. Participant questions are answered so that she or he will feel more comfortable going into this new group.

In weekly group meetings, clients will report on progress on their continuing care goals. These goals will likely include unresolved problem areas from treatment as well as dream goals. The counselor will encourage discussion of progress as time permits in groups, and peers will be encouraged to provide feedback to each other on personal progress. Sometimes peers will confront if there is concern that a participant is engaging in old behavior or not making sufficient progress. Aftercare counselors have to be careful not to permit confrontations to get out of hand and may have to shut down other participants if they become overly zealous in confrontation. Clients sometimes will be assigned homework, such as reading or writing assignments related to relapse prevention, and those assignments will be reviewed in the group meetings as well.

In addition, the participant regularly meets one on one with the aftercare counselor outside the group to evaluate progress toward aftercare goals. These meetings may happen monthly or perhaps bimonthly. The aftercare plan will be reviewed together, and the plan may be collaboratively modified if needed. Review meetings continue at regular intervals throughout aftercare. When the participant approaches the end of aftercare, a more comprehensive review will take place. The counselor may summarize progress and make some recommendations for next steps in the recovery program. The participant sets new goals for the future after discharge from aftercare. The discharge session usually occurs within the group session, and generally involves some type of graduation ritual. During this ritual, counselors, peers, and the participant will each have time to share and reflect upon the aftercare experience. *Closure* is provided for all participants during this ritual. The participant is discharged with a long-term recovery plan in place and with recommendations to continue to participate in support groups.

Spiritual Model for Aftercare: Movement From Healed to Healer

As noted in Chapter 5, the Minnesota model incorporates certain aspects of the spiritual model of recovery. Aftercare within the spiritual model includes continual participation in support groups meant to fill the spiritual void of the client and alter his or her identity so that drugs are no longer wanted to fill that void. During aftercare, participants in Minnesota-model treatment programs are urged to continue working the 12 steps in order to continue to grow spiritually.

In treatment, usually the goal is to have the person complete the first 5 of the 12 steps if possible. The beginning steps are largely dedicated to accepting powerlessness over drug use, accepting that the powerlessness can be overcome by surrender to a higher power that can restore sanity if the client makes that decision, and then resolving to clean house morally by confidentially sharing with another person his or her story and how drugs caused him or her to act in ways that caused guilt and shame. The latter steps remain to be worked after leaving treatment, and this process continues in aftercare programs in the Minnesota model.

However, some clients may choose more religious types of solutions after treatment, and others may continue to develop religious (or spiritual) programs that were used to overcome drug problems instead of utilizing formal treatment. A great many of these practices focus on seeking answers and solutions from universals rather than from drugs, and may tend to be directed toward existential activities to change the person's character permanently so that drugs are no longer a viable option.

The common element among the spiritual approaches seems to be a movement from a personal spiritual healing (common in the early stages of overcoming a drug problem) toward a transforming presence in the world. This shift is reflected quite nicely in Steps 6–12, which move from changing the self with the help of a higher power to helping others change (the last step). Since the person is given a gift of being healed spiritually by the program, the person shares this method of healing with others out of gratitude. In this way, the person becomes a healing presence in the world. The idea of moving from being wounded to becoming a healer is a powerful metaphor for the spiritual model of overcoming a drug problem.

Family Model for Aftercare

Family models for aftercare exist as well, and can be quite useful as the client resumes his or her role in the family. Overcoming a drug problem does not necessarily eliminate problems that exist in relationships or in the family system. Some of these problems and issues may take some time to resolve. Generally speaking, while in treatment, the client spends a great deal of time focusing on solutions to overcoming his or her drug problem. What this means practically speaking is that family and relationship problems often are not addressed systematically until after treatment is completed. This makes aftercare a period of time when relationship and family concerns may rise to the forefront for the client. Therapists and counselors must remain alert to the likelihood that family and relationship issues may become more acute during aftercare and can represent a threat to the client's recovery if not adequately addressed.

Partner Involvement and Couples' Issues After Treatment

Many treatment centers offer family programs, such as weekly family or couple support groups, that may coincide with the aftercare program that the client attends. In addition, the aftercare counselor may decide that meeting jointly with client and partner can be helpful during aftercare to address relationship concerns. This type of meeting can help the partner understand what the client does in aftercare, and can potentially help with relationship or family problems. In addition, many treatment centers also offer partners and other family members continuing family therapy after treatment that may aid in relationship issues.

Many new challenges can arise after treatment for partners. A family therapist can prepare the partner for these challenges as part of a family orientation to aftercare. Such a meeting will occur around the same time as the client develops his or her continuing care plan just prior to discharge from treatment. The family therapist may address adjustment concerns that many partners experience when a client is discharged from treatment. The family therapist can prepare the partner for what to reasonably expect from the loved one after treatment ends.

For example, it is not uncommon for a client to have little to no interest in sex early in recovery from a drug problem, or for the client's interest to fluctuate. Sexual performance is hindered by stress, and obviously the client is under a great deal of stress as she or he learns how to stay drug free. In addition, the client's personality may seem different now that he or she is not using drugs. Although it is likely that many of these changes will be quite positive, the changes also may seem a little strange and unsettling to a partner. Change can be scary, even when it is for the good, and partners are not immune to feeling scared about positive changes in a loved one. Family therapists also will likely want to discuss how relationship dynamics may change now that the loved one has stopped using drugs. Remembering the family model discussed in Chapter 5, as the client changes, the relationship with a partner is likely to change as well. Again, this change will likely be for the best, but even little changes can sometimes feel threatening or disturbing to a partner. Family therapists can alert the partner that these changes may occur and can put into action a plan that will aid the partner to cope with such changes. Change seems much more threatening when a person is under stress, and this statement is as true for partners and family members as it is for clients.

Empirically validated cognitive behavioral therapy for couples can be quite helpful if relationship problems are an issue. Cognitive behavioral couples therapy combines the best of cognitive behavioral and family therapy techniques in order to help couples. The research suggests that use of this type of therapy can be quite helpful in mediating and resolving problems involving couples. Counselors may want to make a referral for this therapy if clients have relationship issues that interfere with aftercare.

Family Involvement and Family Issues

Family therapy programs continue in many treatment programs throughout aftercare, and as mentioned, a family therapist may be available to family members. Children who are having adjustment problems may find therapy beneficial, for example. Including all family members can be helpful for the client and allows other members of the family to work on their own personal growth, too.

The family model of recovery suggests that as the identified client changes in treatment (and beyond), the family dynamics will be altered. The family unit was in a state of equilibrium (albeit dysfunctional) when the client used drugs, but now that the client has changed that behavior, the old family system will be out of balance. Part of the family model for aftercare is to work with the family to create a new, healthy, and functional equilibrium. Practically speaking, the family can expect that the client will want to resume a more active role in the family system now that he or she is not using drugs, and this process of asserting oneself in the family system may ruffle some feathers among other family members.

The family therapist can prepare family members for this likelihood, as well as work with them on their residual feelings about the client's drug use and its effect on family members and the family system. One goal is to prevent family members' toxic feelings from adversely affecting the client's resolve to change the drug problem. *Toxic* in this instance means that expressing the feelings can be harmful to family healing and to the client. On the other hand, a family member may be well justified in having such toxic feelings related to the client's drug use, and the family therapist must be careful not to invalidate those feelings in a way that could harm the therapeutic alliance with the family.

The client likely will benefit from continued involvement of family in the therapeutic process during aftercare. Many commonly reported relapse triggers are related to relationship stress (see Chapter 7), and family therapy may help reduce relationship stress. As the client is learning how to adjust to living drug free after treatment, the family learns how to live with a drug-free loved one.

Phases of Family Recovery

Families can move through phases of recovery just like the clients do. These phases of recovery, however, are more tied to the dynamics of the family. The beginning phase of healing involves personal healing among family members, so the family system at this phase seems somewhat disjointed. Understandably, each member of the family has to place personal healing above family healing during this early stage of recovery. However, after this period of individual recovery takes place, family reintegration becomes possible as members become more focused on working together in a healthy system again.

The middle phase of this process may be turbulent as a new equilibrium is being established, and this period typically coincides with aftercare for the client. Many of the issues discussed previously become a central focus for the family during the aftercare period. As the issues become resolved and family members become more familiar and comfortable with the new, drug-free loved one, then family equilibrium may be restored at a new level. Some family systems do not survive these changes, meaning that a partnership may dissolve. However, many families and partnerships do weather the storms and grow much closer because of this process of separate and collective recovery that takes place after a drug problem has been overcome. The final phase for a family that weathers the storm

USEFUL RESOURCES

National Contact Information for Family Support Groups

Al-Anon/Alateen: Phone: 1-800-356-9996; Web link: http://al-anon-alateen.org/

Co-Anon: Phone: 1-800-898-9985; Web link: http://www.co-anon.org/

CoDA: Phone: (602) 277-7991; Web link: http://www.coda.org/

Families Anonymous: Phone: 1-800-736-9805;
Web link: http://www.familiesanonymous.org/

is a reintegrated family system that is much stronger and healthier than it was when drug use defined its dynamics.

Behavioral Model for Aftercare: Tapering Therapy and Booster Sessions

As mentioned earlier, aftercare is not part of the behavioral model of treating a drug problem. Those clients who are working with a cognitive behavioral therapist will continue to engage in similar therapeutic practices, albeit at a much greater level of skill and self-efficacy, during later stages of psychotherapy as they did in the earlier stages. The number of therapy sessions will slowly be reduced and spaced out over greater intervals of time toward the end of psychotherapy. This is done in order to promote greater generalization of skills on the part of the client and to reduce the client's dependence on therapy and on a therapist for behavior change over the long term. This slow tapering in the number of sessions also tends to promote seeking intrinsic reinforcement for behavior change, so that the client becomes more self-reliant, and that progress is energized by client satisfaction in making changes rather than by therapist satisfaction.

Part of this movement toward self-reliance in cognitive behavioral therapy is to increasingly link natural reinforcers with behavior change. *Natural reinforcers* are positive rewards for behavior change available to the client outside session, as opposed to the reinforcement provided by the therapist in session. Natural reinforcement will have much more power to maintain behavior change over time because it will be consistently available to the client. Since therapy will end, the client must find long-term reinforcement for change elsewhere. Natural reinforcers are the kinds of reward for behavior change that always will be available. They include good feelings, satisfaction, and personal joy for accomplishments as a consequence of engaging in certain behaviors.

Another part of the process of promoting client self-reliance is to teach the client how to become his or her own therapist. Throughout the therapeutic process, a cognitive behavioral therapist will be orienting the client to the model of therapy, how to observe behavior, how to do a particular therapeutic technique and why doing it is theoretically important, and how to practice this technique through role-play and in homework assignments. In-session work trains the client to begin to do these things with prompting by the therapist. Eventually the client will take charge of changing behavior on his or her own time. If a cognitive behavioral therapist has done her or his work well, then the client will assume greater responsibility for controlling his or her own therapy over time.

Periodic progress reviews are made. Often, the timing of these reviews is jointly agreed upon at the beginning of therapy. For example, the client and therapist

CLIENT HANDOUT

The Value of Aftercare

Aftercare can help you consolidate all that you have learned so far in treatment or therapy. This period presents an opportunity for you to practice what you have learned in real-world settings, as well as to enjoy your new freedom from drug use. Use this time to practice the new skills you have learned and experiment with new directions for your life. Also, enjoy yourself as you rediscover who you are without being under the influence of drugs!

Many clients have told me that they found aftercare a liberating time of great self-exploration. Not many people get a chance to redefine themselves later in life, but this is exactly the opportunity that lies before you now. Treatment and therapy have provided you with many skills for overcoming a drug problem, but nowhere is there a manual written on how you must use them to reach your dreams. That manual must be written by you, since you are the expert on yourself. How you use those tools will redefine who you are; in effect, you have the opportunity to become whoever you want.

One of the great joys of aftercare is beginning to enjoy success again. You have already accomplished a miracle by changing your drug use, and you will only get better over time. Congratulations on your success, which is a result of your hard work, but do not forget to acknowledge those who helped you make it to this point. There is a great deal of hard work ahead, but already you are beginning to see that reaching for your dreams may be possible without the ball-and-chain of drug use to slow you down.

Aftercare and beyond will be a time of great change for you, but it will be mostly positive. Certainly some change will not be pleasant, because this is a truism about life, but for the most part what is ahead will be good. The greatest gift in life will be restored to you since you have overcome your drug use: *Hope* will return to you in bucketfuls. Once again you are in charge of your own destiny, and no one can take that away from you. You can give it away, but it cannot be taken. Choose to work very hard not to give away control of your future during aftercare.

may agree to review progress at 4 and 8 weeks. At some point during one of the later reviews, the suggestion is made that, if client progress warrants it, the interval of time between sessions may be extended from every week to every other week, with evaluation of this new arrangement's effectiveness at some point in the future. Eventually the length of time between sessions is lengthened again and again. At some point, a termination date (last session) will be set with client feedback.

Finally, as termination draws near, *booster sessions* may be suggested several months into the future. Research suggests that booster sessions can be effective to check up on client progress and to make adjustments in the recovery plan if needed. In addition, booster sessions can serve to reinforce successful client efforts as well as leave a veiled safety net in place to help the client in the future. The time interval between booster sessions is gradually lengthened until they are no longer needed. Booster sessions tend to be the functional equivalent of aftercare in the behavioral model for treating a drug problem. Using booster sessions recognizes that the client has the skills necessary to succeed but may benefit from a periodic checkup to see how things are going and what can be done to improve on the recovery plan in place.

Crises in Aftercare

Counselors and therapists should be aware that sometimes crises do arise for clients in aftercare. The triggers for such crises generally are problems that existed during treatment but may have reached critical mass during aftercare. For example, it is not uncommon for a relationship problem to escalate once a client has completed treatment. Sometimes partners expect too much from clients after treatment and are disappointed when those expectations are not met. In other cases the partner may have waited to end a relationship until after treatment in some effort to be humane. Regardless of reason, a relationship crisis can be extremely disturbing to a client after completing treatment and must be addressed with intensive psychotherapy using the cognitive and behavioral techniques suggested in Chapter 5. Many clients believe that, since they completed treatment, their partners should see that completion as a good-faith effort to change — but the partner may have other ideas about what he or she wants to do about the relationship.

The obvious concern you may have is for a relapse during such a crisis. As the aftercare counselor or primary therapist, your goal is to convince the client, generally by using cognitive modification techniques, that using drugs will not solve this problem and will, in fact, complicate it. This is a good time to encourage your client to use self-distraction and distress-tolerance skills, to evaluate the situation with as much objectivity as possible using cognitive techniques, and to work on changing the things that can be changed. Relationship problems likely did not begin overnight, so any solutions that may work will take time and patience.

In addition, financial problems can trigger crises during aftercare. Sometimes these crises may actually be brought about because the client has been in treatment. There may be a mountain of bills to face once the client has completed treatment. Again, the change techniques and skills suggested to be used with a relationship crisis can be used under these circumstances. You also can serve as an advocate for the client if bills need to be refinanced or other, more generous arrangements need to be made on repaying the bills. Provide hope to the client that avoiding drug use will only improve the picture over time and enable to client to make better judgments with regard to financial matters.

A change in vocation or career direction may be appropriate to solve such problems over the long term. Aftercare is a good time to consider such a change, and you may want to recommend vocational counseling and make a referral for the client. There are, of course, two basic ways to change financial situations: to decrease spending and to increase income. A change in careers that provides the opportunity for increased income over the long term may be worth enduring short-term financial stress. Cognitive techniques that illustrate how a reduction in income for a relatively short period of time while the person returns to school or gains further vocational training is rapidly overtaken by the lifetime increase of salary that person receives from making the career change can be quite enlightening to clients who may not be able to see the whole picture and may balk at going back to school when finances seem tight. In many instances, the financial pains of going back to school are paid for in a few short years after the completion of training, and then the years that follow merely increase the financial benefits. And these benefits do not even account for the likely increase in quality of life from seeking a career that is more satisfying to your client. Many drug users tend to be underemployed and need new challenges; a challenging career change may be just what is needed.

Finally, other crises can occur that have been mentioned before, such as aggressiveness, suicidality, and perhaps even a psychotic break. Since dealing with these crises was covered in great detail in Chapter 3, I will not cover them again here. Basically, you will want to treat them the same way in aftercare that you would in therapy or treatment. Counselors and therapists should be aware that depression may increase after treatment for some clients, so if you notice the telltale symptoms, you may want to assess your client for suicidality just to be on the safe side, and respond accordingly.

Moral and Ethical Issues Related to Treatment, Therapy, and Continuing Care

Counselors and therapists have to be very careful to defend the rights of their clients who may feel powerless in therapy. As mentioned previously, therapy provides for a significant power imbalance. Sometimes counselors and therapists are tempted by the power available to them, and there are times when this temptation happens subtly enough that the counselor or therapist may not be aware of abuse-of-power occurs. Many ethical violations happen when the professional relationship crosses some sort of invisible line to become a personal relationship. The difficult thing about ethical considerations like these is that the circumstances surrounding any human relationship may be gray rather than clearly black and white. Some people have described ethical problems in therapy as a process of either the client's or the therapist's "crossing a *boundary* of therapy," but in my mind the professional has ultimate responsibility for making sure that such behavior does not occur and, if it does occur, for changing and fixing it now.

There are several areas where a therapeutic relationship can typically go wrong and cause ethical concerns. The first area of concern has to do with finances. Since counseling and therapy often involve payment, it is important to try to divorce therapy as much as possible from the financial aspects of the business of therapy. However, this is not always possible, especially if you are in private practice *and* you are your own accountant, too! A rule of thumb is this: If you cannot treat a client without bias because bills are not being paid, then you have no business treating the client any longer. A therapeutic referral must be made. There is no possible way that you can give your best effort to a client when you are sore about not getting paid.

On the other hand, a client's problems paying the bills will adversely affect therapy even if you are not personally involved with bill collection. You have an obligation to advocate for your client under such circumstances, but you may be in a spot where administrators in your clinic are pressing both you and the client

CASE STUDY

Let's Make a Deal. . . .

Joan is a chemical dependency counselor working with Raquel both in treatment and in aftercare. They have a wonderful working relationship in therapy and Raquel has made good progress toward overcoming her drug problem. Raquel was having financial problems even before treatment began and continues to struggle financially. These problems have caused her to get far behind in paying for her aftercare sessions.

Joan is a single parent and has been having trouble keeping a consistent daycare worker for her toddler, Jason. She knows that Raquel has a goal to someday teach kindergarten and says that she loves young children. At the next progress review meeting Joan brings up the issue of the unpaid aftercare bills. Raquel apologizes for this situation, explains her difficulty finding a job, and then states she will eventually pay the bills "if it takes the rest of my life, I promise." Joan makes a new suggestion that instead of paying money for the bills and for future aftercare, perhaps Raquel might be interested in caring for Jason in exchange for aftercare services past and present and for experience working with children of that age. Raquel agrees and the deal is struck. Although both Joan and Raquel are delighted, do you see any potential problems with this arrangement?

for resolution on these bills. Again, your role as a counselor or therapist requires that you advocate for your client, and if you feel you cannot do this under these circumstances, a therapeutic referral should occur. As mentioned in Chapter 3, you also should consider whether the expenses of treatment or therapy outweigh its benefits. If so, then you may owe it to your client to suggest an alternative that may be as helpful to her or him, but less expensive.

A second area of concern may involve sexual or romantic relationships between a counselor or therapist and a client. There are clearly circumstances in which such a relationship can disturb a therapeutic relationship and do harm to a client. Many clients and careers have been devastated by these types of relationships, some of which seemed genuine at the moment but failed to last. A sexual or romantic relationship with a client you see now is considered by most professional organizations to be grounds for *disciplinary action,* and with good reason. The potential for harm greatly outweighs any potential for good. The situation gets more complicated if the therapeutic relationship has ended. Certainly an argument can be made that, if the therapeutic relationship ended recently, it may have ended precisely so a romantic relationship could be established. Even if the counselor or therapist did not end therapy for these reasons, it may have been that the client felt pressured to do so. Again, the risk for harm may outweigh the possibility for good if therapy ended abruptly for a relationship to occur.

When does it become okay to have a relationship with a former client? There is much debate about when it may be ethically okay for a therapist or counselor to have such a relationship, with some professionals expressing the opinion that such a relationship may be possible, without risk of compromise or coercion, several months or years after therapy has ended. I do not have an easy answer to this question. As a therapist I know there is something unique about a therapeutic relationship that creates or enhances human vulnerability. My feeling is that counselors and therapists must respect the client amid this vulnerability by not taking advantage of that moment. Does this vulnerability between a therapist and a client ever go away? I honestly do not know, but a therapist should consider the vulnerability factor in any relationship with a client, even an ex-client, very strongly and deliberately before acting on emotional attractions, even many years after therapy ends. Even if you are convinced sufficient time has passed for that vulnerability to diminish, it may not have diminished from the standpoint of your ex-client.

Another area of ethical concern relates to the personal agendas of a counselor or therapist. Sometimes a counselor or therapist will have a personal stake in an idea, a product, or even a particular style or technique of therapy. What I am speaking of here goes far beyond a clear preference for a model of therapy; this agenda concerns more of a vested interest in the therapy's being used and in establishing its effectiveness. For example, let's imagine that Counselor Trey has developed a technique, which combines the use of rapid, nonstop eye-blinking with listening to softly played Mozart, that he believes helps people overcome drug problems. But his interest has gone beyond merely whether the technique works, because he has been marketing this technique all over the country and now is sponsoring a school that teaches this technique for a price. The problem is that he has a conflict of interest between his own practice and a business that causes him to have a personal agenda. Now he pushes his therapy on every client he sees, with little regard to what the presenting set of problems may be. Since Trey's combination technique has not been empirically validated, there is no way to know whether his clients really benefit from this agenda.

Another example I've heard about did not involve a conflict of interest so much as an obsession with one strategy. The rumors had it that a physician was treating all of his patients for depression no matter what they presented with, simply assuming that *everyone* was depressed. Because of this, the state license board investigators were quite surprised when they discovered that everyone this physician was treating was on the exact same antidepressant. Before you dismiss this problem as one that can happen only to physicians, let me mention a similar example of a counselor who was convinced that everyone he saw likely had been abused sexually as children, and then used sessions systematically to "bring out" those hidden and forgotten memories in all clients. Many clients who had never been abused were subtly or overtly coerced into believing that they had been by this counselor. Agendas take the form of counselor or therapist obsessions that interfere with clinical judgment and with clients' getting individualized care. Needless to say, professionals who engage in this type of misconduct are at risk for losing licenses and are subject to malpractice litigation.

A much more subtle but insidious agenda occurs when a therapist or counselor has an ax to grind with a particular type of client. In these instances, therapists and counselors can react in a couple of ways that are not helpful to the client. First, the therapist or counselor may be abusive toward the client, in some cases without realizing it. The professional's behavior may range from surly and disrespectful to downright mean toward a specific type of client because of a lack of therapist control over the emotional agenda with such a client. Second, the therapist or counselor simply may not do his or her best work with the client. This can occur in very insidious ways, such as not spending as much time preparing for sessions with the client, or ignoring or neglecting to work hard with the client in session. A therapist or counselor may not be willing to go out of his or her way to help this client because of this emotional agenda, and therefore treats this client significantly different than he or she treats other clients.

Sometimes these emotional agendas reflect prejudice, or worse. For example, a male counselor or therapist may have difficulties working with women, so when he works with a female client, he talks down and sometimes lectures to her about drug use, does not prepare for sessions with her in the same way he prepares for his male clients, is abrupt and unfriendly in session, and finds he is annoyed with her more than with his male clients. Ethically speaking, the counselor should reflect upon these behaviors, look for a pattern, identify his bias, and realize that he has no business treating women with this type of bias. Theoretically, if he really believed in the efficacy of psychotherapy to help people change, he would seek it for himself to overcome these *misogynistic* feelings toward women.

The same type of reaction can result from overt or covert racial prejudice. A large body of research supports the idea that ethnic-minority clients frequently receive qualitatively worse care and quantitatively less attention from health care professionals in clinics and hospital. Sometimes a professional is not even aware of treating ethnic-minority clients differently than White clients. Again, counselors and therapists need to observe their own clinical behavior and note when they may be treating clients differently to identify whether there is a racial pattern to that trend. Another way to check on biases is to observe your personal behavior outside the office: If you are engaging in biased behavior outside work, you likely will be engaging in biased behavior while at work, even if you attempt not to be.

Similarly, counselors and therapists can be tempted to chastise or to try to alter cultural values or practices in which clients may engage. For example, maybe a client is a member of an ethnic-minority group that uses traditional healers in

DOS AND DON'TS

Ethical Behavior Toward Clients

- Do treat your client with respect and empathy.
- Do show your client that you care and will be an advocate for his or her well-being.
- Do use empirically validated therapies whenever appropriate to provide the best care possible.
- Do orient your client to your model and style as a therapist or counselor at intake to allow for informed consent.
- Do know your biases that can adversely affect clients and keep them out of therapy.

On the other hand . . .

- Don't allow financial matters to interfere with the care of your client.
- Don't use the therapeutic relationship for self-gratification.
- Don't use the power you have as a therapist or counselor to coerce your client into doing something not in his or her best interest.
- Don't let any of your personal agendas interfere with the individualized care of your client.
- Don't allow your personal problems and lifestyle imbalances to interfere with quality care.

addition to your treatment services. A counselor or therapist strongly acculturated into mainstream U.S. society may have strong feelings about these traditional practices, perhaps considering them unnecessary and counterproductive to progress. The temptation may exist to act on these biases and try to convince the client to give up these traditional services in favor of more mainstream services. However, a counselor or therapist acting on this type of bias is engaging in highly unethical behavior by trying to impose his or her worldview on the client, and certainly this type of behavior will harm the therapeutic alliance. Counselors and therapists should avoid imposing their views of the world on their clients. If a counselor or therapist is unwilling to allow ethnic-minority clients to seek traditional cultural practices, then that counselor or therapist should sincerely reevaluate whether she or he should be working with ethnic-minority clients.

Another common agenda involves religious or spiritual beliefs. Since religious and spiritual beliefs are quite personal, the potential for abuse in this area is great. There are two general ways that a counselor or therapist can exert power in session with regard to religious or spiritual beliefs that can be harmful to clients. The first way occurs when the counselor or therapist uses therapy as a forum to push her or his beliefs on the client. Counselors or therapists who have strong religious or spiritual ideas should be aware of the temptation to want to share those with a client.

Therapy is an inappropriate forum for sharing your unsolicited personal religious or spiritual beliefs if the client has not given informed consent prior to the beginning of therapy for you to do so. I have heard of many instances over the years in which clients were religiously coerced by counselors and therapists in session. This is highly unethical without informed consent, not to mention a very poor way to establish a healthy and respectful therapeutic alliance. Avoid sharing your personal religious and spiritual beliefs in session, since those beliefs carry the weight of your power as the therapist and can be coercive because of that weight. Remember that your clients likely are vulnerable in this area of their lives when they enter drug treatment, too.

There are some notable gray areas to this black-and-white suggestion to avoid discussion of personal religious and spiritual beliefs with your clients. For example, what do you do when your clients ask you what you believe? In this case, your beliefs *are* being solicited by the client. Under these conditions, it may appropriate to discuss your beliefs if you are comfortable doing so — but under very tight restrictions. For one, you should make it clear that these are *your* beliefs and that, although they work for you, they may not work for the client. In this way, you are not sharing your beliefs in a way that suggests they should be the absolute truth for the client, too, nor are you suggesting that the client share these beliefs. Second, this request for information is specific to this moment in therapy and does not give you a blanket invitation to share your beliefs whenever you want. Third, the discussion should be conducted in such a way that the client is encouraged to discover his or her own beliefs apart from yours.

CLIENT HANDOUT

When You Feel Mistreated in Therapy

You have certain rights in therapy that have been described by your therapist. Speaking globally, you do not have any obligation to act or believe in a way suggested by a therapist or counselor, ever. There will be times when a therapist or counselor may suggest certain strategies for behavior change, but you have choices about whether you want to use those strategies. Even when the counselor or therapist implies that you have no choice but to comply, you have the choice to end therapy. The only exception would be if you have been mandated to treatment or therapy by legal authorities — but even then you have legal rights, including the right to remain silent in therapy!

If you feel that a counselor or therapist has violated your rights, you have several options available to help you. To begin with, if you feel that the violation is minor, and you feel that the relationship between you and your therapist can be repaired, you may want to discuss this with your counselor first before taking up the issue with a third party. The counselor or therapist may respond by changing his or her behavior as you requested and may repair the damage to the relationship to your satisfaction without any outside intervention. However, if correcting the violation needs outside intervention in your opinion, or if you do not feel comfortable confronting your counselor or therapist, seek help. If the counselor works for a clinic, you may want to discuss the violation with a supervisor as a first step. If that does not seem to correct the problem or you feel that the violation is too severe, many professionals are required to be licensed or certified in the states in which they practice. Many of the license or certification boards have Web sites and/or phone hotlines available for consumers to report complaints against counselors or therapists. You may want to register a compliant with the appropriate professional organization that has oversight of the counselor or therapist. Most governing bodies take these complaints quite seriously in order to protect the prestige of the profession and the quality of care provided to consumers.

If these suggested recourses are not available, or if the counselor is not a member of or licensed by a professional organization, then legal recourse may be appropriate. If a criminal act has been committed, you may wish to contact law enforcement officials. If a law has not been broken, but you feel your rights have been violated, then you may wish to seek an attorney for civil action, such as malpractice.

An important thing to remember is that you did not invite this violation of the therapeutic relationship, so there is no reason to feel responsible for what has happened or to downplay your rights. Instead, I encourage you to stand up for your rights as a client and consumer so that this type of situation will not occur in the future, to you or to someone else.

Another exception to the black-and-white suggestion that you avoid sharing your beliefs in session occurs when there *is* informed consent prior to the beginning of therapy that you will be sharing your beliefs and that this is an okay style for the client. Informed consent may occur because you advertise your practice or your clinic as religiously or spiritually oriented. Your orientation also should be reiterated and explained at intake so that the client is well aware of your intent to discuss religious or spiritual beliefs freely in session. However, even when informed consent is in place, counselors and therapists in such settings should remember two important points: Do no harm, and remember that the person is there because he or she wants therapy. Even when both client and therapist/counselor are religiously or spiritually like-minded, there is the potential for abuse of the client's belief system by an overzealous therapist or counselor, or the potential for neglect of therapy at the expense of theological discussions not related to therapy. It is up to counselors and therapists under these circumstances to make sure they pursue their clients' needs first.

On the other hand, abuse also can occur when a counselor or therapist is prejudiced against a client's religious or spiritual views. Counselors and therapists may have biases toward certain religious or spiritual beliefs just as they can have biases toward gender or race. The key, again, is to be aware of those biases by monitoring personal and professional behavior to determine patterns of bias. The danger is that the counselor or therapist will allow this bias to interfere with therapy through the neglect of clients with specific belief systems, through outright abuse (such as hostility) toward this type of client, or even through attempting to change the client's belief system. Counselors or therapists with such biases either need to seek help to change those biases, or should avoid working with clients who have belief systems that are not respected by the counselors or therapists in question.

The only exception to challenging religious or spiritual beliefs that may not be unethical would include beliefs rooted in psychosis or beliefs that threaten the client with imminent harm. For example, if your client is a member of a cult that is seriously considering suicide, not only might you have ethical grounds to challenge those beliefs, but you also have legal grounds in most states to suspend the rules protecting confidentiality because of the imminent risk of harm to the client.

Mandated Treatment and Aftercare

Some clients are sent to treatment or therapy, and to aftercare, under legal mandates by the courts. Other clients may be sent to treatment or therapy, and to aftercare, by employers or even by school officials. These clients often are referred to as *mandated* clients. Mandated clients generally have special needs that other clients may not have.

For example, mandated clients may be required to account for their participation in treatment or therapy, in aftercare, and even in support groups. Usually this is done through signed attendance slips or by communication with representatives of the courts, schools, or worksites that the person has been present at meetings or sessions. As a counselor or therapist working with a mandated client, you may be required to have regular contact with an official of the organization mandating the treatment, which may be a court official such as a probation officer, a university or school official, or an EAP representative from a business. You also may be required to submit documentation of progress to that official in the form of treatment plans, summary updates of progress, and other forms and reports as required by the mandating group.

It is important to explain to your mandated client carefully how his or her particular situation affects privacy and confidentiality during treatment and aftercare. The client should be made aware of the legal limits of his or her rights under these circumstances, since many times mandated treatment allows for great restrictions on the rights of the client. The therapeutic alliance also depends on honesty from you as the therapist or counselor under these circumstances. The client will likely feel extremely powerless under these conditions, and probably resentful, so it will be very important to acknowledge these feelings as well as to be brutally honest about the mandated circumstances of treatment. Brutal honesty is likely the only path that will allow your client to trust you, given the circumstances.

When working with a mandated client, it will be important for you to determine exactly what the rights of the client are under the circumstances, as well as what is expected from you as the counselor or therapist. Some professionals prefer not to work with mandated clients, sometimes because they believe that the clients will likely be dishonest and unmotivated under these conditions. Although that may be true at the beginning of therapy or treatment, this pattern does not have to continue throughout therapy. Whether a person remains dishonest, guarded, and distrustful throughout therapy will likely depend upon how you treat him or her. Being brutally honest, acknowledging the unfavorable circumstances, and being respectful toward the client will go a long way toward reducing client resistance. See Chapter 3 for more ideas about how to motivate behavior change under these circumstances.

Summing Up

Aftercare is a time of transition between treatment and life after treatment. This period of time allows clients to practice what they have been taught under less therapeutic supervision. As they use their skills in the real world, behavior change becomes habit, and confidence to remain drug free rises. Counselors and therapists use this time to encourage clients who are taking control of their own recovery programs while practicing relapse prevention methods. Crises can arise even in aftercare, so counselors and therapists must remain on their therapeutic toes. In addition, professionals want to make sure that they do not cause crises for their clients by acting irresponsibly or unethically. Treat clients with respect throughout the therapeutic process so that they have the opportunity to overcome their drug problems with dignity on their own terms.

Key Terms

Aftercare. A type of continuing care after treatment has ended that focuses on relapse prevention and longer term goals. Aftercare is generally less intensive than treatment.

Booster session. An equivalent to aftercare in cognitive behavioral therapy, booster sessions are regular checkups after therapy concludes to make sure the client is doing well.

Boundary. The idea that therapists and clients define their relationships in professional ways rather than in personal.

Closure. Bringing something in therapy to a meaningful conclusion.

Continuing care plan. The equivalent to a treatment plan for aftercare.

Discharge: A medical term for ending treatment.

Disciplinary action. The imposing of sanctions on a professional by his or her professional organization for violation of laws or ethical codes.

Existentialism. Deep philosophical and spiritual questions about meaning and purpose.

Mandated. Clients who are forced to seek treatment by an authority.

Misogyny. Strong bias against or hatred toward women.

Natural reinforcers. Pleasurable consequences that are the natural result of a behavior.

Termination. Essentially the same as discharge, except this is the psychotherapeutic term used for ending therapy.

Recommended Reading

I would recommend the book *Group Treatment for Substance Abuse: A Stages-of-Change Therapy Manual,* by Mary Velasquez, Gaylyn Maurer, Cathy Crouch, and Carlo DiClemente (New York: Guilford Press, 2001), because it illustrates ways to match group-therapy strategies to the level of motivation and phase of recovery of a client. The book includes details on maintenance of behavior change and relapse-prevention strategies to be used in groups.

TRUTH OR FICTION

QUIZ ANSWERS

1. False; 2. True; 3. True; 4. True; 5. True; 6. False; 7. True

CHAPTER 7

Posttreatment Recovery Management

TRUTH OR FICTION QUIZ

After reading this chapter, you should be able to answer the following questions:

1. Relapses after treatment or therapy are not unusual and can teach important new lessons about recovery. True or False?
2. Interpersonal conflict is a major trigger for relapses. True or False?
3. Stimulus control should be used instead of cue exposure whenever possible. True or False?
4. Poor coping in high-risk situations may cause lowered self-efficacy and increased positive expectancies for drug use. True or False?
5. A slip back into old behavior inevitably ends in a relapse. True or False?
6. You should plan for how to reduce the duration and severity of a lapse or relapse even before one may occur. True or False?
7. Feeling guilty after a lapse is always very helpful for the client. True or False?

Answers on p. 284.

Critical to client success after treatment is the ability to cope successfully with high-risk situations without resorting to drug use. Preparing a client to successfully negotiate these situations begins in treatment; in aftercare, these new skills are practiced routinely, and the client's ability to cope with a variety of high-risk situations can be evaluated. Counselors and therapists work very hard during therapy with their clients to prevent relapse and to make certain they reach their personal goals regarding behavior change.

Relapse prevention is an integral part of therapy and treatment for drug problems. Relapse prevention as a therapy relies on cognitive and behavioral modification techniques and skills training to avoid relapse. Relapse prevention includes educating the client about warning signs for high-risk situations and for behavior that may result in subsequent drug use, as well as training in new skills that help the client avoid a slip back into old behavior. Another aspect of relapse prevention addresses how to respond if a slip back into old behavior occurs, and how to return clients to healthy behaviors in the event of such a slip. Although the origins of relapse prevention are cognitive behavioral, its strategies fit nicely with many other models, including the Minnesota model, which has incorporated relapse prevention into its treatment and aftercare protocols. In addition, family and friends can be involved in helping their loved ones stay the course after treatment. The rest of this chapter will focus on relapse and its prevention, and on strategies that may shorten or manage the course of a relapse if it occurs.

Relapse Model

Relapse does not just suddenly happen without warning or without reason. Research into the processes of relapse has identified a rather predictable chain of events that lead up to it (see Figure 7.1). Moreover, the fact that a client slips into old behavior once does not mean all is lost. On the contrary, a slip offers a tremendous opportunity for both client and therapist or counselor to improve upon the recovery plan. A slip identifies a weakness in the recovery plan and offers an indication of how to improve it. Remembering the transtheoretical stages of change model (see Chapter 3), a relapse is viewed as part of the change cycle and as a fairly common occurrence when a person learns how to overcome a drug problem. So there is no need to panic if a relapse occurs.

Vulnerabilities for Relapse

Research has found that certain vulnerabilities can place a client in a high-risk situation for a relapse (Marlatt & Donovan, in press; Marlatt & Gordon, 1985).

The first of these vulnerabilities is called *lifestyle imbalance*. Lifestyle imbalances occur when a person spends too much time in one life domain, such as working too much without a balance of recreation, or having too much free time and not enough structure. There are several life activities that seem important for lifestyle balance, including eating healthy and exercising, spirituality, intellectual endeavors, healthy emotional expression, social activities and relationships,

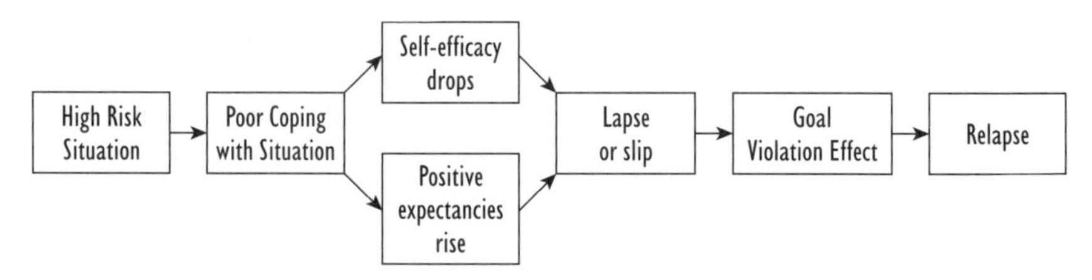

Figure 7.1: The relapse model.

Source: Marlatt (1985).

private time, work, and play. Ideally, a client will not spend an inordinate amount of time in one life activity at the expense of others. If a person spends too much time in one activity, and this imbalance adversely affects other activity areas, then the person is likely to become stressed and worn down, and perhaps experience negative moods or emotions that make him or her vulnerable if confronted with a high-risk situation. Lifestyle imbalance is a common misstep in early recovery by many clients, who are tempted to channel all the time and energy that used to be spent in drug-using behavior into another type of behavior (such as work). In an effort to fill the time, the client may inadvertently stress him- or herself by not seeking balance in activities.

The second vulnerability that can place clients in high-risk situations is a *desire for indulgence*. Many times a client will feel like he or she should be rewarded with something pleasurable for his or her strong efforts in overcoming a drug problem, but sometimes the rewards that are sought place the client in an awkward situation that tempts him or her to use drugs. Other times the client may experience stress or a poor mood and may want to alter the stress or mood with an indulgence. Sometimes the desire for indulgence constitutes an attempt to compensate for lifestyle imbalances.

An indulgence may not even be directly associated with drug use behavior, but frequently it places the client in a situation in which drug use may be an option. For example, the client may simply desire to see old friends as an indulgence without any clear intent to use drugs, but the old friends may be using drugs when she or he arrives (also see the discussion of apparently irrelevant decisions, later in this section). The indulgence may not start out to be related to the use of drugs, but it can place the client in a high-risk situation for doing so.

A third vulnerability can arise when the client experiences *cravings* or urges to use. As mentioned in Chapter 1, cravings can be triggered by social cues as well as physical cues. Obviously, cravings or urges to use can place a client in a high-risk situation for drug use, sometimes before the client is aware of the danger. In other cases, a client may cause a high-risk situation (e.g., a fight with a loved one) out of frustration related to a craving or urge, or in some instances as a pretext to using drugs again. The client may be unaware that the discomfort caused by a craving or urge has contributed to the interpersonal conflict.

Clients also can make *apparently irrelevant decisions* that can send them into high-risk situations. Such decisions are made without awareness or concern for the potential for risk that may result. One example of an apparently irrelevant decision affects the many people who are dieting. One day they find themselves walking into a mall, and then walking by their favorite bakery to peer in the window. To the dieting person, the behavior seems benign when it begins, but when he or she sees those chocolate éclairs, the person may be at great risk for ending the diet. The behavior seemed to start off innocently enough with a trip to a mall, but eventually led to a high-risk situation that tempted the person greatly. That is why these decisions are called *apparently irrelevant* — because, although the initial step seems irrelevant at first, it ends up triggering a chain of events that can quickly complicate matters.

Many drug relapses begin with such decisions, when a client seeks an apparently irrelevant social situation or starts an apparently irrelevant quarrel. Many times the client cannot link the beginning of the behavior chain with the potentially risky outcome. Even if others can see the potential for risk, sometimes the client cannot, so it is important for counselors and therapists to teach about these decisions and help clients identify when they are making them and what to do to stop the behavior chain.

High-Risk Situations: The Triggers

The high-risk situations that can trigger a return to drug use usually fall into three different areas of concern. The first area of concern arises when a client experiences strong or negative moods and emotions. As mentioned in Chapter 1, people with drug problems frequently have problems regulating their moods and many times will use drugs to cover or alter them. Anger, sadness, guilt, and shame all can place the person at risk for drug use if he or she is unprepared for how to respond effectively to ameliorate or tolerate the feelings that occur. However, even happiness can be foreign and awkward to a newly recovering client.

A second area of concern can arise from client-environment interactions that may stress the client in some way. Some examples include adverse conditions that contribute to lifestyle imbalances, such as excessive work-related stress, unemployment, or poverty. Many drug users find it difficult to cope with adverse environmental conditions after treatment, and such conditions can increase their

CASE STUDY

What to Do With Curly's Cues?

You are working with Curly on developing a relapse prevention plan related to overcoming his heroin problem. As part of this plan, you are asking him what cues or situations trigger in him a desire to use heroin. He tells you that he notices that when he sees a spoon, he does think about using drugs and about how nice it would be to get high. He also notices that he has the same reaction when he sees fire or a flame. He mentions that there are things like fighting with his partner or having a problem with his boss that cause him to become upset, and that he is more likely to use under those conditions. He also mentions that seeing his dealer makes him think about using, and that he sees him a lot because he is a coworker. Finally, he identifies that there is a shooting gallery downtown that he used to go to that he is sure would trigger a desire to use if he went there, but he really has no reason to go to that part of town any more. As you develop Curly's relapse prevention plan, what kinds of strategies will you use in and out of session to help Curly address his concerns about these high-risk cues?

stress levels greatly. Unfortunately, many people with drug problems often live out their lives under such stressful environmental conditions, so addressing these conditions while they are still in treatment is critical.

A third area of concern involves interpersonal conflict, usually with a partner, children, or other family members. Relationship stress makes overcoming a drug problem much more difficult, but not impossible. Arguments and other forms of conflict do place the client at risk, however, if she or he has not prepared for how to respond effectively to such situations ahead of time. Other types of relationships, such as with employers or colleagues, also can generate stress that can begin a chain of risky events for the client, so these types of social relationships should not be ignored in a relapse prevention plan.

Interpersonal interactions do not need to involve conflict to present a risk to clients. For example, many clients have told me that, prior to treatment or therapy, they experienced significant pressure from friends, and sometimes from other family members, to use drugs. The pressure exerted by others to use drugs does not necessarily go away after treatment, and these pressures can represent a real challenge to clients as they learn to cope without drugs in early recovery.

How Well the Client Copes Determines What Happens Next

When confronted with a high-risk situation like the ones just described, the client has choices for how to cope. If the client has been instructed well in the use of skills, has spent significant amounts of time rehearsing how she or he will respond to such situations, and has practiced those responses under real conditions, then she or he will likely cope with a high-risk situation without using drugs. However, sometimes the client does not cope well, perhaps because she or he has not anticipated such a situation, has not learned the appropriate skill, has not learned to use that skill in this situation, or has chosen not to use a skill she or he knows.

For whatever reason, the client may not successfully negotiate the high-risk situation in a way that averts the risk. Unsuccessful coping may cause two unfortunate events to occur. The first is a reduction in her or his self-efficacy to successfully cope with the situation without drug use. As you may remember, self-efficacy involves the sense of mastery of a situation that results from competence and confidence. Client competence and confidence can take a beating when a high-risk situation is not handled effectively.

The second unfortunate event is this: At the same time self-efficacy may be dropping, the client may have an increase in positive expectancies associated with drug use. If the client feels little competence or confidence for coping with the situation without drugs, drug use may become a more attractive option. Positive expectancies for drug use may rise as a result, leaving the client in a precarious situation. On the one hand, the client feels more powerless to cope with the circumstances *without* drug use and may see drug use as a solution. As you can imagine, a client is quite vulnerable if she or he reaches this stage in a potential relapse chain. However, relapse is not inevitable, even under these circumstances.

Lapses

Lapses or slips can occur as a result of the lowered self-efficacy and increased positive expectancies related to drug use. Lapses represent a return to use of drugs but not necessarily a return to a drug problem. The distinction between a lapse and a relapse can be quite vague at times, but generally a lapse is not considered a return to old drug use behavior. A lapse tends to be more transitory than a relapse, but a lapse can represent a critical moment of decision for many clients. The way a client and the therapist or counselor prepare for and respond to a lapse is absolutely critical to whether a lapse becomes a relapse or the client returns to maintenance of behavior change and resumes a course toward her or his post-treatment goals.

When a client experiences a lapse, she or he often feels remorse, guilt, shame, and other negative emotions. Frequently a client will blame her- or himself and engage in *self-attack* because of the slip. The experience of negative emotions related to a lapse is referred to as an *abstinence-* or *goal-violation effect* (AVE or GVE, respectively). When a client experiences a GVE, there is a natural tendency to get down on her- or himself. This discouragement can be malignant to a client. If the client allows the discouragement to lead to thinking errors, such as black-and-white thinking (e.g., "What the heck, I have totally blown it now"), then he or she may return to a more regular pattern of drug use. If the client cannot cope with the negative emotions of a GVE, then she or he may be tempted to use again to alter or suppress those emotions, which can return the client to a cycle of drug use to avoid the negative feelings once again. A lapse followed by a GVE can lead to a relapse for an unprepared client.

Relapse represents a return to old behavior for a client. Drug use becomes routine, and old drug use behavior patterns may return in earnest. The duration of a relapse can vary, and can be influenced by the response of both the counselor/therapist and the client. However, even when a client enters a relapse phase as opposed to a simple lapse, there are still many ways to intervene upon it. A relapse does not represent a failure, as mentioned earlier, and may represent a great opportunity to strengthen the client's recovery plan. In the following section, how to manage a relapse will be described — but strategies for preventing a relapse in the first place will also be detailed, as well as ways to implement strategies ahead of time to shorten the duration and reduce the severity of a potential relapse.

Relapse Prevention Strategies

As mentioned in the beginning of this chapter, relapse prevention was originally developed within the behavioral model of treating drug problems and is recognized as a cognitive behavioral therapy used to treat multiple disorders, including drug problems. The model defines various opportunities to intervene all

CLIENT HANDOUT

Are You at Risk for Relapse?

1. Do you find that you are hungry, angry, lonely, or tired frequently?
2. Have you been testing your will or resolve by going places or doing things that you used to do when using drugs?
3. Are you experiencing a great deal of conflict or stress at home, at school or work, or somewhere else in your life?
4. Are you losing your confidence in you ability to cope with your problems without using drugs?
5. Have you been experiencing urges or cravings and not telling anyone about them?
6. Do you think more and more about how good it would be to use drugs again?
7. Do you find yourself withdrawing from people who strongly support your staying away from drugs?
8. Do you find yourself thinking, "What is the use of staying clean, anyway?"
9. Have you slipped recently and felt very bad about it, but haven't told your counselor or therapist?

The more *yes* answers to these questions, the greater your risk. Even one yes tells you that you need to make some adjustments to your continuing care or posttreatment/posttherapy plans. Talk with your therapist or counselor about your answers.

along the chain of events that may lead to a relapse. A counselor or therapist may teach a client skills in treatment, aftercare, or individual psychotherapy that address the vulnerabilities preceding a high-risk situation; that cover a wide variety of high-risk situations before or even as they occur; that increase self-efficacy in those situations before or even as they occur; and that challenge positive drug use expectancies. In addition, counselors and therapists may address a lapse and its accompanying GVE before and as they occur, as well as develop plans for what to do in case the chain of events does result in a relapse. The following sections address each of these areas in some detail in order to prevent a relapse, and describe how to manage one if it does occur.

Restoring Lifestyle Balance

Counselors and therapists need to develop continuing-care and posttreatment plans with lifestyle balance in mind. Make sure you suggest to clients how to provide for a more balanced lifestyle in these plans. First, make an assessment in the life domains mentioned earlier to see whether the client is engaging in a balance of activities in each of those areas. Will your client be doing things to improve her or his physical, spiritual, emotional, and intellectual health and well-being during and after treatment, aftercare, or therapy? Does the plan balance work with play? Does it include serious and challenging activities with pleasurable returns? Is there a balance of alone-time with social interactions? Determine whether the client is spending too much time in one area of her or his life, and if so, suggest ways to correct that imbalance. Suggest activities that fit into the client's schedule and are attractive to the client, and evaluate over time how well the client's activities remain balanced and whether the plans are effective at maintaining such a balance.

In addition, assess the client's beliefs and behavior to make sure that he or she has a balance between the "shoulds" and the "wants" in his or her life (remember rule-governed behavior, discussed in Chapter 5). There are many life rules that need to be abided by in order to provide structure, harmony, and perhaps even meaning to a client's life. However, lifestyle balance suggests that rules, which breed obligations, should be balanced with the desires and needs of the client. If the client is giving too much to others, then he or she may feel frustrated, stressed, and resentful — emotions that can place the client at risk. On the other hand, if the client takes more than gives, this imbalance may contribute to relationship stress and overindulgence that also can place the client at risk. Balance between wants and shoulds is just as important as a balance between the times spent in the different life domains mentioned previously.

Substitute Indulgences

In addition, teach the client to seek out substitutes for drugs or behaviors/situations that were related to drug use in the past. *Substitute indulgences* are activities that are pleasurable but not related to past drug use behavior. These behaviors and practices are meant to respond to the vulnerability that a client may experience when desiring to indulge in something pleasurable. Substitute indulgences also are meant to be healthy alternatives. One example is safe sex with a willing partner. Another example might be self-soothing behavior such as a warm shower or a massage. The sky is the limit when determining what constitutes a substitute indulgence for a client. Suggest indulgences that are enjoyable and relevant for the individual. Try to find indulgences that fit easily into his or her lifestyle, that are affordable and accessible, and that are not too complicated for the client to generate or achieve.

Some have suggested that a negative addiction such as a drug problem can be supplanted by a positive addiction such as compulsive exercise, and certainly exercise is one helpful way to fill the time left vacant when drug use is curtailed. However, a substitute indulgence does not have to be a repetitive activity or even a compulsion. In fact, lifestyle balance suggests that varying the types of substitute indulgences in which a client engages may be quite stimulating and healthy for the client, if they span several life domains. Variety is indeed the spice of life. The best substitute indulgences provide physical, spiritual, emotional, and intellectual stimulation simultaneously.

Coping Imagery

In order to prepare a client for facing high-risk situations during or after treatment, aftercare, or therapy, a counselor or therapist can teach a client to use imagery as a tool to improve his or her ability to cope. The counselor or therapist may use guided imagery (also discussed in Chapter 5), describing the situation and the successive steps of how the client successfully copes with that situation while he or she sits and listens, maybe with eyes closed. The goal is to suggest a skillful course of action in that situation that will lead to positive outcome while illustrating how the client can succeed in using this particular coping strategy.

In addition, the imagery also tends to imaginally enhance the client's self-efficacy. The client succeeds at coping in the imagery; the skills training that occurs by the use of this imagery increases his or her competence to cope with that situation; while the imagery also enhances confidence in his or her ability to succeed under these circumstances. Eventually the client learns how to take control of his or her own imagery experience, first by describing it in session, then eventually using the technique in vivo outside of session to mentally guide him- or herself through the situation in real life.

Stimulus Control and Cue Exposure

In addition, stimulus-control and cue-exposure techniques (see Chapter 5) can be used effectively as relapse prevention strategies. *Stimulus control* means that the client learns how to control her or his level of exposure, and under what conditions, to a particular cue that had been associated with drug use. Cue exposure, as you may remember, uses exposure and response-prevention strategies in session to reduce the power of a drug-use cue to trigger cravings or urges to use.

Cue exposure should be the strategy of choice if the cue cannot possibly be avoided in the real world. For example, it is likely that a client who used to abuse heroin will not be able to avoid seeing spoons in the real world, so you should definitely consider cue exposure to spoons in session, probably with a flame involved to increase the realism of the exposure. However, it may be possible for a client who abuses marijuana to avoid exposure to bongs. Under these circumstances, you may want to suggest a stimulus-control strategy instead of cue exposure, and have your client dispose of his or her bongs during treatment, in aftercare, or in session (or perhaps have a loved one dispose of these, which controls the stimulus exposure even further). Then have your client avoid driving by or entering paraphernalia shops and interacting with friends who have bongs in the future.

> "The overall aim of such stimulus control procedures can be summarized in the old maxim: Out of sight, out of mind."
>
> —G. ALAN MARLATT

When in doubt, though, use cue exposure whenever possible to reduce the power of a cue.

Labeling and Detachment

Counselors and therapists also can teach clients to identify out loud when they feel a desire to use drugs. The process of labeling the craving or urge aloud may disentangle the client from the desire, allowing him or her to become a detached observer of it rather than feeling an obligation to act on it. Labeling and detaching from the desire become even more powerful if done in the presence of others, because the craving or urge becomes a problem not just for one but for two or more to address. There is strength in numbers!

Interestingly, NA and other support groups encourage this strategy (without calling it "labeling and detaching") by suggesting that support-group participants talk about their urges to use with other members (maybe their sponsors, or maybe in a meeting). Counselors and therapists may wish to suggest, if they are comfortable, that clients call them when experiencing these cravings *before* acting upon the urges. The professional can coach the client on how to label and detach from those urges while talking on the phone. Labeling and detaching are quite useful for relapse prevention in high-risk situations, because they can be effectively used by clients when alone, in session, with concerned others, or on the phone (or even online!).

One caveat regarding this strategy: Labeling and detaching is meant to be a technique to reduce the pressure to use drugs, rather than a statement of threat to use drugs in order to manipulate someone else. Some clients may be tempted to use the threat to use in order to control a discussion or argument with a family member or partner. Counselors and therapists need to instruct clients that using the strategy in that way is abusive and likely to harm both the clients and their loved ones.

Self-Monitoring

Self-monitoring can be used to assess for potential high-risk relapse situations. You can assign your client to keep track of stress related to high-risk cues (e.g., relationships or work) or to track mood changes or emotions. Teach the client to track these stressors on a sliding scale so that he or she can see fluctuations in the amount of stress or in the strength of moods or emotions experienced. Sometimes counselors or therapists like to teach clients to rate stress and moods/emotions on a scale of 1 to 100, and to link each rating to a situation or thought. You may even want your client to identify any thinking error he or she is making (Chapter 5) and include alternative ways of responding to and thinking about the situation. Review the self-monitoring every session to see if there are any signs of problems, and help the client to respond accordingly.

Behavioral Assessment

Behavioral assessment can be quite helpful in determining whether a client has the skills to respond effectively in a particular high-risk situation. The Situational Competency Test (SCT) is a very effective way to assess whether the client can respond appropriately to specific high-risk situations, and as mentioned in Chapter 4, the test can be adapted to fit the specific high-risk areas that your client may face. The test was originally developed with relapse prevention in mind and can be a very effective therapeutic tool to help professionals help clients. Behavior can be assessed in other ways, as mentioned in Chapter 4, and these other methods may provide valuable insight into whether your client has unidentified roadblocks to reaching posttreatment goals.

If the client has skills deficits in coping effectively with a high-risk situation, then the next step is to ascertain whether the skill set is present but not being generated in this particular situation. If the skill set is present, then skills generalization is the next step, and the client should rehearse the skills under the conditions that best simulate the situation in question. If the skills are absent, then you must teach them, and after the skills are taught, the client must practice, practice, practice, under a variety of conditions to promote generalization.

Relapse Fantasies

Many clients have fantasies about drug use that they may keep to themselves. You should ask your clients what kinds of fantasies they may have about drug use so you can address those particular high-risk situations preemptively. As discussed earlier, in Chapter 1, sometimes beliefs (like these fantasies) can produce a self-fulfilling prophecy. Understanding these fantasies about drug use may provide tips not only on potential high-risk relapse situations that will need intervention, but also on apparently irrelevant decisions, positive expectancies related to drug use, and thinking errors as well.

Relapse Roadmaps

One strategy to help counselors and therapists understand high-risk situations is to learn from a client's past by creating a relapse roadmap. A *relapse roadmap* helps determine past relapse behavior chains, and may aid the client in avoiding future high-risk situations that can jeopardize progress. The counselor or therapist conducts a behavioral analysis to investigate past relapse episodes that the client may have experienced. The different links along the chain are determined in an effort to discover the client's highways to relapse. As those highways are discovered, the counselor or therapist helps the client develop detours from each one, so that lapse and relapse do not necessarily follow.

Each link in the chain, or intersection on the roadmap, provides an opportunity for a detour or intervention. The roadmap analogy shows that there are many routes to treatment and posttreatment goals, but that some are riskier for lapse and relapse than others. The point is to identify the risky routes so that alternatives can be planned in case the road becomes bumpy for the client.

Relapse roadmaps also can be used to increase awareness about apparently irrelevant decisions. Using the roadmap, you can walk the client down the path she or he has planned for her- or himself so that the long-term consequences of choosing this path become illuminated. The client may not be aware of how the first turn on the map is risky, but when you start asking the client about each subsequent decision about where she or he goes next, then the risk of the chosen path may become more apparent. The relapse roadmap can be quite a useful method for understanding both past and future relapse chains of events.

Relapse Rehearsal

Relapse rehearsal is a way to plan ahead for how your client will successfully negotiate a lapse or relapse, should one occur. The goal is to circumvent the duration and severity of the lapse or relapse event by practicing for how to respond to such an event ahead of time. In addition, the relapse rehearsal can include a plan for circumventing the relapse chain of events before a client slips. The relapse rehearsal also can reduce the risk of a poor coping response, or even a slip or relapse should the chain progress that far. The goal is to develop a "stay-safe" plan for the client before he or she is even at risk, in hopes that the plan can be implemented quickly if needed when the risk arises.

The counselor or therapist helps the client develop a step-by-step response to a lapse/relapse scenario. Clients are oriented by being told that lapses or relapses are common among many people attempting to change drug problems, but that such events are not inevitable. Then clients are told that planning ahead for possible slips is prudent, since it allows for safety plans to be developed in case of emergency. The plans may never be implemented, but they are there if needed.

A relapse plan should include instructions to a client not to panic after a lapse, and then to contact you after it happens. The plan also may include instructions to seek immediate help from a support group or other support network, to do something else immediately (get out of the situation), or some other type of behavior modification. Cognitive modification strategies described later in this chapter addressing the GVE also should be part of this plan. The relapse prevention plan should be comprehensive but easy to follow. In addition, you should rehearse this plan over and over again with your client so that the response will be automatic even in a new and stressful situation (such as a lapse). You can use both imaginal and in vivo rehearsal methods to prepare your client for such an event, even if relapse seems unlikely to occur. Teaching clients to be prepared for the unlikely and the unexpected is a smart strategy.

Skills for Coping With High-Risk Situations

Many of the skills that will help a client successfully negotiate a high-risk situation have been described in Chapter 5, so I will not reiterate those here in any great detail. For example, interpersonal effectiveness, or social skills, can help reduce tension in relationships with family, friends, and coworkers. Emotional regulation skills can aid clients in managing emotional extremes and moodiness without resorting to drug use. Distress-tolerance skills help the client to endure environmental conditions that may be difficult to avoid and to change, as well as ride out cravings and urges without acting on them. Average daily living skills can prevent other stress, such as lifestyle imbalances and financial problems, from building. Many of the same skills that are taught in therapy or treatment work well to prevent relapse. As mentioned earlier in this chapter, assessments like the SCT can help identify high-risk areas for clients where additional skills training may be justified.

One distress-tolerance skill specifically developed for relapse prevention is called *urge surfing* (see also Chapter 5) and can be used by clients to endure cravings or urges. Teach your client to imagine that the craving or urge to use is like an ocean wave. Many clients in the midst of a craving or urge to use cannot imagine that it will subside. However, cravings and urges do eventually dissipate. The key for your client is to avoid acting on the craving or urge when it occurs. Clients are taught to envision the craving or urge as a wave that will rise up, but eventually will fall away. The client is taught to imagine him- or herself surfing the wave rather than being bulled over by it. If the client rides the crest, then she or he finds calmer waters ahead as the craving or urge naturally subsides. This strategy can be used for other uncomfortable situations that your clients need to ride out, such as uncomfortable symptoms related to pain, other mental disorders, and even medicines that may have unpleasant side effects. In these instances, urge surfing becomes *discomfort surfing*.

In addition, others types of skills can be very effective to aid clients when they encounter high-risk situations. For example, relaxation training and stress management can be very good skills to help the client negotiate high-risk situations without resorting to drug use. These skills also can calm the client in the moment so that he or she can access the skills necessary to act effectively in the situation. Many suggestions for relaxation and stress-reduction skills that may be helpful for relapse prevention are described in Chapter 5.

Decision Matrix

A strategy that can be used to renew commitment to the posttreatment recovery plan is called the *decision matrix*. The decision matrix is quite similar to a pros-and-cons list used when a client or potential client is in the contemplation stage of change to enhance motivation. This strategy is particularly useful to challenge the rise of positive expectancies during a chain of events that place the client at risk for a lapse.

The decision matrix allows the client to focus on the costs and benefits of lapse/relapse versus maintaining the changes for which she or he has worked so hard in therapy. An additional element to the decision matrix is an attempt to have

THINGS TO REMEMBER

Decision-Matrix Questions

Questions focusing on the immediate consequences of drug use:

- What would be the good things about using drugs if you did it right now?
- What would be the not-so-good things about using drugs if you did it right now?
- What would be the good things about *not* using drugs right now?
- What would be the not-so-good things about not using drugs right now?

Questions focusing on the delayed consequences of drug use:

- What would be the good things that would happen for you tomorrow morning if you used drugs right now?
- What would be the not-so-good things that would happen for you tomorrow morning if you used drugs right now?
- What would be the good things that would happen for you tomorrow morning if you did *not* use drugs right now?
- What would be the not-so-good things that would happen for you tomorrow morning if you did not use drugs right now?

the client see the long-term consequences of a slip or relapse rather than simply focusing on the short-term gratification of drug use. This process allows the client to walk through the behavior chain to see the ultimate consequences of her or his lapse/relapse behavior (see Chapter 5 as well). Positive expectancies often focus on immediate desired effects of substance use rather than long-term consequences. Although the decision-matrix strategy focuses on the immediate effects to provide balance, it also promotes examination of the long-term effects of substance use as well in an effort to weaken the power of the expectancies to influence the client's immediate behavior.

Identifying Warning Signs

Psychoeducation in relapse prevention includes teaching about the various warning signs that a client could be in a high-risk situation, making apparently irrelevant decisions, coping ineffectively, having lowered self-efficacy to succeed, and having increased positive expectancies for drug use. Part of this process is to personalize this education so that it fits the client's individual circumstances. Relapse warning signs for one client may be very different than the warning signs for another client. The counselor or therapist uses the information gathered by the aforementioned tools to determine what those individual warning signs are for this client, and then teaches the client to be able to identify these as they arise under real-world conditions.

In addition, this information can be written out to remind the client of particular warning signs, with suggestions for how the client should respond to them. For example, you and your client have identified that becoming cynical is a warning sign linked to a relapse chain for him. In response to the warning sign, you and he generate suggestions in session for how he should respond when confronted with feeling and acting cynical. The warning sign can be printed on a piece of paper or card as a table or chart and displayed in prominent places where he will be able to see and remember it (perhaps with all the other warning signs). Next to the warning sign on the chart will be listed the action responses generated in session so he is reminded how to respond if he realizes his cynicism is on the rise.

Such warning signs should be put in prominent places where the client is reminded of them. This can include places at home, like on the refrigerator, favorite chair, bedside table, or television cabinet. It also may include places like at work (discrete places, of course), in the car, or other places frequented by the client. The point is to have the warning signs placed in an area that reminds the client to be aware of risky situations, and to be constantly reminded of alternative ways to respond if those situations arise.

Relapse Contracts

If a client does slip or relapse, it does not mean that progress is arrested or that treatment has not succeeded. Remember, lapses and relapses provide opportunities for clients to grow and for recovery plans to be improved. In addition, there are strategies that can be used to reduce the duration and severity of a lapse or relapse. The first intervention upon a lapse or relapse occurs well before it happens, when you and your client develop a relapse plan and use relapse rehearsal in session. In this way, you teach the client to respond to a lapse or relapse by actively seeking help and by doing something differently.

When your client contacts you after a lapse or relapse, make sure that she or he comes in to see you if possible (although a contract can be made on the phone or online, too). During this contact, you can use a relapse contract to control the severity or duration of the lapse or relapse. A *relapse contract* is an agreement that you negotiate with your client on the limits of the relapse behavior. First, you want to try to negotiate with the client to get an agreement on stopping the lapse or relapse as soon as possible. You may want to use strategies mentioned in Chapter 3 for eliciting a commitment from a client, and a decisional matrix as well. If the client is unwilling to end the lapse or relapse at that moment, then gain a verbal or written commitment for when, specifically, he or she is willing to stop the old behavior. In this way, you have placed some limits on the duration of the return to old drug use behavior. The relapse contract is one way to encourage a stay-safe plan with the client in the event a relapse does occur.

In the same way, you also want to negotiate how much the client will use during this relapse. Try to gain commitment from the client to limit use to a certain amount for the duration of the relapse. Another consideration is to try to contain the relapse to use of less harmful substances, if possible. So if the client is a multiple-drug user, try to gain commitment to use only less harmful substances (i.e., if there are qualitative differences between the client's drugs of choice, such as between marijuana and heroin, try to limit use to marijuana). The goal is to reduce the risk of the relapse event so that return to health will be easier for the client.

> "If there is no struggle, there is no progress."
>
> — FREDERICK DOUGLASS

When the relapse event has ended, then do a deconstruction of the relapse chain of events so as to understand its circumstances. Revise the posttreatment plan to address any new risk areas identified. Teach new skills as needed, and make sure that the skills are generalized to new risk areas. Use the time also to reframe the relapse as an opportunity to learn more about recovery, and to discuss how the client is now one step closer to reaching posttreatment goals (see the section on cognitive restructuring later in this chapter).

Reminder Cards in Case of Emergency

The relapse plan includes reminder cards on how to respond in the event of a relapse or slip. The cards often are small enough to fit in a pocket, wallet, or purse, and therefore are easily accessible to a client when she or he needs to see them. Usually the cards have brief instructions, such as "call your therapist," "go to a meeting," "call your sponsor or friend," "get away from the situation," and other reminders like these. Sometimes a person may have multiple cards, and have these placed in strategic areas. There may be a reminder card in a shirt pocket, in the desk at work, and in the car.

Remember that using the reminder card has to be practiced like any other strategy before a relapse event occurs. You will want to have your client practice carrying it and using it in session. You may wish to randomly ask the client to produce the card in session just to see whether he or she is carrying it. If you do this enough times, the client will make carrying and looking at the card a habit. The reminder card represents another way to develop and implement a stay-safe plan with a client.

Programmed Relapse

Under some circumstances, if a client fully intends to relapse, then you may want to control how this event unfolds. One strategy for doing so is called a *programmed relapse*. A programmed relapse often is conducted in session, if possible. If the client intends to lapse no matter what you do or say, then you might as well use that lapse in an educational fashion in session while having some control over it as well. Programmed relapses have been effectively used with some addictive behaviors to control the severity and duration of the event.

An example of a programmed relapse conducted in this way would be with someone who intends to lapse on smoking cigarettes after a period of cessation. In this instance, the programmed relapse would take place in session. The therapist would first ask the client to talk about the positive expectancies (and other beliefs) related to smoking prior to lighting up. The point is to get the expectancies out on the table for discussion later in the session. Then the client lights up, smokes, and discusses thoughts and feelings as the smoking continues. After the cigarette has been smoked, the client talks about the experience of smoking the cigarette, and that experience is later compared with the expectancies that preceded lighting up. Usually the expectancies are very different than the reality of smoking, which is your hope as a therapist. Many times the client will find that the smoking was not as good as expected, which then provides plenty of grist for the millstone of therapy. Sometimes the client decides to return to recovery after such a programmed relapse because the reality of using was not as good as expected.

Using programmed relapse for illegal substances in session is a little dicier for counselors and therapists because of legal concerns. If your client absolutely plans to relapse, there may be ways to use this strategy out of session, though, that could potentially help your client. For one thing, you may reach agreement with the client on a specific date for the planned lapse, with the idea that the client will talk with you on the phone about the experience as it occurs. In that way you can assess expectancies and other beliefs directly before the drug is used, and then ascertain the actual consequences later. The difficulty with conducting this strategy by phone will be the intoxicating effects, which may cause

CASE STUDY

Falling Star?

Roberto has shined throughout his treatment. At every step in the process, you have been impressed with how hard he has worked on his treatment plan, and how committed he is to overcoming his problems associated with methamphetamine use. Now that he is actively involved in aftercare, Roberto has become heavily involved with the alumni group at your center, and is held in very high esteem by his peers. There is talk that he should serve as an officer in that group once he finishes aftercare, which will be in a couple of weeks. You have been meeting with him to develop his posttreatment recovery plans the last few weeks, but he looks much less bright tonight and more circumspect than usual. After exchanging greetings, he tells you (without looking you in the eye) that he had a bad week this week, that his partner walked out on him yesterday, and that after that happened he used some crank last night, and he feels like, "I've blown it all now and almost did not come in tonight." How do you answer Roberto? What will you do with him tonight in session?

perceptual and communication problems that prevent a meaningful discussion about effects at that particular moment. It might make more sense for the client to discuss those at a later time. One potential alternative is to have the client monitor expectancies prior to using on his or her own, then track thoughts, emotions, and consequences after the event through self-monitoring, to be discussed at the next session. If you choose this method, make sure to instruct the client to continue to self-monitor well after the intoxicating effects have dissipated so that a more balanced picture of immediate and long-term effects is obtained.

Although programmed relapse has been found to be quite effective with smoking, alcohol use, and gambling, for example, using this strategy with a client using an illegal substance may be more problematic. However, there are ways to use the spirit of this strategy, which is to encourage the client to compare expectancies with actual outcomes in order to challenge those expectancies effectively outside session. The goal is to contain a relapse that is inevitable and to have the client learn from that experience so that drug use seems less glamorous.

Cognitive Restructuring

Cognitive restructuring effectively addresses GVEs, and includes reframing the lapse so that the client views it in a more positive manner. For example, clients often associate a lapse with personal failure on their part, and the guilt and shame associated with goal violation relates to this sense of failure. As a counselor or therapist, you want to challenge your client's perceptions of failure by normalizing the experience. After all, relapse is part of the change process and tends to happen commonly among people learning something new. For example, how many people learn how to ride a bike perfectly the first time they get on one? Chances are there will be at least one fall, with perhaps a few scrapes or bruises from the experience. If falling off a bike is not an unexpected experience while learning how to ride, then it follows that a lapse would not be an unexpected experience when a person attempts to overcome a drug problem. Arguably, overcoming a drug problem is more difficult than riding a bike, too.

In addition, lapses and relapses provide important information on how to strengthen a recovery program. They provide guidance to counselors and therapists on how to improve the plan, and they allow clients to learn new skills in order to be one step closer to reaching posttreatment goals. There is no reason to overreact to a lapse or relapse when it occurs, because it is not the end of the change process but signals the beginning of another stage of growth.

Finally, therapists and counselors want to teach clients to change their attributions for how the relapse occurred. Most clients tend to blame themselves and attribute the relapse to personal shortcomings or personal mistakes. One problem with this type of attribution is that clients tend to make overgeneralization errors that suggest somehow that they are flawed at their very cores. However, you as the counselor or therapist must challenge these thinking errors, and teach the client to attribute the relapse to the situation rather than the self. Attributing the relapse to the self causes the client to be the problem, and leaves few options for correcting the problem. If the relapse is viewed as a problem in negotiating a particular situation, then the answer is to learn new skills to overcome those circumstances in the future. Attributing a relapse to the situation rather than to the client allows for the problem to be defined by the situation rather than the person, and makes the problem capable of being solved behaviorally.

Changing the attribution of a relapse from self to situation is a strategy that can be used prior to and after a relapse. Counselors and therapists will want to orient clients very early in treatment and throughout aftercare to the model that views relapses as problem-negotiation situations so that clients will remember this information later if needed. Teach that people overcoming drug problems do well in some situations but maybe not as well in others. A relapse occurs in the context of only one small slice of the client's world. The client may cope without drugs well in many areas, then slip under this particular circumstance. The client must understand that the circumstance is the trigger, not him or her.

Minnesota-Model Relapse Prevention

Relapse prevention, as mentioned, is compatible with a variety of treatment models. For example, many Minnesota-model facilities have incorporated aspects of cognitive behavioral relapse prevention into their treatment and aftercare programs. There have been efforts to combine the relapse prevention model with disease-model instructions to maintain abstinence after treatment is completed. Minnesota-model relapse prevention is generally begun late in treatment and then continued into aftercare. There are numerous books and manuals that have incorporated relapse prevention methods into this particular model.

Relapse Prevention Among Diverse Populations

Relapse prevention within ethnic-minority communities can look somewhat different than it does in a typical treatment center. Relapse prevention methods with ethnic-minority clients often include involvement in traditional cultural activities as part of the therapy. One important theme may be the restoration of the client into her or his rightful place within the family and the community. Another potentially important cultural issue to address with many ethnic-minority clients will be difficulties overcoming shame. High-risk situations may vary across cultures, and a therapist or counselor should know the community well enough to understand cultural nuances related to risky relapse situations.

Relapse prevention for clients with psychiatric conditions must include treatment of the comorbid conditions in order to be effective. This generally means developing a collaborative relationship with a psychiatrist if the treatment includes pharmacotherapy. The relapse plan must provide checks on adherence to the treatment of the comorbid condition, and if adherence is a problem, then motivation enhancement or skills training to improve adherence to taking the medicines is in order. In a very real way, clients with comorbid disorders will have two relapse prevention plans: one related to drug use and one related to treating the comorbid condition.

Relapse Prevention as Part of Treatment, Aftercare, and Psychotherapy

Since many Minnesota-model treatment centers include relapse prevention as part of their curricula for clients, relapse prevention often is included in the typical treatment protocol. There may be psychoeducation groups dedicated to teaching about warnings of relapse as well as identifying and responding appropriately to potential triggers. In addition, many chemical dependency counselors will include relapse prevention training as part of individual counseling sessions. As mentioned earlier in this chapter, relapse prevention in this model may begin late in treatment, usually after steps 2 and 3 (of the 12-step model) have been completed, and will continue to be a primary focus in aftercare (see Chapter 6), where relapse prevention will be merged with working on steps 6–12.

Relapse prevention therapy is an integral part of cognitive behavioral therapy for treating a drug problem. Cognitive behavioral therapists often will merge relapse prevention with other cognitive and behavioral change strategies mentioned in Chapter 5. Relapse prevention will become a primary focus of therapy when a person draws closer to termination, but the relapse plan will be developed much earlier in the process. As you may remember, the transtheoretical stages of change model (Chapter 3) makes suggestions as to which change strategies may be most appropriate to use, depending on where a client is in the change cycle. Relapse prevention best fits in the later stages of change when a person has resolved ambivalence and is committed to changing behavior. Relapse prevention may be mentioned to clients in the preparation stage as part of a suggested menu of options for helping them. Cognitive behavioral psychotherapists will typically use motivational interviewing in the earlier stages, and other change strategies, including relapse prevention, in the later stages of change when a person is committed to making those changes.

Relapse prevention therapy would ideally be conducted as the person enters into action, and of course as the client attempts to maintain the progress he or she is making over the long-term. This is a major concern with group-based relapse prevention therapy, because groups often include people at different stages in the change process. Relapse prevention will not be very relevant (or even make sense) to a person in the contemplation stage. It is my recommendation that relapse prevention groups (and education) be targeted at those clients who are already changing behavior (and committed to that change!).

Developing Relapse Prevention Plans

With this is mind, the relapse prevention plan probably should not begin until the client has shown commitment to changing a drug problem. This recommendation places many treatment centers in an awkward position, since many of them operate under the assumption that each client should have a relapse prevention plan in place once she or he is discharged. Under these conditions, the counselor can make recommendations for a plan but should not be surprised if the client does not follow through on those recommendations. However, a client who is sincerely walking the walk deserves a comprehensive relapse prevention plan before discharge from treatment, and this plan will make up a large part of the continuing care plan for aftercare (see Chapter 6).

Individual therapists working one on one with clients may have more flexibility in this regard. Psychotherapy may not be as time limited as treatment, and therefore a psychotherapist may have the luxury of waiting longer to develop and implement a relapse plan at the appropriate time in the change process. In the meantime, the psychotherapist can continue to use strategies to enhance motivation and commitment until the client has decided to change. It is worth remembering that sometimes motivation changes drastically, depending on the therapy goal. So if the client is not ready to stop using drugs completely, you may find that he or she is completely ready to reduce the harmfulness of his or her habits. Relapse management (see next section) in conjunction with behavior and cognitive modification strategies may be very useful to help clients reach that goal.

In an ideal world, all clients would be ready for a relapse prevention plan before therapy or treatment was completed, but this not always a certainty. Before we can prevent relapse, change must be underway. As therapists and counselors, we have an obligation to develop plans that will help clients after they finish working with us. But in some cases, client progress may not warrant relapse prevention plans. However, continuing care and posttherapy plans can be developed with clients who have not yet chosen action to change, and these plans should focus on helping clients move closer to making a commitment for change.

Relapse Management

Relapse management involves using relapse prevention strategies with clients who do not seek abstinence as a goal for treatment or recovery. Some clients may have chosen to change their habits but not to quit using entirely. The goal of relapse management is to help these clients maintain behavior change over the long term after the goals for treatment or therapy have been reached.

For example, a client may decide to quit using one substance, such as heroin, but not another, such as marijuana. Relapse management (prevention) techniques can be used to help this client meet his or her goals for abstaining from heroin while still using marijuana. Another example might be the case of a client who wants to reduce the use of all drugs, but may be unwilling to stop using any

CASE STUDY

Patricia's Pain

Patricia is a client of yours who has been using cocaine, heroin, and marijuana. She also has cancer, which is in remission, but the cancer treatment causes her significant physical pain. Early in treatment, she tells you that she is more than ready to stop using the cocaine and heroin, but she wants to continue using marijuana to control her pain and nausea. As you are developing a relapse prevention plan with her, she reports that she has experienced relapses in the past on heroin when her pain became unmanageable. One week before her discharge into aftercare, Patricia reiterates her commitment to refrain from heroin and cocaine use but her unwillingness to refrain from marijuana, because marijuana helps the pain and she is convinced she will relapse on heroin if the pain is too great after therapy. Given the information she has provided, what do you think would be important to include in her relapse plan? What kinds of roadblocks may she face, and what can you do to prepare her for these?

one of them all together. In this instance, relapse management techniques can be used to help the client stay at the targeted use goals that have been established (and not to overuse, for example). For many drug users, abstinence may be the best plan, but for those who are not ready to quit just yet, relapse prevention can help them reach and maintain their current goals for reduction of drug use.

Chronic Relapse Prevention

In other instances, you may have clients who are willing to abstain but will have great difficulty monitoring and controlling their behavior. Clients with these problems often cycle in and out of abstinence in spite of their best intentions to remain clean. For those clients who are chronically at risk, perhaps lifelong risk, for relapse, you may want to include relapse prevention as part of the long-term plan for recovery. There are certain groups of clients with multiple problems who may be at great risk for multiple relapses. For example, if you have a client with a long history of chronic and severe drug abuse, a history of a severe mental disorder, extreme difficulties with impulse control, or signs of cognitive impairment, then you may have to make posttreatment plans that address relapse concerns for the unforeseeable future. Clients who may be at risk for relapse over the long term would be good candidates for scheduled booster sessions so that you can check up on their progress and potentially modify their plans as needed well into the future.

Recovery Plans Following Aftercare

Aftercare counselors will want to develop *posttreatment recovery plans* for clients as they near the end of aftercare. A posttreatment plan can be developed by using the continuing care plan, and any unfinished items may become part of a long-term plan for the client after discharge from aftercare. These items will likely be Tier 4 problem areas that will benefit from long-term strategies for change. You can work with your client to develop these plans, including any dream goals that the client wishes to pursue.

In addition, your role is to gradually shift the responsibility for directing the recovery plan entirely over to the client. By the end of aftercare, the client should feel empowered enough to conduct treatment on him- or herself. Part of directing one's own treatment is to develop a long-term plan for how to avoid relapse in the future. If you are operating within a disease model understanding of a drug problem, this means being able to direct a personal relapse prevention plan one day at a time for the rest of the client's life. The client also should have developed strong social connections with like-minded others who will encourage and support the client in reaching these posttreatment goals after discharge from aftercare.

Posttherapy plans are made when a client is preparing for termination in individual psychotherapy. These are developed in much the same way as posttreatment plans may be developed in aftercare. One difference may be the inclusion of booster sessions (see Chapter 6) as part of the plan. Another difference may be a different outlook on how a self-directed relapse prevention plan may look. Within a behavioral model of psychotherapy, there is hope that a problem — including a drug problem — may be overcome for good. Maintenance of changes in this model may not require relapse prevention for the rest of a client's life, but only as long as the client needs it. The plan is completely under the client's control and can be adjusted as the client changes. There is an assumption in this model that as the client changes, the drug problem will become a part of his or her past, forever. So a posttherapy plan within this model ends when the client has changed for good (i.e., when the changes become habit).

Family Involvement in Relapse Prevention

Family involvement can be quite helpful in the relapse prevention effort. One potentially useful strategy is for families to make efforts to reduce relationship stressors. These efforts will likely require couples or family therapy, which ideally will improve communication within the family system and potentially reduce friction. In addition, family members may learn to reduce any negatively expressed emotions toward the client. Family and couples therapy would be highly recommended if those stressors represent a high-risk situation for the client in question and if the family members or partner are supportive of the client's efforts toward recovery.

Families also can be helpful to monitor adherence for those clients who may have to take medicines to treat a comorbid disorder. If family members note that a client is not taking the medicines as prescribed, they can alert the counselor, therapist, or treating physician to the problem. Family members also may observe

CLIENT HANDOUT

Relapse and Relapse Prevention

If you are working to overcome a drug problem, relapse prevention can help you reach your goals. One question you may wish to ask a potential therapist or counselor before entering treatment concerns how much emphasis the treatment or therapy will place on relapse prevention strategies. As treatment or therapy unfolds, make sure to openly share when you have cravings and urges, so that your counselor or therapist can help you identify what may be triggering those. Also share what have been high-risk situations for using drugs in the past so that you can develop plans to protect yourself from those situations after treatment or therapy is completed.

Your relapse prevention plan will help remind you of what to do to successfully cope with high-risk situations when you are confronted with them. If you are facing a tough situation in which you are tempted to use drugs, your plan will remind you to seek help. Contact your counselor or therapist before you use drugs, if possible. Even if you do have a lapse, remember that it is *not* the end of the world, but rather a chance to improve your recovery plan. Remember to call your counselor or therapist as soon as you can after a lapse. Lapses are not unusual and your counselor or therapist can help you return to recovery.

flare-ups in symptoms that professionals may not see. Flare-ups in symptoms may occur independently of whether the client is adherent in taking the prescribed medicines. Sometimes a medicine that works well for one person will not work as well for another. Again, family members can alert the treating professionals to this problem so that an adjustment in the plan can be considered.

Family members may also want to continue on their own healing paths, which can include continued support-group involvement or even individual therapy. Using support groups or seeking therapeutic help over the long term offers the opportunity for positive change that will likely help both the family member and the client. Family members also may find a need to focus on their own quality-of-life problem areas after treatment has ended for their loved one, and therapy can provide them with this opportunity.

Summing Up

Making mistakes is typical when learning how to do something new, and recovering from a drug problem is no exception to this rule. Relapses are not the end of recovery, but instead represent a new beginning of a better recovery plan. Relapses can be prevented, or even managed if they occur, and plans to circumvent the relapse process must begin in treatment. These plans involve identifying the roadblocks that interfere with your client's reaching posttreatment goals

CLIENT HANDOUT

A Word to Family Members About Lapses and Relapses

Lapses and relapses are very scary to families, but you are not without options when one does occur to a loved one. Try to encourage him or her to contact the counselor or therapist as soon as possible. There is no need to nag, but a gentle and loving suggestion can be quite helpful. Sometimes it helps to wait until your loved one is no longer intoxicated to talk with him or her, since it is more likely that he or she will be able to comprehend your suggestion and see your genuine concern.

Although it may not feel like it at the time, a slip does *not* mean that your loved one is no longer committed to recovery. If you can, avoid overreacting to the situation. Try to be supportive and not to be hostile or overly disappointed. If you remember that a lapse or relapse is typical when learning how to overcome drug problems, and that lapses and relapses can lead to a much stronger recovery program, then maybe you can ride out the slip in a way that shows your loved one hope and support. If you have strong negative feelings about the slip, try to share those with your therapist or support group rather than unloading on your loved one. Unloading will not help him or her and probably will not make you feel any better about the situation. Lapses and relapses tend to be temporary and fleeting if handled well, so find a way to ride out the storm by trusting that the skies will clear eventually.

so that new strategies can be planned, implemented, and practiced before the risks are faced. Stimulus control, cue exposure, monitoring of behavior, and learning new skills are essential elements to an effective relapse prevention plan; and treatment, aftercare, and therapy sessions offer forums to identify and practice overcoming the roadblocks that may lie ahead. Relapse prevention is a team effort, with clients, counselors, therapists, families, and even communities working together to preserve those gains made through hard work during treatment.

Key Terms

Abstinence-violation effect (AVE). The response of feeling shame, guilt, and hopelessness that clients often have following a lapse after a period of abstinence.

Apparently irrelevant decisions. Decisions that clients make that may place them in high-risk situations without their being aware of the risk.

Desire for indulgence. A response that often occurs during recovery in which a client feels the need to reward him- or herself with something pleasurable.

Goal-violation effect (GVE). Similar to an AVE, this effect includes violation of goals that may not be linked to abstinence.

Lapse. The phase in a relapse cycle in which a person has slipped but not returned in earnest to old drug-using behavior.

Lifestyle imbalance. A circumstance in which a client does not spend time caring for her- or himself in all the important life domains.

Relapse management. Using relapse prevention methods to control drug use rather than stop it entirely.

Self-attack. When clients belittle themselves or put themselves down because of frustration or disappointment. This often occurs during a GVE or AVE.

Stimulus control. A strategy to control or limit exposure to a trigger or cue.

Substitute indulgences. Safe alternatives to drug use that reward the client for doing well in recovery.

Recommended Reading

I recommend reading *Relapse Prevention,* by G. Alan Marlatt and Judith Gordon (New York: Guilford Press, 1985). Although many books have been written since this one, this is the original classic that introduced the relapse model and prevention methods we still use today. These strategies have been scientifically validated for many years now. A new edition of this book edited by Marlatt and Dennis Donovan is due out soon.

TRUTH OR FICTION

QUIZ ANSWERS

1. True; 2. True; 3. False; 4. True; 5. False; 6. True; 7. False

CHAPTER 8

New Beginnings: Moving Beyond Addictions

TRUTH OR FICTION

QUIZ

After reading this chapter, you should be able to answer the following questions:

1. Eventually there will be a time when your client's efforts to overcome a drug problem will become an automatic habit rather than a struggle. True or False?
2. All the models for understanding a drug problem posit that treating a drug problem is a lifelong effort. True or False?
3. Biopsychosocial protective factors help clients overcome drug problems. True or False?
4. Being more respectful to the other person is an important way to improve relationships. True or False?
5. Mentoring is not the same as supervision. True or False?
6. Mentoring is meant to be a give-and-take relationship. True or False?
7. Leaving a legacy requires massive resources. True or False?

Answers on page 301.

Overcoming a drug problem takes hard work and time, but eventually the fruits of your clients' labors will become quite obvious. They likely will experience amazing positive changes in their lives that they never thought possible. The early stages of recovery are difficult because the client has to act thoughtfully and deliberately in order to change behavior, but eventually those changes will become habit and his or her use of new skills to face life challenges, automatic. In a very real sense, when the client gets to this stage of recovery, he or she has become a brand-new person. This chapter previews what is ahead for your clients in the months and years after changing their drug use, and will suggest new challenges they may want to consider in the coming years.

Biopsychosocial Recovery

You may remember that Chapter 1 reviewed the biopsychosocial model of drug problems. By now, your clients have replaced or nearly replaced many of those risk factors with new biological, psychological, and social *protective factors* that helped them change their behavior. For example, they have engaged in new and healthy physical activities to improve their health and physical well-being: exercising, eating right, getting enough rest, and eliminating the toxic effects of the drugs they abused in the past. They feel better physically and their outlooks have improved because they have new biological balances in place to protect themselves.

They have learned new coping skills and how to use them in a variety of situations, sometimes without even being aware that they are using them now. They have learned to challenge and change thoughts and beliefs that distort their perceptions of the world around them, learned to feel and express emotions in a healthy fashion, and learned to shape their own behavior over time and use rewards to encourage themselves down the recovery path. Their self-efficacy is high and their feelings of hope even higher, because they have protected themselves with new psychological skills.

They also have added new social support networks in their lives to serve as guides and cheerleaders as they've made significant life changes. The people who surround them now advocate for them. The stress in their social relationships is likely diminishing over time as they have developed confidence in their recovery and as they have worked to improve their interaction styles with others. People like to be around them now, because their real selves have appeared since they stopped using drugs. There are many who care about them in ways that they may not have experienced in many years — maybe even in their lifetimes — because they have protected themselves with new social skills and networks.

Interestingly, their original risk factors and vulnerabilities may still be present. However, the differences between when they had drug problems and today are remarkable because the biopsychosocial risk factors have been placed in check by their learning and developing the biopsychosocial protections discussed previously. These new protections have walled off the risk factors and made your clients less vulnerable to their effects. Their progress also has caused them to change as people: Their personalities may even be very different than before, as well as the way they think about and act within the world. These changes make it significantly less likely that they will return to the old ways, simply because that is not who they are any longer. And with every passing day, their growth is placing more distance between them and their drug problems. They deserve congratulations for a job well done, and encouragement to keep up the good work!

"Reality is a crutch for people who can't cope with drugs."

— LILY TOMLIN

Recovery or Recovered?

The different models of recovery mentioned in Chapter 5 also have different philosophies about whether recovery ends or is a lifelong process. The disease model describes overcoming a drug problem in terms of remission, which suggests that the condition is present but under control or dormant. Within the disease model, recovery is a lifelong process that requires the client to use his or her recovery tools on a daily basis.

The spiritual model is similar, in that the condition that allowed the drug problem — namely, a spiritual void — to arise may always be present in the person. Recovery in this model uses spiritual practices on a daily basis to improve the self, so that the void is reduced over time. There is some debate within this model as to whether the void can ever be completely filled or whether a person can ever be truly spiritually whole or healed. Some may suggest that a person can eventually be "converted" so that he or she is completely transformed. Under this condition it would theoretically be possible to recover for good. However, many others feel that the transformation is a slow and lifelong process. Many people who operate in this model feel the need to associate themselves with support groups or use religious or spiritual practices regularly as part of their lifelong recovery plans.

Within the family model, the family system can be transformed when all its members change. In this process, the family unit may reach a new equilibrium after the drug problem has been eliminated. This new balance in the family dynamics takes some time, since it is thrown out of balance in early recovery because of change of drug use. The family eventually reintegrates at a different (higher) level of function. The transformed and health family system, if it remains in equilibrium, theoretically would prevent the recurrence of a drug problem, although there may be new challenges to the system along the way that are not related to drug use. In this sense, a family — including the loved one who used drugs — could be recovered, if the changes in the family system remain permanent and in balance.

Finally, the behavioral model of drug problems does provide for the possibility for an end of recovery. As the person uses new skills and strategies to change, he or she is changed for good, which makes it very unlikely that the ex-client would return to the old behavior. In the behavioral model, the ex-client is in control of his or her recovery, and therefore has the power to control and overcome drug use. The changes in behavior have eliminated old behavior chains and replaced them with new, healthy ones. The old drug use habit has been exchanged for new habits that do not include drugs, perhaps permanently in this model.

So, to review the differences in perspective, those who feel most comfortable understanding a drug problem within the disease model talk about using recovery methods for a lifetime in order to recognize and address powerlessness over the problem. For those who believe strongly in the spiritual model, recovery may

CLIENT HANDOUT

Choosing to Cut Down Rather Than Quit

Some of you may have chosen to cut down on your drug use rather than quit completely. Now that you have successfully reached your goals for reducing your drug use and maintained those changes for a significant period of time, you may want to set new goals for yourself. One idea may be to have a trial period of abstinence to see if that works for you. Another possible goal is to reduce your drug use to a new, lower level. Now that you have seen the benefits of reducing your drug use, you may entertain the idea of increasing your benefits by setting a new goal for reduction. You can use the same tools that helped you reach your current goal to reach a new goal if you choose. At this stage in your recovery, it is important to set new goals for yourself to improve your health and quality of life. Setting a new goal for reduction can be one way to challenge and help yourself at the same time.

be a lifelong journey to seek meaning and purpose and to improve their characters in order to fill the void with something meaningful. For those who are most comfortable in the family model for understanding drug problems, the answer is to change the entire family system in order to change the problem. This requires change for all family members so that the unit can grow together as a team. And those who feel more comfortable in the behavioral model try to overcome their drug problems once and for all by changing their actions and beliefs, and by learning to use new skills to cope with life effectively and without drugs. Those who overcome their drug problems become different people, in control of their own destinies, leaving their pasts behind as they changed. Depending on the model that you are most comfortable with, your prediction for what eventually happens in recovery and with regard to your clients' drug problems may vary.

The following sections will discuss other ways that your clients' lives will change and provide you with some suggestions for how they can measure their progress in significant areas. Many of these suggestions are meant to prompt the client to think about new challenges ahead and are not meant necessarily as a roadmap — they have the ability to draw their own maps now. However, you should invite your clients to consider how they would like to grow in each of these important areas, and how they can get there from here.

Physical Health and Well-Being

Changing drug use reduces health risks significantly for your clients, but there may be other changes they can make to improve their health. There are several domains of physical health that are worth considering to see whether they are treating their bodies with the respect that they deserve. When recovery efforts to overcome their drug problems have become habit, they are at the stage at which they can take on new challenges to protect and improve their health.

First, are there other behaviors in which the client engages that are harmful to his or her health? One such behavior may be smoking or chewing tobacco products. The health risks associated with tobacco use are well documented and do not need to be repeated here. Many people overcoming their drug problems delay smoking cessation during treatment and early recovery because too many changes may seem overwhelming to tackle. However, at this stage they should seriously consider changing smoking behavior in order to improve their health.

Another compulsive type of behavior that can be harmful is overeating and being overweight. Dieting can help for some people, but often, dieting seems aversive and many diets do not succeed. There are some general rules about eating that can change a person's health and weight without his or her necessarily resorting to the discomfort of crash dieting (which the research suggests does not work very well anyway). For one, your clients should try to change the types of foods they eat rather than how much — for example, trying to avoid processed food (which either is already prepared or can be made in a few minutes) whenever possible, because that kind of food is usually loaded with calories and unhealthy levels of sodium and other chemicals. Encourage clients to eat freshly prepared foods instead, so they can control what goes into the entrées that adorn their tables. Second, the client should try to eat more fresh vegetables and fruits, and if he or she is hungry for a snack, should try eating raw vegetables or fruit instead of a bag of chips or the like. Third, whenever possible, he or she should opt for low-fat, low-calorie, and diet-type products. Fourth, he or she should eat the heavier meals earlier in the day, if possible. The research suggests a couple of

CASE STUDY

Run, Flores, Run!

Flores had been clean from drugs for almost 2 years when she decided she wanted to improve her health and lose some weight. She decided to join her local gym for access to aerobic and weight equipment and started to run around the block when she could. She discovered that it was important to structure the gym time into her day, so she started going at the same time in the morning on Mondays, Wednesdays, and Fridays, and then she would run around the block as soon as she got home from work. As her exercise program became a routine, she noticed some unexpected side effects. First, she did not snack as much during the day, and although she may have been eating a little more at meals she was losing weight. Second, she found that smoking was not enjoyable after running and exercising, and she was considering quitting that, too. Finally, although the exercise was hard in the beginning, it had gotten easier over time, just like what she experienced during her recovery from her drug problem. Because she was using distress-tolerance skills and reinforcement for sticking to the plan at the beginning, the new exercise program was now starting to pay dividends for Flores in ways she had not even considered.

things about the timing of meals and human metabolism. One area of inquiry has found that food eaten earlier in the day tends to be used as energy whereas food eaten later may be stored away as fat. Another area of inquiry has found that eating earlier in the day, and more frequently but with smaller portions, tends to increase the metabolic rate so that the calories are burned more efficiently.

Fifth, and finally, encourage your client to get some exercise. The research suggests that the best diet is exercising more. People who like to eat need to exercise more in order to be able to eat more of what they want. It's not a bad idea to tie eating together with exercise in a contingent relationship (e.g., "*If* I want to eat more, *then* I have to exercise this morning in order to earn the food"). Exercising not only improves cardiovascular health and burns calories, it also increases metabolic rate so that the body burns more calories even when at rest than it did before the exercise program began. Many experts suggest vigorous exercise for an hour at a time at least three times a week. In addition, suggest that the client walk more: walking up and down stairs instead of using the elevator or escalator; getting up and walking during lunch or breaks, especially if he or she has a job that requires a lot of sitting; walking, jogging, or riding a bike regularly around the neighborhood before or after work. Suggest that the client do it with a family member or a friend so that he or she will be more committed and so it will be more enjoyable. Perhaps he or she can also engage in an outdoor hobby that includes exercise whenever possible.

Emphasize to your client that it would do his or her body a favor to get an annual physical from a physician. Most people do not blink an eye to get a car in for a tune-up but for some reason are not as faithful about attending to their bodies. If they have medical conditions that require certain treatments or taking medicine, they should do what they are told to do by their doctors, and reliably. After all, we will only get as far in this life as our bodies will take us!

For each of these areas, clients' treatment and therapy training for overcoming drug problems will help them. They can use the same skills and education that they learned in treatment to change these other health behaviors. In addition, they can use their relapse prevention training to help them maintain changes in these health areas over the long term, so that they are able to reach their goals for each of these targeted behaviors (e.g., diet or exercise).

Intellectual Pursuits: Exercise for the Mind

In addition to improving their physical health, clients should learn to challenge themselves in new ways mentally in order to grow in this important area. It will be a good idea to acquire new hobbies that involve lots of thinking and problem solving in order to exercise the brain. They may want to start reading books regularly or maybe push some other skills that they have to new levels (e.g., maybe becoming even better at woodworking by learning a new technique). One of my ex-clients became an expert on crossword puzzles and other word games as part of his brain-exercise program.

CLIENT HANDOUT

Room for Improvement?

The following assessment is meant to help you determine whether there are areas of your life that you can improve upon. Rate each of the following areas of your life on a scale of 1 (not very satisfied) to 100 (totally satisfied):

I am __________ % satisfied with my health.

I am __________ % satisfied with my fitness level.

I am __________ % satisfied with my habits that affect my health, such as eating or smoking.

I am __________ % satisfied with how much I use my intellect.

I am __________ % satisfied with my educational level.

I am __________ % satisfied with my current job or career.

I am __________ % satisfied with my hobbies and how I spend my free time.

I am __________ % satisfied with my ability to be assertive.

I am __________ % satisfied with my ability to regulate my moods.

I am __________ % satisfied with how I express emotions toward others closest to me.

I am __________ % satisfied with my relationships with family members.

I am __________ % satisfied with my relationships with friends.

I am __________ % satisfied with my ability to forgive others.

I am __________ % satisfied with my ability to be patient.

I am __________ % satisfied with my tolerance of others and other points of view.

I am __________ % satisfied with my character.

I am __________ % satisfied with the legacy I will leave behind.

Areas of lower scores provide you with new opportunities for growth!

Others choose to exercise their brains by moving in new directions vocationally and/or educationally. Setting new goals and challenges at work can be quite satisfying, and can lead to new opportunities. The person may wish to challenge him- or herself to move to the next level at work, or may decide to make a career change. This may require additional training or education. Now is the time for the client to review vocational goals and interests, and see whether his or her quality of life might benefit from new challenges in the career path or even a change of directions at work. Many people find that their vocational interests change along with their behavior after changing a drug problem.

Even if the person does not intend to make a career change it might be time to consider finishing his or her degree. Many people gain great satisfaction about earning a degree at the next level even if they do not intend to change career directions. A degree can become a symbol of success that pleases most people, so it can enhance one's self-efficacy. In addition, many people I have worked with express great joy and satisfaction at having completed *something,* and obtaining a degree provides a concrete symbol of completion. Even if the person has completed one degree, he or she may wish to consider working toward another degree at the next level to challenge him- or herself intellectually. Degrees tend to open doors that he or she may not even know exist.

Emotional Growth

Sometimes people forget to work to improve their emotional lives. Arguably, emotional growth is highly neglected by most people. When people discuss personal growth, usually the topic centers around physical health, intellectual endeavors, and even spirituality; emotional growth may remain an afterthought unless emotional problems are interfering with maintenance of behavior change. You may want to suggest that your client consider how to grow emotionally and move to a new level in this area of life. For example, what can the client do to improve his or her emotional maturity in the coming years?

A person may have particular issues with one or more emotions that need to be addressed. For example, does the person lose his or her temper too easily, even today? What can he or she do to change this particular problem? Can the person find ways to reduce the triggers that may lead to losing his or her temper, such as lowering the expectations threshold so he or she does not easily become frustrated, learning how to become more patient and tolerant with other people, finding ways to reduce cynicism, or learning to see the whole picture rather than the present moment?

> "Healing is a matter of time, but it is sometimes also a matter of opportunity."
>
> — HIPPOCRATES

Does the person tend to have problems expressing emotions appropriately to other people? Are there ways that he or she can become more assertive? What can the person do to be more warm and expressive to those closest to him or her? What can the person do to become more mature about when and how to express emotions? And what can he or she do to reduce moodiness, if that is a pattern? Addressing these issues will require emotional discipline and lots of practice, but changing in these areas can provide great rewards, such as emotional balance and serenity.

Improving Relationships

The person also may wish to work on improving relationships with others at this stage of recovery. Changing a drug problem probably has helped the person's relationships, but it still may be helpful to challenge him- or herself to make even more improvements. Although working on relationship issues takes more than one person, your client can do his or her part to try to improve the way that he or she interacts with others. There are several ways to improve social relationships, including improving communication style, increasing the amount of time spent attending to the other person, increasing emotional responsiveness to that person, increasing the amount of time spent with the person, improving the quality of time spent with the person, and increasing respectfulness toward the other person.

For example, your client may wish to improve a relationship with a romantic partner by improving the way he or she communicates with that partner. This may involve increasing the amount of communication that they have or changing the style by which they communicate. Self-improvement in this area may include improving nonverbal communications, by smiling or touching more in ways that convey affection. It also helps to evaluate how much time the person is giving to the relationship, and to judge whether that time includes a significant amount of quality time in which the partner is the recipient of his or her undistracted and unshared attention. Part of that attention might include doing really nice things for the other person that he or she would view as special. However, another significant part of attending to a partner involves understanding the other person's needs moment by moment and responding to those as they arise.

Attending includes emotional responsiveness. Positive emotional responsiveness would include sharing warmth and love openly with a partner. It also means controlling one's own negatively expressed emotions and learning to use assertiveness skills to share displeasure when it occurs rather than attacking or even retaliating against the other person. For some people, the challenge may be to become more expressive of positive feelings and less expressive of negative ones in order to improve the relationship. Others may be challenged simply by becoming more emotionally open with their partners.

In addition, the person should evaluate the time spent together as a couple. Is it balanced? Do they spend too much time as a couple parenting and not enough together time alone? Do they spend too much time playing and not enough time working together (or vice versa)? Partner time should be balanced across the areas discussed in Chapter 7 (just as it should be for private time), in order to promote lifestyle balance in the partnership. In addition, the person should respect the partner by allowing her or him private time, and sometimes making space for this time in the relationship is important. Couples need to find a good balance between private time, time together, and time with children (if applicable) for a relationship to remain healthy (see Figure 8.1).

You might advise your client to learn to treat his or her partner with greater respect, giving at least as much to the partner as he or she is taking from the relationship. Is your client treating his or her partner as an equal in all aspects of their relationship? It is helpful for one person to treat the other each day as an honored gift that has entered into his or her life. If one or both members of the partnership

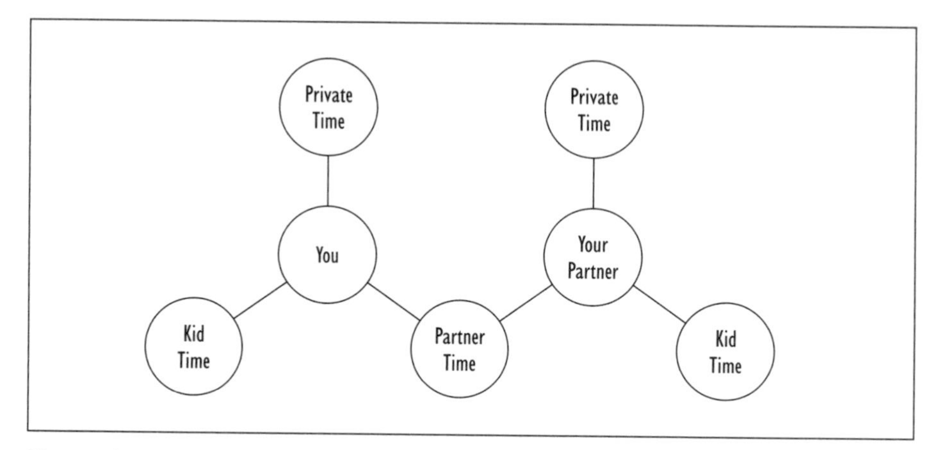

Figure 8.1: Balance in a relationship can be challenging!

does not feel that way, then it may mean they need to reconsider the relationship or how they are approaching it. Remind your clients that couples therapy can help those who are willing to work hard (as they already have for their recovery).

In addition, encourage the client to challenge him- or herself to become a better parent to the children or stepchildren. Parents should learn to listen to their children with genuine interest in what they are doing and where they are going in life. Discuss with your client how to practice assertiveness with children when he or she wants them to do something, and how to use reinforcement (rather than punishment) to shape their behavior. Yelling should be avoided, and conversations with children should be more mutual, rather than a lecture or something that takes place only when there are problems. Remind your client to look at them when they are talking so they know he or she is interested, and to try to show more affection by smiling and hugging more.

The person should also play with the children more often so they can see his or her non-serious side as well, and should turn off the television (and the computer) once in a while. Children need their parents' undivided attention at times. Family meals with conversations that include the children are a start, as is finding ways to help them with their homework. Encourage your client to attend the children's school functions if possible, reminding him or her that where a parent puts in his or her time shows the children that they are important to their parent, and that he or she cares about them. Discuss with your client how to treat his or her children with respect, because they are honored gifts to the client as well. A client's children may be part of his or her legacy in life (see later in this chapter), which is a place of utmost honor.

Also, help your client evaluate whether he or she can improve on friendships as well. Are there ways that the person can improve how he or she communicates with them? Are there imbalances in the amount or type of time spent with friends? Some people in recovery find that they may be spending too much time with friends to avoid dealing with problems at home. Now might be the time to begin to address those problems at home if this is the case. In other cases, clients may find that they are taking more than giving in their friendships (or vice versa), and may want to work toward more balanced relationships. Finally, have the client evaluate the respectfulness in his or her friendships, and make adjustments to those friendships that lack respect. Sometimes relationships are one-sided and need to be ended. In other instances, the person may discover that he or she will want to elevate an established friendship to a new level of respect. Finally, discuss how the client can communicate better with coworkers and grant them the respect that he or she would want from them.

As mentioned in Chapter 7, relationships can be extremely stressful, but they also are the source of some of the greatest joy that one can experience. A person who is willing to invest great amounts of him- or herself into a worthy relationship will find that it returns many times over what he or she has given to it. Investing in healthy relationships, and repairing the less healthy ones, will be an area of great satisfaction and challenge for your clients, with many happy returns in the years to come.

Spiritual Growth

> "Go confidently in the direction of your dreams. Live the life you have imagined."
>
> — HENRY DAVID THOREAU

Many people find that after overcoming drug problems they experience spiritual growth in ways they had never imagined possible. Your clients probably have already noticed many changes in the way they view themselves, others, and the world around them, and these changes likely have affected their spiritual lives. Now may be the time for your clients to challenge themselves to even greater spiritual heights.

For example, one aspect of spiritual growth that many people who have overcome drug problems find helpful is learning to forgive more completely. A client may feel like someone has wronged him or her greatly in life and that those feelings are hard to shake. However, the past, even the painful betrayals and times of distress, has led your client to become the person that he or she is today. Even the pain has been important for growth. This does not dismiss the painfulness, but it does suggest that the client has overcome it. Forgiveness in this sense is letting the past be the past and realizing that surviving the unpleasantness has made the client a better person. You may need to ask your client whether it's time to let the past be put in its proper perspective.

In addition, forgiveness may concern a person's willingness to let a grudge go. Holding on to a grudge in many respects means that a person is joined at the hip with the object of the grudge. It is difficult to make progress in life when you drag along the ball-and-chain of a grudge toward another. Letting go of grudges will make any person's journey a little lighter.

Spiritual growth may involve expanding one's worldview. This can happen in different ways. First, clients may expand their worldviews with regard to the having a broader sense of time. Seeing time as expansive, and understanding that this moment is precious but miniscule in the great ocean of eternity, allows great patience to develop. A person can see that things worth having or waiting for involve a great commitment of time, which means that patience is required. Spiritual growth in this sense means that the person makes the most of this moment, but also that he or she is willing to wait for this moment to bear fruit well into the future. Encourage your clients to think about how their lives would improve if they were more patient.

Second, clients may find their worldviews expanding because they are opening their minds. Tolerance depends on many things. First, tolerance depends on the ability to see beauty and truth in different ways of thinking and of seeing the world. Second, it depends on respecting other people's opinions and different life experiences. Third, it depends on humility, which teaches that one does not know everything, and that receiving one answer in life seems to generate 10 baffling new questions. In fact, it may be that some of the questions have no answers, and as a person's mind opens he or she becomes more comfortable with that, no longer feeling like he or she needs to know all the answers. Certainly people disagree, but even disagreement does not necessarily mean that one is right and one is wrong. Sometimes when two people look at a coin, one focuses on the head while the other focuses on the tail. Neither is wrong in his or her description of the coin; it is the same coin but different views. It may be the time for your clients to reduce their prejudices by increasing their humility.

Spiritual growth also may involve improving one's character by striving to be the best person possible. This should not be confused with perfectionism; rather, becoming the best person one can includes recognizing and embracing one's own natural limits. However, a person does want to understand whether the limits are there naturally or whether the limits have been placed there by that person. *Natural* limits are those things that cause us to be humble, but *self-imposed* limits are those that cause us to stumble. Discuss with your clients how to know that a limit is self-imposed — that is, whether he or she is "settling" rather than challenging him- or herself to new heights. Encourage clients to accept their natural limits but push beyond their self-imposed ones.

Mentoring and Legacies

Perhaps the most important ways to grow spiritually involve leaving gifts for others. There are two important ways that your clients can give to others in a manner that can change the recipients and your clients, too, and these are by *mentoring* another person or by working on a *legacy* that benefits others.

Mentoring means sharing one's experiences and expertise in a particular area of one's life with another person in order to help that person succeed in a similar area. Many mentoring relationships are professional in nature. For example,

CASE STUDY

The Many Hats of Hank

Hank has found that he has a lot to offer others now that he has been clean from drugs for several years. At work, he is now in position to help junior employees learn the trade. There is one young man who has sought out Hank's advice about how to improve his work skills, and Hank shares all that he can. At home, he has found time to be an active participant in his apartment complex's tenant association. And recently he became a Big Brother volunteer to Adam, who is a teen who reminds Hank a great deal of what he was like when he was younger. He spends time on Saturday with Adam shooting hoops or just walking and talking, responding to what Adam needs at the time. Hank reflects on how he has become a role model for others and on the fact that people really respect him now. He feels fantastic about himself today because he can see that his life makes a difference in the world, and it does not cost him much, except his time.

if you are a plumber, mentoring an apprentice would involve not only teaching the tools of the trade but also teaching the young plumber how to excel at the chosen trade. Mentoring often involves modeling successful behavior and offering advice, but also may include friendship and genuine concern for the other person's well-being. Mentors are viewed as wise sages who can really help the mentees (or persons being mentored) be successes.

Mentorship does not have to be in a professional realm, though. For example, in recovery groups, being a good, conscientious sponsor means assuming a mentorship role. In this domain, mentors instruct the people they sponsor not only on how to remain drug free and work their programs, but also on how to improve quality of life in recovery. The sponsoring/mentoring relationship may become a friendship of sorts, although a true mentorship involves a teacher-pupil relationship, which means a power (knowledge) imbalance at least during the early stages. In some ways a mentor may act more parental than like a friend, although a kind of friendship can develop as part of parenting, to be sure. Other life areas in which a mentoring relationship can develop include sports and recreation, education or training, and even very personal domains such as spirituality.

One way to leave a legacy is to share one's experience and knowledge so that they can benefit others. Your clients' experience and knowledge can be spread by mentoring, because if they mentor well, then someday their mentees may mentor others, and the experiences and knowledge are passed on to another generation. There are many areas in one's life in which he or she can mentor another person, some that I have not mentioned. We can mentor in any area where we have developed expertise and where there may be an opportunity to share that expertise with another person in a noncoercive way. *Noncoercive* is an important point to emphasize here, because mentorship relies upon consent. You must want to mentor the person and, in turn, the person must want to be mentored by you.

Let your clients know that mentorship is a great responsibility and quite an honor, and that they should take the role seriously if they are extended the invitation. There are some rules that will help your clients to be good mentors. First, discuss with your clients how to make sure that their teachings and advice are welcome before sharing them with their mentees. We should always check with the other person to find out whether he or she wants to hear our ideas or learn new information from us. There is a qualitative difference between being a supervisor and being a mentor. A supervisor trains and has oversight as a matter of obligation, whereas mentorship is a matter of choice. We can be supervisors without mentoring, and we can mentor without supervising, but it is a great gift and privilege when we both supervise *and* mentor.

Second, mentorship should be done without an ulterior motive. Mentoring is a gift, so the mentorship of the mentee should be the only motive. Mentorship becomes corrupted when there are other goals, such as pushing the mentee to do things we wish we had done or using the relationship for personal gain. Because it is sometimes difficult to avoid these trappings, mentorship is not an easy thing to foster. The satisfaction of mentoring comes from observing how our mentees creatively use what we have taught them in their own lives and careers over the long term.

Third, the goal of mentorship is to help the other person succeed. Let your clients know that if they have goals beyond this one, their mentoring is in danger of becoming a selfish rather than selfless enterprise. It is hard to keep our egos out of a mentoring relationship, but we must try to do so for this relationship to succeed. In this way, mentorship is very much like parenting, because although we may have ideas about what we would like our children to become, many times our children have very different ideas about what they want to become. A good mentor trains and teaches, but also will not interfere when the mentee seeks an independent path.

Mentorship is one kind of legacy that can be timeless in its giving, because if a person mentors well, the information he or she shares will be passed on, perhaps in perpetuity. However, there are other ways to leave a legacy besides mentoring. The fruits of our own labors can represent a legacy if the results can help others in the years to come. Here are some examples of legacies that you can discuss with your clients. If you are an architect, then one legacy will be the buildings that you create from scratch. You have a choice to create mediocrity or to achieve brilliance by always challenging yourself to become a better architect. Working on a legacy suggests you are not willing to settle for mediocrity. If you are a parent, the same would be true. Your children will be one of your legacies, so constantly improve yourself as a parent on a daily basis. If you are a partner, be a better partner today than you were yesterday. If your client chooses to be a

CLIENT HANDOUT

Mentorship

- Mentoring and supervision are not necessarily the same.
- Make sure that your teachings and advice are welcomed by the potential mentee.
- Mentoring is meant to be a gift, so no ulterior motive should be involved in the relationship.
- Mentoring is designed to help the mentee succeed.
- Mentoring is an honor that involves great responsibility, so take your role as a mentor seriously.

mentor, he or she must strive to improve his or her mentorship on a daily basis. Some people choose to make their characters their legacies, so that others may want to emulate them as role models. Encourage your client to choose an area in which he or she has the skills and ability to make a difference, to potentially leave the world a better place than it was before, and make his or her legacy there.

Legacies do not have to be massive undertakings, nor even related to skillfulness, but they do have to be uniquely one's own. Some people use volunteerism to leave a legacy by the gift of time. Others may give resources to develop a legacy. Legacies do involve sacrifices at times, precisely because they are gifts. However, legacies also provide dividends of goodwill and the satisfaction of seeing that our efforts in life may outlive us. Spiritual growth benefits from such efforts. Many people find it important to have multiple legacies, and being able to do this successfully means that they must actively participate in different arenas of social interaction. Some people find they are able to leave legacies in multiple roles as partners, parents, coworkers, friends, and participants in the local and global communities.

An analogy from camping may help you illustrate how to leave a legacy in the different areas of one's life. In camping, there is an unwritten rule that you should leave your campsite in better shape than when you arrive. Practically speaking, that means that when camping, you should leave no trace of your use of the grounds, and that you should pick up after others who came before who did not follow that rule. So after the tent is packed away, a good camper will rake the grounds to get rid of footprints and crushed grass where he or she slept, and pick up litter that others have left, and pack it out. In this way, you have improved the campsite for the next person.

Two life principles flow from this very simple approach to camping, and relate to the leaving of a legacy as well. First, discuss with your clients how we can make our demands on the world low impact. A low-impact life is a great legacy because it enhances present relationships and protects future generations. Clients should try to discover ways to reduce their impact in the different areas of their lives, becoming lower maintenance in relationships with others and traveling light in the world. Encourage your clients to find ways to extend these ideas through family, friendships, work, and every other important area where they influence the world.

Second, encourage your clients to use their time to make the world a better place in those areas where they can, and to think about how their actions may improve the lives of those they touch or how the things they do can help others whom they do not know. Help your clients to try to see life in more global terms, and how their local impact can ripple out to affect the future. Discuss with your clients how to make their lives into statements that stand the test of time, finding ways to clean those campsites that they use even if they did not make the messes.

Your clients will discover that recovery from a drug problem seems very difficult in the beginning but gets easier with time. They can use the skills that helped them overcome their drug problems to overcome all forms of obstacles and problems that they will face in the days and years to come. Life without drugs frees them to pursue new and emerging interests and to engage in new challenges. Treating their drug problems has given them new skills to use as they face future challenges on their own terms. There are always opportunities for improvement and creative ways to improve. They now have the tools to succeed; their growth in the future is limited only by their own imaginations.

Summing Up

Overcoming a drug problem means different things to different people, but clearly overcoming a drug problem will change the way a person acts in, and thinks and feels about, the world. Recovery includes incorporating protective factors into a person's life that make drug use no longer a viable or desirable option. Instead, your client's hard work in recovery has caused fundamental changes that improve his or her quality of life in ways he or she never thought possible. However, there are many challenges ahead that your client can choose to tackle if he or she wishes to continue to improve upon him- or herself. Some suggestions for new challenges were made in this chapter, but your clients likely will come up with their own ideas based on their own unique life circumstances. Many people find great joy in the new challenges that help to make them better people, including those ways in which they are able to give to others. Your clients have control of the paths ahead now that they have overcome their drug problems; help them to choose wisely and enjoy the journey.

Key Terms

Legacy. A gift that will outlive the person who gave it and that will help others.
Mentoring. Tutoring another person in something with the idea of helping the person succeed in that area.
Protective factors. Circumstances or behaviors that tend to prevent harmful consequences from occurring to a person.

Recommended Reading

I would recommend reading *First Things First,* by Stephen Covey, Roger Merrill, and Rebecca Merrill (New York: Simon & Schuster, 1995); this book provides a wonderful blueprint for how to more effectively structure one's time, set priorities in life, and leave an enduring legacy.

TRUTH OR FICTION

QUIZ ANSWERS

1. True; 2. False; 3. True; 4. True; 5. True; 6. False; 7. False

REFERENCES

American Psychiatric Association. (2000). *Diagnostic and statistical manual of mental disorders (4th ed., text revision).* Washington, DC: Author.

Arroyo, J. A., Miller, W. R., & Tonigan, J. S. (2003). The influence of Hispanic ethnicity on long-term outcome in three alcohol-treatment modalities. *Journal of Studies on Alcohol, 64,* 98–104.

Baer, J. S., Sampson, P. D., Barr, H. M., Connor, P. D., & Streissguth, A. P. (2003). A 21-year longitudinal analysis of the effects of prenatal alcohol exposure on young adult drinking. *Archives of General Psychiatry, 60,* 377–385.

Bandura, A. (1997). *Self-efficacy: The exercise of control.* New York: W. H. Freeman.

Beck, A. T., & Emery, G. (1995). *Coping with anxiety and panic.* Bala Cynwyd, PA: Beck Institute for Cognitive Therapy and Research.

Beck, A. T., Rush, A. J., Shaw, B. F., & Emery, G. (1979). *Cognitive therapy of depression.* New York: Guilford Press.

Beck, A. T., Wright, F. D., Newman, C. F., & Liese, B. S. (1993). *Cognitive therapy of substance abuse.* New York: Guilford Press.

Beidel, D. C., Turner, S. M., & Cooley, M. R. (1993). Assessing reliable and clinical significant change in social phobia: Validity of the Social Phobia and Anxiety Inventory. *Behavior Research and Therapy, 31,* 331–337.

Berman, A. L., Shepherd, G., & Silverman, M. M. (2003). The LSARS-II: Lethality of Suicide Attempt Rating Scale — Updated. *Suicide and Life Threatening Behaviors, 33,* 261–276.

Bernstein, N. (2002). The drug war's littlest victims. Retrieved August 4, 2004 from http://www.salon.com/mwt/feature/2002/10/30/drug_measures/print.html.

Blume, A. W., & Marlatt, G. A. (2000). Recent important losses predict readiness-to-change scores in people with co-occurring psychiatric disorders. *Addictive Behaviors, 25,* 461–464.

Blume, A. W., & Schmaling, K. B. (1998). Regret, substance abuse, and readiness to change in a dually diagnosed sample. *Addictive Behaviors, 23,* 693–697.

Blume, A. W., Schmaling, K. B., & Marlatt, G. A. (2001). Motivating drinking behavior change: Depressive symptoms may not be noxious. *Addictive Behaviors, 26,* 267–272.

Brown, S. A., Myers, M. G., Lippke, L., Tapert, S. F., Stewart, D. G., & Vik, P. W. (1998). Psychometric evaluation of the Customary Drinking and Drug Use Record (CDDR): A measure of adolescent alcohol and drug involvement. *Journal of Studies on Alcohol, 59,* 427–438.

Bureau of Justice Statistics (1992). Correctional Populations in the United States, 1992. Washington, DC: U.S. Department of Justice.

Bureau of Justice Statistics. (1999). Prisoners in 1999. Washington, DC: U.S. Department of Justice, August 2000.

Cervantes, E. A., Miller, W. R., & Tonigan, J. S. (1994). Comparison of Timeline Follow-Back and averaging methods for quantifying alcohol consumption in treatment research. *Assessment, 1,* 23–30.

Chaney, E. F., O'Leary, M. R., & Marlatt, G. A. (1978). Skills training with alcoholics. *Journal of Clinical and Consulting Psychology, 46,* 1092–1104.

Chiauzzi, E. J., & Liljegren, S. (1993). Taboo topics in addiction treatment: An empirical review of clinical folklore. *Journal of Substance Abuse Treatment, 10,* 303–316.

Derogatis, L. R., Lipman, R. S., & Covi, L. (1973). SCL-90: An outpatient psychiatric rating scale — preliminary report. *Psychopharmacology Bulletin, 9,* 13–28.

Derogatis, L. R., & Melisaratos, N. (1983). The Brief Symptom Inventory: An introductory report. *Psychological Medicine, 13,* 595–605.

DiClemente, C. C., & Hughes, S. O. (1990). Stages-of-change profiles in outpatient alcoholism treatment. *Journal of Substance Abuse, 2,* 217–235.

Ellis, A., & Grieger, R. (1977). *RET: Handbook of rational-emotive therapy.* New York: Springer.

Engelhart, C., Eisenstein, N., Johnson, V., Wolf, J., Williamson, J., Steitz, D., Girard, V., Paramatmuni, K., Ouzounian, N., & Losonczy, M. (1999). Factor structure of the Neurobehavioral Cognitive Status Exam (COGNISTAT) in healthy and psychiatrically and neurologically impaired, elderly adults. *Clinical Neuropsychology, 13,* 109–111.

First, M. B., Gibbon, M., Spitzer, R. L., & Williams, J. B. W. (1995). *Structured clinical interview for* DSM-IV *(SCID).* New York: NY State Psychiatric Institute.

Foa, E.B., & Tolin, D.F. (2000). Comparison of the PTSD Symptom Scale — Interview Version and the Clinician-Administered PTSD Scale. *Journal of Traumatic Stress, 13,* 181–191.

Folstein, M. F., Robins, L. N., & Helzer, J. E. (1983). The Mini-Mental State Examination. *Archives of General Psychiatry, 40,* 812.

Friedman, A. S., & Utada, A. (1989). A method for diagnosing and planning the treatment of adolescent drug abusers (the Adolescent Drug Abuse Diagnosis [ADAD] instrument). *Journal of Drug Education, 19,* 285–312.

Heaton, R. K., Chelune, G. J., Talley, J. L., Kay, G. G., & Curtiss, G. (1993). *Wisconsin Card Sorting Test Manual: Expanded and revised.* Odessa, FL: Psychological Assessment Resources.

Herron, E. W., Bernstein, L., & Rosen, H. (1968). Psychometric analysis of the multiple affective adjective check list: MAACL-today. *Journal of Clinical Psychology, 24,* S448–S450.

Institute of Medicine. (1990). *Broadening the base of treatment for alcohol problems.* Washington, DC: National Academy Press.

Jellinek, E. M. (1960). *The disease concept of alcoholism.* New Haven, CT: College and University Press.

Kadden, R., Carroll, K., Donovan, D., Cooney, N., Monti, P., Abrams, D., Litt, M., & Hester, R. (1999). Cognitive-behavioral coping skills therapy manual: A clinical research guide for therapists treating individuals with alcohol abuse and dependence. In M. E. Mattson (Ed.), *Project MATCH Monograph Series, 4.* Bethesda, MD: National Institute on Alcohol Abuse and Alcoholism.

Kaminer, Y., Bukstein, O., & Tarter, R. (1989). Teen Addiction Severity Index (T-ASI): Clinical and research implications: A preliminary report. *National Institute on Drug Abuse Research Monograph, 95,* 363.

Kari & Associates (2004). Legalization-Prohibition: The "WAR" and its effects. Retrieved August 4, 2004 from http://www.karisable.com/c

Kessler, R.C., McGonagle, K.A. Zhao, S., et al. (1994). Lifetime and 12-month prevalence of *DSM-III-R* psychiatric disorders in the United States. *Archives of General Psychiatry, 51,* 8–19.

Knight, J. R., Shrier, L. A., Bravender, T. D., Farrell, M., Vander Bilt, J., & Shaffer, H. J. (1999). A new brief screen for adolescent substance abuse. *Archives of Pediatric Medicine, 153,* 591–596.

Linehan, M. M. (1993). *Cognitive-behavioral treatment of Borderline Personality Disorder.* New York: Guilford Press.

Mack, J. E. (2002). Addictions: Individual and societal. Paper presented at the 25 Years of Addiction Treatment Conference, February 2, Boston, MA. Cited in Shaffer, H. J., & Albanese, M. J. (2005). Addiction's defining characteristics. In R. H. Coombs (Ed.), *Addiction Counseling Review.* Mahwah, NJ: Lahaska Press.

Marlatt, G. A. (1985). Relapse prevention: Theoretical rationale and overview of the model. In G. A. Marlatt & J. R. Gordon (Eds.), *Relapse prevention: Maintenance strategies in the treatment of addictive behaviors* (pp. 3–70). New York: Guilford Press.

Marlatt, G. A., Demming, B., & Reid, J. B. (1973). Loss-of-control drinking in alcoholics: An experimental analogue. *Journal of Abnormal Psychology, 81,* 233–241.

Marlatt, G. A., & Donovan, D. M. (in press). *Relapse prevention: Maintenance strategies in the treatment of addictive behaviors* (2nd ed.). New York: Guilford Press.

Marlatt, G. A., & Gordon, J. (1985). *Relapse prevention.* New York: Guilford Press.

McLellan, A. T., Luborsky, L., Cacciola, J., Griffith, J., Evans, F., Barr, H. L., & O'Brien, C. P. (1985). New data from the Addiction Severity Index: Reliability and validity in tree centers. *Journal of Nervous and Mental Diseases, 173,* 412–423.

McNair, D. M., Lorr, M., & Droppleman, L. F. (1992). *POMS manual: Profile of Mood States.* San Diego: Educational and Industrial Testing Services.

Meyers, K., McLellan, A. T., Jaeger, J. L., & Pettinati, H. M. (1995). The development of the Comprehensive Addiction Severity Index for Adolescents (CASI-A): An interview for assessing multiple problems of adolescents. *Journal of Substance Abuse Treatment, 12,* 181–193.

Mignault, J. P., Pallonen, U. E., & Velicer, W. F. (1997). Decisional balance and stage of change for adolescent drinking. *Addictive Behaviors, 22,* 339–351.

Miller, W. R. (1996). Form 90: A structured interview for drinking and related behaviors. In M. E. Mattson (Ed.), *Project MATCH Monograph Series, 5.* Bethesda, MD: National Institute on Alcohol Abuse and Alcoholism.

Miller, W. R., & Rollnick, S. (2002). *Motivational interviewing: Preparing people for change* (2nd ed.). New York: Guilford Press.

Miller, W. R., Sovereign, R. G., & Krege, B. (1988). The check-up: A model for early intervention in addictive behaviors. *Behavioural Psychotherapy, 16,* 251–268.

Miller, W. R., & Tonigan, J. S. (1996). Assessing drinkers' motivations for change: The Stages of Change Readiness and Treatment Eagerness Scale (SOCRATES). *Psychology of Addictive Behaviors, 10,* 81–89.

Miller, W. R., Tonigan, J. S., & Longabaugh, R. (1995). Drinker Inventory of Consequences: An instrument for assessing adverse consequences of alcohol abuse. In M. E. Mattson (Ed.), *Project MATCH Monograph Series, 4.* Bethesda, MD: National Institute on Alcohol Abuse and Alcoholism.

Miller, W. R., Walters, S. T., & Bennett, M. E. (2001). How effective is alcoholism treatment in the United States? *Journal of Studies on Alcohol, 62,* 211–220.

Miller, W. R., Zweben, A., DiClemente, C. C., & Rychtarik, R. G. (1999). *Motivational enhancement therapy manual: A clinical research guide for therapists treating individuals with alcohol abuse and dependence.* In M. E. Mattson (Ed.), *Project MATCH Monograph Series, 2.* Rockville, MD: National Institute on Alcohol Abuse and Alcoholism.

Millon, T. (1994). *Manual for the MCMI-III.* Minneapolis: National Computer Systems.

National Center for Injury Prevention and Control. (2003). *Ten leading causes of death, United States, 2000.* http://webapp.cdc.gov/cgi-bin/broker.exe

Nowinski, J., Baker, S., & Carroll, K. (1995). Twelve step facilitation therapy manual: A clinical research guide for therapists treating individuals with alcohol abuse and dependence. In M. E. Mattson (Ed.), *Project MATCH Monograph Series, 4.*Bethesda, MD: National Institute on Alcohol Abuse and Alcoholism.

Office of National Drug Control Policy. (2001). *The economic costs of drug abuse in the United States, 1992–1998* (Publication No. NCJ-190636). Washington, DC: Executive Office of the President.

Prochaska, J. O., DiClemente, C. C., & Norcross, J. C. (1992). In search of how people change: Applications to addictive behaviors. *American Psychologist, 47,* 1102–1114.

Rahdert, E. (1991). *The adolescent assessment/referral system manual.* Rockville, MD: National Institute on Drug Abuse.

Reitan, R. M., & Wolfson, D. (1985). *The Halstead-Reitan neuropsychological test battery: Theory and clinical interpretation.* Tucson, AZ: Neuropsychology Press.

Roberts, L. J., Shaner, A., & Eckman, T. (1999). *Overcoming addictions: Skills training for people with schizophrenia.* New York: W. W. Norton.

Robins, L. N., Helzer, J. E., Croughan, J., & Ratcliff, K. S. (1981). National Institute of Mental Health Diagnostic Interview Schedule: Its history, characteristics, and validity. *Archives of General Psychiatry, 38,* 381–389.

Rollnick, S., Heather, N., Gold, R., & Hall, W. (1992). Development of a short "readiness to change" questionnaire for use in brief, opportunistic interventions among excessive drinkers. *British Journal of Addiction, 87,* 743–754.

Shaffer, D., Fisher, P., Lucas, C. P., Dulcan, M. K., & Schwab-Stone, M. E. (2000). NIMH Diagnostic Interview Schedule for Children Version IV (NIMH DISC-IV): Description, differences from previous versions, and reliability of some common diagnoses. *Journal of the American Academy of Child and Adolescent Psychiatry, 39,* 28–38.

Skinner, H. A. (1982). The Drug Abuse Screening Test. *Addictive Behaviors, 7,* 363–371.

Sklar, S. M., Annis, H. M., & Turner, N. E. (1997). Development and validation of the Drug-Taking Confidence Questionnaire: A measure of coping self-efficacy. *Addictive Behaviors, 22,* 655–670.

Smith, A. (1991). *Symbol Digit Modalities Test.* Los Angeles: Western Psychological Services.

Smith, K., Conroy, R. W., & Ehler, B. D. (1984). Lethality of Suicide Attempt Rating Scale. *Suicide and Life Threatening Behaviors, 14,* 215–242.

Snyder, D. K. (1979). Multidimensional assessment of marital satisfaction. *Journal of Marriage and the Family, 41,* 813–823.

Spanier, G. B. (1976). Measuring dyadic adjustment: New scales for assessing the quality of marriage and similar dyads. *Journal of Marriage and the Family, 38,* 15–28.

Stephens, R. S., Roffman, R. A., & Curtin, L. (2000). Comparison of extended versus brief treatments for marijuana use. *Journal of Consulting and Clinical Psychology, 68,* 898–908.

Stinchfield, R., & Winters, K. C. (1997). Measuring change in adolescent drug misuse with the Personal Experiences Inventory (PEI). *Substance Use and Misuse, 32,* 63–76.

Stott, N. C. H., Rollnick, S., & Pill, R. M. (1995). Innovation in clinical method: Diabetes care and negotiating skills. *Family Practice, 12,* 413–418.

Stroop, J. S. (1935). Studies of interference in serial verbal reaction. *Journal of Experimental Psychology, 18,* 643–662.

Substance Abuse and Mental Health Services Administration. (2003). *2001 national household survey on drug abuse (NHSDA).* http://www.samhsa.gov/oas/nhsda/

Wechsler, D. (1997). *WAIS-III WMS-III: Technical manual.* San Antonio: Psychological Corporation.

Weed, N. C., Butcher, J. N., McKenna, T., & Ben-Porath, Y. S. (1992). New measures for assessing alcohol and drug abuse with the MMPI-2: The APS and the AAS. *Journal of Personality Assessment, 58,* 389–404.

INDEX